Shotcrete

Modern Concrete Technology Series

A series of books presenting the state-of-the-art in concrete technology.

Series Editors

Arnon Bentur
National Building Research Institute
Faculty of Civil and Environmental
Engineering
Technion-Israel Institute of
Technology
Technion City
Haifa 32 000
Israel

Sidney Mindess
Department of Civil Engineering
University of British Columbia
6250 Applied Science Lane
Vancouver, B.C. V6T 1Z4
Canada

For more information about this series, please visit: https://www.routledge.com/series-title/book-series/MCT

Shotcrete

Materials, Performance and Use

Dudley Robert ('Rusty') Morgan
and
Marc Jolin

CRC Press
Taylor & Francis Group
Boca Raton London New York

CRC Press is an imprint of the
Taylor & Francis Group, an **informa** business

First edition published 2022
by CRC Press
6000 Broken Sound Parkway NW, Suite 300, Boca Raton, FL 33487-2742

and by CRC Press
4 Park Square, Milton Park, Abingdon, Oxon, OX14 4RN

© 2022 Taylor & Francis Group, LLC

CRC Press is an imprint of Taylor & Francis Group, LLC

Library of Congress Cataloging-in-Publication Data
Names: Morgan, D. R. (Dudley R.), author. | Jolin, Marc author.
Title: Shotcrete : materials, performance and use / Dudley
Robert Morgan, Marc Jolin.
Description: First edition. | Boca Raton : CRC Press, 2022. | Series:
Modern concrete technology, 1746-2959 | Includes bibliographical
references and index.
Identifiers: LCCN 2021031643 (print) | LCCN 2021031644 (ebook) | ISBN
9781482264104 (hbk) | ISBN 9781032039718 (pbk) | ISBN 9780429169946
(ebk)
Subjects: LCSH: Shotcrete.
Classification: LCC TA446 .J65 2022 (print) | LCC TA446 (ebook) | DDC
620.1/36--dc23
LC record available at https://lccn.loc.gov/2021031643
LC ebook record available at https://lccn.loc.gov/2021031644

ISBN: 978-1-482-26410-4 (hbk)
ISBN: 978-1-032-03971-8 (pbk)
ISBN: 978-0-429-16994-6 (ebk)

DOI: 10.1201/9780429169946

Typeset in Sabon
by SPi Technologies India Pvt Ltd (Straive)

*To Orlis Morgan without whose support this
book would not have been written*

and

*To all the Éloïses in the world who are ceaseless in their fortitude and
perseverance while remaining true to their self and their passions*

Contents

Preface

This idea of taking part in the writing of a book on shotcrete came about 5 years ago when Dr. Rusty Morgan invited me to participate as a co-author on the project. It made perfect sense; he has been responsible for some of the most impressive shotcrete technology applications in the world and has shared his passion for shotcrete with many of us for over 40 years. On my part, I have been in shotcrete R&D for my entire university career and felt like I also have a few things to contribute. Moreover, a *book* on shotcrete seems a perfect tool for helping educate interested persons on shotcrete on its many possible (and impressive!) uses. As you, the reader, will hopefully discover in these pages, shotcrete is more than just a method to spray concrete; it encompasses in fact a large industry of hard-working and dedicated people who take great pride in their work. As much as anywhere in the construction industry, the persons on the job site are key players in the success of any shotcrete application. In fact, it could probably be argued that to be passionate about shotcrete, you need to get your hands dirty.

As my co-author started drafting out pages on shotcrete technology and particularly engaging case studies, I was confronted with reality: finding time and energy to *write* is not as easy and simple as I thought it would be. After a number of false starts and hurdles, it became evident that this book project would become an opportunity to learn about myself and share some of my understanding and discoveries on shotcrete technology with others.

I have been privileged to work with someone as knowledgeable and passionate about his work as Dr. Rusty Morgan. I have learned a lot while working on the manuscript, and for this I will always be grateful to have been included in this project. I sincerely hope that the passion that Rusty and I share for shotcrete will be of benefit to you.

Enjoy the reading.

Marc Jolin

Acknowledgements

The authors would like to acknowledge the guidance and encouragement to write this book provided by Dr. Sidney Mindess, Professor Emeritus in the Department of Civil Engineering at the University of British Columbia. The information provided in this book is drawn primarily from the authors' project files and research and development experience. We would, however, like to acknowledge and thank the following organizations and individuals, in particular, for the material and case history examples presented, which have contributed immeasurably to this book.

Abbott, Roger: Shotcrete shoring, underpinning buildings and cut-and-cover tunnels

American Concrete Institute (ACI): Guides, standards and specifications

American Shotcrete Association (ASA): *Shotcrete Magazine* publications and position statements

American Society for Testing and Materials (ASTM International): Specifications and test methods

Armelin, Hugo: Rebound in dry-mix shotcrete

Atkinson, Richard: Shotcrete in Ekati Diamond Mine, NWT, Canada

Balck, Lars: Prestressed shotcrete water tanks

Banthia, Nemkumar: A decade of shotcrete research at the University of British Columbia

Barton, Nick: Q-system for underground shotcrete

Basso Trujillo, Pasquale: Bond strength of reinforcing bars encased with shotcrete with varying encapsulation qualities

Beaupre, Denis: Rheology, pumpability and air entrainment in wet-mix shotcrete

Bernard, Stefan: Shotcrete early strength development and fibre shotcrete toughness testing

Bertrand, Jacques: Metropolitan Boulevard, Montreal Quebec, shotcrete repairs

Bérubé, Simon: The Influence of the nozzle tip on shotcrete spray
Bissonnette, Benoît: Understanding the pumpability of concrete and shrinkage cracking of shotcrete
Bolduc, Louis-Samuel: Evaluating the service life of shotcrete
Bridger, Patrick: Shotcrete application equipment including pumps, predampeners and nozzles

Canadian Standards Association: Concrete materials and methods of concrete construction/test methods and standard practices for concrete
Crom, Theodore: Dry-mix shotcrete nozzling
Czajka, Wlodzimierz: Museum of History of Polish Jews

Drakeley, William: Shotcrete vanishing edge pool and competition pool, Connecticut
Duckworth, Oscar: Shotcrete safety, artificial rockscapes and wine caves
Duffield, Stephen: Shotcrete in Northparkes E26 mine and Cadia Mine, NSW Australia
Dufour, Jean-Francois: Deicing chemicals scaling resistance of shotcrete and cold weather shotcreting in Kattiniq Mine Quebec

EFNARC: European specification for sprayed concrete
Engineering Conferences International (ECI): Shotcrete for underground support
Engineering Foundation (US): Shotcrete for underground support
Ezzet, Mazin: Shotcrete rehabilitation of Stanley Park and Devonian Park Seawalls, Vancouver and Ruskin Dam steel fibre shotcrete retrofit

Fily-Paré, Isabelle: The use of recycled glass in shotcrete
Flanagan, Jason: Shotcrete acoustic shells, UK
Ford, K.: Remote control shaft lining with shotcrete
Forrest, Michael: Seismic retrofit of Littlerock Dam with steel fibre shotcrete
Fulford, John: Elephant Lands, Oregon Zoo

Gagnon, Antoine: Sustainable shotcrete and fibre-reinforced shotcrete
Gagnon, Frédéric: Pumping concrete: a fundamental and practical approach
Gendreau, Martin: Haute-Frond Prince Lighthouse repair with steel fibre shotcrete
Gilbride, Paul: Port of Saint John, New Brunswick shipping berth face repair with steel fibre shotcrete
Ginouse, Nicolas: Investigation of spray pattern in shotcrete applications
Grimstad, Eystein: Norwegian Method of Tunnelling, Q-system graphs

Hanskat, Charles: Liquid containing shotcrete structures and cold joints
Hasler, Hans: Architectural shotcrete, Goetheanum, Dornach, Switzerland
Heere, Roland: Shotcrete retrofit of dams and a mechanically stabilized earth wall
Huesler, Beat: Ayla Golf Resort Aqaba, Jordan, shotcrete shell structures
Hutter, Joseph: Shotcrete in Vale Inco Mines, Sudbury, Ontario

International Concrete Repair Institute (ICRI): Repair methods
International Tunnelling Association (ITA): Shotcrete for underground support

Keller, Lloyd: High-volume slag shotcrete mixes and thermal control plans for shotcrete
King, Ross: Structural shotcrete mock-ups and structural shotcrete construction
Kirsten, Hendrik: South African Water Bed Test and shotcrete in mining
Knipe, Dave: Mayan Empire Exhibit, Jacksonville and Palm Beach Zoo, Florida
Kusterle, Wolfgang: Alkali-free shotcrete accelerators and early age strength testing

Larson, John: Shotcrete in Vale Inco Mines, Sudbury, Ontario
Lemay, Jean-Daniel: Ultra-high early strength shotcrete and many shotcrete reports

Marchand, Jacques: Transport properties in concrete
Martin, Brad: Shotcrete construction of the bobsleigh/luge tracks for the Whistler 2010 and Beijing 2022 Winter Olympic Games
McAskill, Neil: Shotcrete repair of World War I and II concrete ships
McComas, Alice (American Shotcrete Association): procurement of photographs from *Shotcrete Magazine* for figures in this book
McFadden, Shane: Shaft repair with shotcrete
Menu Gandhi, Bruce: Effect of mixture parameters on shrinkage and cracking resistance of dry-mix shotcrete
Millette, Dan: Shotcrete accelerators
Mindess, Sidney: A decade of shotcrete research at the University of British Columbia

Nitschke, Axel: NATM tunnel lining design
Noland, Bill: Scottsdale Arch bridge at Indian Bend Wash, Arizona

Oakes, Ryan: Shotcrete mountain pool, North Carolina

Parker, Harvey: Dry-mix shotcrete rebound and steel fibre shotcrete
Pigeon, Michel: Durability of dry- and wet-process shotcrete
Poole, Ryan: Shotcrete domes
Power, Patrick: Service life of shotcrete

Rabcewicz, L.: New Austrian tunnelling method
Radomski, Shaun: Mass shotcrete and hybrid shotcrete, and overhead shotcrete reshaping of hydroelectric draft tubes with steel fibre shotcrete
Reny, Simon: Improve your shotcrete: use coarse aggregates
Ripley, Bruce: Stave Falls hydroelectric tunnel lining with steel fibre shotcrete
Rispin, Michael: Shotcrete application with remote control manipulator arms and re-entry under shotcrete in tunnels and mines

Schallom, Ray: Shotcrete equipment selection
Siccardi, Pierre: The influence of the nozzle tip on shotcrete spray performance and the best new dry-mix nozzle
South, Jason: Architectural shotcrete domes and shotcrete dome construction

Tatnall, Pete: Synthetic fibre shotcrete and fire resistance of shotcrete
Teichert, Pietro: History of Carl Akeley and architectural shotcrete in the Goetheanum, Dornach, Switzerland
Totten, Larry: California Memorial Stadium seismic retrofit and structural shotcrete specifications
Town, Raymond: Wachussets aqueduct shotcrete lining
Townsend, Frank: Shotcrete lining of wine caves

Vandewalle, Marc: Steel fibre shotcrete in tunnels
Verma, Louisa: Tracking down of unique photograph of early shotcrete gun
von der Hofen, Marcus: Oregon City Bridge seismic retrofit and architectural finishes for shotcrete walls

Warner, Jim: Seismic retrofit of structures in California with shotcrete
Wolsiefer, John: Silica fume shotcrete

Yoggy, George: History of shotcrete, shotcrete wisdom, shotcrete in mining and shotcrete equipment

Zhang, Lihe (John): Shotcrete in tunnelling and mining, shotcrete transport properties, shotcrete cracking, accelerator addition in shotcrete and thermal control plans for mass shotcrete
Zweifel, Chris: Shotcrete domes
Zynda, Chris: Forming for shotcrete and structural shotcrete

Finally, the first author would like to thank Wood PLC and its predecessor companies, AMEC Environment and Infrastructure, AGRA Inc. and R.M. Hardy & Associates Ltd., for providing him with the opportunity to pursue a 45-year consulting career in concrete and shotcrete technology and supporting him in participation in international technical committees and presentation of papers at international conferences.

Authors

Dr. Dudley Robert ('Rusty') Morgan is a civil engineer with over 55 years' experience in concrete and shotcrete technology, and the evaluation and rehabilitation of civil engineering infrastructure. After 10 years in academia in South Africa, Canada and Australia, he returned to Vancouver, Canada, where he worked as a consultant for Wood PLC and its predecessor companies on over 1200 projects all over the world. He was a founding member and past president of the American Shotcrete Association.

Dr. Marc Jolin is a professor in the Department of Civil and Water Engineering at Université Laval in Québec City, Canada. He received his PhD from the University of British Columbia, Canada in 1999. An active member of the Centre de Recherche sur les Infrastructures en Béton – CRIB, his research focuses on shotcrete. A recognized and appreciated researcher and educator, Dr. Jolin is an active member of the American Concrete Institute and the American Shotcrete Association.

Part I

History, material, performances, research and development, equipment and applications

Chapter 1

Introduction

While shotcrete has been with us for over 100 years and there are literally thousands of publications on various aspects of shotcrete technology, unlike concrete technology, there is a surprising dearth of general textbooks on the subject. There are a number of comprehensive shotcrete publications written by technical committees, such as the American Concrete Institute *ACI 506R Guide to Shotcrete*,[1] EFNARC *European Specification for Sprayed Concrete*, and Australian Shotcrete Society, *Shotcreting in Australia*, publications. There is also a textbook edited by Simon Austin and Peter Robins, *Sprayed Concrete, Properties, Design and Application* (1995) in which, interestingly, what were then considered to be *special shotcretes*[2] have now, for the most part, become mainstream.

In addition to the above-mentioned publications, there are also a number of topic-specific shotcrete publications, such as the book by Marc Vandewalle (1996) on *Tunneling the World*, which is primarily focused on the use of steel fibre-reinforced shotcrete in tunnels and the International Tunnelling and Underground Space Association ITA Working Group 12: *Permanent Sprayed Concrete Linings* (2020) publication. Also, since 1999, the American Shotcrete Association has published *Shotcrete Magazine* four times a year and with between five and eight feature articles per issue, it has contributed over 500 publications to the shotcrete literature between 1999 and 2021.

So, while there is a wealth of available information on various aspects of shotcrete technology, it is scattered throughout a wide range of documents, some of them not readily available to persons interested in some particular aspect of the technology. Also, there have been a number of advances in shotcrete technology since the Austin and Robins book was published in 1995. This was the impetus for this textbook: *Shotcrete; Materials, Performance and Use*. It is designed to be a comprehensive textbook, covering the current state-of-the-art of shotcrete technology and providing information on a broad spectrum of the many and various uses of shotcrete in industry. It contains 16 chapters, with a comprehensive reference list at the end of each chapter. In this way, the interested reader can delve into any particular topic in more detail by consulting the references of interest.

DOI: 10.1201/9780429169946-2

This *Shotcrete Book* is intended to be of interest not only to academics (undergraduate and graduate students and teachers) interested in learning more about the topic, but also to design engineers and architects considering use of the technology. It should also be useful as a guide to contractors using shotcrete to build structures or use it in one or more of its many and various applications. The reader will find some repetition of material between different chapters. This is intentional in order to make the book more reader-friendly, i.e. avoid having to keep being referred to other chapters to get specific details on any particular topic.

The book is divided into two parts. *Part I* is composed of nine chapters. It provides *Shotcrete Definitions and Terminology* and then a brief *History of Shotcrete* from 1907 to 2020. There are then chapters on *Shotcrete Materials, Mixture Proportioning* and *Performance Requirements*. This is followed by a chapter on *Shotcrete Research and Development* (mainly based on R&D work carried out at Université Laval in Quebec and the University of British Columbia over a three-decade period). The last chapter in Part I deals with *Shotcrete Application*.

Part II provides a broad overview of *Shotcrete Uses and Case Histories*. Included in the seven chapters in Part II are chapters on shotcrete use in: *Buildings and Structures, Infrastructure Repair and Rehabilitation, Ground Support and Shoring, Underground Support in Tunnels, Shotcrete in Mining, Swimming Pools* and *Spas and Architectural Shotcrete*. Part II provides a general overview of a wide spectrum of applications for this versatile construction material/method.

NOTES

1 Dr. Morgan, the first author of this *Shotcrete Book*, was Secretary of the *ACI 506 Shotcreting* Committee for 25 years and the second author, Dr. Jolin, has been a member for over 20 years, and chair for 6 years, of the same committee.
2 Chapter 11 on the topic of special shotcretes in Austin and Robins (1995) was written by Dr. Morgan.

REFERENCES

ACI 506R. 2016. *Guide to Shotcrete. American Concrete Institute.*
Austin, S. and Robins, P. 1995. *Sprayed Concrete, Properties, Design and Application.* Whittles Publishing Services. 382.
Australian Shotcrete Society. 2010. *Shotcreting in Australia.* Concrete Society of Australia. Second ed. 84.
EFNARC. 1999. *Guidelines for Specifiers and Contractors.* European Specification for Sprayed Concrete. 31.
ITA Working Group no 12 and ITAtech. 2020. Permanent Sprayed Concrete Linings. *International Tunnelling and Underground Space Association.* 56.
Vandewalle, M. 1996. *Tunneling the World.* Zwevegem, Belgium, N.V. Bekaert, S.A. Fourth ed..

Chapter 2

Shotcrete definitions and terminology

2.1 WHAT IS SHOTCRETE?

The American Concrete Institute CT-18 ACI Concrete Terminology defines shotcrete as follows: "concrete placed by a high velocity pneumatic projection from a nozzle". The ACI 506.2–13(18) "Specification for Shotcrete" is a bit more specific and defines shotcrete as follows: "concrete or mortar conveyed through a hose and pneumatically projected at high velocity onto a surface to achieve compaction". The American Shotcrete Association defines shotcrete as "a method of placing concrete with sufficient velocity to achieve compaction".

In Europe and some other parts of the world, the term *Sprayed Concrete* rather than *Shotcrete* is used to describe the process. For example, the EFNARC "European Specification for Sprayed Concrete" (1996) uses the term *Sprayed Concrete*, rather than *Shotcrete* and defines Sprayed Concrete as "a mixture of cement, aggregate and water projected pneumatically from a nozzle into place to produce a dense homogeneous mass. Sprayed concrete normally incorporates admixtures and may also include additions of fibres or a combination of these".

The above definitions all describe the same process, albeit with varying terminology and detail in description of the process. For the purpose of this book, however, the authors have elected to use the term *Shotcrete to* describe the process, as much of the content of this book is based on North American practice and experience. It should also be noted that depending on the context, the term *Shotcrete* is used in North America and elsewhere as both a noun and a verb, as it is used to describe both the material and the process of application of the material. It will be used interchangeably in this manner throughout this book.

2.2 SHOTCRETE PROCESSES

There are basically two different shotcrete processes: the wet-mix and the dry-mix processes. Wet-mix shotcrete is a process in which all of the

DOI: 10.1201/9780429169946-3

ingredients, including water, are mixed before introduction into the delivery hose and compressed air is introduced to the material flow at the nozzle. Dry-mix shotcrete is a process in which most of the mixing water is added at the nozzle. It should be noted that the term "Gunite" is sometimes used in parts of North America and elsewhere in the world in lieu of dry-mix shotcrete. The reasons for this are discussed in Chapter 3. The term *dry-mix shotcrete*, rather than *gunite* will, however, be used throughout this book, as it is the term recommended for use for this process by the American Concrete Institute and American Shotcrete Association, as well as other organizations in North America.

The corresponding terminology used in the EFNARC "European Specification for Sprayed Concrete" is "Wet-Mix Sprayed Concrete" and "Dry-Mix Sprayed Concrete". This specification describes the wet-mix process as follows:

> a technique in which cement, aggregate and water are batched and mixed together prior to being fed into a purpose-made machine and conveyed through a pipeline to a nozzle where the mixture is pneumatically and continuously projected into place. The mixture normally incorporates admixtures and may also include additions of fibers or a combination of these.

This same specification also describes the dry-mix process as follows:

> a technique in which cement and aggregate are batched, mixed and fed into a purpose-made machine wherein the mixture is pressurized, metered into a compressed air stream and conveyed through hoses or pipes to a nozzle where water is introduced as a spray to wet the mixture which is then projected continuously into place. The mixture may also incorporate admixtures or fibers or a combination of these.

It should be noted that the above definitions and descriptions for the shotcrete process involve the use of compressed air to pneumatically project the shotcrete material at high velocity onto the receiving surface. Other methods of projecting concrete onto a receiving surface at high impacting velocity, such as "Centrifugally Sprayed Concrete" (Morgan et al. 2010), are not included in this definition of shotcrete and will thus not be dealt with in this book.

2.3 SHOTCRETE TERMINOLOGY

While much of the terminology used in the shotcrete industry is the same as that used in conventional reinforced concrete design, specification, construction and testing, there is certain terminology that is unique to the shotcrete industry. In addition to the terminology provided in Sections 2.1 and 2.2 preceding, the following is a brief glossary of such shotcrete-related terminology.

Air lance (also called blowpipe): compressed air jet operated by a nozzle-man's helper during shotcrete application to help keep the shooting area free of build-up of overspray and rebound.

Air ring: a perforated manifold in the body of the wet-mix shotcrete nozzle through which air is added to pneumatically convey the shotcrete onto the receiving surface

Bench shooting: a method used to shoot thick vertical walls by benching or stack shooting

Brooming or broom finish: a finishing procedure in which a bristle broom is drawn across a fresh smooth-finished shotcrete face to provide surface texture

Build-up thickness: thickness of freshly applied shotcrete

Cutting screed (also called cutting rod): a sharp-edged finishing tool which is used to trim freshly applied shotcrete back to a designated line and grade

Cuttings (also called trimmings): shotcrete material applied beyond the finished face and cut back to the required face

Finish coat (also called flash coat): final thin layer of shotcrete applied to even out the shotcrete surface prior to final finishing operations

Ground wire (also called screed wire or shooting wire): small gauge, high tensile strength steel wire used to establish line and grade for shotcrete work

Gun: Dry-mix shotcrete delivery equipment

Gun-finish: natural applied shotcrete finish that has had no finishing operations

Gun operator: person on the shotcrete crew who operates the dry-mix shotcrete delivery equipment (gun)

Gunning: the act of applying dry-mix shotcrete

Nozzle: attachment at the end of the delivery hose in which (1) air is added in the wet-mix shotcrete process or (2) water is added in the dry-mix shotcrete process, from which a continuous stream of shotcrete is ejected at high velocity (before conveying the shotcrete to the receiving surface at a high impacting velocity)

Nozzleman (also called nozzle operator): craftsman on the shotcrete crew who controls air addition at the nozzle in the wet-mix shotcrete process, and water addition at the nozzle in the dry-mix shotcrete process to control consistency, and manipulates the nozzle to control deposition of the material on the receiving surface

Nozzle velocity: velocity of the shotcrete material (in m/s) as it exits the nozzle

Overspray: shotcrete material deposited away from the intended receiving surface

Predampening: in dry-mix shotcrete the process of adding part of the mix water to the dry shotcrete materials to predampen them to about 3 to 6% moisture content immediately prior to introduction into the shotcrete gun

Rebound: shotcrete materials comprised mainly of coarse aggregate, with some paste and sand, that bounces away from the receiving surface

Rolling: a wavy textured uneven shotcrete surface resulting from applying the shotcrete at angles less than 90° to the receiving surface

Sagging (also called sloughing): subsidence of freshly applied shotcrete, usually caused by shooting shotcrete which is too wet and/or applying too thick or too great a height of shotcrete at one time

Shooting: The act of applying shotcrete

Water ring: a perforated manifold in the dry-mix shotcrete nozzle at which water is added under pressure to the shotcrete material stream

Wetting: the addition of water at the nozzle in the dry-mix shotcrete process just before the material exits the nozzle

REFERENCES

ACI CT-18. 2018. *Concrete Terminology.* American Concrete Institute. 80.

ACI-506.2-13(18). 2013, reapproved 2018. *Specification for Shotcrete.* American Concrete Institute. 12 p.

EFNARC. 1996. *European Specification for Sprayed Concrete.* 30.

EFNARC. 1999. Guidelines for specifiers and contractors. *Concrete.* Vol. 44. No. 0. 31.

Morgan, D. R., Loevlie, K., Kwong, N. and Chan, A. 2010. Centrifugal placed concrete for lining horizontal pipes, culverts, and vertical shafts. *Shotcrete: Elements of a System – Proceedings of the 3rd International Conference on Engineering Developments in Shotcrete.* doi:10.1201/b10545-27.

Chapter 3

History of shotcrete

3.1 THE INVENTION

It is now generally recognized that Carl Ethan Akeley (1864–1926) was the *inventor* of shotcrete. Teichert (2002) provides a fascinating historical overview of Carl Akeley the man and his contributions to the invention of *shotcrete*. Akeley was first and foremost a naturalist, and world-renowned taxidermist who specialized in building life-like presentations of animals in natural history museums in the USA, first at the Milwaukee Public Museum, Wisconsin (1888–1895), followed by the Field Columbian Museum, (now the Field Museum of Natural History) in Chicago (1895–1909). In 1909, Carl Akeley was hired by the American Museum of Natural History in New York, where some of his most impressive work is still displayed in the Akeley Hall of African Mammals (Teichert, 2002) (Figure 3.1).

It is perhaps thus not surprising that many references in the literature attribute the invention of shotcrete to a desire by Akeley to improve upon the process of dermoplastic, i.e. the process of building faithful anatomical models of animals by using tubes covered with wire, cloth and plaster. Hand application of plaster was meticulous and time-consuming work and various references have suggested that the dry-mix *shotcrete* process was developed by Akeley to improve upon this process. It is true that others later used shotcrete for this process, but Teichert (2002) reports that Akeley never actually used shotcrete for this purpose.

The incentive for the invention of the shotcrete process originated while Akeley was at the Field Columbian Museum in Chicago. In the spring of 1907 a colleague, Clarence Dewey, was using a compressed air-driven enlarged atomizer built by Akeley to spray coloured plaster of Paris to *paint* artificial rockscapes being built as part of a museum exhibit. At that time the museum was housed in a building that had been erected for the 1892 World Exhibition. The director of the museum, Frederick Skiff, was concerned about the deteriorating condition of the façade of the building. He had observed Dewey at work and asked Akeley if he could develop a *plaster spray gun* to re-coat the façade. He rose to the challenge and in June 1907

DOI: 10.1201/9780429169946-4

Figure 3.1 Carl Akeley, the inventor of the dry-mix shotcrete (gunite) process.

revealed a rudimentary machine he called a *plastergun*. This *gun* operated on the principle of a double chamber. The chambers were placed one on top of the other and were alternatively pressurized with compressed air. Dry plaster material was fed into the gun and conveyed pneumatically by the compressed air to a nozzle where mix water was added to wet out the material as it was pneumatically projected onto the receiving surface. And so, the double chamber gun was born (Figure 3.2).

Akeley continued to work on the gun during 1908 and 1909, adapting it for application of Portland cement and sand mixtures. Typical mixture proportions consisted of one-part Portland cement to three parts (by mass) of concrete sand. He applied for a patent on the machine in September 1909, finally being awarded with a patent for it in May 1911. In the meantime, others, impressed with his invention, exhibited it as a *cement gun* at the Cement Show at Madison Square Garden in New York in December 1910. It was a sensation at the Cement Show and garnered a great deal of interest. One of its earliest uses was for lining the Hunter's Brook Siphon for New York Water Supply. Another early use was for encasement of structural steel at New York's Grand Central Station for protection against corrosion and fire. By 1911, it was being used by the US Army Corps of Engineers for rock slope stabilization work during construction of the Panama Canal (Figure 3.3).

In addition to invention of the *cement gun*, Akeley had no fewer than 37 patents awarded between 1895 and 1921. These included the first rotary

Figure 3.2 Carl Akeley's original cement gun, *circa* 1908.

Figure 3.3 Slope stabilization with dry-mix shotcrete (gunite) by US Army Corps
of Engineers during building of Panama Canal in 1911.

(Photo courtesy of the Panama Canal Authority.)

motion picture camera and a powerful searchlight, which was used by the US Army during the First World War. Remarkable achievements for a self-made man who had only three or four years of grade school education (Teichert, 2002).

3.2 THE FIRST 50 YEARS

George Yoggy (2000, 2001) provides a comprehensive review of the first 50 years of shotcrete development in North America and elsewhere. In 1912, the Cement Gun Company in Allentown, Pennsylvania acquired the rights to Akeley's patents for the *Cement Gun* and coined the term *gunite* to describe the process that we today refer to as *dry-mix shotcrete (or dry-mix sprayed concrete)*. Formed, cast-in-place concrete in the early 1900s was largely consolidated by methods such as tamping, *puddling* and rodding. Engineers quickly recognized the superior consolidation provided by the pneumatic placement of sand/cement mortars at high impacting velocity and the potential of this method to provide enhanced durability and service life. The gunite process immediately found use in a wide variety of applications, including construction and repair of buildings; protection of structural steel against corrosion and fire damage; lining of sewers, water and railway tunnels; repair of bridges, dams and canals; rock slope stabilization; and construction of water-retaining structures.

An excellent early example of the early use of *gunite* is in construction of the Oregon City Bridge spanning the Willamette River near Portland, Oregon (von der Hofen, 2012). Figure 3.4 shows a photo of the bridge under construction in 1922. This C.B. McCullough designed steel box girder arch bridge was lined with *gunite* to protect the steel from corrosion from emissions from a nearby paper mill. An article published in *Engineering World* in December 1922 provided a detailed description of the *gunite* work and concluded with the statement:

> The efficiency of the cement gun and accessory equipment on this piece of work was demonstrated to the satisfaction of those assumed responsibility for the character and speed of construction. The aesthetic features as they appear in the general view will commend themselves to those who like to see a touch of the artistic imparted to a structure of severe utility.

The original *gunite* construction provided nearly 90 years of performance. From 2010 to 2012, as part of a major rehabilitation of the bridge by the Oregon Department of Transportation, the original *gunite* coating that encapsulated the steel components of the bridge was removed and replaced with a modern high-performance wet-mix shotcrete (von der Hofen, 2013).

Figure 3.4 View of the Oregon City Bridge under construction in 1922.

(Photo courtesy Marcus von der Hofen.)

By 1915, the Cement Gun Company had grown to become a large contracting organization. By the early 1920s, the use of *gunite* was widespread throughout North America and had expanded to Germany (1921), the United Kingdom (1924) and by the end of the decade to other countries in Europe, as well as India and South Africa and elsewhere. Considerable research and testing was conducted at Lehigh University in Pennsylvania as early as 1917, and subsequently at the University of California to quantify the physical properties of *gunite*. Early tests concentrated on characterizing compressive strength development, density and bond. Watertightness was also an important consideration for water-retaining or conveyance structures. Substantial additional research and testing was carried out at organizations such as the University of Toronto in Ontario, the US Bureau of Standards and the US Department of the Navy, as well as many others, all before the 1940s (Yoggy, 2000).

The use of the *gunite* process continued to expand throughout the world during the 1930s and 1940s, with the double pressure chamber gun concept invented by Akeley still being the predominant method used to convey material. Various companies developed their own dry-mix guns. A few examples of equipment are shown in Chapter 8. In addition to *gunite*, various trademark terms were used by different companies to describe the process including *guncrete, blastcrete* and *jetcrete*. In the early 1930s, the American Railway Engineering Association adopted the term *shotcrete* to describe the dry-mix process and in 1951, the American Concrete Institute (ACI), in an effort to standardize terminology, also adopted the term *shotcrete*. Initially, the term *shotcrete* applied only to the dry-mix process, but after the Second World War, with the development of the wet-mix process, the ACI used the term *wet-mix shotcrete* to describe the wet-mix process.

In the 1950s, new types of dry-mix guns were developed. A rotary feed bowl type gun was developed in the USA and different types of rotary barrel guns were developed in the USA and Europe. Detailed descriptions of these types of guns are provided in Chapter 8. The development of these new types of guns had a major impact on the shotcrete industry. Not only did they improve productivity, but they also allowed for the use of coarse aggregate (typically 10 mm maximum size) in the shotcrete mixture proportioning. A typical dry-mix shotcrete mix was composed of one-part Portland cement to one-part coarse aggregate to three parts concrete sand by mass. These more concrete-like mixtures (as opposed to the more mortar-like old *gunite* mixtures) rapidly found favour with engineers and contractors, as reflected in the ACI 506 Shotcrete Committee *Grading No.2* grading limits for combined aggregates (ACI 506 Guide to Shotcrete) (see Chapter 4).

The Long Beach earthquake in California in 1933 had a major effect on the subsequent use of reinforced shotcrete for seismic retrofit of masonry buildings at hospitals and schools. For the next four decades, many hundreds of buildings were seismically retrofitted with reinforced shotcrete, with increasingly heavily reinforced sections being constructed after the Tehachapi Earthquake in 1952 and the San Fernando Earthquake in 1971 (Warner, 2004). Initially, this work was carried out with the double chamber dry-mix gun, but with time, work started to be done with the rotary barrel dry-mix gun and eventually with the wet-mix shotcrete process. Today most of this seismic retrofit is done with the wet-mix shotcrete process.

3.3 THE NEXT 50 YEARS

3.3.1 Wet-mix shotcrete

The major revolution in the shotcrete industry was the development of the wet-mix shotcrete process, i.e. where the shotcrete materials were all pre-mixed with water (and chemical admixtures) before being pumped down a line/hose to a nozzle, where compressed was added to pneumatically project the material onto the receiving surface at a high impacting velocity. Various individuals and companies had experimented with this process as far back as the 1920s (Sprayed Concrete Association, 1999), but it was not until the mid-1950s that the wet-mix process started to find significant industrial application. Initial applications were carried out using conventional concrete pumps. While they worked, they were not ideally suited to wet-mix shotcrete application.

A number of equipment manufacturers experimented with modifying concrete pumps to make them more suited to wet-mix shotcrete application. A number of improvements were made to pumps in the 1960s, but it was the development of the swing-tube concrete pump in the late 1970s that really made wet-mix shotcrete practical (Yoggy, 2002). The material cylinders were sized to make them suitable for conveying shotcrete at a rate that could be managed by a nozzleman for hand application. The rate of cycling of the swing tube controlled the *surge* and volume of shotcrete delivered per minute. With these refinements, the nozzleman was now able to maintain precise control over deposition of shotcrete in a wide range of different shooting conditions (e.g. vertical, overhead, downward, open shooting or shooting congested reinforcing) at a rate of productivity of about four times that possible by the dry-mix shotcrete process. With hydraulic assisted applications, which typically use bigger equipment and larger diameter hoses, even greater rates of production are achievable. While exact numbers are not available, the indications are that the ratio of wet-mix to dry-mix shotcrete in North America has gone from about 70% dry and 30% wet in the late 1970s to about 25% dry and 75% wet by 2020.

3.3.2 Steel fibre

The next major advance in shotcrete technology was the development of steel fibre-reinforced shotcrete (SFRS). The concept of reinforcing shotcrete with discreet, discontinuous fibres was first developed by the Batelle Research Corporation in the USA in 1971 (Morgan, 2000). Research applications of SFRS were conducted by Lankard and also by Parker in 1971 (ACI 506.1R Guide to Fibre Reinforced Shotcrete). The first practical application of SFRS in North America was in 1972, when it was used by the US Army Corps of Engineers for rock slope stabilization and lining a tunnel adit at the Ririe Dam on Willow Creek, a tributary of the Snake River in Idaho (Kaden, 1974). The first use of SFRS in Canada was in 1976, when a dry-mix shotcrete mixture designed by the first author was used to stabilize a sloughing railway embankment in Burnaby, British Columbia (Figure 3.5).

The first SFRS work was done using the dry-mix shotcrete process, but SFRS using the wet-mix process is now widely used in North America and around the world (Vandewalle, 1990). Many hundreds of thousands of cubic metres of SFRS are used annually in projects such as rock slope stabilization, support of underground openings in tunnels and mines, canal linings and remediation of dams, bridges and marine structures (Morgan, 1995). The use of steel fibre reinforcement in lieu of other forms of reinforcing, such as welded wire mesh, chain link mesh or conventional reinforcing

Figure 3.5 Ririe Dam slope stabilization and Burnaby railway embankment stabilization with steel fibre reinforced dry-mix shotcrete.

Figure 3.6 Shipping berth face rehabilitation in Port of Saint John with wet-mix steel fibre reinforced shotcrete.

bars, has led to the construction of more economic and durable structures. Figure 3.6 shows a good example of this in the use of wet-mix steel fibre-reinforced shotcrete for rehabilitation of shipping berth faces at the Port of Saint John in New Brunswick.

3.3.3 Silica fume

The next significant development in shotcrete technology was the incorporation of condensed silica fume as a supplementary cementing material in the shotcrete mix. This was first undertaken in Norway in 1975 (Garshol, 1990). The first application of silica fume in shotcrete in Canada was in 1984, when a dry-mix shotcrete designed by the first author was used in shotcrete rehabilitation of a pier in the intertidal region in Vancouver harbour, British Columbia (Morgan, 1995). It was found that the silica fume had major benefits for both the plastic (fresh) and hardened shotcrete. In the plastic phase it provided enhanced adhesion, cohesion and thickness of build-up without sloughing. It also provided substantial reductions in rebound, particularly in the dry-mix shotcrete process. It also provided enhanced wash-out resistance when working in intertidal regions or wet areas. In the hardened state, the silica fume has been found to provide the same attributes expected when it is used in high quality concretes, e.g. increased compressive strength, reduced permeability, increased resistance to chloride ion intrusion and chemical attack, improved sulphate resistance and mitigation of alkali aggregate reactivity (Morgan, 1995).

3.3.4 Synthetic fibre

Chronologically the next significant advance in shotcrete technology was the development of synthetic fibre-reinforced shotcrete (SnFRS) in the 1980s. There are basically two types of synthetic fibres: microfibres and macro fibres (see Figure 3.7). Synthetic microfibres can be used in both wet-mix and dry-mix shotcretes, but synthetic macro fibres are mainly only used in wet-mix shotcrete. ACI 506.1R provides a description of the differences between these two fibre types. Macrofibres have an equivalent diameter greater than 0.3 mm and microfibres are anything below, although they typically have an equivalent diameter of about 30 μm to 50 μm. The vast majority of synthetic fibres used in shotcrete are made from polypropylene, but some work has been done with other fibre types, including nylon, carbon and polyvinyl alcohol (PVA) fibres. Synthetic microfibres are typically used at low addition rates (1 to 2 kg/m^3). They are used mainly to improve resistance to plastic shrinkage cracking but have also been found to be valuable in increasing resistance to explosive spalling in tunnel linings subjected to high-temperature fires (Tatnall, 2002). Synthetic macrofibres are used at much higher addition rates (5 to 9 kg/m^3 being common) and are used for many of the same reasons as steel fibre reinforcement, e.g. to improve toughness (residual load-carrying capacity after cracking) and impact resistance (Morgan et al., 1999). Synthetic macrofibre reinforced shotcrete is now widely used around the world in tunnelling and mining applications, as well as for slope stabilization, creek channelization and marine structures rehabilitation (Morgan, 1995, 2000).

Figure 3.7 Macrosynthetic and microsynthetic fibres.

3.3.5 Chemical admixtures

Air-entraining admixtures: Air-entraining admixtures have been used in wet-mix shotcrete to provide freeze/thaw durability since the development of wet-mix shotcrete in the mid-1950s. With respect to dry-mix shotcrete, as recently as the 1990s the ACI 506 Shotcrete Committee was of the opinion that it was not possible to adequately entrain air in dry-mix shotcretes. Research at Université Laval in Quebec City in the late 1980s and early 1990s, however, showed that it was possible to entrain sufficient air in dry-mix shotcrete to provide good freeze/thaw durability and resistance to deicing salt scaling (Beaupré et al., 1994). The air-entraining admixture could be added either to the mixing water before it was injected at the nozzle, or as a dry powdered admixture, batched in with the dry shotcrete materials (Dufour et al., 2006). Nowadays, most dry-bagged shotcrete materials for exterior applications in frost exposure environments are batched with dry powdered air-entraining admixtures (Vezina, 2001).

Water-reducing admixtures: Conventional water-reducing admixtures have been used in wet-mix shotcretes since the 1950s. However, with the introduction of silica fume into shotcrete applications in North America in the mid-1980s, which has a high-water demand, the use of conventional water-reducing admixtures alone was often not sufficient to reduce water demand to a sufficient extent to provide a sufficiently low water/ cementing materials ratio. So, in the mid-1980s high range water-reducing admixtures (also called superplasticizers) started to be used in conjunction with conventional water-reducing admixtures in wet-mix silica fume shotcretes. Nowadays, so-called *All-Range Water Reducing Admixtures* are commonly used.

Retarders and hydration-controlling admixtures: Wet-mix shotcretes typically take longer to discharge from transit mixers than conventional concretes, because of the requirement to control the rate at which shotcrete is supplied to the nozzle. Thus, set retarding admixtures have often been added to wet-mix shotcrete mixtures to extend the workability (pumpability) of the mixture, particularly in hot weather conditions. Conventional set retarders have, however, had their limitations, particularly in tunnel and mining applications, where there are often long times (sometimes 4 to 8 hours) from batching to completion of discharge of the shotcrete. The introduction of *Hydration-Controlling Admixtures* in the 2000s has had a major beneficial effect on the shotcrete industry. It is now possible to *put the shotcrete to sleep* for 12 hours (or even longer, if required) and then instantly *wake it up* with shotcrete accelerator addition at the nozzle.

Shotcrete set accelerators: Shotcrete set accelerators are mainly used in underground applications, particularly in overhead applications in tunnels and mines. In dry-mix shotcrete they are added as dry powdered materials to the dry shotcrete materials, before introduction into the shotcrete gun. Early (*circa* 1960s to 1990s) dry-mix shotcrete accelerators were mainly highly alkaline (>12 pH) sodium or potassium aluminate, or carbonate-based dry powdered products. Liquid versions of the sodium and potassium aluminates, as well as liquid sodium silicate-based accelerators were added at the nozzle in wet-mix shotcretes. They worked reasonably well in terms of providing rapid setting and stiffening of the shotcrete and very early strength gain (1 to 2 hours). These high alkaline accelerators, however, tended to have detrimental effects on the longer-term compressive strength, permeability and durability of the shotcrete, with the effect being more pronounced the greater the accelerator addition rate. They also had negative health, safety and environmental influences and their use has now been banned in a number of countries. A major advance in shotcrete technology was the introduction in the 2000s of so-called *Alkali Free* shotcrete accelerators. These liquid accelerators are mainly based on aqueous suspensions of aluminum sulphate compounds and have a pH of about 3. They have a less negative effect on the compressive strength, permeability and durability of shotcrete (Millette and Jolin, 2014) and are compatible with most hydration-controlling admixtures. They are now being used widely throughout the world in underground and other wet-mix shotcrete applications. A good example of this is the retrofit of a hydroelectric draft tube ceiling in a US Army Corps of Engineers project in Washington State in 2019 (Radomski, et al., 2019).

3.4 SHOTCRETE QUALITY

It was recognized from the earliest days that the quality of the in-place shotcrete product was highly influenced by the competence of the shotcrete nozzleman and crew. One could have perfectly good shotcrete materials and mixture proportions and shotcrete batching, mixing, delivery and supply, but if the skills of the nozzleman and crew were found to be wanting, an inferior in-place shotcrete product could result. In the early days (*circa* 1920s to 1940s) the Cement Gun Company controlled the patents to the *gunite* process and much of the contracting work (Yoggy, 2001). They provided comprehensive education programmes and exercised strict control over shotcrete nozzleman and crew training and implemented rigorous quality control programs. The net result was the construction of a wide range of shotcrete projects which were well regarded by recognized specifying and testing authorities. Yoggy (Yoggy, 2001), however, reports that after the Second World War, things changed. With new types of shotcrete machines entering the market and the Cement Gun Company no longer have tight control over shotcrete contracting, issues with shotcrete quality started to emerge. Yoggy describes it as a *shotcrete mid-life crisis*. Many engineers and specifying authorities lost faith with the shotcrete process and excluded it from their project specifications.

It took several decades for the shotcrete industry to recover from this image. Prominent in this recovery process was the American Concrete Institute (ACI). The ACI 506 Shotcrete Committee was formed in 1957. It formed several sub-committees and has produced a Specification and a number of Guides and educational documents, which are frequently updated. They are used throughout North America and many other countries around the world. Also active in this recovery process has been ASTM International which has published a number of Standard Specifications, Practice documents and Test Methods for shotcrete.

In addition to these ACI and ASTM International initiatives, in 1998 the American Shotcrete Association (ASA) was formed. It was established by contractors, materials and equipment suppliers, engineers, academics and others with a common interest in promoting the safe and beneficial use of the shotcrete process. One of the first initiatives of the ASA was to establish a *Shotcrete Nozzleman Education and Training* program. This was followed by the establishment of a *Shotcrete Nozzleman Certification* program in 2000. This certification initiative was subsequently taken over by ACI Committee C660 with implementation of the *ACI Shotcrete Nozzleman Certification* program in 2001. The certification is for hand application of shotcrete and since its initiation, many hundreds of shotcrete nozzlemen have been certified for the wet-mix and/or dry-mix shotcrete processes (see Chapter 9). Many specifying authorities now require the use of ACI Certified Shotcrete Nozzlemen on their shotcrete projects and there has been a considerable increase in the quality and volume of shotcrete construction in North America in the past two decades.

In Europe, EFNARC took a different tack. Recognizing that much of the use of shotcrete in Europe was for underground support, using remote placement hydraulic arms for applying wet-mix shotcrete, in 2009 they launched a Nozzleman Certification Scheme centred mainly around the safe operation of remote placement equipment. In 2014, there were over 200 certified nozzlemen. Most of them are from Europe, but they report that some of them are from North and South America, South Asia and Australasia (EFNARC, 2014).

3.5 SHOTCRETE RESEARCH AND DEVELOPMENT

As previously mentioned, in much of the early 1920s *gunite* research and development work was carried out at Lehigh University in Pennsylvania, with additional work, up to the 1940s, being carried out at the University of California and at the University of Toronto (Yoggy, 2000). Shotcrete research was also conducted during this period by the US Bureau of Reclamation, the US Department of the Navy and US Army Corps of Engineers. During the next several decades there appears to have been relatively little shotcrete research and development work conducted at universities in the US and Canada. The majority of new developments in shotcrete technology arose from research and development work carried out by materials and equipment suppliers, either in-house, or contracted out to materials engineering testing laboratories (Morgan, 2008). Good examples of this are the new developments in chemical admixtures for use in shotcrete, steel and synthetic fibre-reinforced shotcrete technology and the use of new supplementary cementing materials, such as silica fume and calcined metakaolin.

It was not until the 1990s and 2000s that universities in North America started to look seriously at the science of wet and dry-mix shotcrete. Funding from the Canadian Network of Centres of Excellence on High-Performance Concrete enabled fundamental research into shotcrete technology to be conducted at the University of British Columbia and at Université Laval in Quebec City. Banthia and Mindess (Banthia and Mindess, 2006) provided a summary of a decade of shotcrete research at the University of British Columbia and Jolin (Jolin and Bissonnette, 2006) summarized a decade of shotcrete research at Laval University. Many Masters and Doctoral students graduated in these programs (see Chapter 7) and subsequently went on to practice in various sectors of the shotcrete industry. This had a profound effect on the shotcrete industry, bringing more *science to the art* and advancing the credibility of shotcrete in the engineering community. Université Laval continues to support a shotcrete research and development laboratory, which is unique amongst North American universities.

In summary, shotcrete has come a long way since its invention by Carl Akeley in 1907. Modern shotcrete technology is a considerably more advanced method of placing concrete than the early *gunite* method. It should continue to enjoy increasing recognition and use, provided all those involved in the industry continue to support education, training, certification and an emphasis on quality assurance and quality control. In addition, it is the hope of the authors of this book that the shotcrete industry should continue to support shotcrete research and development at universities and other institutions, so that the next generation of advances in shotcrete technology can be realized.

REFERENCES

ACI 506.1R-21. 2021. *Guide to Fiber Reinforced Shotcrete*. American Concrete Institute. 20 p.

ACI 506R-16. 2016a. *Guide to Shotcrete*. American Concrete Institute. 52p.

Banthia, N. and Mindess, S. 2006. *Bringing Science to an Art: A Decade of Shotcrete Research at the University of British Columbia*. Whistler, British Columbia. ASCE Shotcrete for Underground Support X. 30–45.

Beaupré, D., Talbot, C., Gendreau, M., Pigeon, M. and Morgan, D. R. 1994. Deicer Salt Scaling Resistance of Dry- and Wet-Process Shotcrete. *ACI Materials Journal*. Vol. 91. No. 5. September–October. 487–494.

Dufour, J. -F., Reny, S. and Vezina, D. 2006. State-of-the-Art Specifications for Shotcrete. *Shotcrete Magazine, American Shotcrete Association* Fall 2006. 4–11.

EFNARC. 2014. *Introduction to Nozzleman Certification. EFNARC Sprayed Concrete Nozzleman Certification Scheme*. 2014. 14.

Garshol, K. 1990. Development of Mechanised Wet Mix Shotcrete Application in the Norwegian Tunneling Industry. *ASCE Shotcrete for Underground Support V*, Uppsala, Sweden, 113–124.

Jolin, M. and Bissonnette, B. 2006. A Decade of Shotcrete Research at Laval University. *ASCE Shotcrete for Underground Support X*, Whistler, British Columbia, 46–62.

Kaden, R. 1974. Slope Stabilized with Steel Fibrous Shotcrete. *Western Construction* April 1974. 30–33.

Millette, D. and Jolin, M. 2014. Shotcrete Accelerators for Wet-Mix. *Shotcrete Magazine, American Shotcrete Association* Fall 2014. 44–46.

Morgan, D. R. 1995. Special Sprayed Concretes. *Sprayed Concrete: Properties, Design and Application*, Edited by Austin, S. & Robins, P., Scotland, Publisher by Whittles Publishing, 229–265.

Morgan, D. R. 2000. Evolution of Fibre Reinforced Shotcrete. Shotcrete Magazine, American Shotcrete Association May, 2000. 8–11.

Morgan, D. R. 2008. Shotcrete: A Compilation of Papers. *American Shotcrete Association* 424 p.

Morgan, D. R., Heere, R., McAskill, N. and Chan, C. 1999. Comparative Evaluation of System Ductility of Mesh and Fibre Reinforced Shotcretes. *ASCE Shotcrete for Underground Support VIII*, Campos do Jordao, Brazil, 1999, 216–239.

Radomski, S. M., Morgan, D. R., Zhang, L. and Graham, D. 2019. *Structural Modifications to Hydroelectric Turbine Draft Tube Ceiling. Shotcrete Magazine, American Shotcrete Association* Summer, 2019. 22–34.

Sprayed Concrete Association. 1999. *Introduction to Sprayed Concrete.* 34 p.

Tatnall, P. C. 2002. Shotcrete in Fires: Effect of Fibres on Explosive Spalling. *Shotcrete Magazine, American Shotcrete Association* Fall, 2002. 10–12.

Teichert, P. 2002. Carl Akeley- A Tribute to the Founder of Shotcrete. Shotcrete Magazine, American Shotcrete Association Summer, 2002. 10–12.

Vandewalle, M. 1990. *Tunneling the World.* Zwevegem, Belgium, N.V. Bekaert, S.A..

Vezina, D. 2001. Development of Durable Dry-Mix Shotcrete in Quebec. *Shotcrete Magazine, American Shotcrete Association* Spring, 2001. 18–20.

von der Hofen, M. H. 2012. The Oregon City Bridge, Part I. *Shotcrete Magazine, American Shotcrete Association* Fall, 2012. 30–32.

von der Hofen, M. H. 2013. The Oregon City Bridge, Part II. *Shotcrete Magazine, American Shotcrete Association* Spring, 2013. 22–24.

Warner, J. 2004. History of Shotcrete in Seismic Retrofit in California. *Shotcrete Magazine, American Shotcrete Association* Winter, 2004. 14–17.

Yoggy, G. 2000. The History of Shotcrete, Part I. *Shotcrete Magazine, American Shotcrete Association* Fall, 2000. 28–29.

Yoggy, G. 2001. The History of Shotcrete, Part II. *Shotcrete Magazine, American Shotcrete Association* Spring, 2001. 22–23.

Yoggy, G. 2002. The History of Shotcrete, Part III. *Shotcrete Magazine, American Shotcrete Association* Winter, 2002. 20–23.

Chapter 4

Shotcrete materials

4.1 INTRODUCTION

Shotcrete is essentially concrete and so, with the odd exception, the same ingredients are used for the production of shotcrete as are used in modern high-performance concretes. The basic constituents of shotcrete are as follows: Portland cement (various types); supplementary cementing materials (fly ash, silica fume, ground granulated blast-furnace slag, calcined metakaolin and other natural pozzolans); coarse and fine aggregates; various types of chemical admixtures (water-reducing admixtures, high-range water-reducing admixtures, air-entraining admixtures, set-retarding admixtures, hydration-controlling admixtures, set-accelerating admixtures and others), and water of suitable quality. With respect to set accelerators, two different types can be used: conventional concrete set accelerators that are added to wet-mix shotcrete mix during batching and shotcrete accelerators that are added at the nozzle during shooting.

In addition to the above materials, a variety of special additions are often used in shotcrete. Such additions include different types of fibre (steel fibre, macro synthetic fibres, micro synthetic fibres, natural fibres and occasionally other types of fibre, such as glass fibre, carbon fibres and polyvinyl alcohol fibres) and rheology modifying ingredients such as magnesium aluminium silicates. The sections of this chapter which follow elaborate on the use of these materials in shotcrete.

4.2 CEMENT

Portland cement is the main binder used in shotcrete. Table 4.1 lists the various types of Portland cement available in North America (ASTM C150).

ASTM Type I (CSA Type GU) is the most commonly used cement in shotcrete in North America. Some cements are designated as ASTM Type I/II as they meet the ASTM performance requirements for both an ASTM Type I and ASTM Type II cement. Such cements are widely used in shotcrete in Western North America. ASTM Type III (CSA Type HE) high early strength

DOI: 10.1201/9780429169946-5

Table 4.1 ASTM and CSA equivalent portland cements available in North America

ASTM designation	CSA designation	Classification
Type I	Type GU	General use
Type II	Type MS & MH	Moderate sulphate Resistance & heat of hydration
Type III	Type HE	High early strength
Type IV	Type LH	Low heat of hydration
Type V	Type HS	High sulphate resistance

cements are sometimes used in shotcrete where rapid early strength development is required, e.g. in underpinning buildings and structures, tunnel lining and shotcrete application in intertidal regions in marine projects. ASTM Type IV (CSA Type LH) Low Heat of Hydration cement is typically only used in mass concrete structures and is not readily available. It is not well suited to most shotcrete applications and so is seldom used in shotcrete, with the possible exception of shooting of mass concrete plugs to seal underground openings. ASTM Type V (CSA Type HS) High Sulphate Resistance concrete is sometimes used in potash mines and other applications where the shotcrete comes into contact with sulphate-bearing soils and/or water.

In addition to the above Portland cement types, a variety of different blended cements are used in concrete production in North America. Such cements are described in publications such as ASTM C595 *Standard Specification for Blended Hydraulic Cements* and CSA A3000 *Cementitious Materials for Use in Concrete*. The different types of blended cements detailed in these publications are not elaborated upon in this chapter, as they are not often used in shotcrete. Shotcrete engineers generally prefer to have the ability to custom design the proportions of Portland cement and supplementary cementing materials in the shotcrete mix design, rather than being restricted by the proportions available in proprietary blended cements.

Another type of cement that has found specialized applications in shotcrete is Calcium Aluminate Cement (CAC, also known as High Alumina Cement). Details regarding the chemistry and pros and cons of the use of this cement in concrete can be found in (Hewlett, 2003; Scrivener, 2003). Due to its rapid setting and early strength development characteristics, it has found use in a variety of different shotcrete projects, including shotcrete application on frozen ground and control of water in shotcrete lining of tunnels. Calcium aluminate cement shotcrete has also been found to provide higher acid and chemical resistance than Portland cement, and has as a consequence, been widely used in lining sewer pipes, where it displays high resistance to biogenic sulphide corrosion. Design and testing of concrete made of CAC for structural application requires care and expertise as various time-dependent microstructure phase changes can take place, not necessarily leading to a monotonic increase of strength over time (Adams et al., 2018).

Calcium aluminate cements have also been widely used in refractory shot-crete applications, where strength is required at high temperatures. This use of calcium aluminate cement in shotcrete is not elaborated upon in this book, as it could be a book unto itself. Details regarding refractory shotcrete mix designs and applications can be found in the Spring 2008 edition of Shotcrete Magazine, which was devoted to Refractory Shotcrete. (Shotcrete Magazine, Spring 2008).

4.3 SUPPLEMENTARY CEMENTING MATERIALS

4.3.1 Fly ash

The most widely used supplementary cementing material in shotcrete is fly ash. It is used for the same reasons that fly ash is used in concrete. In the plastic phase fly ash imparts benefits such as improved pumpability and hence *shootability* in shotcrete. In the hardened phase, fly ash use results in reduced heat of hydration (which can be beneficial in shooting thick sections, where high shotcrete temperatures, or differential thermal gradients could be of concern). In cool ambient temperatures, however, the percentage of fly ash used may have to be limited, as the reduced heat of hydration may result in slow setting and hardening and rates of early strength development in the shotcrete. Thus, while fly ash contents of 30% or more by mass of Portland cement are common in cast-in-place concrete, fly ash contents in shotcrete are generally limited from 15 to 25%.

Fly ash should conform to the requirements of ASTM C618, or CSA A3001(in CSA, 2018). ASTM C618 defines two classes of fly ash: Class F, produced from harder, older, anthracite or bituminous coals, and Class C, produced from younger lignite and sub-bituminous coals. Class F fly ash typically has less than about 7% lime (CaO) and has no self-cementing properties, i.e. when mixed with water it does not set and harden and gain strength like Portland cement. Rather, it acts as a pozzolan in concrete or shotcrete. (i.e. the fly ash reacts with calcium hydroxide produced in the hydration of Portland cement to produce additional calcium silicate hydrate, which is the main *glue* or binder in concrete or shotcrete). Class C fly ash typically has more than about 20% lime (CaO) and, in addition to having pozzolanic attributes, has self-cementing properties.

CSA A3001 defines three different types of fly ash: Type F low calcium content (< 15%) (similar to ASTM C618 Class F); Type CI intermediate calcium content (> 15% and < 20%) and Type CH high calcium content (>20%).

Fly ash is widely used in shotcrete in North America, primarily because of the enhanced durability it imparts to the shotcrete. The pozzolanic effects, which produce additional calcium silicate hydrate (CSH), result in reduced permeability in the shotcrete and this contributes to making the shotcrete less susceptible to leaching and efflorescence, sulphate attack, chloride ion penetration, frost damage and alkali-aggregate reactivity (AAR). Durability considerations are dealt with in Chapter 6. While both ASTM Class F and Class C fly ash have been used in shotcrete, it has been found that Class F fly ash is considerably more effective in suppressing AAR (Thomas, 2011). Since many of the aggregate sources in North America are alkali reactive, Class F fly ash has enjoyed the most widespread use in shotcrete in North America.

4.3.2 Silica fume

Next to fly ash, the most widely used supplementary cementing material in shotcrete in North America is silica fume. Silica fume is a by-product of the production of silica metal in a submerged electric arc furnace. Very pure quartz rock, with wood chip as a fluffing agent, is melted in the furnace and the molten silica metal is tapped out of the bottom of the furnace. The silica fume is the *smoke* that goes up the stack. It is collected in electro-static bag houses and then conveyed to process tanks where it is converted to *condensed silica fume* by tumbling air currents. In this densified form, it is suitable for transport and handling and mixing in ready mix concrete or dry-bagged concrete products production plants (Silica Fume Association, 2005; ACI 234R).

Silica fume is an amorphous, ultrafine material with spherical particles with average diameters of about 0.15 μm. This is about twice as fine as tobacco smoke and about 100 times smaller in diameter than the average Portland cement particle. The silica fume is composed of between 87% and 98% silicon dioxide (SiO_2) with the bulk of the remaining material being carbon from the wood chips used in the smelting process (this is what imparts the dark grey colour to silica fume). Being ultrafine and amorphous, silica fume is a *super-pozzolan*. It readily reacts to consume the calcium hydroxide (CH) from Portland cement hydration reactions, creating new calcium silicate hydrate (CSH). This markedly reduces permeability and enhances the durability of the shotcrete.

Silica Fume was first used in shotcrete in North America in the early 1980s (Morgan, 1988). It was first used for repair of reinforced concrete elements in a pier structure in intertidal regions in Vancouver Harbour, Canada, because of the superior wash-out resistance it provided to the shotcrete. During this project, and in subsequent laboratory studies and field applications, it was noted that at addition rates of around 8% (per mass of binder), silica fume remarkably increased the adhesion and cohesion and consequent thickness of build-up of shotcrete in a single pass achievable on both vertical and overhead surfaces, in both wet-mix and dry-mix shotcretes. It also substantially reduced the amount of shotcrete rebound, particularly with dry-mix shotcrete (Wolsiefer and Morgan, 1993).

In addition to the benefits that silica fume imparts to plastic (fresh) shotcrete, it also provides a number of benefits to the hardened shotcrete. Not only does it reduce permeability and increase early and later age compressive strength development, but also it increases resistance to chloride ion penetration (thus enhancing resistance to corrosion of reinforcing steel in structures), and also increases resistance to sulphate attack (Wolsiefer and Morgan, 1993; Zhang and Morgan, 2016). Silica fume also helps mitigate damage from AAR.

Because of the benefits that silica fume brings to shotcrete in both the plastic and hardened shotcrete, it is now almost universally used in North America for ground support in tunnelling and mining applications and infrastructure rehabilitation. It is particularly helpful in shotcrete used for marine structures repair in intertidal regions (Gilbride, Morgan and Bremner, 1988; Morgan, Rich and Lobo, 1998; Giroux and Reny, 2006).

4.3.3 Ground Granulated Blast Furnace Slag

There has been some use of Ground Granulated Blast Furnace Slag (GGBFS) in shotcrete in North America, but mainly in areas where fly ash is not readily available. It is used for much the same reasons that fly ash is used in shotcrete. In concrete, GGBFS is often used at cement replacement values of 40% to as much as 70%. Wet-mix shotcrete with such high cement replacement value is now also being used in thick structural shotcrete applications because of thermal control requirements. It is possible in such shotcrete to keep peak temperatures in structural elements 1.0 to 1.8 m thick below 60°C, which is important in mitigating differential thermal stress-induced cracking. Care is, however, required in the shotcrete mixture design to provide a mix with suitable *shootability* and *finishability* (resistance to sagging or sloughing). Incorporation of hydrophilic natural microfibres (either cellulose or hemp-based) has been found to be important in this regard. A case history example of the use of such high volume slag shotcrete mixes in heavily reinforced structural shotcrete walls in an underground station is presented in Section 10.3. Performance requirements for GGBFS can be found in ASTM C989 and CSA A3001(in CSA, 2018).

4.3.4 Natural pozzolans

A variety of different natural pozzolans have been used in shotcrete in North America, but only in a limited way. Consistency of quality and availability of supply have been factors that have limited their use in shotcrete. Perhaps the most successful of these natural pozzolans has been calcined metakaolin. Shotcrete with calcined metakaolin displays performance characteristics in the plastic and hardened phases intermediate in performance between fly ash and silica fume. As such, it has found use in tunnelling and mining applications on some North American projects. Morgan et al. (2010) describe one project where centrifugal sprayed concrete incorporating calcined metakaolin was successfully applied to line a 3.5 m diameter 290 m deep raise-bore shaft at a gold mine in British Columbia. The calcined metakaolin was used at a 20% cement replacement level. The same calcined metakaolin was used in wet-mix shotcrete, robotically applied, for underground support in the same gold mine for several years.

4.4 AGGREGATES

4.4.1 Grading requirements

Essentially the same aggregates are used in shotcrete as in conventional cast-in-place concrete, with the exception that a smaller maximum size of aggregate is used in shotcrete. The ASTM C1436 Standard Specification for Materials for Shotcrete (which is referenced in the ACI 506.2 Specification for Shotcrete), recognizes two different *Grading Limits for Combined Aggregates for Shotcrete:* Grading No. 1 and Grading No. 2. Grading No. 1 is essentially the same as that required for fine aggregate (concrete sand) in ASTM C33 and has a nominal maximum aggregate size of 4.75 mm. Grading No. 2 has a nominal maximum aggregate size of 9.5 mm and is typically produced by combining about 70% by mass of Grading No. 1 fine aggregate with about 30% by mass of a nominal 9.5 mm coarse aggregate. The grading limits for these two different aggregate sizes are shown in Table 4.2.

These grading limits are graphically depicted in Figure 4.1 which follows.

Historically, the original dry-mix shotcretes (*gunite*) used in the early 1900s and for many decades thereafter, used Grading No. 1 aggregates. In essence, these were *mortar* mixes. Most modern dry-mix shotcretes now, however, use Grading No. 2 aggregates (i.e. produce more concrete-like mixtures). There are still some projects which use Grading No. 1 aggregates in dry-mix shotcretes, such as encapsulating prestressing strands in water tank construction (Hanskat, 2010) and certain shotcrete repair materials.

Table 4.2 Grading limits for aggregates for shotcrete

Percent by mass passing individual sieve

Sieve size U.S. standard	Grading No. 1		Grading No. 2	
	Lower limit	Upper limit	Lower limit	Upper limit
12.5 mm	—	—	100	100
9.5 mm	100	100	90	100
4.75 mm	95	100	70	85
2.36 mm	80	98	50	70
1.18 mm	50	85	35	55
600 μm	25	60	20	35
300 μm	10	30	8	20
150 μm	2	10	2	10

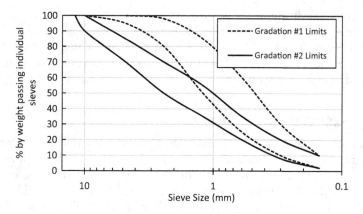

Figure 4.1 ACI 506 grading limits for aggregates for shotcrete.

The vast majority of wet-mix shotcretes, however, use Grading No. 2 or even larger size combined aggregate gradations. For wet-mix shotcrete, pumping in small diameter hoses (37.5 mm and 50 mm internal diameter) often imposes stringent requirements on mix design, and particularly on the *combined* aggregate gradation. It should be cautioned that meeting either of these Gradations may not necessarily be sufficient to guarantee easy pumping. It is the packing density of the combined aggregate phase's skeleton that needs to be considered (Jolin et al., 2009).

In much of Western North America, thick structural walls are constructed using wet-mix shotcrete with nominal 14 mm maximum size aggregate. There are reasons for this. Firstly, the larger the maximum aggregate size, the more *concrete-like* the shotcrete and the lower the water demand of the mix; hence, the lower the cementing materials content required to achieve a given water/cementing materials ratio. Also, the lower the water demand of the mix, the lower the drying shrinkage capacity of the mix, and hence a reduced potential for restrained drying shrinkage cracking. In addition, most ready-mix concrete suppliers have stockpiles of nominal 14 mm maximum size aggregate for their routine concrete production. Many ready-mix concrete suppliers do not keep stockpiles of nominal 9.5 mm maximum size aggregate (unless they are producing special concretes like exposed aggregate concretes for sidewalks and driveways). Thus, using 14 mm maximum size aggregates can lower the cost of wet-mix shotcrete mixes. It should, however, be noted that in hand application of shotcrete on overhead surfaces, such as in tunnels and mines, there is reluctance on the part of the nozzlemen to use larger than 9.5 mm maximum size coarse aggregate because of aggregate rebound. A rebounding 14 mm size aggregate can impact a nozzleman with more momentum than a 9.5 mm size aggregate particle. In short, it can hurt.

In an article "Improve your shotcrete: Use coarse aggregates" (Reny and Jolin, 2011), they make a good case for using coarse aggregate in shotcrete. In addition to the reasons listed above, they note that the larger maximum size aggregates provide a higher impacting velocity during shooting, which results in better compaction and consolidation of the shotcrete and encasement of reinforcing steel. This results in structures with enhanced durability.

4.4.2 Aggregate durability

In addition to the aggregate grading considerations discussed in the preceding paragraphs, shotcrete aggregates should conform to the requirements for physical properties and limits on deleterious substances for concrete aggregates detailed in publications such as ASTM C33 and CSA A23.1/A23.2. In particular, the aggregates should be petrographically suitable for use in concrete/shotcrete. They should be free of excessive amounts of soft or deleterious particles such as lumps of clay; low-density granular materials such as coal or lignite particles; ironstone; and swelling materials such as certain types of shalestone, mudstone and siltstone.

Aggregates should also be inherently durable. They should not be susceptible to breakdown from exposure to repeated cycles of freezing and thawing, or deicing chemicals. Freeze-thaw durability of the produced shotcrete can be evaluated in the ASTM C666 test, where shotcrete prisms are subjected to 300 cycles of freezing and thawing in a saturated condition (Morgan et al., 1988; Morgan, 1989; Morgan, 1991a). Resistance to deicing chemicals can be evaluated in the ASTM C672 salt scaling test, where shotcrete specimens are subjected to 50 cycles of freezing and thawing in a salt exposure condition (Beaupré et al., 1994; Dufour et al., 2006). In addition, aggregates should not be alkali reactive to the extent that they cause deleterious expansion in concrete/shotcrete from the alkalis in Portland cement, or from exposure to external sources of alkali. The inherent alkali-aggregate reaction (AAR) susceptibility of aggregates can be evaluated in tests such as ASTM C 1260, or CSA A23.2-25A accelerated mortar bar test (test results in 14 days), and CSA A23.2-14A concrete prism test (test results in one year).

Aggregates should also be free of excessive quantities of flat and/or elongated particles. Such aggregate particles do not pump or shoot well. Guidance as to what constitutes excessive amounts of flat and elongated particles can be found in ASTM C33 and CSA A23.1/A23.2. Experience has shown that naturally rounded gravels and sands, such as river gravels, with a limited amount of crushing tend to work best in pumping and shooting and display the least rebound. Crushed quarried rocks and occasionally manufactured sands are sometimes used in shotcrete production in regions where naturally rounded sands and gravels are not available. They, however, produce *harsher* mixes and require careful attention to mix designs and pumping and shooting equipment and procedures if pumping and placement difficulties are to be avoided.

In situations where shotcrete abrasion resistance is important, such as spillways, draft tubes and stilling basins in dams, where shotcrete has been used for remedial works (Zhang, et al., 2011), or in ore passes in mines, it is important that aggregates with high abrasion resistance be used. The abrasion resistance of aggregates can be evaluated in tests such as the Micro Deval abrasion test for fine aggregates (ASTM D7428 and CSA A23.2-23A) and Micro Deval abrasion test for Coarse aggregate (CSA A23.2-29A). The Los Angeles Abrasion test for small-size coarse aggregate (ASTM C131 and CSA A23.2-16A) can also be used. In addition to selecting aggregates with high abrasion resistance, the abrasion resistance of the mortar fraction in shotcrete can be substantially enhanced by the incorporation of an integral mineral hardener in the shotcrete.

4.5 CHEMICAL ADMIXTURES

4.5.1 Introduction

Modern shotcretes rely heavily on the addition of various types of chemical admixtures to provide the shotcrete with optimal performance in both the plastic (fresh) and hardened states. Different types of admixtures are used in wet and dry-mix shotcretes. ASTM C494 provides a specification for admixtures used in cast-in-place concrete. ASTM C1141 provides a specification for nine different types of admixtures for use in wet and dry-mix shotcretes. Table 4.3 which follows lists these various types of admixtures in the ASTM C1141 standard.

Table 4.3 ASTM C1141 shotcrete admixture requirements

Type I—Dry-mix shotcrete

Grade	Admixture	ASTM standard
1	Accelerating	D98, C494/C494M type C or E
2	Retarding	C494/C494M type B or D
3	Pozzolanic	C618, C989/C989M, C1240
4	Metallic iron	Not established
5	Colouring	C979/C979M
6	Organic polymer	C1438

Grade	Admixture	ASTM Standard
1	Accelerating	D98, C494/C494M types C or E
2	Retarding	C494/C494M, type B, D or G
3	Pozzolanic	C618, C989/C989M, C1240
4	Metallic iron	Not established
5	Colouring	C979/C979M
6	Organic polymer	C1438
7	Water reducing	C494/C494M, types A, D, E, F, or G
8	Air-entraining	C260/C260M

Not all of these admixture types are, however, routinely used in shotcrete and there are some other types of admixtures which are used, which are not listed in the ASTM C1141 standard. Thus, the discussion which follows concentrates on the most commonly used admixtures and the reasons for their use.

In dry-mix shotcrete, the most commonly used admixtures are dry-powdered accelerators added during batching and, in frost exposure environments, air-entraining admixtures added either to the mixing water added at the nozzle, or as dry powdered admixtures added during batching. (Note: The use of pozzolans is dealt with in Section 4.3 of this chapter.)

In wet-mix shotcrete, the most commonly used admixtures are as follows:

a) Water-reducing admixtures, including normal, mid-range and high-range water reducers (Note: high-range water reducers are often referred to as superplasticizers);
b) Air-entraining admixtures;
c) Accelerating admixtures added at the nozzle;
d) Retarding admixtures;
e) Hydration control admixtures;

Other types of admixtures, such as shrinkage reducers, corrosion inhibitors and alkali-silica reactivity inhibitors are also sometimes added, but their use is not common. In architectural shotcretes, particularly in artificial rockscapes and like projects, colouring admixtures are frequently used.

4.5.2 Dry-mix shotcrete admixtures

Dry-mix shotcrete admixtures can be added either in a dry powdered form during batching, or as a liquid added at the nozzle during shooting. When shotcrete is supplied in an *oven-dry* form in paper bags, or bulk bin bags, the admixture is usually pre-blended into the mix during dry batching and is activated when water is added to the batch in the predampener and at the nozzle. Dry powdered accelerators and air-entraining admixtures are commonly added in this way.

4.5.2.1 Water reducers

Note that there is no need to add a dry powdered water-reducing admixture (or superplasticizer) to dry-mix shotcrete. For like mixtures the water demand is inherently lower in dry-mix shotcrete, compared to an equivalent wet-mix shotcrete without a water reducer, since there is no need to have extra *water of workability* to facilitate conveying the shotcrete by pumping. In fact, the addition of a powdered water reducer or superplasticizer to dry-mix shotcrete can have very detrimental effects. The powder can activate in situ after the shotcrete has been applied, resulting in sagging, sloughing and fall-out of the shotcrete.

4.5.2.2 Air entrainment

Air entrainment is beneficial for enhancing the resistance of shotcrete to freeze/thaw damage and deicing salt scaling. Prior to the 1990s, the conventional wisdom, as stated in the ACI 506 Guide to Shotcrete and other publications, was that it was not possible to effectively entrain air in dry-mix shotcrete. Extensive research conducted at Université Laval in Quebec in the 1990s, however, debunked this myth (Jolin and Bissonnette, 2006). They demonstrated that there were effectively two ways in which to entrain air in dry-mix shotcrete. The first was to add a liquid air-entraining admixture to the mix water supplied to the nozzle (Lamontagne et al., 1996). The second way was to add a dry powdered air-entraining admixture to the dry shotcrete mix during batching operations. Both of these methods were capable of producing in-place shotcrete with a satisfactory air content and in-place air void system. Dufour, however, expressed a preference for the use of dry powdered air-entraining admixtures as better control over the admixture dosage was possible, compared to the use of a liquid air-entraining admixture added to the mix water introduced at the nozzle, since nozzlemen frequently adjust the amount of liquid added at the nozzle to cater to shooting conditions (Dufour, 2008). Organizations such as the Quebec Ministry of Transportation (Dufour et al., 2006) and ACI (ACI 506R-16 Guide to Shotcrete) now specify the use of air entrainment in dry-mix shotcrete in freeze/thaw and deicing chemical exposure environments.

A variety of different chemical compounds have been used as air-entraining admixtures in concrete/shotcrete, including vinsol resins, salts of sulfonated lignin, salts of petroleum acids, salts of proteinaceous acids, alkylbenzene sulfonates and sulfonated hydrocarbons. Users should consult with their admixture supplier, as some types of air-entraining admixtures create more stable air bubbles during the shotcrete shooting process than others.

4.5.2.3 Accelerators

Accelerating admixtures can be added to dry-mix shotcrete as dry powdered admixture preblended in with the dry-mix materials during batching. In wet-mix shotcrete, accelerating admixtures are added in a liquid form at the nozzle. They are predominantly used for overhead applications in tunnels and mines and in intertidal projects in marine applications. Accelerators are added to rapidly accelerate the plastic shotcrete setting and hardening characteristics, which in turn allows for the build-up of thicker layers of shotcrete more rapidly, with reduced potential for sagging, sloughing and fall out. They also increase the resistance to wash-out of shotcrete applied in wet conditions. In the hardened state, they increase the rate of early strength development in the shotcrete (up to about 24 hours). This can accelerate the time permitted for man re-entry into underground space in tunnelling and mining applications (Rispin, 2005). The accelerator dosage should, however, be carefully controlled as the higher the accelerator dosage, the greater the reduction in later age compressive strength and durability parameters such as Boiled Absorption (BA) and Volume of Permeable Voids (VPV) (ASTM C642) and rapid chloride permeability (ASTM C1202), (Jolin et al., 1997; Zhang and Morgan, 2016).

There are a variety of different types of accelerators which have been used in dry-mix shotcretes:

a) Alkaline silicate-based accelerators (e.g. sodium silicates and modified sodium silicates), with a pH in the 12 to 13 range, available in liquid form;
b) Alkaline aluminate-based accelerators (e.g. sodium and potassium aluminates), with a pH typically in the 13 to 14 range, available in powder and liquid form;
c) Carbonate based accelerators, available only in powdered form;
d) Calcium chloride, available in powder and liquid form;
e) Alkali-free accelerators commonly based on suspensions of aluminum sulphate compounds, with a pH in the 2.5 to 3.5 range, available in powder and liquid form.

The alkaline silicate-based accelerators were amongst the earliest types of accelerators added to dry-mix shotcrete at the nozzle. Some of the first versions were simply waterglass (sodium silicate). They were reasonably effective in providing the shotcrete with enhanced adhesion and cohesion, allowing for more rapid build-up of shotcrete without sagging and sloughing. Unfortunately, they were sometimes abused, being added at dosage rates of up to 20% by mass of cement. While this enabled great thicknesses of shotcrete to be applied overhead in a single pass (up to 500 mm), it had serious detrimental influences on the later age-hardened shotcrete properties. Compressive strengths at 28 days were often below 20 MPa with BA values in excess of 10% and VPV values in excess of 20%. Such shotcretes proved to be non-durable and deteriorated in a few years from the deleterious effects of leaching and frost action. Modern modified sodium silicates are generally more effective at lower dosage rates than the earlier versions and less detrimental to later age-hardened shotcrete performance. They are now mainly used in developing countries (because of their lower cost per litre), and in locations where there are incompatibilities between the types of Portland cement available and alkali-free accelerators.

Up until 2000, both liquid and powder alkaline-based accelerators were widely used in dry-mix shotcrete throughout the world. They were generally effective in promoting rapid setting and hardening and early-age strength development when used at dosages ranging from about 4 to 7% by mass of Portland cement. At these addition rates, shotcretes of acceptable quality could generally be produced. There have, however, been a number of projects where the dosage has been increased to 8 to 10% and at these addition rates the strength and durability of the shotcrete can be compromised. Also, with a pH of 13 to 14, the alkaline mist created during shooting using these materials can create an unsafe working environment. Protective clothing, respirators and eye protection should be worn at all times. Exposed skin can suffer alkaline burns. As a consequence of such safety concerns, a number of countries now prohibit the use of such alkaline accelerators in shotcrete.

Calcium chloride is an economical and effective set accelerator. It should, however not be used in any shotcrete with embedded metals such as reinforcing steel, rock bolts and lattice girders, because of the potential for the rapid onset of corrosion of the steel. Its use has been limited to special applications, such as installation of shotcrete in permafrost ground in a mine in Northern Canada (Dufour, 2000). In this case, a chloride brine solution was added to the prebagged dry-mix shotcrete at the nozzle. This allowed the shotcrete to set, harden and gain sufficient strength before freeze-back stopped hydration reactions (and inhibited steel corrosion reactions). On another project in a potash mine in Saskatchewan, it was not permissible to apply dry-mix shotcrete with potable water added at the nozzle, because such water resulted in dissolution of the potash, compromising shotcrete bond. Thus, chloride accelerator was added to the shotcrete to counteract this dissolution effect and acceptable bond was achieved. Because of the temporary nature of the mine, the rate of corrosion of embedded metals was deemed to be acceptable. Calcium chloride is also not recommended for use in unreinforced concrete/shotcrete, as it markedly increases the drying shrinkage capacity of the mix and hence potential for restrained drying shrinkage cracking and delamination (Morgan, 1975).

The now most commonly used shotcrete accelerators (for both dry- and wet-mix shotcretes) are alkali-free accelerators. Not only have they substantially enhanced the health and safety in the working environment, but they have also proven to be very beneficial for the shotcrete production process. When used at suitable addition rates they provide acceptable setting and hardening and early-age strength development characteristics to the shotcrete and have less detrimental effect on the later age compressive strength development and durability characteristics of the shotcrete (Zhang and Morgan, 2016). Most of the underground support projects now carried out with wet-mix shotcrete in North America now use alkali-free accelerators added at the nozzle.

4.5.3 Wet-mix shotcrete admixtures

4.5.3.1 Water reducers

Water-reducing admixtures are almost universally used in wet-mix shot-cretes. With its inherently high cementing materials content, water-reducing admixtures are required to keep the water demand of the mix at a sufficiently low level. A good target range for the water demand is 180 to 200 L/m^3. If this is not done, the plastic shotcrete can display poor shootability. At water demands below about 180 L/m^3 the mixture may be too stiff to provide good pumpability and shootability to provide optimal consolidation and encasement of reinforcing steel and embedded items. At water demands above about 200 L/m^3 the shotcrete may become vulnerable to sagging and sloughing. Also, in the hardened state the compressive strength and durability characteristics may be compromised, and the mix would likely display higher drying shrinkage capacity, with an increased potential for restrained drying shrinkage cracking.

With Portland cement as the binder, or in Portland cement plus fly ash mixes, or Portland cement plus slag mixes, the use of a standard *ASTM Type A Water Reducing Admixture, or ASTM Type D Water Reducing and Retarding Admixture* will likely suffice to produce an acceptable water demand in the shotcrete mix. In mixes with Portland cement and silica fume, it will probably be necessary to use an *ASTM Type F High Range Water Reducing Admixture* (superplasticizer), or *ASTM Type G Water Reducing, High Range, and Retarding Admixture* (ASTM C494) to provide an acceptable water demand in the shotcrete mix, as silica fume has a high water demand.

Prior to the 1980s, lignosulfonates (a by-product of the pulp and paper industry) were the most commonly used water reducers in concrete and shotcrete (Morgan, 1975). Since then, a wide range of different types of chemicals have been used as water-reducing admixtures, including hydroxylated carboxylic acids and various types of carbohydrates. Earlier types of high-range water reducers included sulfonated melamine formaldehyde condensates and sulfonated naphthalene formaldehyde condensates. The dosage level at which these admixtures could be used was generally limited, as excessively high dosages could result in adverse effects, such as extended set retardation. Modern so-called full-range water reducers have now been developed, which can act like standard Water-reducing Admixtures at lower dosage levels and like high-range water-reducing admixtures at higher dosage levels, without adverse effects on the concrete/shotcrete. Such admixtures are commonly based on polycarboxylates and are proving to be popular in modern wet-mix shotcretes.

4.5.3.2 Retarders and hydration-controlling admixtures

ASTM Type B Retarding Admixtures (ASTM C494) (Also referred to as ASTM *Group II Grade 2 Retarding Admixture* in ASTM C1141) have been used on many shotcrete projects over the decades, where extended workability and delayed setting time are required. A wide variety of different products have been used as retarders, including various types of lignin, borax, sugars and tartaric acids and salts. The limitations of most of these types of retarding admixtures are that while they can delay set for many hours (or even days), depending on the dosage level, they are limited in how long they can extend the workability (slump) of the plastic concrete/shotcrete. Recognizing this limitation, extensive work was conducted by admixture manufacturers to develop a new generation of admixtures referred to as hydration-controlling admixtures.

These hydration-controlling admixtures act as chelating agents, i.e. they coat the cement grains to inhibit the cement hydration reactions. Depending on the hydration-controlling admixture dosage, they can extend the workability and setting time by several hours, or even days. When their effect wears off, setting and hardening and strength development reactions develop in a normal way. One of their major advantages in shotcrete, particularly in shotcrete for underground support in tunnels and mines, is that their hydration-controlling effect can be *switched off* instantaneously by the addition of a suitable shotcrete accelerator at the nozzle. Shotcrete batched on a day shift can be sent underground and then held in a remixer unit for 12 or more hours, until the night shift is ready to use it. Shotcrete with a slump in the 170mm to 220 mm range can be pumped to the nozzle and then *woken up* by the accelerator addition at the nozzle (Radomski et al., 2019). This instantaneously converts the shotcrete to a stiff mix (with no slump) which can adhere to vertical and overhead surfaces without sagging, sloughing and fall-out. Cement hydration reactions immediately commence. Initial set times are reached in a few minutes and rapid early and later age compressive strength are developed. The advent of hydration-controlling admixtures has been a boon for the shotcrete industry, as they have revolutionized what is now possible by way of shotcrete delivery and application.

4.5.3.3 Set accelerators

There are two different types of accelerators that can be added to wet-mix shotcrete. The first is accelerating admixtures which are added to the shotcrete mix during batching, in the same way as used in concrete mixes. ASTM C1141-15 describes these as *Type II, Grade 1 Accelerating Admixtures*. Chemicals such as calcium chloride, triethanolamine, calcium formate, calcium nitrite and calcium nitrate have been used for this purpose. The accelerators decrease the setting time and increase the rate of early strength development. They can be useful in cold weather conditions, where lower ambient and shotcrete temperatures can cause delays in setting and hardening of the shotcrete. Their major disadvantage, however, is that they increase the rate of loss of workability. Shotcrete mixtures generally take longer to discharge from ready mix concrete trucks than cast-in-place concrete, and so excessively rapid rates of loss of workability can be a problem. For this reason, other than in cold weather conditions, ASTM *Type II, Grade 1 Accelerating Admixtures* are not often used in wet-mix shotcrete.

The second type of wet-mix shotcrete accelerators are liquid accelerators added at the nozzle. Essentially the same types of accelerators added at the nozzle described in the preceding section on accelerators in dry-mix shotcrete are also used in wet-mix shotcrete. The same pros and cons for the different types of accelerators detailed for dry-mix shotcretes also apply to wet-mix shotcretes. Most impressive, however, is their ability to transform a high workability mix with a 170 mm to 220 mm slump into instantly stiff shotcrete when sprayed onto the receiving surface. While shotcretes without accelerator addition at the nozzle are typically sprayed at slumps in the 50 to 90 mm range, mixes with such slumps are not well suited to uniform accelerator addition at the nozzle. Indeed, mixes with lower slumps (stiffer mixes) may lead to incomplete filling of the pump cylinders and a more pronounced interruption of concrete flow at the nozzle when the swing valve moves from one cylinder to the other (i.e. surge effect). While this is not a problem when spraying wet-mix shotcrete *without* accelerator, it has the potential to create non-uniform dispersion of accelerator through the mix since the accelerator is added at the nozzle at a constant flow, resulting in in-place shotcrete with accelerator-rich and accelerator-poor layers (Millette, 2011 and Section 7.3.3).

The most commonly used wet-mix shotcrete accelerators now used in North America are alkali-free accelerators. Not only are they more user-friendly and safer for the shotcrete crew from a health perspective, but they also have less detrimental effect on the compressive strength and durability of the hardened shotcrete, compared to the earlier generation alkali-based accelerators, particularly when used at high addition rates (Beaupré and Jolin, 2002). The *New Austrian Guideline on Sprayed Concrete* provides requirements for chemical properties and strength performance for "non-alkaline" shotcrete set accelerators for use in both wet and dry-mix shotcretes (Kusterle, 1999).

4.5.3.4 Air-entraining admixtures

Wet-mix shotcrete exposed to cycles of freezing and thawing in a saturated condition needs to be properly air entrained to provide freeze/thaw durability (Morgan et al., 1988; Morgan, 1989; Morgan, 1991a). It is important to note that the shooting process *knocks out* a large proportion of the larger bubbles, reducing the air content into the range of 5+/–1.5% and providing a high-quality air-void system. While in practice the target should be between 7% and 10% for pumping efficiency, it is interesting to note that shotcrete with as high as 19% air content has been successfully pumped and sprayed, yielding an in-place air content of only 5% (Beaupré et al., 2001). Note: the air content of the in-place shotcrete is best determined by digging the shotcrete out from the receiving surface and reconsolidating it in an air pressure meter base as if it were plastic concrete, and then running the ASTM C231 test (Jolin and Beaupré, 2003; Zhang, 2012). The parameters of the air void system in the hardened shotcrete can be determined on cores extracted from the in-place shotcrete, tested to ASTM C457. This test measures the air content in the hardened concrete, as well as the specific surface and spacing factor of the air void system. To be freeze/thaw durable, the hardened in-place shotcrete needs to have an acceptable air content and spacing factor. More details regarding this issue are provided in Section 6.3.

It is well recognized in the shotcrete industry that a high initial air content will increase the slump of the as-batched shotcrete. This can make the shotcrete easy to pump and shoot. As the shotcrete impacts on the receiving surface and about half of the air content is lost, the slump of the in-place shotcrete goes down instantaneously. This so-called *slump killer* effect, which was documented by Beaupré in his Doctoral thesis (Beaupré, 1994), is very beneficial to the shotcrete process as, as it results in improved adhesion and cohesion of the shotcrete on the receiving surface, permitting greater thicknesses of build-up without sagging and sloughing (Zhang, 2012).

The same types of chemicals listed for air entrainment in dry-mix shotcrete have also been used in wet-mix shotcrete. The admixture suppliers should, however, be consulted in selecting an air-entraining admixture for wet-mix shotcrete, as some types of admixtures produce a more stable air bubble with a resultant better in-place air void system.

4.5.3.5 Other admixtures

A variety of other types of admixtures are sometimes used in wet-mix shotcrete, including shrinkage reducing admixtures, corrosion inhibitors, colouring admixtures, organic polymer admixtures, etc. Care should, however, be taken in using such products to determine not only their influence on the prime reason(s) for which they are promoted but also for their effects on all the application and physical properties of both the plastic and hardened shotcrete. For example, some types of latex polymer shotcrete admixtures produced shotcretes which proved to be vulnerable to debonding between shotcrete layers when submerged in seawater.

4.6 FIBRES

4.6.1 Introduction

ASTM C1116 defines four categories of fibres for use in concrete:

Type I   Steel Fibres (includes stainless, alloy and carbon steel fibres)
Type II   Glass Fibres (alkali-resistant glass fibres)

Type III   Synthetic Fibres
Type IV   Natural Fibres (cellulose-based fibres)

The American Concrete Institute (ACI CT-18) offers the following definitions for fibres:

- Fibre: a slender and elongated solid material, generally with a length at least 100 times its diameter;
- Fibre aspect ratio: the ratio of the length to diameter of a fibre in which the diameter may be an equivalent diameter; and
- Equivalent fibre diameter: diameter of a circle having an area equal to the average cross-sectional area of a fibre.

With regard to the size of the fibres, the following two definitions are also provided by ACI:

- Macrofibre: a fibre with an equivalent diameter greater than or equal to 0.3 mm for use in concrete; and
- Microfibre: a fibre with an equivalent diameter less than 0.3 mm for use in concrete.

And finally, with regard to material, ACI defines:

- Steel fibres: discrete fibres made of steel, used as reinforcement in concrete; and
- Synthetic fibres: chopped fibres made of polyolefin, such as polypropylene and polyethylene materials, used as reinforcement in concrete.

These ACI definitions illustrate the scope of products a specifier may have to deal with: macrofibres with typical lengths varying from 30 to 60 mm and of diameters ranging from 0.3 to 1 mm, made of either steel or synthetic material. The various nuances of steel or types of polyolefin in turn make fibres available over a wide range of physical properties, and the various shapes or surface textures offered completes the picture of an industry that has hundreds of different types of fibre products available. Furthermore, microfibres of various types may be included in the mixes to help improve resistance to early-age cracking and in the case of synthetic microfibres, enhance resistance of concrete or shotcrete to explosive spalling in fires.

A variety of different types of fibres have been used in wet and dry-mix shotcretes (ACI 506.1R; Morgan and Heere, 2000; Vandewalle, 1996; RTC, 2019). Chapter 3 provides a historical background to the introduction and use of fibres in shotcrete. The most commonly used fibre types in shotcrete include:

a) Steel fibres
b) Synthetic macrofibres (fibres with equivalent diameters > 0.3 mm)

c) Synthetic microfibres (fibres with equivalent diameters < 0.3 mm)

d) Natural microfibres

The majority of synthetic fibres used have been made from polypropylene, but some nylon fibres and blends of polypropylene and polyethylene fibres have also been used. Natural fibres used include hemp-based fibres and cellulose fibres. An interesting new development is a treated hemp-based natural fibre, designed to be used in the same applications as synthetic microfibres (Morgan et al., 2017). Other types of fibres have also been used, but less commonly. These include glass fibres, carbon fibres and polyvinyl alcohol fibres. More details regarding the more common fibre types used in shotcrete are provided in the sections which follow.

4.6.2 Macrofibres

In concrete technology, macrofibres are used to improve the properties of concrete *after* cracking. In practice, the effects of fibres on this *post-cracking behaviour* are to control the opening of the cracks, absorb or dissipate energy at the crack location and improve impact resistance. While the detailed mechanisms by which fibres work in concrete are detailed elsewhere (Bentur and Mindess, 2019), it must be stressed that the extent of these effects will greatly depend on *both* the quality of the concrete or shotcrete matrix and the type and dosage of fibre used. This explains why manufacturers have been so inventive over the years by developing fibre textures and shapes that improve adhesion and friction with the surrounding hydrated cement paste. These fibre improvements generate a better uptake of the loads after cracking and/or a higher energy absorption in the concrete/shotcrete element, and/or reduction in the required fibre addition rate for a given specified performance.

Apart from the properties of the fibre itself, perhaps the most useful parameter describing a fibre is the *aspect ratio*, which is defined as length/equivalent diameter. The higher the aspect ratio and volume concentration of the fibre, the better the performance of the fibre reinforced shotcrete (FRS) with respect to parameters such as toughness, crack resistance and impact resistance. There are, however, practical limits to the aspect ratio and volume concentration of fibres that can be used, because as it becomes higher, the shotcrete becomes more difficult to mix, convey and shoot. Some of the earliest generation steel fibres were straight, with aspect ratios in the 50 to 83 range (Banthia et al., 1992). They were often difficult to convey and shoot and provided less than impressive toughness performance. Manufacturers then devised ways to improve the effective aspect ratio of steel fibres by techniques such as: hooked ends, stamped enlarged ends, stamped continuous deformations and crimping. Another technique successfully used is to glue the fibres together (like staples) with a water-soluble glue, to create an artificially low aspect ratio for easy batching, with the individual fibres then getting dispersed in the mix during mixing. In parallel,

Table 4.4 Typical fibre properties

	Steel fibre	Macrosynthetic fibre
Young's modulus	200–210 GPa	3–12 GPa
Tensile strength	350–2500 MPa	350–650 MPa
Melting points	1500°C	165°C
Significant thermal creep limit	370°C	> 20°C

synthetic fibre manufactures have improved performances by using fibrillating and collated fibres; nowadays most of the modern higher performance synthetic macrofibres are, however, supplied in a monofilament form with various types of deformations or embossing on them to enhance bond.

For a given toughness performance level (see Sections 6.9 and 13.4), the fibre volume addition rate required will vary, depending on the fibre tensile strength and *equivalent aspect ratio* and concrete matrix quality. Typical macrofibre properties are shown in Table 4.4 (RTC, 2019).

The question of the appropriate fibre type and dosage is often the source of animated discussions. Given what has been said so far, it should be understood that the right choice of fibre (type and dosage) will be the result of an approach combining the properties of the shotcrete to be produced and the expected performances.

Macrofibres also modify the rheology of the fresh shotcrete, providing more cohesive mixtures with greater resistance to sagging, sloughing and fall-out. It should also be noted that the high velocity of the sprayed material has a positive effect on the orientation of fibres as they tend to align in a predominantly 2D plane parallel to the substrate. This favourable orientation functions well, as the fibres are positioned to intercept potential cracking going through the thickness of the shotcrete. It is considered that a predominantly 2D plane orientation may improve efficiency by as much as 100% when compared to a purely 3D random spatial distribution (Bentur and Mindess, 2019).

4.6.2.1 Steel fibres

The majority of steel fibres used in shotcrete have been made from carbon steel, but in very aggressive exposure conditions and/or where higher tensile strengths are required to provide high *toughness* performance (residual load-carrying capacity after cracking), alloy and stainless-steel fibres have been used. Various processes have been used for the manufacture of steel fibres, including cutting cold-drawn steel wire, slitting steel sheet, milling steel block, shaving prestressing steel wire and the melt extraction process (Figure 4.2). By far the vast majority of steel fibres used in shotcrete have, however, been produced from cut cold-drawn steel wire (Morgan, 1991b).

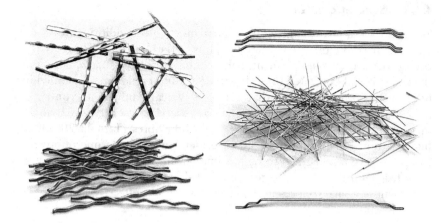

Figure 4.2 Examples of steel fibres used in shotcrete.

Deformed fibres with lengths of 30 to 38 mm and aspect ratios ranging from 40 to 60 are now common. Steel fibre addition rates typically range from 40 to 60 kg/m^3 (0.51 to 0.76% volume) with values as high as 80 kg/m^3 (1.02% volume) occasionally being used. (Morgan et al., 1995). It should, however, be noted that some fibre can be lost as rebound during the shooting process, particularly in the dry-mix shotcrete process. See Chapter 6 for more detail on this issue.

4.6.2.2 Synthetic fibres

The majority of synthetic macrofibres used have been made from polypropylene, but some nylon fibres and blends of polypropylene and polyethylene fibres have been used. Synthetic macrofibres are mainly used in wet-mix shotcrete. They are typically used in fibre addition rates of 5 to 9 kg/m^3 (about 0.5 to 1.0% by volume of the shotcrete). They have been produced in a variety of different forms, including monofilament, fibrillated, partially fibrillating and collated. Lengths and equivalent aspect ratios vary, but lengths in the 30 to 50 mm range are common.

4.6.3 Microfibres

While microfibres also have a positive effect on the rheology of the freshly applied shotcrete, increasing resistance to sagging, sloughing and fall-out, they are mainly used to provide:

a) Plastic shrinkage cracking control (Morgan et al., 2017)
b) Resistance to explosive spalling in fire exposure conditions (Tatnall, 2002)

4.6.3.1 Synthetic fibres

Synthetic microfibres are generally used in much lower addition rates of only 1 to 2 kg/m³ (about 0.1 to 0.2% by volume of the shotcrete). They have also been produced in monofilament, collated and fibrillated forms. On mixing the collated and fibrillated fibres break down into predominantly individual fibres. It has been calculated that 1 kg of a typical synthetic microfibre will have about 114 million fibres. By comparison, 1 kg of a typical synthetic macrofibre will have about 20,000 to 30,000 fibres (Tatnall, 2002). The fine size and large number of fibres present in synthetic microfibre rein-forced shotcrete is claimed to be a prime reason why synthetic microfibres are effective in enhancing the resistance of shotcrete to explosive spalling in fires. Synthetic macrofibres and steel fibres are not effective in this regard (Tatnall, 2002).

4.6.3.2 Natural fibres

Relatively new natural microfibres (hemp or cellulose based) are also now being used in lieu of the synthetic microfibres in wet-mix shotcrete (Morgan et al., 2017). Their major advantage is that they are hydrophilic (absorb water), compared to synthetic fibres, which are hydrophobic (repel water).

Benefits which accrue from their use in shotcrete include:

a) The fibre is readily dispersible in wet-mix shotcrete, providing uni-form distribution of the fibre during mixing, pumping and shooting and this helps prevent segregation.
b) The applied shotcrete is easier to finish than mixes with synthetic microfibre (no fibres are evident in the finished surface).
c) Water absorbed by the fibre during batching and mixing acts as an "internal curing agent" in that it releases moisture to the cement hydration reactions as the shotcrete dries and this helps mitigate early age plastic and drying shrinkage induced cracking. (Morgan et al., 2017; see Section 6.11)

4.7 WATER

Water added to the predampener and at the nozzle in dry-mix shotcrete, and all curing water, should preferably be of drinking water quality (pota-ble). Similarly, water added during batching and mixing, and any water added at the site to wet-mix shotcrete, and used for curing, should prefer-ably be potable. If potable water is not available (as occurs on some mine sites and remote locations), then the mixing and curing water should be free of any substances that could be injurious to shotcrete or embedded metals. For example, water containing chlorides should not be used, unless the maximum water-soluble chloride-ion concentration in the shotcrete

Table 4.5 Maximum water-soluble chloride-ion concentration in shotcrete to protect steel reinforcement from corrosion, percent by mass of shotcrete (ACI 318)[1]

Prestressed concrete	0.06
Reinforced concrete exposed to chloride in service	0.15
Reinforced concrete that will be dry or protected from moisture in service	1.0
Other	0.3

[1] Adapted from ACI 318.

produced using such water is below the limits specified in ACI 318 as detailed in Table 4.5, in order to protect reinforcing steel and embedded metals from corrosion.

Non-potable water should only be used if it can be demonstrated that it does not adversely affect plastic and hardened shotcrete properties. It should not have detrimental effects on the setting time and slump retention, or the compressive strength and durability of the shotcrete. For example, CSA A23.1 requires that concrete (shotcrete) made with non-potable water produce a compressive strength at 28 days of at least 90% of that produced by a control concrete (shotcrete) made using a known acceptable water. ACI 318, Section 3.4 requires that mortar cubes made with non-potable water produce a compressive strength of at least 90% of mortar cubes made with distilled water.

With respect to durability, care should be exercised to not use water containing excessive amounts of organic substances. Some organic substances can cause set retardation and/or excessive air entrainment, which can interfere with shotcrete quality. Non-potable water with excessive amounts of alkalis should also be avoided; it can cause rapid loss of workability and set acceleration. It can also increase the alkali content in the shotcrete to the extent that it could be injurious when potentially alkali reactive aggregates are being used (i.e. result in deleterious AAR) (CSA A864). Excessive amounts of alkalis in the mix and curing water can also result in objectionable efflorescence and staining in the hardened shotcrete. Similarly, excessive amounts of sulphates should be avoided, as they can interfere with setting time and promote internal sulphate attack in the shotcrete. ASTM C1602 provides limits for chlorides, alkalis (expressed as Na_2O equivalent) and sulphates in mix water. These limits are summarized in Table 4.6.

With respect to curing water, if potable water is not available, water with ferrous compounds or other chemicals which could cause discoloration and staining should be avoided, particularly in architectural quality shotcrete. Also, any water used for curing should not be more than 10°C cooler than the shotcrete to which it is applied, in order to protect against thermal shock-induced cracking (ACI 506R).

Table 4.6 Chemical limits for mixing water (ASTM C1602)

Maximum concentration in combined mixing water, ppm[1]	Limits
A. Chloride as Cl–, ppm	
1. In prestressed concrete, bridge decks, or otherwise designated	500
2. Other reinforced concrete in moist environments or containing aluminum embedments or dissimilar metals or with stay-in-place galvanized metal forms	1000
B. Sulfate as SO_4, ppm	3000
C. Alkalis as $(Na_2O + 0.658 K_2O)$, ppm	600

[1] ppm is the abbreviation for parts per million

REFERENCES

ACI 234R. 2006. *Guide for Use of Silica Fume in Concrete. American Concrete Institute.*

ACI 506.1R-21. 2021. *Guide to Fiber Reinforced Shotcrete.* American Concrete Institute. 20 p.

ACI 506R-16. 2016. *Guide to Shotcrete.* American Concrete Institute. 52 p.

ACI CODE-318-19. 2019 *Building Code Requirements for Structural Concrete and Commentary.* American Concrete Institute. https://doi.org/10.14359/51716937

ACI-506.2-13(18). 2013, reapproved 2018. *Specification for Shotcrete.* American Concrete Institute. 12 p.

ACI CT-18. 2018a. *Concrete Terminology.* American Concrete Institute. 80.

ASTM C457. 2016a. *Standard Test Method for Microscopical Determination of Parameters of the Air-Void System in Hardened Concrete.* 7p. ASTM International. https://doi.org/10.1520/C0457_C0457M-16

ASTM C494. 2019. *Standard Specification for Chemical Admixtures for Concrete.* 15p. ASTM International. https://doi.org/10.1520/C0494_C0494M-19

ASTM C618. 2019. *Standard Specification for Coal Fly Ash and Raw or Calcined Natural Pozzolan for Use in Concrete.* 5p. ASTM International. https://doi.org/10.1520/C0618-19

ASTM C1116. 2019a. *standard Specification for Fiber-Reinforced Concrete.* 7p. ASTM International. https://doi.org/10.1520/C1116_C1116M-10AR15

Adams, M. P., Lute, R. D., Moffatt, E. G. and Ideker, J. H. 2018. Evaluation of a Procedure for Determining the Converted Strength of Calcium Aluminate Cement Concrete. *Journal of Testing and Evaluation.* Vol. 46. No. 4. https://doi.org/10.1520/JTE20160277

ASTM C1141. 2015. *Standard Specification for Admixtures for Shotcrete.* 4 p. ASTM International. https://doi.org/10.1520/C1141_C1141M-15

ASTM C1202. 2019. *Standard Test Method for Electrical Indication of Concrete's Ability to Resist Chloride Ion Penetration.* 8 p. ASTM International.https://doi.org/10.1520/C1202-19

ASTM C1260. 2021. *Standard Test Method for Potential Alkali Reactivity of Aggregates (Mortar-Bar Method).* 5 p. ASTM International. https://doi.org/10.1520/C1260-21

ASTM C131. 2020 *Standard Test Method for Resistance to Degradation of Small-Size Coarse Aggregate by Abrasion and Impact in the Los Angeles Machine.* ASTM International. 5 p. https://doi.org/10.1520/c0131_c0131m-20

ASTM C1436. 2013. *Standard Specification for Materials for Shotcrete.* 2 p. ASTM International. https://doi.org/10.1520/C1436-13

ASTM C150. 2021. *Standard Specification for Portland Cement.* ASTM International. 9 p. https://doi.org/10.1520/c0150_c0150m-21

ASTM C1602. 2018. *Standard Specification for Mixing Water Used in the Production of Hydraulic Cement Concrete.* 5 p. ASTM International. https://doi.org/10.1520/C1602_C1602M-18

ASTM C33. 2018 *Standard Specification for Concrete Aggregates.* ASTM International. 8 p. https://doi.org/10.1520/c0033_c0033m-18.

ASTM C595. 2021. *Standard Specifications for Blended Hydraulic Cements.* ASTM International. 10 p. https://doi.org/10.1520/c0595_c0595m-21

ASTM C642. 2013. *Standard Test Method for Density, Absorption and Voids in Hardened Concrete.* 3 p. ASTM International. https://doi.org/10.1520/c0642-13.

ASTM C666. 2015. *Standard Test Method for Resistance of Concrete to Rapid Freezing and Thawing.* 7 p. ASTM International. https://doi.org/10.1520/C0666_C0666M-15

ASTM C672. 2012. *Standard Test Method for Scaling Resistance of Concrete Surfaces Exposed to Deicing Chemicals.* 7 p. ASTM International.

ASTM C989. 2018 *Standard Specification for Ground Blast-Furnace Slag for Use in Concrete and Mortars.* 7 p. ASTM International. https://doi.org/10.1520/C0989_C0989M-18A

ASTM D7428. 2015. *Standard Test Method for Resistance of Fine Aggregate to Degradation by Abrasion in Micro-Deval Apparatus.* 6 p. ASTM International. https://doi.org/10.1520/D7428-15

Banthia, N., Trottier, J.-F., Wood, D. and Beaupré, D. 1992. Steel Fiber Dry-Mix Shotcrete: Influence of Fiber Geometry. *Concrete International.* Vol. 14. No. 5. 24–28.

Beaupré, D. 1994. *Rheology of High Performance Shotcrete,* Doctoral Thesis, University of British Columbia, Vancouver, Canada.

Beaupré, D. and Jolin, M. 2002. Efficiency of Shotcrete Accelerator: A Fundamental Approach. *Proceedings of the Conference on Shotcrete for Underground Support IX,* 99–111.

Beaupré, D., Pigeon, M., Jolin, M. and Lacombe, P. 2001. Recent Developments in the Field of Shotcrete: The Quebec Experience. *Shotcrete: Engineering Developments,* Edited by Bernard, E. S., Lisse, Netherlands; Exton, PA, Published by A.A. Balkema.

Beaupré, D., Talbot, C., Gendreau, M., Pigeon, M. and Morgan, D. R. 1994. Deicer Salt Scaling Resistance of Dry and Wet-Process Shotcrete. *ACI Materials Journal.* Vol. 91. No. 5. September–October. 487–494.

Bentur, A. and Mindess, S. (2019). Fibre Reinforced Cementitious Composites. CRC Press 624 p.

CSA. (2005). *A864 Guide to the evaluation and management of concrete structures affected by alkali-aggregate reaction.* 108p. Canadian Standard Association.

CSA. (2018). *A3000 Cementitious materials compendium.* 253 p. Canadian Standards Association.

CSA. (2019). *A23.1/A23.2 Concrete materials and methods of concrete construction/Test methods and standard practices for concrete.* 690 p. Canadian Standards Association.

Dufour, J. -F. 2000. Performance of Dry-Mix Shotcrete in Permafrost Environment. *Shotcrete Magazine* August, 2000. 1–8.

Dufour, J. -F. 2008. Can Dry-Mix Shotcrete be Air Entrained? *Shotcrete Magazine* Fall, 2008. 28–30.

Dufour, J. -F., Reny, S. and Vezina, D. 2006. State-of-the-Art Specifications for Shotcrete Rehabilitation Projects. *Shotcrete Magazine* Fall, 2006. 4–11.

Gilbride, P., Morgan, D. R. and Bremner, T. W. 1988. Deterioration and Rehabilitation of Berth Faces in Tidal Zones at the Port of Saint John. *American Concrete Institute, Concrete in Marine Environment, SP-109*, 1988, 199–227.

Giroux, P. and Reny, S. 2006. Pointe de la Prairie Lighthouse. *Shotcrete Magazine* Fall 2006. 30–32.

Hanskat, C. S. 2010. Shotcrete in Liquid Containing Concrete Structures. *Shotcrete Magazine* Summer 2010. 24–28.

Hewlett, P. C., et al. 2003. *Lea's Chemistry of Cement and Concrete.* Elsevier Science & Technology Books. Fourth ed.

Jolin, M. and Beaupré, D. 2003. Understanding Wet-Mix Shotcrete: Mix Designs, Specifications and Placement. *Shotcrete Magazine* Summer, 2003. 6–12.

Jolin, M., Beaupré, D., Pigeon, M. and Lamontagne, A. 1997. Use of Set Accelerating Admixtures in Dry-Mix Shotcrete. *Journal of Materials in Civil Engineering.* Vol. 9. No. 4. doi: 10.1061/(ASCE)0899-1561(1997)9:4(180)

Jolin, M. and Bissonnette, B. 2006. A Decade of Shotcrete Research at Laval University. *Shotcrete for Underground Support X*, Edited by Morgan, D.R. & Parker, H. W., Whistler, British Columbia, Canada, Published by ASCE, 46–62.

Jolin, M., Burns, D., Bissonnette, B., Gagnon, F. and Bolduc, L. S. 2009. Understanding the Pumpability of Concrete. *Shotcrete for Underground Support XI*, Edited by Felix Amberg, M.O.S. Ethz, SIA, Switzerland & Knut F Garshol, BASF Construction Chemicals, LLF, USA Eds, ECI Symposium Series, 2009. https://dc.engconfintl.org/shotcrete/17.

Kusterle, W. 1999. The New Austrian Guideline on Sprayed Concrete. *Shotcrete for Underground Support VIII*, Edited by Celestino, C. & Parker, H.W., ASCE, Sao Paulo, Brazil, April 11–15, 1999, 16–26.

Lamontagne, A., Pigeon, M. and Beaupré, D. 1996. Use of Air-Entraining Admixture in Dry-Mix Shotcrete. ACI Materials Journal. Vol. 93. No. 1. 69–74.

Millette, D. 2011. Using Accelerator for Shotcreting. *Shotcrete Magazine, American Shotcrete Association* Spring 2011 36–39.

Morgan, D. R. 1975. Effects of Chemical Admixtures on Creep and Shrinkage in Concrete. *Proceedings, Workshop on the Use of Chemical Admixtures in Concrete*, Edited by D.R. Morgan, University of New South Wales, Australia, 113–148.

Morgan, D. R. 1988. Dry-Mix Silica Fume Shotcrete in Western Canada. *Concrete International.* Vol. 10. No. 1. January. 24–32.

Morgan, D. R. 1989. Freeze-Thaw Durability of Shotcrete. Concrete International. Vol. 11. No. 8. August. 86–93.

Morgan, D. R. 1991a. Freeze-Thaw Durability of Steel and Polypropylene Reinforced Shotcretes. *CANMET/ACI International Conference on Durability of Shotcrete, SP-126*, 1991, 901–911.

Morgan, D. R. 1991b. Steel Fiber Reinforced Shotcrete for Support of Underground Openings in Canada. *Concrete International*. Vol. 13. No. 11. November. 56–64.

Morgan, D. R., Chen, L. and Beaupré, D. 1995. Toughness of Fiber Reinforced Shotcrete. *Shotcrete for Underground Support XII, Telfs, Austria*, Edited by Klappperich, H., Pottler, R. & Willocq, J., Published by ASCE, 66–87.

Morgan, D. R. and Heere, R. 2000. Evolution of Fiber Reinforced Shotcrete. *Shotcrete Magazine* May, 2000. 8–11.

Morgan, D. R., Heere, R., McAskill, N. and Chen, C. 1999. Comparative Evaluation of System Ductility of Mesh and Fiber Reinforced Shotcretes. Shotcrete for Underground Support VIII, Edited by Celistino, T. B. & Parker, H.W., Sao Paulo, Brazil, Published by ASCE, 216–239.

Morgan, D. R., Kirkness, A. J., McAskill, N. and Duke, N. 1988. Freeze-Thaw Durability of Wet-Mix and Dry-Mix Shotcretes with Silca Fume and Steel Fibers. *Cement, Concrete and Aggregates*. Vol. 10. No. 2. Winter. 96–102.

Morgan, D. R., Loevlie, K., Kwong, N., Chan, A. 2010. Centrifugal placed concrete for lining horizontal pipes, culverts, and vertical shafts. *Shotcrete: Elements of a System – Proceedings of the 3rd International Conference on Engineering Developments in Shotcrete*, https://doi.org/10.1201/b10545-27.

Morgan, D. R., McAskill, N., Richardson, B. W. and Zellers, R. C. 1989. A Comparative Evaluation of Plain, Polypropylene Fiber, Steel Fiber, and Wire Mesh Reinforced Shotcretes. Transportation Research Record 1226, Transportation Research Board, National Research Council, Washington, DC, 1989, 78–87.

Morgan, D.R. and Rich, L. 1998. High Volume Synthetic Fiber Reinforced Shotcrete. *Synthetic Fiber Reinforced Concrete Association Symposium*, Orlando, Florida, January 16, 1998, 18.

Morgan, D. R., Rich, L. and Lobo, A. 1998. About-Face, Repair at the Port of Montreal. *Concrete International*. Vol. 20. No. 9. September. 66–73.

Morgan, D. R., Zhang, L. and Pildysh, M. 2017. New Hemp-based Fiber Enhances Wet-Mix Shotcrete Performance. *Shotcrete Magazine* Spring, 2017. 36–45.

Neville, A. M. and Wainright, P. J. 1976. *High Alumina Cement Concrete*. John Wiley & Sons. 201 p.

Radomski, S. M., Morgan, D. R., Zhang, L. and Graham, D. 2019. Structural Modifications to Hydroelectric Turbine Draft Tube Ceiling. *Shotcrete Magazine, American Shotcrete Association* Summer, 2019. 22–34.

Reny, S. and Jolin, M. 2011. Improve your Shotcrete: Use Coarse Aggregates. *Shotcrete Magazine* Winter, 2011. 26–28.

Rispin, M. 2005. Reentry into a Shotcreted Underground Heading. *Shotcrete Magazine* Spring, 2005. 26–30.

RTC. (2019). Guideline on the Applicability of Fibre-Reinforced Shotcrete for Ground Support in Mines. Rock Tech Centre – MIGS III – WP 24, 53 p.

Ryan, T. F. 1975. Steel Fibres in Gunite: An Appraisal. *Tunnels and Tunneling*. Vol. 7. No. 7. 74–75.

Scrivener, K. 2003. Calcium aluminate Cements. chapter 2 in *Advance Concrete Technology, Volume 3-Constituent Materials*, edited by Newman, J. & Choo, B.S., published by Butterworth-Heinemann publishers, 30 p.

Shotcrete Magazine Spring, 2008, Published by American Shotcrete Association.

Silica Fume Users Manual. 2005. Published by Silica Fume Association, 193 p.

Tatnall, P. 2002. Shotcrete in Fires: Effects of Fibers on Explosive Spalling. *Shotcrete Magazine* Fall, 2002. 10–12.

Thomas, M.D.A. 2011. The Effect of Supplementary Cementing Materials on Alkali-silica Reaction: A Review. *Cement and Concrete Research*. Vol. 41. 1224–1231.

Vandewalle, M. 1996. *Tunneling the World*. Bekaert S.A., 247 p.

WHRP. 2014. Wisconsin Highway Research Program, Laboratory Study for Evaluation of Class C vs Class F Fly Ash for Highway Pavement, Report 0092-12-04, 2014, 154 p.

Wolsiefer, J. and Morgan, D. R. 1993. Silica Fume in Shotcrete. *Concrete International*. Vol. 15. No. 4. April. 34–39.

Zhang, L. 2012. Air Content in Shotcrete: As-Shot Versus As-Batched. *Shotcrete Magazine* Winter, 2012. 50–54.

Zhang, L., Ezzet, M., Shanahan, N., Morgan, D. R. and Sukumar, A. P. 2011. Ruskin Dam Spillway Assessed. *Concrete International*. Vol. 33. No. 2. February. 37–43.

Zhang, L. and Morgan, D. R. 2016. Comparative Evaluation of Transport Properties of Shotcrete Compared to Cast-in-Place Concrete. *ACI Materials Journal*. Vol. 113. No. 3. May–June. 373–384.

Chapter 5

Shotcrete mixture proportioning

5.1 INTRODUCTION

At first glance shotcrete mixture proportioning used in early years would appear to have been a fairly simple exercise. The dry-mix shotcrete (back then called *gunite*) was simply composed of Portland cement, a suitably graded sand and water. Shotcrete mixture proportions were expressed, for example, as follows: 1 Part Cement to 4 Parts Sand, measured by volume. The water content in the mix was expressed as gallons per bag of cement, or sometimes as a percent by mass of cement (Stewart, 1933).

While some contractors still use volumetric proportioning for dry-mix shotcrete mixtures, most dry-mix shotcrete is now proportioned using mass proportioning methods. This is particularly true for dry-bagged shotcrete products. Nearly all wet-mix shotcrete is now designed using mass proportioning methods. The sections, which follow, provide guidance on how to carry out dry-mix and wet-mix shotcrete mixture proportioning using mass proportioning.

5.2 WET-MIX SHOTCRETE PROPORTIONING

5.2.1 Basics

Wet-mix shotcrete mixture proportioning is similar to conventional concrete mixture proportioning in that the basic methods provided in ACI 211.1 and ASTM C94 for mass proportioning or ASTM C1116 for volume proportioning can be used. There are, however, some significant differences between the requirements for cast-in-place concrete mixture proportioning and wet-mix shotcrete mixture proportioning. These differences include the following items:

a) Shotcrete mixes typically have smaller maximum size aggregates than cast-in-place concrete. Some designers permit the use of nominal 14 mm maximum size aggregate in shotcrete mixtures used for

DOI: 10.1201/9780429169946-6

construction of thick structural walls and other structural elements. Most wet-mix shotcrete used in North America is, however, designed with a composite blend of coarse and fine aggregate which conforms to the ACI 506 Grading No. 2 requirements, i.e. has a nominal 10 mm maximum size aggregate. Mortar-like mixes with fine aggregate gradations conforming to ACI 506 Grading No. 1 requirements, i.e. with a 5 mm nominal maximum size aggregate, are still used in some finish coats and special applications. Larger size aggregates, such as 20 mm or 28 mm nominal maximum size aggregates, as used in cast-in-place concrete, are not suited to use in the shotcrete process. Aggregate rebound with such aggregates is excessive and the large size aggregate particles would cause deep cratering in the freshly applied shotcrete. Also, large size aggregates rebounding could cause injury to nozzlemen and the adjacent work crew (blow-pipe operators, finishers and labourers).

b) The proportion of coarse aggregate to fine aggregate (sand) is much lower in shotcrete mixtures compared to conventional cast-in-place concrete mixtures. Cast-in-place concrete mixtures typically have fine aggregate contents (percent by mass of material passing the 5 mm sieve) of 35 to 45% by mass of the total blend of coarse and fine aggregates. By contrast, wet-mix shotcrete mixtures typically have fine aggregate contents of 70 to 75% by mass of the total blend of coarse and fine aggregates. The main reason for this is that rebound would be grossly excessive if one attempted to shoot conventional concrete mixtures. In the shotcrete process, a layer of paste (cementing material, water and entrained air) is first built up on the shooting surface being shot against. The coarse aggregate and some of the fine aggregate particles rebound from the receiving surface. As the depth of mortar (paste plus fine aggregate) bed thickens, coarser aggregate particles start to embed in the mortar and become captured as the shotcrete build-up thickens, and the amount of rebound diminishes. With a well-designed wet-mix shotcrete, with suitably sized and graded aggregate, the total amount of rebound can be very low (as low as 5 to 10% by mass of total material shot on vertical surfaces) (Austin and Robins, 1995; Wolsiefer and Morgan, 1993).

c) Shotcrete mixes typically have higher total cementing materials contents than typical from 25 to 35 MPa structural cast-in-place concrete mixes. Whereas a 25-MPa cast-in-place concrete mix with a 14 mm maximum size aggregate might have a total cementing materials content of about 280 kg/m³, and a 35 MPa concrete mix with a 14 mm maximum size aggregate might have a total cementing materials content of 350 kg/m³, most wet-mix shotcretes will have a total cementing materials content of at least 425 kg/m³. In shotcrete applications in tunnels and mines, where there is a lot of overhead shooting, and in challenging working environments, such as rehabilitation of marine infrastructure in intertidal zones, total cementing materials contents may be as high as 480 kg/m^3 or even more. Such shotcrete mixtures typically achieve 28-day compressive strengths, on cores extracted from test panels, well in excess of 40 MPa. The main reason for the relatively high cementing materials content in shotcrete (compared to typical structural cast-in-place concretes) is that shotcrete needs sufficient paste for the applied product to have suitable adhesion (ability to stick to the receiving surface), cohesion (ability to stick to itself, without sagging and sloughing), resistance to fall-out and to minimize rebound. It is futile to specify and try and apply a 20 MPa shotcrete. Such shotcrete would have such a low cementing materials content (and hence paste content) that it would be difficult to pump and shoot and would display poor adhesion and cohesion and excessive rebound, and be vulnerable to sagging, sloughing and fall-out.

d) Wet-mix shotcretes with exposure to freezing and thawing conditions and/or deicing chemicals should be air entrained to at least 7% to 10% in the shotcrete as discharged into the pump hopper. This is because most of the larger air bubbles are lost during the shooting process, i.e. the air content in the in-place shotcrete would typically be in about the 3.5% to 5% range (Jolin and Beaupré, 2000; Zhang, 2012). It has been demonstrated in numerous laboratory studies (Morgan et al., 1988; Beaupré et al., 1994) as well as field observations (Gilbride et al., 1988; Morgan, 1989; Morgan, 1991a; Gilbride et al., 1996), that when properly designed and applied, such air-entrained shotcrete has good freeze/thaw durability and resistance to scaling from deicing chemicals.

e) Wet-mix shotcretes without accelerators added at the nozzle are normally supplied at slumps in the 60 +/– 20 mm range. By contrast, wet-mix shotcretes with liquid accelerator addition at the nozzle are typically supplied at slumps in the 190 +/– 20 mm range. Indeed, mixes with lower slumps (stiffer mixes) may lead to incomplete filling of pump cylinders and a more pronounced interruption of concrete flow at the nozzle when the swing valve moves from one cylinder to the other (i.e. surge effect). While this is not a problem when spraying wet-mix shotcrete without accelerator, it has the potential to create non-uniform dispersion of accelerator through the mix since the accelerator is added at the nozzle at a constant flow, resulting in in-place shotcrete with accelerator-rich and accelerator-poor layers (Millette, 2011 and Section 7.3.3). Accelerator addition at the nozzle in mixtures with suitable plasticity (slump) instantaneously converts the shotcrete mixture from nearly flowing consistency to a uniformly stiff mixture which can adhere to the applied surface without sagging, sloughing and fall-out and have suitable quality and uniformity (Millette, 2011; Millette and Jolin, 2014).

Table 5.1 Examples of CSA A23.1 classes of concrete exposure

C-XL	Structurally reinforced concrete exposed to chlorides or other severe environments with or without freezing and thawing conditions, with higher durability performance expectations than the C-1 classes.
C-1	Structurally reinforced concrete exposed to chlorides with or without freezing and thawing conditions. Examples: bridge decks, parking decks and ramps, portions of structures exposed to seawater located within the tidal and splash zones, concrete exposed to seawater spray, and salt-water pools. For seawater or seawater-spray exposures the requirements for S-3 exposure also have to be met.
C-2	Non-structurally reinforced (i.e. plain) concrete exposed to chlorides and freezing and thawing. Examples: garage floors, porches, steps, pavements, sidewalks, curbs, and gutters.
C-3	Continuously submerged concrete exposed to chlorides, but not to freezing and thawing. Examples: underwater portions of structures exposed to seawater. For seawater or seawater-spray exposures the requirements for S-3 exposure also have to be met.
C-4	Non-structurally reinforced concrete exposed to chlorides, but not to freezing and thawing. Examples: underground parking slabs on grade.
F-1	Concrete exposed to freezing and thawing in a saturated condition, but not to chlorides. Examples: pool decks, patios, tennis courts, freshwater pools, and freshwater control structures.
F-2	Concrete in an unsaturated condition exposed to freezing and thawing, but not to chlorides. Examples: exterior walls and columns.
N	Concrete that when in service is neither exposed to chlorides nor to freezing and thawing nor to sulphates, either in a wet or dry environment. Examples: footings and interior slabs, walls, and columns.

5.2.2 Wet-mix shotcrete mixture design

The section which follows provides examples of how to design shotcrete mixtures for different types of applications. The steps to be followed in designing a shotcrete mix are as follows:

1. Consider the shotcrete exposure conditions. Table 1 of CSA A23.1-19 *Concrete Materials and Methods of Concrete Construction* provides definitions for different concrete exposure conditions. These same criteria can be applied to shotcrete. Excerpts from this Table are summarized in Table 5.1 for convenience of referral.

2. Table 2 of CSA A23.1-19 provides performance requirements for concretes for the different exposure conditions detailed in Table 5.1 above. Key amongst these performance requirements are:
   a) Maximum allowable water-to-cementing materials ratio;
   b) Minimum compressive strength at 28 or 56 days;

Table 5.2 CSA A23.1 concrete performance requirements for exposure categories listed in Table 5.1

Class of exposure	Maximum water-to-cementing materials ratio	Minimum specified compressive strength (MPa) and age (d) at test	Air Entrained	Chloride ion penetrability requirements and age at test
C-XL or A-XL	0.40	50 within 56 d	Yes	<1000 coulombs within 91 d
C-I or A-I	0.40	35 within 56 d	Yes	<1500 coulombs within 91 d
C-2	0.45	32 at 28 d	Yes	—
C-3	0.50	30 at 28 d	n/a	—
C-4	0.55	25 at 28 d	n/a	—
F-1	0.50	30 at 28 d	Yes	—
F-2	0.55	25 at 28 d	Yes	—
N	As per the mix design for the strength required	For structural design	n/a	—

c)   Chloride ion penetrability requirements in Coulombs (as measured in the ASTM C1202 test); and

d)   Air content category as detailed in CSA A23.1-19.

All of the above criteria can be applied to shotcrete, except for the required air content (as discussed in Section 5.2.1 (d)). Excerpts from this table are summarized in Table 5.2.

3. Consider any other special provisions that might apply to the shotcrete, such as:

a)   Limits on the water-soluble chloride ion content permissible in the mixture (mostly applies to limiting the chloride ion content in chemical admixtures used, e.g. avoid use of chloride-based accelerators where reinforcing steel corrosion is a concern);

b)   Limits on the amount of supplementary cementing materials that may be used (e.g. do not use high volume fly ash additions in shotcrete applied in cold weather conditions, or in shotcrete that will be exposed to deicing chemicals);

c)   Flexural strength requirements, where specified;

d)   Inclusion of steel or macrosynthetic fibres where flexural toughness requirements are specified (e.g. Joules energy in ASTM C1550 round panel tests, or Toughness Performance Level or Flexural Toughness in ASTM C1609 beam tests); and

e)   Whether a shotcrete accelerator will be added at the nozzle and the implications that this will have on parameters such as early and later age compressive strength development, boiled absorption and volume of permeable voids in the ASTM C642 test, and the susceptibility of chloride ion penetration in the ASTM C1202 test.

After considering all the above items, the numeric calculation of the shotcrete mixture proportions can proceed. Two examples are provided in the sections which follow. The first example is for a wet-mix shotcrete for use in construction of structural shotcrete walls in an in-ground parking structure in a northern climate with exposure to cycles of freezing and thawing and deicing chemicals. The second example is for a macrosynthetic fibre-reinforced shotcrete with accelerator addition at the nozzle, for underground support in a mine.

5.2.2.1 Structural shotcrete mix design for parking structure

Shotcrete performance requirements:

- Exposure condition: CSA A23.1-19 Class C-1
- Maximum water/cementing materials ratio: 0.40
- Minimum specified compressive strength: 35 MPa at 28 days
- Chloride ion penetrability (ASTM C1202): less than 1500 coulombs at 91 days
- Air content: as-batched 7% to 10%
- Air content: as-shot 3.5% to 5%
- 14 mm maximum size coarse aggregate

Select a cement content and water content that will produce a water/cementing materials ratio not exceeding the specified 0.40 and produce shotcrete which meets the specified minimum 35 MPa compressive strength at 28 days with a suitable margin of safety. Good guidance in this regard is provided by methods such as the Popovic equation (Popovic, 1998), as shown in Figure 5.1 which follows.

The values for A, B and y shown in Figure 5.1 are empirical constants developed for typical natural aggregates available in Western Canada and have been developed from decades of feedback between shotcrete mixture designs and actual compressive strength achieved on cores extracted from quality control test panels in laboratory and field testing for many structural shotcrete projects. The value "a" represents the in-place (as-shot) air content. Equivalent cement efficiency factors are assigned to supplementary cementing materials such as fly ash and silica fume. For the ASTM Class F fly ashes most commonly used in Western Canada, an equivalent cement efficiency factor of 0.85 is commonly used. For the silica fumes most commonly used in Western Canada, an equivalent cement efficiency factor of 1.15 is commonly used. Shotcrete users in other parts of the world can use the empirical

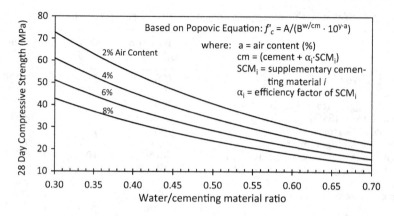

Figure 5.1 Relationship between compressive strength at 28 days and water/cementing materials ratio for different in-place air content values, based on Popovic equation (for typical shotcrete mixes in Lower Mainland, British Columbia, Canada: A = 208.4, B = 18.53 and y = 0.0384).

constants shown in Figure 5.1 as general guidelines, but should fine-tune them based on actual laboratory and field performance observed in their regions.

Table 5.3, which follows, shows a wet-mix shotcrete mix design used for construction of structural walls on a large in-ground parking structure in Western Canada. The steps used in preparation of this mix design were as follows:

1. From experience, it is known that such shotcretes characteristically have a water demand of about 185 L/m³;
2. Select a cement content of 400 kg/m³ and fly ash content of 80 kg/m³;
3. The calculated water/(cement + fly ash) ratio = 0.385;
4. The calculated 28-day compressive strength from the Popovic equation for an as-shot air content of 5.0% is 42 MPa (This provides a margin of 7 MPa over the specified 35-MPa compressive strength);
5. Based on examination of the gradation of the 14–5 mm coarse aggregate and fine aggregate (sand), select a fine aggregate content of 75% by mass of the total aggregates;
6. Based on knowledge of the density values (kg/m³) for the constituent materials, and assuming an as-shot air content of 5.0%, select quantities of coarse and fine aggregate to produce a yield of 1.01 ± 0.01m³.

Figure 5.2 shows shotcrete construction in a parkade wall with this mixture design. The shotcrete mix satisfied all the above specified performance parameters and performed well. It was well suited to its application.

Table 5.3 Wet-mix shotcrete mix design for use in parking structure

Material	Mass per m^3 SSD agg. kg	Density, kg/m^3	Volume m^3
Cement type GU	400	3150	0.1270
Fly ash – Type F	80	2070	0.0386
Coarse aggregate (14–5 mm, SSD)	400	2670	0.1498
Coarse sand (SSD)	1200	2620	0.4580
Estimated water, L	185	1000	0.1850
Water-reducing admixture, L	1.20	1000	0.0012
High-range water-reducing adm.[1], L	note 1	1000	0.0000
Air-entraining agent[2], L (for 7–10% as batched)	note 2	—	—
Air content ± 1% (as shot)	5.0	—	0.0505
Total	2266	Yield (m^3) =	1.0102
Calculated Mix Design Parameters			
Fine aggregate content	75.0%		
Water/cementitious ratio	0.385		
Plastic density (kg/m^3)	2243		
Fly ash content (% by mass of cement)	20.0%		

[1] Add high-range water-reducing admixture at appropriate dosage required to achieve the maximum allowable *water/cementitious* ratio and required slump

[2] Adjust air-entraining admixture dosage as required to meet the air content of 7–10% as batched, and 3.5 to 6.5% as-shot.

Figure 5.2 Reinforced shotcrete construction of a parkade wall in Western Canada. (Photo courtesy Shaun Radomski.)

5.2.2.2 Shotcrete mix design for underground support in mine

Mixture designs for shotcretes used for underground support in mines typi-cally differ from shotcrete mixture designs used in construction of structural shotcrete walls (as shown in Table 5.3), in the following respects:

a) Much of the shotcrete in underground mines is applied to overhead surfaces. Thus, measures that enhance the ability of the shotcrete to stick to the rock surfaces and be built up without sagging, sloughing and fall-out become very important. The use of silica fume and accel-erators added at the nozzle is very beneficial in this regard.

b) Silica fume addition markedly improves the thickness of build-up achievable per pass of shotcrete applied and reduces fall-out and rebound (Wolsiefer and Morgan, 1993).

c) Much the shotcrete applied in modern underground mines is com-monly reinforced with either steel fibre (Morgan 1991b, or with macrosynthetic fibre (Morgan and Heere, 2000; Bernard et al., 2014; Bernard and Thomas, 2020).

d) Times from shotcrete batching to completion of discharge can be quite long, particularly where shotcrete supply is by transit mixers which have to travel many kilometres down declines to the point of shooting. As such, hydration-controlling admixtures are commonly used to con-trol the rate of slump loss and prevent the shotcrete from prematurely setting. Shotcrete is often kept alive for 6 to 8 hours (and sometimes even as much as 24 hours), depending on the logistics of shotcrete sup-ply and application.

e) Shotcrete accelerators are routinely added at the nozzle to overcome the slump retention effects of the hydration-controlling admixture and cause the shotcrete to instantaneously stiffen and build up without sagging, sloughing and fall-out as it impacts on the rock surface. As mentioned previously, shotcrete with accelerator added at the nozzle is typically supplied at slumps in the 180–200 mm range.

f) Early age strength development is an important consideration in shot-crete in mining applications, so that personnel and equipment re-entry under shotcreted areas can proceed as early as possible, so that the mining cycle of rock bolt installation, wire mesh installation (where required), drilling, blasting and mucking (clearing out blasted rock or ore) can proceed in a timely manner (Rispin, 2005). Also, in many ground conditions, early age shotcrete strength development is impor-tant to stabilize the opening, help control convergence and protect against ground fall-out. Accelerator addition at the nozzle is very important in accelerating early-age (say up to 24 hours) compressive strength development (Morgan et al., 1999; Rispin, 2005; Bernard and Geltinger, 2007).

g) Air entrainment is usually not required in shotcrete applied in underground mines, as the shotcrete is seldom exposed to cycles of freezing and thawing. Exceptions are where shotcrete is applied in permafrost ground conditions (Dufour, 2000), or intentionally frozen ground in tunnelling or shaft sinking operations (Madsen, 2014).

From the above, it can be seen that shotcrete used in mining (and many tunnelling applications) differs in many respects from typical structural shotcretes used above ground. The same basic procedures used for structural shotcrete mixture design can be used with design of shotcretes for underground support, but with some significant differences/additions. For example:

1. Workability tests need to be conducted to establish the slump retention characteristics of the hydration-controlling admixture.
2. Tests need to be conducted to demonstrate that shotcrete made with the selected accelerator type and addition rate will meet the specified setting times and early age (up to 24 hours) and later age (7 and 28 days) compressive strength requirements.
3. Fibre contents have to be selected such that the shotcrete can meet the specified toughness performance criteria in the ASTM C1550 round panel test, or ASTM C1609 beam test.
4. Limits are set for values of boiled absorption and Volume of Permeable Voids in the ASTM C642 test. This test is used to guard against excessive accelerator addition at the nozzle, which can seriously downgrade the quality and durability of the shotcrete.

Table 5.4, which follows, provides an example of a robotically applied wet-mix shotcrete that was used for underground support in a base-metal mine in Western Canada. The specified performance parameters were:

a) Blend of coarse and fine aggregate which satisfies the ACI 506 Grading No.2 limits;
b) Maximum 0.40 water/cementing materials ratio;
c) Slump of 180 +/–20 mm at discharge into shotcrete pump;
d) Air content 2.5 +/–1.5%;
e) Minimum 2 MPa at 6 hours compressive strength;
f) Minimum 30 MPa at 7 days and 40 MPa 28 days compressive strength
g) Minimum 320 Joules energy at 40 mm deflection in ASTM C1550 round panel test at 7 days
h) Maximum Boiled Absorption of 9% and Volume of Permeable Voids of 18% at 7days in ASTM C642 test.

If this mix design is analysed in the Popovic equation it produces a theoretical compressive strength of 56.8 MPa at 28 days. At first glance, this would

Table 5.4 Fibre-reinforced shotcrete mix design for use in underground mine

Material	Mass per m³ SSD aggregate, kg	Density, kg/m³	Volume, m³
Cement type GU	430	3150	0.1365
Silica fume	45	2200	0.0205
Coarse aggregate (10–2.5 mm, SSD)	380	2744	0.1385
Fine aggregate (SSD)	1310	2649	0.4945
Estimated water, L	185	1000	0.1850
High water-reducing admixture[1], L	2.500	1000	0.0025
Hydration-controlling admixture[2], L	1.200	1000	0.0012
Macrosynthetic fibre[3]	6.000	910	0.0066
Air content – at pump	2.5	—	—
Air content – as shot	2.0	—	0.0202
Total	2354	Yield (m³) = 1.0105	

[1] Adjust high-range water-reducing admixture dosage as required to provide a slump of 180 ± 20 mm at discharge into shotcrete pump.
[2] Adjust hydration-controlling admixture dosage as required to maintain slump life. Add shotcrete accelerating admixture at nozzle at approximately 7% by mass of cement.
[3] Adjust fibre addition rate as required to meet specified toughness in Joules in ASTM C1550 test.

appear to be excessively high relative to the specified compressive strength of 40 MPa at 28 days. Experience on numerous tunnelling and mining projects has, however, shown that significant reductions in 28-day compressive strength can be expected, as a result of accelerator addition at the nozzle (Millette and Lessard, 2007). The amount of strength reduction will be influenced by the accelerator type and dosage rate. Figure 5.3 and Table 5.5 show an example of the relationship between the dosage rate for a modern

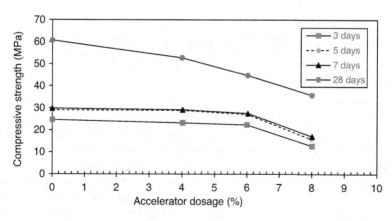

Figure 5.3 Effect of alkali-free accelerator dosage (% by mass of cement) on compressive strength.

(Graph courtesy Lihe (John) Zhang, LZhang Consulting & Testing Ltd.)

Table 5.5 Effect of alkali-free accelerator addition rate on compressive strength

Accelerator dosage (by mass of cement %)	3 days	7 days	28 days
4	33.5	44.2	48.7
6	23.3	30.2	39.3

alkali-free accelerator and compressive strength with time for a tunnelling project in Western Canada. It can be seen that relative to a shotcrete with no accelerator addition at the nozzle, reductions in compressive strength of 25% (14 MPa) occurred at 28 days with 6% accelerator addition at the nozzle. At 8% accelerator addition, a reduction in compressive strength of 40% (25 MPa) occurred at 28 days. With older type alkali-based accelerators (e.g. sodium and potassium-based aluminates), even greater reductions in compressive strength can occur. Thus, it is important to design the base shotcrete mix with a sufficient margin of safety to cater to the strength reductions resulting from accelerator addition at the nozzle.

In another tunnelling project in Western Canada (Zhang et al., 2019) increasing the alkali-free accelerator addition rate at the nozzle from 4% to 6% resulted in a 19% reduction in compressive strength, as shown in Table 5.5.

Chapter 14 in this book provides some case history examples of the use of shotcrete in mines in North America and Australia. Several million cubic metres of fibre-reinforced wet-mix shotcrete (in conjunction with rock bolts, cable bolts and other forms of reinforcement, where needed) have provided successful ground support in underground mines and tunnels over the past 30 years (Bernard et al., 2014). Indeed, Bernard indicates that about 1.5 million cubic metres of fibre-reinforced shotcrete is being used for ground support applications worldwide every year.

5.3 DRY-MIX SHOTCRETE PROPORTIONING

5.3.1 Basics

In its simplest form, the proportioning of dry-mix shotcrete only requires selecting an aggregate to cement ratio, for example, a 4:1 mix (by volume). Indeed, given that it is the nozzleman that controls the amount of water added at the nozzle to the dry-mixture material coming down the hose (see Figure 8.1), there is no point in selecting or specifying a water-to-cementing materials ratio, as is usually done in conventional concrete, or wet-mix shotcrete design. Although there is no recognized rational method for proportioning dry-mix shotcrete for strength or durability (ACI 5060R-16), over 100 years of experience shows that it is possible to relatively easily produce high quality and high strength dry-mix shotcrete. That being said, there are a few practical findings that can be put forward:

1. As for wet-mix shotcrete, the maximum aggregate size will be limited in order to control rebound and facilitate transport of dry-mix shotcrete materials through the dry-mix gun and hose. The recommended combined aggregate gradation is that of the ACI 506R-16 Gradation No. 2, which has a nominal 10 mm maximum aggregate size. Mortar-like mixes with fine aggregate gradations conforming to ACI 506R-16 Gradation No. 1 requirements (i.e. with a 5 mm nominal maximum size aggregate), are, however, still used in some finish coats and special applications. There is an argument that can be made, however, for the value of having the coarser aggregate found in ACI 506R-16 Gradation No. 2 as it helps with consolidation and reduces the early age shrinkage cracking potential of the dry-mix shotcrete (Reny and Jolin, 2011; Menu et al., 2022).

2. The fact that the dry-mix shotcrete mixture design is not based on water/cement ratio may come as a surprise to materials engineers; however, it should be explained that while placing dry-mix shotcrete, the nozzleman relies on visual clues to adjust the amount of water added to the mixture, such as the imprints of larger aggregates on the fresh surface, the slight sheen of the freshly placed material, and the behaviour of the fresh shotcrete when it goes around obstacles such as reinforcing bars. There is a limit to the amount of water that can be added by the nozzleman, as an excess of water in the mixture would lead to sagging, sloughing or even debonding from the surface upon which it is sprayed. Typical 28-day compressive strengths are normally in excess of 30 MPa.

3. In reality, dry-mix shotcrete mixture proportioning by volume is somewhat more complex than appears at first glance. This is because of the phenomenon known as bulking. Bulking is a process in which the presence of films of moisture around aggregate particles in damp aggregates pushes the aggregate particles apart, resulting in an increase in volume for a given mass of sand (Neville, 1996). The extent of bulking that occurs depends on the moisture content present in the sand and is also influenced by the fine aggregate (sand) gradation (fineness) and texture (crushed sands tend to bulk more than natural sands). Sands in a Saturated Surface Dry (SSD) condition have no free surface moisture and thus by definition have 0% bulking. As the moisture content of the fine aggregate increases, the bulking increases, with maximum bulking typically occurring at moisture contents in the 5% to 8% range. Upon further addition of water, the films of water merge and bulking diminishes. There is no bulking in completely saturated fine aggregates.

Thus, in dry-mix shotcrete mixture proportioning by volume, it is important to determine the relationship between moisture content and bulking in the fine aggregate (sand) so that the correct volume of sand can be batched relative to the amount of Portland Cement, and other cementing materials, added to the mixture. Neville, 1996 shows how to determine the Bulking Factor for aggregates at different moisture contents and so to adjust the volume of fine aggregate (sand) required to be batched for varying moisture contents. With some sands showing a Bulking Factor as high as 30%, this volume correction of sand is important, as neglecting it would lead to an unwanted increase in the net cement content in the mixture, which in turn may lead to an increase in the potential for early-age cracking and higher heat of hydration.

4. While dry-mix shotcrete mixture proportioning by volume is directly done on job sites, it is more and more popular, and often mandatory, to use oven-dry pre-bagged dry-mix shotcrete mixtures (ASTM C1480). The pre-bagged mixtures obviously include cement and combined aggregates and may also contain a number of other ingredients found in concrete such as supplementary cementing materials, fibres, powdered accelerator, powdered air-entraining admixture and other admixtures that are available in a powdered form. It is because all the ingredients are combined in an industrial size planetary mixer that it is possible to introduce and properly disperse low volume additions of materials such as silica fume or powdered chemical admixtures. These prepackaged materials are available in a number of sizes, the most popular being small 30 kg bags (typical in repair jobs) or 1000 kg bulk-bags (commonly used in mining and ground support applications). A note of caution, however, oven-dry material will require some form of pre-dampening (see Section 8.2), either before the introduction of the dry shotcrete material into the gun, or by using a hydromix nozzle. It is considered bad practice to spray oven-dry prebagged dry-mix shotcrete without any form of pre-dampening (ACI 506R-16), as it leads to increased dust and rebound and increases the level of placement difficulty (e.g. reduced visibility in the tunnel). It can lead to the formation of sand lenses and inhomogeneities in the in-place shotcrete (see Appendix 2 in ACI CPP660.1-20, 2020). Also, shooting oven-dry materials can result in a build-up of static electricity in the hose, which on discharge can give the nozzleman an unpleasant shock.

5.3.2 Dry-mix shotcrete mixture design

This section provides examples of how to design dry-mix shotcrete mixtures for different types of applications. The steps to be followed in designing a dry-mix shotcrete mix are as follows:

1. Select the proper cement or binder content for the expected exposure conditions (see Table 5.1);
2. Select the proper combined aggregate gradation to meet the requirements of ACI 506 Gradation No. 2 (or No. 1 if needed);
3. Consider any other special provisions that might apply to the shotcrete, such as:

a. Limits on the water-soluble chloride ion content permissible in the mixture, which mostly applies to limiting the chloride ion content in chemical admixtures used (e.g. avoid use of chloride-based accelerators where reinforcing steel corrosion is a concern);

b. Limits on the amount of supplementary cementing materials that may be used (e.g. do not use high volume fly ash additions in shotcrete applied in cold weather conditions, or in shotcrete that will be exposed to deicing chemicals);

c. Flexural strength requirements, where specified;

d. Inclusion of steel or macrosynthetic fibres where flexural toughness requirements are specified (e.g. Joules energy in ASTM C1550 round panel tests, or Toughness Performance Level or Flexural Toughness in ASTM C1609 beam tests);

e. Inclusion of microsynthetic fibres to increase resistance to early-age plastic shrinkage induced cracking and resistance to explosive spalling in fires.

f. Whether a shotcrete accelerator has been added to the prebagged mixture, and the implications that this will have on parameters such as early and later age compressive strength development, boiled absorption and volume of permeable voids in the ASTM C642 test, and the susceptibility of chloride ion penetration as measured in the ASTM C1202 test.

Examples of dry-mix shotcrete mixture designs are provided in Tables 5.6 and 5.7. The first example in Table 5.6 is for a dry-mix shotcrete for use in repair of structural shotcrete walls in a northern climate, with exposure to cycles of freezing and thawing and deicing chemicals. The second example in Table 5.7 is for a dry-mix shotcrete with an included set-accelerator for use in underground support in a mine.

Table 5.6 Dry-mix shotcrete mix design for the repair of structural walls

Material	% of dry mass	Mass* per m³ kg/m³
Cement type GU	19	405
Silica fume	2	44
Coarse aggregate (10–2.5 mm, SSD)	15	320
Fine aggregate (SSD)	64	1365
Water	—	180
Microsynthetic fibre	neg.	0.9
Air content (using powdered air-entraining admixture)	—	**
Total	100%	2340 kg/m³

* Given that the water-cementing materials ratio is not known *a priori* in dry-mix shotcrete, the mass per m³ reported assumes a w/cm = 0.40

** As required for 5% air content in hardened shotcrete

Table 5.7 Dry-mix shotcrete mix design for ground support in a mine

Material	% of dry mass	Mass* per m³ kg/m³
Cement type HE	19	405
Silica fume	2	42
Coarse aggregate (10–2.5 mm, SSD)	12.5	267
Fine aggregate (SSD)	65	1386
Water	—	179
Macrosynthetic fibre	0.5	10
Powdered set-accelerating admixture	1	21
Total	100%	2310 kg/m³

* Given that the water–cement ratio is not known *a priori* in dry-mix shotcrete, the dosage per m³ reported assumes a w/cm = 0.40; assumed air content of 3%.

REFERENCES

ACI 211.1R-19(09). 2009. *Standard Practice for Selecting Proportions for Normal, Heavyweight, and Mass Concrete*. American Concrete Institute. 38p.

ACI 506R-16. 2016b. *Guide to Shotcrete*. American Concrete Institute. 52p.

ACI CPP660.1-20. 2020. *Certification Policies for Shotcrete Nozzleman and Shotcrete Nozzleman-In-Training*. American Concrete Institute. 36 p.

ASTM C94. 2021. *Standard Specification for Ready-Mixed Concrete*. 15p. ASTM International. https://doi.org/10.1520/C0094_C0094M-21B

ASTM C1116. 2019b. *Standard Specification for Fiber-Reinforced Concrete*. 7p. ASTM International. https://doi.org/10.1520/C1116_C1116M-10AR15

ASTM C642. 2013a. *Standard Test Method for Density, Absorption and Voids in Hardened Concrete*. 3p. ASTM International. https://doi.org/10.1520/C0642-13

ASTM C1202. 2019a. *Standard Test Method for Electrical Indication of Concrete's Ability to Resist Chloride Ion Penetration*. 8p. ASTM International. https://doi.org/10.1520/C1012_C1012M-18B

ASTM C1480. 2012. *Standard Specification for Packaged, Pre-Blended, Dry, Combined Materials for Use in Wet or Dry Shotcrete Application*. ASTM International.

ASTM C1550. 2020a. *Standard Test Method for Flexural Toughness of Fiber-Reinforced Concrete (Using Centrally Loaded Round Panel)*. 14p. https://doi.org/10.1520/C1550-20

ASTM C1609. 2019a. *Standard Test Method for Flexural Performance of Fiber Reinforced Concrete (Using Beam with Third Point Loading)*. 9p. https://doi.org/10.1520/C1609_C1609M-19A

Austin, S. and Robins, P.J. 1995. *Sprayed Concrete: Properties, Design and Application*. Whittles Publishing Services, 41–47.

Beaupré, D., Talbot, C., Gendrau, M., Pigeon, M. and Morgan, D. R. 1994. Deicer Salt Scaling Resistance of Dry and Wet-Process Shotcrete. *ACI Materials Journal*. Vol. 91. No. 5. September–October. 487–494.

Bernard, E. S. and Geltinger, C. 2007. Determination of Early-Age Compressive Strength for FRS. *Shotcrete Magazine* Fall, 2007. 22–27.

Bernard, E. S., Clements, M. J. K., Duffield, S. B. and Morgan, D. R. 2014. Development of Macrosynthetic Fibre Reinforced Shotcrete in Australia.

Seventh International Symposium on Sprayed Concrete for Underground Use, Sandefjord, Norway, June 16–19, 2014, Published by Norwegian Concrete Association.

Bernard, E. S. and Thomas, A. H., 2020. Fibre Reinforced Sprayed Concrete for Ground Support. *Tunnelling and Underground Space Technology*. Vol. 98. No. 2020. 103302. 14 p.

CSA. 2019a. *A23.1/A23.2 Concrete materials and methods of concrete construction/Test methods and standard practices for concrete*. 690p. Canadian Standards Association.

Dufour, J. -F. 2000. Performance of Dry-Mix Shotcrete in Permafrost Environment. *Shotcrete Magazine* August, 2000. 28–31.

Gilbride, P., Morgan, D. R. and Bremner, T. W. 1988. Deterioration and Rehabilitation of Berth Faces in Tidal Zones at the Port of Saint John, ACI SP-109. *Concrete in Marine Environment*, 199–227.

Gilbride, P., Morgan, D. R. and Bremner, T. W. 1996. Performance of Shotcrete Repairs to Berth Faces at Port of Saint John. *Gjorv Symposium, CANMET/ACI International Conference on Performance of Concrete in Marine Environment*, St. Andrews-by-the-Sea, New Brunswick, August 4–9, 1996, 163–171.

Jolin, M. and Beaupré, D. 2000. Temporary High Initial Air Content Wet Process Shotcrete. *Shotcrete Magazine* Fall 2000. 22–23.

Madsen, P. H. 2014. Shotcreting on Frozen Ground. *Shotcrete Magazine* Summer, 2014. 42–45.

Menu, B., Pépin-Beaudet, A., Jolin, M. and Bissonnette, B. 2022. Experimental Study on the Effect of Key Mixture Parameters on Shrinkage and Cracking Resistance of Dry-Mix Shotcrete. Construction and Building Materials, Vol. 320. https://doi.10.1016/j.conbuildmat.2021.126216

Millette, D. 2011. Using Accelerators for Shotcreting. *Shotcrete Magazine* Spring, 2011. 36–39.

Millette, D. and Jolin, M. 2014. Shotcrete Accelerators for Wet-Mix. *Shotcrete Magazine* Fall, 2014. 44–46.

Millette, D. and Lessard, M. 2007. Development of a Wet-Mix Shotcrete for a Deep Mine. *Shotcrete Magazine* Winter, 2007. 16–23.

Morgan, D. R., Kirkness, A. J., McAskill, N. and Duke, N. 1988. Freeze-Thaw Durability of Wet-Mix and Dry-Mix Shotcretes with Silica Fume and Steel Fibres. Published by ASTM. *Cement, Concrete and Aggregates*. Vol. 10. No. 2. Winter. 96–102.

Morgan, D. R. 1989. Freeze-Thaw Durability of Shotcrete. *Concrete International*. Vol. 11. No. 8. August. 86–93.

Morgan, D. R. 1991a. Freeze-Thaw Durability of Steel and Polypropylene Fibre Reinforced Shotcrete: A Review, ACI SP-126. *CANMET/ACI International Conference on Durability of Concrete*, 901–911.

Morgan, D. R. 1991b. Steel Fiber Reinforced Shotcrete for Support of Underground Openings in Canada. *Concrete International*. Vol. 13. No. 11. 56–64.

Morgan, D. R., McAskill, N. and Heere, R. 1999. Determination of Early-Age Compressive Strength of Shotcrete. *3rd International Symposium on Sprayed Concrete*, Gol, Norway, September 26–29, 1999, Published by Norwegian Concrete Association, 9 p.

Morgan, D.R. and Heere, R. 2000. Evolution of Fiber Reinforced Shotcrete. *Shotcrete Magazine* May, 2000. 8–11.

Neville, A. M. 1996. *Properties of Concrete*. John Wiley & Sons Inc. 844 pages.

Popovic, S. 1998. History of a Mathematical Model for Strength Development of Portland Cement Concrete. *ACI Materials Journal*. Vol. 95. No. 5. 593–600.

Reny, S. and Jolin, M. 2011. Improve Your Shotcrete: Use Coarse Aggregates!, *Shotcrete Magazine, American Shotcrete Association* Winter 2011. 26–28.

Rispin, R. 2005. Reentry into a Shotcreted Underground Heading. *Shotcrete Magazine* Spring, 2000. 26–30.

Stewart, E. P. 1933. New Test Data Aid Quality Control of Gunite. *Engineering News Record* November, 1933, Re-published in Shotcrete Magazine Fall, 2014, 66–70.

Wolsiefer, J. and Morgan, D. R. 1993. Silica Fume in Shotcrete. *Concrete International*. Vol 13. No. 4. April. 34–39.

Zhang, L. 2012. Air Content in Shotcrete: As-Shot Versus As-Batched. *Shotcrete Magazine* Winter, 2012. 50–54.

Zhang, L., Morgan, D. R., Moali, S., Gagnon, D. and Dugas, D. 2019. Tunnel Shotcrete Lining for Hydroelectrical Projects. *Shotcrete Magazine, American Shotcrete Association* Summer, 2019. 36–42.

Chapter 6

Shotcrete performance requirements

6.1 INTRODUCTION

The performance requirements for shotcrete can basically be divided into *Plastic Shotcrete Properties* and *Hardened Shotcrete Properties*. While the performance requirements for hardened shotcrete properties are essentially the same as those for cast-in-place concrete, plastic shotcrete has several unique performance attributes which are not applicable to cast-in-place concrete. For example, while both cast-in-place concrete placed by pumping and wet-mix shotcrete require a rheology suitable for pumping, wet-mix shotcrete needs to have a rheology such that on shooting on a vertical or overhead surface, it will have sufficient adhesion and cohesion such that it does not sag, slough or fall off (Beaupré, 1994). With conventional wet-mix shotcrete, this requirement is usually achieved by having mixture designs with higher cementitious contents and lower coarse aggregate contents than in cast-in-place concretes, and lower workability (slump).

6.2 WORKABILITY

Wet-mix shotcretes are typically pumped at lower workability (slump) than most pumped concretes, with slumps in the 50 to 80 mm range being common. This is, however, not always the case. In wet-mix shotcrete applied to overhead surfaces in tunnels and mines, or in intertidal regions in marine applications, where it is often necessary to use shotcrete accelerators added at the nozzle, higher slumps are required. In such cases, the shotcrete is pumped at a near-flowing consistency (slump of 180–200 mm). While having such high workability makes pumping easier, the high slump is mainly required to facilitate efficient and uniform dispersion of the accelerator throughout the shotcrete mix at the nozzle. Some contractors have attempted to add accelerators at the nozzle to shotcrete pumped at low slumps (50 to 80 mm) in the mistaken belief that this will enhance shotcrete build-up overhead. At such low slumps, the accelerator becomes difficult to

DOI: 10.1201/9780429169946-7

uniformly disperse throughout the mix and layers of *accelerator-rich* and *accelerator-poor* shotcrete can result.

The accelerator addition at the nozzle converts the near-flowing consistency shotcrete to an instantly stiff product on the wall with resistance to sagging, sloughing and fall-out, provided the shotcrete is not applied too thick. Typically, properly accelerated shotcrete can be built up in about 100-mm-thick layers at a time on overhead surfaces; thicker layers are more susceptible to debonding and fall-out (Radomski et al., 2019). Where greater thicknesses are required, the initial layer shot should be allowed to attain initial set before application of the next layer. Depending on factors such as the accelerator type and addition rate and the shotcrete and ambient temperatures, this can take as little as 5 minutes, to as much as 15 minutes or even more.

6.3 AIR CONTENT

Another factor affecting the workability and shooting characteristics of wet-mix shotcrete is the air content. Any concrete technologist knows that, for a given mix, as you increase the plastic air content (through the addition of an air-entraining admixture during batching and mixing), the workability (slump) of the mix will increase, i.e. it acts like a plasticizer. Conversely, as the air content is reduced (e.g. through addition of an air-detraining agent), the workability (slump) of the mix will decrease. Beaupré in his Doctoral thesis at the University of British Columbia (Beaupré, 1994) found that advantage could be taken of this phenomenon to enhance the pumpability and *shootability* of wet-mix shotcrete. Here the term *shootability* is used to describe the ability of shotcrete to stick to a receiving surface (adhesion) and to itself as it is built up in layers (cohesion). Thus, if air entrainment is added to the wet-mix shotcrete during batching and mixing to increase the plastic air content from say 3% to 10% (or even more), there will be a substantial increase in the workability (slump) of the shotcrete, which will make it easier to pump. This can be particularly beneficial in difficult-to-pump mixes, such as mixes with high steel fibre or macrosynthetic fibre contents. It can also be highly beneficial for wet-mix shotcrete mixes which require high slumps because of accelerator addition at the nozzle.

A concrete technologist might say that this is all well and good with respect to pumpability, but what about the adverse effects of high air contents on compressive strength of the hardened product? It is well known that about 4% to 5% of compressive strength is lost for every 1% of air content above the specified air content. Beaupré (1994) discovered that during shooting about half of the *as-batched air content* is lost on impact on the receiving surface; in fact, given that it is the larger air bubbles that are expelled, the in-place air content is always reduced to approximately 3% to

5%, even if the initial air content is much higher than 10% (see Chapter 7). For example, shotcrete batched at an air content in the 7%–10% range will typically end up with an *as-shot air content* of about 3.5% to 5% (Zhang, 2012). The as-shot air content can be determined by shooting directly into an ASTM C231 air pressure meter base, or preferably by shooting onto a wall, digging out the plastic shotcrete and reconsolidating it in the air pressure meter base and conducting the air-content test in the usual manner prescribed for concrete. This takes care of the concerns about the adverse effect of high air content in the in-place product on compressive strength. However, in practice, given the robustness of this higher initial air-content approach, air content is typically only measured at the point of concrete discharge into the pump.

With respect to *shootability*, as air content is knocked out on impact of the shotcrete on the receiving surface, the workability (slump) of the in-place shotcrete is instantaneously reduced. This substantially enhances the adhesion and cohesion characteristics of the shotcrete and increases resistance to sagging, sloughing and fall-out. Beaupré (1994) referred to this as a *slump-killer effect*. Jolin and Beaupré (2003) used the term *high initial air content* to describe the process. A schematic of this process is presented in Chapter 7 (Figure 7.8).

With respect to durability, two different studies by Morgan (Morgan et al., 1988; Morgan, 1991) demonstrated that although the residual air content in the hardened wet-mix shotcrete might be as low as 3.7%, the air-void parameters (spacing factor and specific surface) were such that the shotcretes provided excellent freeze-thaw durability ratings when tested to ASTM C666, Procedure A. i.e. 300 cycles of freezing and thawing in water.

With dry-mix shotcrete, until as recently as the late 1990s, conventional wisdom was that it was not possible to adequately entrain air in dry-mix shotcrete for the purposes of providing freeze-thaw durability. It was not until 2005 that the ACI 506 Guide to Shotcrete recognized that it was indeed possible to entrain air in dry-mix shotcrete. This recognition was largely based on the research conducted at Université Laval in Quebec in the mid-1990s (Beaupré, et al., 1996; Dufour, 1996). The Ministry of Transportation Quebec (MTQ) shotcrete specification requires dry-mix shotcrete in the plastic and hardened states to have an air content in the plastic and hardened states to be in the range of 3.5% to 7.0% for shotcrete exposed to cycles of freezing and thawing and deicing chemicals (Dufour, et al., 2006).

There are basically two ways to entrain air in dry-mix shotcrete:

a) Add an air-entraining admixture to the mix water that is added at the nozzle.
b) Add a dry-powdered air-entraining admixture to the dry-batched materials during batching.

While both methods work, method (b) is now generally preferred and is routinely used in prepackaged dry-mix shotcrete materials supply (Dufour, 2008). Method (a) requires the provision of special water tanks on site and a measuring device for accurate dispensing of liquid air-entraining admixture into the mix water (Lamontagne, Pigeon and Beaupré, 1996).

6.4 REBOUND

ACI CT-18 defines rebound as *shotcrete that bounces away from the surface against which the shotcrete is being projected.* Rebound is comprised mainly of coarser aggregate particles, with some adhering finer particles (sand grains and paste). Rebound is not bad; it is a natural part of the shotcrete process. When shotcrete first impacts on the receiving surface, the coarser aggregate particles have no paste or mortar into which to become embedded and bounce off, falling to the ground. As the paste and mortar layer thickness builds, more and more of the coarser aggregate particles can become embedded and the rate of rebound diminishes. This phenomenon has been studied in detail for both dry-mix shotcrete (Armelin, 1997; Jolin, 1999; Parker, 1999) and wet-mix shotcrete (Beaupré, 1994). Figure 6.1 shows rebound test data for dry-mix mortars and shotcrete from Jolin's doctoral thesis at the University of British Columbia (Jolin, 1999). Figure 6.2 shows similar data for wet-mix shotcrete from Beaupré's doctoral thesis at the University of British Columbia (Beaupré, 1994).

The overall rebound in a given shotcrete application is influenced by a variety of factors, including:

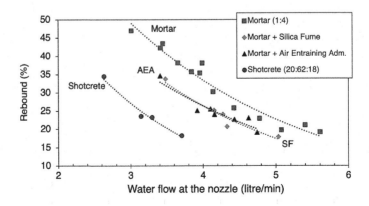

Figure 6.1 Rebound test data for dry-mix shotcrete.

(Jolin, 1999.)

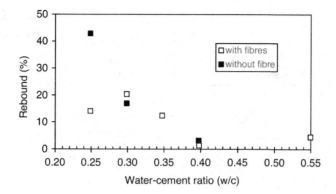

Figure 6.2 Rebound test data for wet-mix shotcrete.

(Beaupré, 1994.)

a) The shotcrete type: rebound is much higher in dry-mix shotcrete compared to wet-mix shotcrete (Wolsiefer and Morgan, 1993);
b) The shotcrete orientation; rebound is typically higher in overhead applications, compared to vertical applications (Wolsiefer and Morgan, 1993);
c) The consistency of the shotcrete: rebound is higher in shotcretes applied at a drier (stiffer) consistency. This is particularly evident for dry-mix shotcrete (Armelin et al., 1997);
d) The orientation of the shotcrete stream to the receiving surface; lowest rebound occurs in shotcrete applied at right angles (90 degrees) to the receiving surface. The more acute the angle of the impacting shotcrete stream, the higher the rebound. See Figure 6.3; and
e) Incorporation of rheology modifying additions to the shotcrete, such as silica fume (Wolsiefer and Morgan, 1993), metakaolin, hydrous magnesium aluminate-silicates and suspensions of nanometric amorphous silica particles in a stable liquid form (Yurdakul and Reider, 2015) can result in marked reductions in rebound in both wet and dry-mix shotcrete.

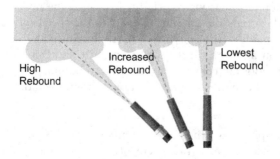

Figure 6.3 Effect of shooting orientation on shotcrete rebound.

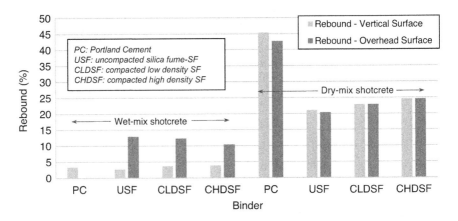

Figure 6.4 Plastic properties of wet and dry-mix shotcrete, including rebound test data.

(Wolsiefer and Morgan, 1993.)

Figure 6.4 provides a comparison of rebound for wet and dry-mix shotcretes applied in a wood rebound test chamber for both vertical and overhead applications for shotcrete mixes with and without various forms of silica fume addition (Wolsiefer and Morgan, 1993). Lowest rebound (around 3% to 4%) occurs in wet-mix shotcrete applied to a vertical surface. On an overhead surface, the wet-mix shotcrete rebound increased to about 10% to 13%. In dry-mix shotcrete, the rebound of silica fume modified shotcretes was in the range of 21% to 25% on a vertical surface and 19% to 25% on an overhead surface. The plain control Portland cement dry-mix shotcrete had around 43% to 45% rebound when applied to vertical and overhead surfaces.

While these data were generated in a systematic laboratory study, the same trends can be observed in the field. Some project specifications place a limit on the maximum amount of rebound for which a contractor will be compensated. For example, in some tunnel lining projects, as a cost control item, tarpaulins are placed on the ground in the shooting area and the rebound gathered and weighed and expressed as percent by mass of the total amount of shotcrete that was discharged through the nozzle. If the calculated rebound exceeds the amount allowed in the specification, then a cost adjustment is made to the payment for shotcrete to the contractor. This approach encourages the contractor to optimize shotcrete mixture designs and use good shooting technique to minimize rebound.

The amount of overall rebound and fibre rebound will depend on several factors, including:

a) Shotcrete placement method (wet-mix or dry-mix shotcrete process),
b) Type of shotcrete mix (plain cement, or silica fume modified),
c) Shooting orientation (vertical or overhead)

d) Thickness of the shotcrete layer.

e) Shooting technique

Overall, rebound and hence fibre rebound, is relatively low in the wet-mix shotcrete process but can be quite high in the dry-mix shotcrete process. Also, silica fume addition to the mix can dramatically reduce the amount of overall rebound and hence fibre rebound, particularly in the dry-mix shotcrete process. Fibre rebound will tend to be higher in thinner shotcrete layers (Parker, 1976, 1999). Also, shooting technique is important in that the least rebound will occur in shotcrete that impacts at right angles (90 degrees) to the receiving surface. The more acute the impacting angle, the higher the overall and fibre rebound. Also, for dry-mix shotcrete, mixtures shot at drier consistencies will develop greater overall and fibre rebound.

6.5 SETTING TIME

Setting time is an important consideration for many shotcrete applications. While setting times similar to that achieved in conventional concretes without accelerator addition may suffice for many shotcrete applications (e.g. structural shotcrete walls, canal linings, swimming pools, skateparks, rock slope stabilization, etc.), there are applications such as underground support in tunnels and mines, remedial work in marine intertidal regions and shotcrete application overhead in infrastructure rehabilitation, where more rapid setting times may be required to facilitate the shotcrete construction process and satisfy design requirements.

Setting time can be measured using the *ASTM C 1117-89 (1994) Standard Test Method for Time of Setting of Shotcrete Mixtures by Penetration Resistance*. This test method is based on the *ASTM C 403/C 403 M-99 Standard Test Method for Time of Setting of Concrete Mixtures by Penetration Resistance*. ASTM C1117 was withdrawn in 2003 (because of a lack of a precision and bias statement) but is still widely used in the shotcrete industry. In this test method shotcrete is shot into a standard ASTM C 1140 test panel and setting time is determined using standard penetration needles. Two states of setting are defined:

a) **Initial setting:** a penetration resistance of 500 psi (3.5 MPa)

b) **Final setting:** a penetration resistance of 4000 psi (27.6 MPa)

Figure 6.5 shows equipment that can be used to conduct a setting time test. When initial setting has been reached the shotcrete will have lost all workability and would be difficult to cut, trim or otherwise finish. When final setting has been reached, the shotcrete will be hard and suitable for application of additional layers of shotcrete. With conventional concrete accelerators added to the mix during batching, final setting times may be reduced from

Figure 6.5 Measuring setting time of shotcrete using ASTM C1117 penetration needles.

2 to 3 hours to as little one hour. By contrast, with shotcrete accelerators added at the nozzle, depending on the accelerator type and addition rate, initial setting can be achieved in a matter of only a few minutes (5 to 10 minutes) and final setting within half an hour. For example, in a hydroelectric draft tube retrofit project recently completed in Washington State, USA (Radomski et al., 2019), the addition of 6% by mass of cement of an alkali-free accelerator at the nozzle resulted in an initial setting time of 8 minutes and final setting time of 32 minutes. Even more rapid setting times can be achieved with higher accelerator addition rates, but such practice should generally be avoided, as high accelerator addition rates can adversely affect the compressive strength and durability of the shotcrete.

The ASTM C1117-89 (1994) penetrometer needles test method is a useful and relatively simple test to use for quality control purposes to check whether the required amount of accelerator is being added at the nozzle. Calibration tests can be done at the start-up phase of a project to establish the relationship between accelerator addition rates and setting time. Once the desired accelerator addition rate has been established, the setting time for this mix forms the benchmark against which setting times on the job can be compared. Excessively rapid setting times are an indicator that too much accelerator is being added at the nozzle; conversely, excessively slow setting times indicate that not enough accelerator is being added at the nozzle, or a cement-accelerator incompatibility. It should be noted that on large projects, modern alkali-free accelerator can be specifically adapted to a given binder to help balance initial set and strength development (Juilland et al., 2011). In tunnelling and mining work this is important, as people should not be allowed under shotcrete applied overhead before it has reached final set and a specified minimum compressive strength. Depending on ground conditions, shotcrete may be required to develop early-age compressive strength of 1 or 2 MPa before man entry is permitted (Rispin, 2005). See Section 6.6 for more detail on this issue.

6.6 EARLY-AGE COMPRESSIVE STRENGTH

Compressive strength of shotcrete is normally determined by shooting standard ASTM C1140 test panels and extracting and testing drilled cores using the ASTM C1604 test method. This method, however, only works satisfactorily with shotcrete that has developed compressive strength of at least 10 MPa. At compressive strengths below this, drilled cores will tend to ravel during the coring process and core compressive strength test results are likely to be unreliable. And yet there is a need on many tunnelling and mining projects to know what the shotcrete compressive strength is for strengths in the 1 to 10 MPa range. A number of different test methods have been developed to address this issue. Bernard (Bernard and Geltinger, 2007) provides an excellent review of different types of tests that have been used to attempt to measure early-age compressive strength development in shotcrete. These are summarized below.

a) Soil penetrometer
b) Meynadier needle penetrometer
c) Hiliti Gun (pull-out probe)
d) Beam End Tester

Bernard carried out a systematic comparative study of early-age (1 to 24 hours) compressive strength of shotcretes, using the above testing devices. He found that the soil penetrometer could measure compressive strengths until the shotcrete strength exceeded about 1.3 MPa. While the test was easy to use, the comparative study showed that it overestimated compressive strength by a significant margin. Thus, it should be used with caution in field work.

The Meynadier Needle Penetrometer is frequently used in Europe but not much in North America. It consists of a 3 mm diameter steel needle at the end of a spring that is forced into the surface of the setting and hardening shotcrete. Figure 6.6 shows the needle penetrometer in use. The force

Figure 6.6 Meynadier needle penetrometer in use.

(Photo courtesy E. Stefan Bernard.)

required to drive the needle into a depth of 15 mm is used to determine the approximate compressive strength with the aid of a calibration chart. Bernard stated that this test method is suitable for determining compressive strengths up to about 1.2 MPa. He, however, indicated that it had several disadvantages, including test results being influenced by coarse aggregate particles and fibres getting in the way, and the nuisance of having to use a calibration chart.

The Hilti Gun method is frequently used in Europe and is sometimes used in North America. It involves firing a steel fastener into the surface of shotcrete, measuring the depth of penetration and then using a separate device to pull the fastener out of the shotcrete surface. The force required to pull the fastener out is combined with the depth of penetration using a

Figure 6.7 Hilti Gun.

calibration chart to determine the strength of the shotcrete. There are different types of Hilti Guns available, but Bernard cautions that only the Hilti DX450 gun should be used. Figure 6.7 shows a Hilti Gun. The main advantage of the method is that it can measure compressive strength in the 2 to 18 MPa range. Disadvantages cited by Bernard include the requirement to use explosive cartridges and the relatively high costs of the equipment and fasteners compared to other test methods. Also, the method does not provide a direct measurement of compressive strength but requires the use of a calibration chart to estimate compressive strength.

The Beam End Tester method is based on the (now withdrawn) ASTM C116 test method for determining the compressive strength of portions of concrete beams broken in flexure. It was adapted by Morgan (Morgan et al., 1999) for use in shotcrete. Shotcrete is sprayed into easy release 75 mm × 75 mm × 350 mm beam moulds (although other sizes can be used). As soon as the shotcrete reaches a compressive strength of about 0.5 MPa (as measured using a needle penetrometer), the beam sides can be stripped, and portions of the beam tested as equivalent cubes for compressive strength. Typically, three tests can be done on one beam. Figure 6.8 shows a nozzleman shooting into beam moulds. Figure 6.9 shows the equipment used for testing the ends of beams (as equivalent cubes) for compressive strength. It can be used to test shotcrete with compressive strength ranging from 0.5 MPa to 20 MPa (and even higher with a sufficiently high-capacity hydraulic pump). It is the only early-age testing method which measures compressive strength directly. Indeed, indirect test methods are now commonly calibrated against results from the Beam End Tester. As such it has found favour and is now widely used in tunnelling and mining projects in North America, Australia and elsewhere. Morgan (Morgan et al., 1999)

Figure 6.8 Nozzleman shooting into Beam End Tester moulds.

Figure 6.9 Beam end tester in use.

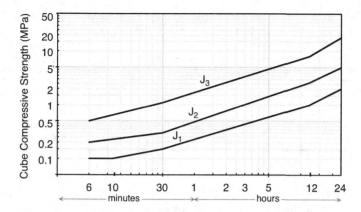

Figure 6.10 Austrian Concrete Society Sprayed Concrete Guidelines J₁, J₂ and J₃ early-age compressive strength envelopes and test results for a mix meeting J₂ performance requirement.

and Bernard (Bernard and Geltinger, 2007) provide more details regarding the use of this test method. Bernard does, however, caution that the shot beams should be stored in a temperature environment that is similar to the in-place shotcrete if the tests are to accurately represent in-place shotcrete compressive strength development.

The results of early-age strength tests (up to 24 hours) are frequently compared against the Austrian Shotcrete Standard J_1, J_2 and J_3 envelopes, as shown in Figure 6.10 (Austrian Concrete Society Sprayed Concrete Guidelines, 2013). Depending on ground conditions, and factors such as re-entry times under freshly applied shotcrete, design engineers may specify that early-age compressive strengths conform to J_1, J_2 or J_3 performance requirements. Minimum J_2 performance is often specified in tunnel lining and mining projects and is readily achievable in well-designed shotcrete mixtures with a suitable type and addition rate of shotcrete accelerator at the nozzle.

In the J_2-envelope, the minimum required compressive strength is 0.5 MPa at 1 hour and 1.0 MPa at 2 hours. A minimum shotcrete compressive strength of 1.0 MPa before allowing manpower re-entry underground is commonly specified in North America (Rispin, 2005). In severe ground conditions (e.g. NATM construction in loose ground), more stringent J_3 performance requirements may be specified.

6.7 LATER-AGE COMPRESSIVE STRENGTH

After shotcrete has reached a compressive strength of about 10 MPa, it can be cored from shot test panels (or if needed from the in-place shotcrete works). ASTM C1140 provides *Practice for Preparing and Testing*

Table 6.1 Strength correction factor required to estimate the compressive strength of concrete cores, when the length to diameter ratio is less than 2.0

Ratio of length to diameter (L/D)	Strength correction factor
1.75	0.98
1.50	0.96
1.25	0.93
1.00	0.87

Specimens from Shotcrete Test Panels, including cores for compressive strength testing. ASTM C1604 provides *Test Method for Obtaining and Testing Drilled Cores of Shotcrete*, including compressive strength and tensile splitting strength. Project specifications typically require the extraction and testing of three cores at each age of interest, with reporting of individual and average core strengths at each age. ASTM C1604 requires that if the core *Length to Diameter Ratio (L/D)* is 1.75 or less (which is often the case) that the following *Strength Correction Factors* be applied (Table 6.1). Where the L/D ratio does not correspond with values provided in the above table, interpolation should be used to calculate the *Strength Correction Factor*.

There is some controversy in the shotcrete industry as to what constitutes acceptable core compressive strengths for cores drilled and extracted from either a standard shotcrete test panel, or the in-place shotcrete. For conventional cast-in-place concrete, cast cylinders form the basis for determination of conformance to the design compressive strength. When there is a question about the results of the cylinder tests, cores are sometimes drilled and extracted from the concrete. The standard *CSA A23.1/23.2-19 Concrete materials and methods of concrete construction/ Test methods and standard practices for concrete*, requires that:

> The compressive strength of the concrete in the area of the structure represented by the core tests shall be considered adequate if: (a) the average set of three cores from the portion of the structure in question is equal to at least 85% of the specified strength and (b) no single core is less than 75% of the specified strength.

ACI 318-19: Building Code Requirements for Structural Concrete and Commentary has similar requirements for cast-in-place concrete.

The logic behind the above strength acceptance criteria for cast-in-place concrete appears to be that structural design is based on compressive strength of cast concrete cylinders, made and tested in a prescribed standard manner. Bloem (1965) and others have, however, shown that drilled cores typically exhibit lower compressive strengths than cast concrete cylinders made from the same concrete and cured in the same manner. Hence, the above-reduced acceptance values for compressive strength of drilled cores from cast-in-place concrete.

With shotcrete, however, cast cylinders do not form the basis for determining compressive strength for structural shotcrete. Rather, compressive strength is always based on drilled cores extracted from standard shotcrete test panels (or the in-place shotcrete). There is a good reason for this. The shooting process changes the nature of the shotcrete, compared to the shotcrete that was discharged into the shotcrete pump in the wet-mix shotcrete process. For example:

a) Some of the coarse aggregates will be lost during shooting because of rebound, and
b) About half of the air content of the material discharged into the shotcrete pump will be lost during the shooting process.

The reduction in air content can markedly increase compressive strength when it is considered that there is about a 4% to 5% reduction in compressive strength for every 1% of additional air content in the hardened product. Thus, if the ready-mix concrete supplier were to make cylinders from the shotcrete discharged into the shotcrete pump, they would likely have considerably lower compressive strengths than companion cores extracted from shot test panels (particularly for mixes with high initial air contents). On the basis of the above considerations, most design engineers will specify that shotcrete acceptance or rejection be based on the actual drilled core compressive strength results and that the 85% and 75% strength reduction acceptance criteria described above for cast-in-place concrete not be applied to shotcrete.

Well-designed and applied wet and dry-mix shotcretes, made with quality materials, will typically satisfy compressive strengths of 35 to 40 MPa at 28 days (Zhang et al., 2016). Much higher compressive strengths, up to 70 MPa or even more, are possible with suitable mixture designs and materials and the use of supplementary cementing materials such as silica fume and high addition rates of high range water-reducing admixtures (Morgan et al., 1999). Indeed, the first author was involved in multi-million dollar repair of an off-shore concrete oil platform where the design compressive strength of the substrate concrete was 90 MPa at 28 days and the structural design engineer required the repair shotcrete to have a minimum 28-day compressive strength of 100 MPa. A suitable shotcrete mixture was designed and applied.

Some contractors, particularly in the swimming pool industry, have attempted to save money by reducing cement content and using shotcretes with design strengths as low as 20 MPa. This is a retrograde practice, as such shotcrete will not shoot and consolidate well. It will have high rebound (a lack of sufficient paste content), reduced adhesion and cohesion and be vulnerable to sagging and sloughing. In addition, the hardened product is likely to be permeable and have poor durability. The American Shotcrete Association has published a Position Statement on this topic (ASA Position Statement #4, 2015) and recommends that swimming pool shotcrete have a minimum compressive strength of at least 28 MPa, and preferably 34 MPa, in order to permit the construction of watertight and durable pools.

6.8 FLEXURAL STRENGTH

Flexural strength is not frequently specified as a performance requirement for plain (non-fibre reinforced) shotcrete, but when it is, sawed beams should be procured from shotcrete test panels in accordance with the ASTM C42 *Standard Test Method for Obtaining and Testing Drilled Cores and Sawed Beams of Concrete* and tested in accordance with ASTM C78 *Standard Test Method for Flexural Strength of Concrete (Using Simple Beam with Third Point Loading)*.

By contrast, with fibre-reinforced shotcrete, flexural strength is a frequently specified performance parameter. Indeed, if the design has a requirement to meet a certain *Toughness Performance Level* (Morgan et al., 1995), then flexural strength is a necessary specified performance requirement. Initially, flexural strength of fibre-reinforced shotcretes was determined using the ASTM C1018 *Standard Test Method for Flexural Toughness and First Crack Strength of Fibre-Reinforced Concrete Using Beam with Third Pont Loading*. While this test method was fully capable of accurately determining flexural strength of shotcrete, it was found to have some deficiencies in determining toughness using the *Toughness Indices* calculation method and was withdrawn by ASTM in 2006. It was replaced in 2005 by ASTM C1609 *Standard Test Method for Flexural Performance of Fibre-Reinforced Concrete (Using Beam With Third Point Loading)*. This is a complex test method and has undergone several modifications since originally published, and so the latest version of the document should be referenced.

In the ASTM C1609 test, saw-cut shotcrete beams should have dimensions of 100 mm × 100 mm × 350 mm. If the European standard EN 14488-3 is used then saw-cut beams should have dimensions of 75 mm × 125 mm × 600 mm. Figure 6.11 shows an ASTM C1609 test in progress on a servo-controlled testing machine. It should be cautioned that flexural strength test results from ASTM C1609 and EN 14488-3 are not directly comparable, not only because of the differences in beam dimensions but also because a notch is saw cut in the centre of the bottom of the beam in the EN 14488-3 test.

Figure 6.11 ASTM C1609 flexural beam test in progress.

(Photo courtesy Lihe (John) Zhang, LZhang Consulting & Testing Ltd.)

6.9 FLEXURAL TOUGHNESS

Conceptually, flexural toughness can be thought of as the ability of fibre-reinforced concrete or shotcrete to continue to carry load after cracking. There are a variety of different types of test methods that have been used in different countries to measure flexural toughness of fibre-reinforced concretes and shotcretes. In North America, the available methods are as follows:

a) ASTM C1609 *Flexural Performance of Fibre-Reinforced Concrete (Using Beam With Third Point Loading)*.

b) ASTM C1399 *Standard Test Method for Obtaining Average-Residual Strength of Fibre-Reinforced Concrete.*
c) ASTM C1550 Flexural Toughness of *Fibre*-Reinforced Concrete (Using Centrally Loaded Round Panel).

In Europe, the most commonly used test methods are as follows:

a) EN 14488-3 Testing Sprayed Concrete: Flexural Strengths (first peak, ultimate and residual) of Fibre-Reinforced Beam Specimens.
b) EN 14488-5 Testing Sprayed Concrete: Determination of Energy Absorption Capacity of Fibre-Reinforced Slab Specimens.

In civil engineering tunnel lining projects and other structural shotcrete applications in North America, the most frequently specified flexural toughness test method is the ASTM C1609 beam test. This is, in part, because this test method is most useful for defining flexural toughness performance parameters at smaller deflections, with narrow crack widths (Permanent civil works generally try to avoid large deformations and limit permissible crack widths). By contrast, in many mining applications the fibre-reinforced shotcrete lining is subjected to large deformations with consequently wider crack development and the preferred flexural toughness test method is the ASTM C1550 round panel test. Figure 6.12 shows a picture of the ASTM C1550 test in progress on a servo-controlled testing machine.

The ASTM C1550 round panel test method is useful for defining flexural toughness at both small and large deformations and at both narrow and wider crack widths. The area under the load–deflection curve is defined as the energy absorbing capacity of the panel in Joules, and this value is of interest to the mining engineer in ground support design. For example, the publication Australian Shotcrete Society: Recommended Practice: Shotcreting in Australia, 2010, provides a table showing toughness values specified in recent Australian mining projects as shown in Table 6.2. Note that these

Figure 6.12 ASTM C1550 round panel test in progress.

Table 6.2 Typical toughness values specified in recent Australian mining projects

Type of support	Specified toughness[1]
Non-structural or low deformation	280 Joules
Moderate ground support	360 Joules
High-level ground support	450 Joules

[1] 40 mm deflection in ASTM C-1550.

toughness values are based on test results at 40 mm end point deflections in the round panel test.

A ground support design chart compiled by Barton and Grimstad (Barton and Grimstad, 2014) provides energy absorption recommendations for fibre-reinforced shotcretes for different ground conditions in underground openings (see Figure 13.6). Values are provided in Joules and are based on tests conducted using the EN 14488-5 edge supported rectangular plate test with an end-point deflection of 25 mm. Bernard (Bernard, 2002) carried out an extensive comparative evaluation of fibre-reinforced shotcretes tested in accordance with both the EN 14488-5 plate test and the ASTM C1550 round panel test. He concluded that the energy in Joules in the EN 14488-5 test at 25 mm deflection was equivalent to 2.5 times the energy in Joules in the ASTM C1550 round panel test at 40 mm deflection. Recent data obtained with modern steel fibres have however reported varying equivalence factors (Gagnon and Jolin, 2018). Supplemental information on possible sources for the differences observed can be found in RTC (2019).

The ASTM C1399 test method is not often used with shotcrete. It is mainly used in testing of cast concretes with low fibre addition rates that would not perform well in either the ASTM C1609 beam test or ASTM C1550 round panel test.

6.10 BOND STRENGTH

In freestanding structural shotcrete elements such as walls, columns and pilasters, where shotcrete is typically applied to sealed plywood forms, bond strength is not a pertinent performance requirement. However, in many shotcrete applications, such as the following, it is important:

a) Bond to prepared concrete substrates in infrastructure rehabilitation and seismic retrofit. e.g. buildings, dams, tunnels, bridges, industrial and marine structures (Morgan, 2008).
b) In multilayer shotcrete construction where shotcrete is required to bond to previously applied shotcrete layers (Radomski et al., 2019).
c) Bond to prepared rock substrates in underground tunnels and mines and rock slope stabilization (Austin and Robins, 1995).

In conventional cast-in place concrete construction, the Canadian Standards Association CSA A23.1/23.2-19 requires a minimum tensile bond strength of 0.9 MPa at 28 days for topping concretes bonded to slabs below when tested in accordance with the CSA A23.2-6B test method. The American Concrete Institute ACI 506R-16 *Guide to Shotcrete* states: *Properly applied shotcrete with sufficient compaction on a well-prepared substrate usually develops a bond strength over* 145 psi (1.0 MPa).

With respect to concrete substrates, the question arises: What constitutes a well-prepared substrate? This issue was studied in depth in a research project at Université Laval (Talbot et al., 1994). They tested the direct tensile bond strength of wet and dry-mix shotcretes, with and without silica fume and steel fibres, applied to a substrate concrete prepared in different ways, using the test set-up shown in Figure 6.13.

The following types of concrete surface preparation were used:

a) Hydrodemolition;
b) Sandblasted;
c) Jackhammered;
d) Jackhammered and sandblasted;
e) Grinding.

The prepared concrete surfaces were predampened prior to shotcrete application. Extensive experience in bond testing in the laboratory and in the field has demonstrated that the optimal moisture condition for the substrate concrete (and for that matter substrates such as masonry and rock) for maximizing bond strength is *the Saturated Surface Dry (SSD) condition*. If the substrate surface is excessively wet (has free surface water on it) at the time of shotcrete application, this can result in a high water/cement ratio

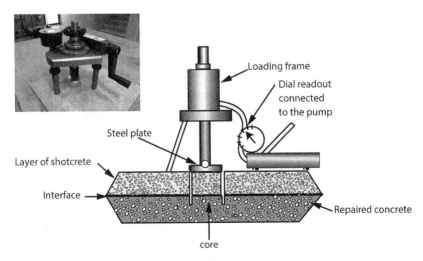

Figure 6.13 Test set-up for direct tensile bond strength testing at Université Laval.

at the critical bond interface and a substantial reduction, or even loss of bond strength, altogether. Conversely, if the substrate surface is excessively dry at the time of shotcrete application, water can be sucked out of the freshly applied shotcrete and the consequent desiccation at the critical bond interface can reduce bond strength. Hence the importance of having the substrate in an SSD condition at the time of shotcrete application.

In the Université Laval study (Talbot et al., 1994), no significant difference in bond strength at age 2 months and 6 months was observed between the wet- or dry-mix shotcrete processes for shotcrete applied to a substrate prepared by hydrodemolition. Measured bond strengths were consistently in excess of 1.0 MPa and characteristically in the 1.4 to 1.9 MPa range. Chipping with a jack hammer, followed by sandblasting also resulted in good bond strengths in the 1.7 to 2.0 MPa range. While chipping alone produced bond strength of around 1.0 MPa at 2 months, it was not recommended, as it appeared to result in a degradation of bond with time as the bond strength was below 1.0 MPa at 6 months. Sandblasting alone resulted in good bond strengths of 2.3 to 2.6 MPa at 2 months, but test results reduced to 1.7 to 2.0 MPa at 6 months. Worst bond test results were attained on surfaces that were ground. Test results ranged from 0.4 MPa to 1.4 MPa at 2 months but degraded to 0 to 0.2 MPa at 6 months.

Clearly, the surface roughness profile is an important consideration in maximizing bond. Guidance in this regard can be found in the International Concrete Repair Institute (ICRI) Technical Guideline 310.2R-2013. This guideline provides a range of different concrete surface profiles ranging from CSP-1 (smoothest) to CSP-9 (roughest), produced as indicated in Table 6.3.

Polymer templates with all of these surface roughness profiles are available from the ICRI. While they were developed for *Selecting and specifying concrete surface preparation for sealers, coatings and polymer overlays*, they have also been used to characterize required surface profiles for bonded concrete overlays and shotcretes applied to a variety of different substrates. In seismic retrofit of dams and other structures, ICRI CSP-7 to CSP-9 concrete surface profiles have been specified.

Table 6.3 Preparation methods

Concrete surface profile	Surface preparation method
CSP-1	Acid-etched
CSP-2	Grinding
CSP-3	Light abrasive blast
CSP-4	Medium blast
CSP-5	Medium/heavy blast
CSP-6	Heavy blast
CSP-7	Heavy shotblast
CSP-8	Extreme shotblast
CSP-9	Extreme shotblast

In multilayer shotcrete construction, shotcrete has to bond to previously applied shotcrete. The shotcrete can be applied the same day to a previous shotcrete layer that has stiffened and hardened sufficiently to resist sagging and sloughing under the weight of the new shotcrete layer. Shotcrete that has attained initial setting will usually be satisfactory for this purpose. The next layer of shotcrete can also be applied days, or if necessary, weeks later, provided the substrate shotcrete is properly prepared (Hanskat, 2014). Preparation methods include water pressure blasting (a 35 MPa water pressure blaster is recommended), and wet grit blasting, to remove any materials detrimental to good bond, such as hardened overspray, dust, dirt or any other contaminants. The substrate shotcrete should also be in an SSD state at the time of application of the next layer of shotcrete. When this is properly done, direct tension test results well in excess of 1.0 MPa at 28 days are commonly achieved. It is often difficult to even find the bond plane in many of the test samples. Failure may occur within the most recently applied shotcrete layer and so the test result may reflect the direct tensile strength of the shotcrete, rather than the bond strength, which would be even higher.

In actual shotcrete multilayer construction projects, where bond strength values are specified, the construction schedule does often not allow waiting for 28 days before testing for bond strength. On such projects, contractors will often test for bond strength at earlier ages (7 to 14 days) and if the test result meets the specified minimum 28-day bond test result, then the work is accepted. Table 6.4 shows results from a hydroelectric project (Radomski et al., 2019) where a wet-mix, steel fibre-reinforced silica fume shotcrete, with accelerator addition at the nozzle was used to build up shotcrete up to 2 m thick overhead in 100 mm thick layers. The specified minimum bond strength at 28 days was 0.7 MPa. Mean bond strengths at 9 to 11 days ranged from 1.0 to 1.3 MPa and were 1.6 MPa at 15 days.

In underground tunnelling and mining and rock slope stabilization projects, shotcrete is frequently applied to rock substrates. The rock substrates may have been produced by methods such as drill and blast, tunnel boring machines (TBM), or *roadheader* boring machines. Some authorities specify minimum bond strengths to rock substrates of 0.5 MPa at 28 days (Austin and Robins, 1995). While shotcrete bond to rock substrates is clearly an important objective, the Australian Shotcrete Society *Recommended Practice, Shotcreting in Australia* cautions against specifying a minimum tensile bond strength for rock substrates. This is because of the highly variable character of naturally occurring rock. While shotcrete bond strengths in excess of 1.0 MPa may be achieved in strong, hard, rock types such as granites and quartzites, it may not be possible to attain bond strengths of even 0 MPa in layered rocks such as schists, shales and slates and in weaker rock types such as weathered sandstones and mudstones. Rather, the Australian Shotcrete Society recommends the specification of surface preparation methods that maximize the opportunities for bond development to

Table 6.4 Direct tensile bond strength test results for multilayer shotcrete construction

Turbine unit No. 2 barrel A			Turbine unit No. 2 barrel C		
Bond strength, MPa			Bond strength, MPa		
Test no.	Age, days		Test no.	Age, days	
	9	15		9	11
1	1.20	—	1	1.47	—
2	0.89	—	2	1.68	—
3	—	1.88	3	1.04	—
4	—	1.69	4	1.18	—
5	—	1.27	5	—	1.30
6	—	1.52	6	—	1.26
Mean	1.05	1.59	Mean	1.34	1.28
Standard deviation	0.219	0.259	Standard deviation	0.288	0.028
Specs	Min 0.7		Specs	Min 0.7	
ACI 506	Min 1.0		ACI 506	Min 1.0	

Note: 1 MPa = 145 psi

the substrate. In this regard, the use of surface preparation methods such as *hydroscaling* is recommended (Clements et al., 2004). It should, however, be cautioned that if hydro-scaling is used, that the rock be allowed to dry back to an SSD condition before shotcrete is applied. Shotcrete applied to dripping wet rock surfaces can have severely compromised bond.

With respect to testing bond, the Australian Shotcrete Society recommends that rather than using direct tensile bond pull-off tests, that the adequacy of bond be determined using hammer sounding of the shotcrete layer. A *drummy* sound indicates a loss of bond. They also note that in deforming ground that bond can be reduced to zero with time. Hence the importance of having suitably designed rockbolt connections between the shotcrete and substrate rock (see, for example, the Grimstad and Barton ground support chart in Figure 13.4).

6.11 SHRINKAGE AND CRACKING

When it is considered that drying shrinkage occurs predominantly in the paste (cementing materials plus water) component of the mix (Morgan, 1973), shrinkage tends to be higher in shotcrete than conventional structural cast-in-place concretes of similar strength for the following reasons:

a) Shotcrete is characteristically made with a smaller maximum aggregate size (10 to 14 mm) than cast-in-place concrete (20 to 28 mm);

smaller maximum size aggregates require a higher paste content to provide a workable mix.

b) Shotcrete is characteristically made with a much higher fine aggregate (sand) content (70% to 75% by mass) compared to conventional cast-in-place concretes (35% to 45% by mass); the higher the fine aggregate content, the higher the paste content required to provide a workable mix.

c) Shotcrete has a considerably higher water demand (170–200L/m³) than an equivalent strength cast-in-place concrete (140–160 L/m³); the higher the water demand, the higher the shrinkage capacity of the mix.

d) Shotcrete requires a higher paste content than cast-in-place concrete, in order to provide the shotcrete with suitable adhesion and cohesion and resistance to sagging and sloughing and to reduce rebound.

Conventional 30 to 40 MPa compressive strength cast-in-in place concretes tend to have unrestrained drying shrinkage in the 0.04% to 0.06% range at 28 days and the 0.05% to 0.07% range at 90 days (Morgan, 1975). In comparison, wet-mix shotcrete with similar compressive strength has unrestrained drying shrinkage in the 0.08 to 0.09% range at 28 days and 0.09 to 0.10% range at 90 days. This is illustrated in Figure 6.14 (Wolsiefer and Morgan, 1993).

Dry-mix shotcrete with similar 28-day compressive strengths to the wet-mix shotcretes noted above had unrestrained drying shrinkage in the 0.05% to 0.07 % range at 28 days and 0.07% to 0.08 % range at 90 days. This is illustrated in Figure 6.15 (Wolsiefer and Morgan, 1993). The lower drying shrinkage in the dry-mix shotcrete, compared to the wet-mix shotcrete, is attributed primarily to the lower water demand of the dry-mix shotcrete

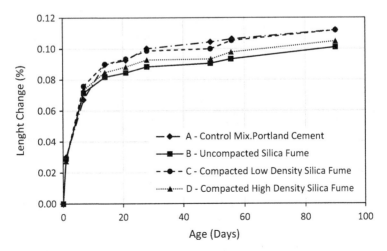

Figure 6.14 Drying shrinkage of wet-mix shotcrete with and without silica fume.

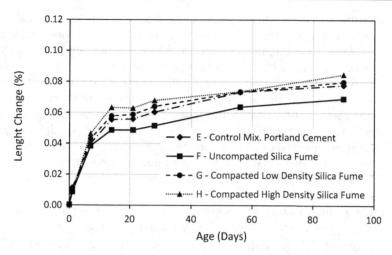

Figure 6.15 Drying shrinkage of dry-mix shotcretes with and without silica fume.

(165 L/m³) compared to the wet-mix shotcrete (177 L/m³). Interestingly, the silica fume modified mixes tended to have slightly lower unrestrained drying shrinkage values than mixes with Portland cement as the only binder (see Figures 6.14 and 6.15).

Austin and Robbins (Austin and Robins, 1995) summarize the results of drying shrinkage studies on wet and dry-mix shotcretes conducted by other researchers. Test results are generally within the ranges reported above from the Wolsiefer and Morgan study. In summary, it is clear that characteristically shotcretes have higher unrestrained drying shrinkage capacity than equivalent compressive strength cast-in-place concretes.

Having said this the first author has recently been involved in the development and application of new low shrinkage wet-mix shotcretes with 70% slag, with 28-day shrinkage values below 0.04%, which are now being used in construction of mass shotcrete structural walls in underground stations, with good results (hardly any restrained drying shrinkage cracking) (see Chapter 7 and Section 7.5).

Morgan and Chan (Morgan and Chan, 2001) published a paper *Understanding and Controlling Shrinkage and Cracking in Shotcrete*. They raised the following questions and provided responses:

a) Why is shrinkage a potential problem in shotcrete?
b) What causes shrinkage?
c) What causes cracking?
d) What shotcrete mixture design factors affect shrinkage and cracking?
e) What should be done to control shrinkage-induced cracking?

The sections which follow address these questions.

a) Shrinkage is a potential problem in shotcrete (and concrete) design and construction in that it can lead to restrained drying shrinkage cracking. Cracking in turn can provide a path for ingress of aggressive chemicals such as chlorides in bridges and parking, industrial and marine structures. This can lead to accelerated rates of corrosion of reinforcing steel in such structures, with consequent shotcrete cracking, delamination and spalling. In addition, cracking can provide a path for penetration of deleterious products such as sulphates and other aggressive chemical solutions in environmental structures (e.g. sewage treatment plants and sewers), pulp and paper mills and mine infrastructure. This can result in accelerated deterioration of such structures.

b) The prime cause of shrinkage in concrete and shotcrete is a loss of water from the mix. There are various types of shrinkage:

Plastic shrinkage: Shrinkage that occurs in the fresh shotcrete before it has set and hardened, as a result of loss of moisture to the ambient environment.

Drying shrinkage: Shrinkage that occurs in the hardened shotcrete as a result of the loss of moisture to the ambient environment. Drying shrinkage can continue for many years, although about 70% of it occurs within about 3 months (Neville, 1996).

Autogenous shrinkage: Also referred to as chemical shrinkage, or self-desiccation, is caused by consumption of water by the cement hydration reactions. Autogenous shrinkage is usually only about 10% of the long-term drying shrinkage, except in very low water/cementing materials mixes, where it can be considerably higher (Neville, 1996; Aitcin, 1999).

Thermal contraction: In addition to the various types of shrinkage caused by a loss of moisture as described above, shotcrete can contract as the result of thermal effects.

c) Just as there are various types of shrinkage, there are also various types of cracking.

Plastic shrinkage cracking: This cracking is caused by plastic shrinkage and is the result of freshly applied shotcrete drying excessively (as a result of inadequate protection) before it has had a chance to develop any significant tensile strength.

Drying shrinkage cracking: This cracking is caused by drying shrinkage in the hardened shotcrete and occurs if the shrinkage-induced tensile stress exceeds the tensile strength of the shotcrete. This is graphically illustrated in Figure 6.16 (Morgan and Chan, 2001). Shotcrete exposed to drying at an early age (12 hours to 7days), before it has developed sufficient tensile strength, is vulnerable to drying shrinkage cracking. Also, shotcrete mixtures with a high

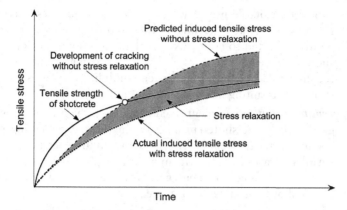

Figure 6.16 Cracking occurs when shrinkage-induced tensile stress exceeds tensile strength of shotcrete.

shrinkage capacity, such as poorly designed mixes with an excessively high cementing materials content and/or water demand, are more susceptible to drying shrinkage cracking. Note that such mixes may develop drying shrinkage-induced cracks at a later age, even if they were initially properly cured. In addition, shotcretes with excessively high accelerator addition, are more susceptible to drying shrinkage cracking (Beaupré and Jolin, 2002).

Autogenous shrinkage cracking: This type of cracking is relatively rare in conventional shotcretes but can occur in very high strength, say 70 MPa silica fume modified shotcretes with very low water/cementing materials ratios, if they are not thoroughly wet-cured at early ages (from the time of final set, to at least 3 days and preferably 7 days) (Aitcin, 1999).

Thermal cracking: While not moisture related, shotcrete can crack if it is subjected to thermal shock. If a strong thermal gradient is allowed to develop between the surface and interior of the shotcrete before it has developed sufficient tensile strength to resist the imposed thermal stresses, then it can crack. CSA A23.1-19, Table 20, provides guidance as to what constitutes acceptable thermal gradients for concrete for different structural configurations.

d) Mixture design factors affecting shrinkage and cracking

Cementing materials content: The higher the cementing materials content, the greater the shrinkage capacity of the shotcrete. Thus, mixture designs with excessively high cementing materials contents (say over 500 kg/m³) should be avoided.

Water content: The higher the water demand of the shotcrete, the higher the shrinkage capacity of the shotcrete. Thus, for wet-mix shotcrete, suitable use of water-reducing admixtures and/or high range (or so-called all-range) water-reducing admixtures should be implemented to control water demand. Note that for dry-mix shotcrete, the use of powdered water-reducing admixtures is not recommended, as the admixture can mobilize in the freshly applied shotcrete, resulting in sloughing and fall-outs.

Aggregate gradation: As mentioned previously, the finer the aggregate gradation in the shotcrete mix, the higher the cementing materials and water (paste) content of the mix and hence the higher the shrinkage capacity. Thus, from a shrinkage perspective, the use of ACI 506 Grading No.2 aggregates is preferred to the more mortar-like ACI 506 Grading No.1 aggregates.

Air-entraining admixtures: As previously discussed, air-entraining admixtures can be useful with respect to minimizing water demand and hence reducing shrinkage, in that they act like plasticizers to increase workability and pumpability of wet-mix shotcrete.

Accelerators: Research (Morgan, 1975; Neubert and Manns, 1993; Jolin et al., 1997; Beaupré and Jolin, 2002) and practical experience (Morgan and Neill, 1991), have shown that most accelerators will increase the shrinkage of concrete and shotcrete, particularly at early ages. The higher the accelerator addition, the greater the shrinkage capacity of the mix. In particular, never use calcium chloride as a shotcrete accelerator. While it can be very effective in providing rapid early set, it can increase *early-age* (up to 3 days) drying shrinkage by as much as 50%. This can lead to cracking and delaminations. This occurred on a bridge rehabilitation project in Oregon, where the designer required the addition of calcium chloride to the mix-water added at the nozzle in dry-mix shotcrete. This was done in an attempt to create chloride compatibility between shotcrete repairs and the surrounding concrete, for electrochemical reasons in this cathodic repair application. The repairs, however repeatedly failed by cracking and delamination. It was only when the calcium chloride addition at the nozzle was discontinued that the cracking and delamination were eliminated (Morgan and Chan, 2001).

Shrinkage-reducing admixtures: Shrinkage can be significantly reduced by the use of shrinkage-reducing admixtures (SRAs). They act by reducing the surface tension in the pore water solution. This reduces the contraction forces exerted by the pore water menisci on the capillary pore walls which in turn reduces shrinkage. This was well demonstrated in a study conducted by Morgan et al. (2001) in which the addition of 2% and 4% SRA by mass of cement resulted in significant reductions in drying shrinkage in both wet-mix shotcrete, as shown in Figure 6.17, and dry-mix shotcrete, as shown in Figure 6.18. Similar products

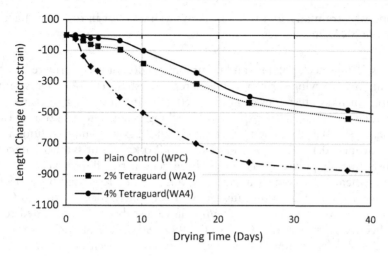

Figure 6.17 Drying shrinkage in wet-mix shotcretes produced with and without shrinkage-reducing admixtures.

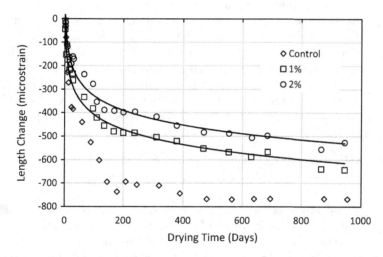

Figure 6.18 Drying shrinkage in dry-mix shotcrete produced with and without shrinkage-reducing admixtures.

were found to greatly reduce the cracking potential of dry-mix shotcrete (Menu et al., 2020).

In a companion study (Morgan et al., 2001), in tests conducted in an environmental chamber with severe drying conditions, the plain control wet-mix and dry-mix shotcretes developed restrained drying shrinkage cracks but mixes with 2% SRA addition by mass of cement displayed no cracking. It should, however, be cautioned that there have been in the past compatibility issues between SRA's and air-entraining admixtures (a difficulty to properly entrain air), and this has likely been a factor in the limited acceptance of SRA's in shotcrete in the field.

Fibres: While steel, polymer and natural fibres do not necessarily reduce the amount of drying shrinkage in concrete and shotcrete in an unrestrained free shrinkage test, they can be very effective in controlling, or even eliminating restrained drying-shrinkage cracking in concrete (Gryzbowski and Shah, 1990) and shotcrete (Campbell, 1999). Low volume addition rates of around 0.1–0.2% by volume (1.0 to 2.0 kg/m³) of synthetic microfibers (mainly polypropylene) have been demonstrated to be very effective in mitigating plastic shrinkage cracking in shotcrete (Campbell, 1999). Higher volume addition rates of synthetic macrofibres of around 0.5% to 0.9% by volume (5 to 9 kg/m³) have also been demonstrated to be effective in this regard (Campbell, 1999). Steel fibre at addition rates of 0.2–0.4% by volume (15 to 30 kg/m³) have also been shown to suppress plastic shrinkage cracking (Campbell, 1999).

Natural hemp-based fibre was demonstrated to be very effective in mitigating plastic shrinkage cracking in wet-mix shotcrete in tests conducted in accordance with the ASTM C1579 *Standard Test Method for Evaluating Plastic Shrinkage Cracking of Restrained Fibre-Reinforced Concrete (Using a Steel Form Insert)* (Morgan et al., 2017). This test method requires a Plain Control Mix without fibre to develop a minimum crack width of 0.5 mm in a controlled wind tunnel test. It then compares the crack widths in fibre-reinforced concrete against the Plain Control concrete using a parameter called the *Crack Reduction Ratio (CRR)*, where:

$$CRR = [1 - \text{average crack width of Fibre} - \text{Reinforced Concrete/average crack width of Plain Control Concrete}] \times 100\%.$$

In this study, the wet-mix shotcrete with synthetic fibre had a fibre addition rate of 0.15% (1.35 kg/m³) and a CRR of 84%. The wet-mix shotcrete with natural hemp-based fibre had a fibre addition rate of 0.15% (2.0 kg/m³) and was more effective in suppressing plastic shrinkage cracking, as it had a CRR of 92%. In subsequent field applications in industrial shotcrete walls and skatepark bowls, the natural hemp-based fibre has been found to be very effective, eliminating both plastic and drying shrinkage cracking when ACI 506R-16 recommended curing practices were followed.

Gryzbowski (Gryzbowski and Shah, 1990) studied the effects of steel and polypropylene synthetic macro fibres in mitigating drying shrinkage cracking in concretes in a restrained ring-shrinkage test. Crack development with time in steel fibre-reinforced concretes for fibre addition rates of 0.25%, 0.5%, 1.0% and 1.5% by volume are shown in Figure 6.19. Similar tests on polypropylene fibre-reinforced concretes at fibre addition rates of 0.1%, 0.25%, 0.5% and 1.0% by volume are shown in Figure 6.20. It is apparent

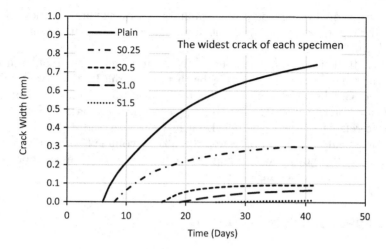

Figure 6.19 Crack width development with time in steel fibre-reinforced concretes in ring shrinkage test.

(Authorized reprint from 1990 ACI Materials Journal, Vol.87 Shrinkage Cracking
in Fibre-Reinforced Concrete by Gryzbowski and Shah; courtesy American
Concrete Institute.)

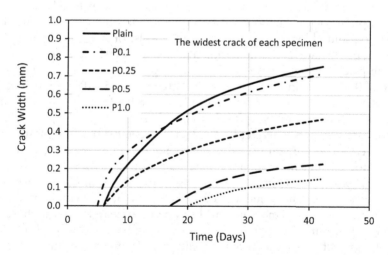

Figure 6.20 Crack width development with time in polypropylene fibre-reinforced concrete in ring shrinkage test.

(Authorized reprint from 1990 ACI Materials Journal, Vol.87 Shrinkage Cracking
in Fibre-Reinforced Concrete by Gryzbowski and Shah; courtesy American
Concrete Institute.)

that on an equal volume percentage addition rate, steel fibres are more effective than polypropylene synthetic fibres in restraining drying shrinkage crack widths.

This effect has also been observed in wet-mix shotcretes applied in the field in rehabilitation of shipping berth faces at the Port of Montreal in Quebec. Cracks were fewer and tighter in steel fibre-reinforced shotcrete than in shotcrete made with polypropylene synthetic macrofibres. In the seismic retrofit of the Littlerock Dam in California, the use of steel fibre reinforcement at an addition rate of 0.76% by volume (60 kg/m³), in conjunction with rigorous wet curing, was effective in completely suppressing drying shrinkage cracking (Forrest et al., 1996).

6.12 FREEZE-THAW DURABILITY

6.12.1 Wet-mix shotcrete freeze-thaw durability

As mentioned in Section 4.5.3, just like cast-in-place concrete, wet-mix shotcrete exposed to cycles of freezing and thawing in a saturated condition needs to be properly air entrained to provide freeze/thaw durability. CSA A23.1-19 requires that cast-in-place concrete meet a maximum allowable water/cementing materials ratio of 0.50 and minimum compressive strength of 30 MPa at 28 days for a *CSA A23.1-19 Class F-1 Exposure* for concrete exposed to freezing and thawing in a saturated condition. For structurally reinforced cast-in-place concrete exposed to both freezing and thawing in a saturated condition and chlorides from deicing chemicals, or seawater in intertidal regions, or seawater spray in marine structures, CSA A23.1-19 requires that cast-in-place concrete have a maximum allowable water/cementing materials ratio of 0.40 and minimum compressive strength of 35 MPa within 56 days, for a *CSA Class C-1 Exposure*, as detailed in CSA A23.1-19 Tables 1 and 2. These same criteria can be applied to wet-mix shotcrete.

For cast-in-place concrete, CSA A23.1-19 requires that the plastic concrete have an air content of 5–8% for 10 mm maximum size aggregate and 4–7% for 14 mm maximum size aggregate for CSA A23.1-19 Class F-1 and C-1 exposure conditions. With respect to air entrainment in wet-mix shotcrete, as previously mentioned in Section 6.3, about half of the as-batched air content as measured at the point of discharge into the shotcrete pump is lost during the pumping and shooting process (most of it is lost during impact onto the receiving surface) (Jolin and Beaupré, 2003), (Zhang, 2012). Thus, it is common to specify that as-batched plastic shotcrete air content be in the 7%–10% range, in order to provide in-place shotcrete air contents in the approximately 3.5% to 5% range. While these plastic shotcrete air-content values for the in-place shotcrete are a bit below that required in CSA A23.1-19 for cast-in-place concrete, there is evidence in several studies (Morgan et al., 1988; Morgan, 1989; Morgan, 1991; Beaupré, 1994), that such wet-mix shotcrete can provide excellent

Table 6.5 Wet and dry-mix shotcrete air-void and durability parameters

Mix no.	28-day compressive strength, MPa	Plastic air content, %	Hardened air content, %	Air-void spacing factor, mm	Specific surface, mm^{-1}	Durability factor at 300 cycles	Durability rating
I D	49.6	—	5.39	0.27	18.4	97.3	Excellent
2D	51.8	—	6.00	0.29	16.6	99.2	Excellent
9D	41.9	—	6.51	0.31	14.8	97.4	Excellent
I W	55.8	3.8	5.57	0.17	27.3	101.6	Excellent
2W	65.7	3.7	4.54	0.28	17.8	99.1	Excellent
3W	65.0	3.8	5.15	0.27	18.5	96.9	Excellent

freeze-thaw durability in the ASTM C666 Procedure A test, in which shot-crete prisms are subjected to 300 cycles of freezing and thawing in a saturated condition. This is well demonstrated in Table 6.5 from a study by Morgan et al (Morgan et al., 1988).

For cast-in-place concrete subjected to freezing and thawing, CSA A23.1-19 requires the air content in the hardened concrete equal to or exceed 3.0 % and the average spacing factor to not exceed 0.23 mm, with no single value greater than 0.26 mm. For cast-in-place concretes with water-to-cementing materials ratios of 0.36 or less, they relax these limits and require an average spacing factor of 0.25 mm with no single value exceeding 0.30 mm. For wet-mix shotcrete, there is evidence (Morgan et al., 1988) that shotcrete with an average spacing factor as high as 0.28 mm provides *Excellent Durability* in the ASTM C666 Procedure A test (i.e. 300 cycles of freezing and thawing in water), as shown in Table 6.3. In another study, (Morgan, 1989) reviewed the results of air-void parameters and ASTM C666 Procedure A testing for a wide range of different wet-mix shotcretes from different projects and concluded that for wet-mix shotcretes with a water/cementing materials ratios of 0.40 or less, an average air-void spacing factor of up to 0.30 mm can provide adequate freeze-thaw durability.

In summary, there is plenty of evidence, both in laboratory testing, and observations of the behaviour of properly designed and applied air-entrained wet-mix shotcretes in the field, that they can provide good durability on exposure to cycles of freezing and thawing in a saturated condition (Morgan, 1989; Gilbride et al., 1996). A good example of this is the shipping berth face rehabilitation at the Port of Saint John in New Brunswick, Canada (Gilbride et al., 1988). The concrete shipping berth faces are subjected to a tidal range of 8.5 m and over two hundred freezing and thawing cycles in a year, with temperatures often falling as low as –30°C in the winter, with sheets of ice forming on the berth faces. This represents one of the most severe freeze/thaw exposure environments anywhere in the world. Nearly two km of the 50- to 70-year-old concrete berth faces had suffered severe deterioration from frost, ice scour and wave action. A remedial programme was implemented to rehabilitate the berth faces over a 10-year period, using wet-mix, air-entrained, steel fibre reinforced, silica fume modified shotcrete. Details regarding the project are provided in Section 11.10. In 1995, after nearly 10 years in service, the oldest shotcrete applications to the berth faces were examined (Gilbride et al., 1996). There was no evidence of freeze/thaw damage of the shotcrete resurfacing of the shipping berth faces, in spite of the shotcrete having been subjected to over 2000 cycles of freezing and thawing. Communications with Gilbride in 2015, after nearly 30 years in service, indicated that the shotcrete resurfacing was still performing well.

6.12.2 Dry-mix shotcrete freeze-thaw durability

As mentioned in Section 3.5, prior to the late 1990's nearly all dry-mix shotcrete in North America was made without air entrainment. Studies at the Portland Cement Association in Chicago (Litvin and Shideler, 1966), the US Army Corps of Engineers (Reading, 1981), (Schrader and Kaden, 1987) and in Canada (Morgan, 1989) indicated that while it was possible for some dry-mix shotcretes made without air entrainment to provide satisfactory freeze/thaw durability in ASTM C666 Procedure A testing, and in the field, this was not universally true and some non-air-entrained dry-mix shotcretes did not provide satisfactory freeze/thaw durability. It was not until 2005 that the ACI 506R-05 *Guide to Shotcrete* recognized that it was possible to entrain air in dry-mix shotcrete, for the purpose of improving freeze/thaw durability and resistance to deicing salt scaling. This realization was based largely on research conducted at Université Laval in Quebec (Lamontagne, Pigeon and Beaupré, 1996; Dufour, 1996; Beaupré et al., 1996). Air entrainment could be achieved either by adding an air-entraining admixture to the mix water added at the nozzle, or by adding a dry powdered air-entraining admixture to the dry mix during batching. The latter method is now generally preferred and is routinely used in dry-mix shotcrete production (Dufour, 2008; Dufour et al., 2006).

With respect to freeze/thaw durability, the Ministry of Transportation Quebec (MTQ) requires that the air content in the plastic and hardened dry-mix shotcrete be in the 3.5 to 7% range, and the average air-void spacing factor not exceed 0.30 mm, with no individual test result exceeding 0.32 mm (Dufour et al., 2006). With respect to resistance to deicing salt scaling, Dufour (Dufour, 1996) demonstrated that dry-mix shotcrete with an air content in the plastic and hardened states of 3.5% to 7%, which satisfied the above air-void spacing factor requirements, provided satisfactory salt scaling resistance. This was demonstrated in deicing salt scaling tests conducted by Dufour (Dufour, 1996) in accordance with ASTM C672 to 50 cycles of freezing and thawing in a deicing salt solution. Figure 6.21 shows that a properly air-entrained dry-mix shotcrete experienced only 0.11 kg/m^3 mass loss. By contrast, Figure 6.22 shows that a non-air-entrained dry-mix shotcrete suffered severe scaling, with a mass loss of 8.81 kg/m^3 after 50 cycles of freezing and thawing. Organizations such as the MTQ limit the

Figure 6.21 Air-entrained dry-mix shotcrete with mass loss of 0.11 kg/m³ in ASTM C672 test.

Figure 6.22 Non-air-entrained dry-mix shotcrete with mass loss of 8.81 kg/m³ in ASTM C672 test.

allowable amount of mass loss in the ASTM C672 test to a maximum of 1.0 kg/m^3 (Dufour et al., 2006).

6.13 DURABILITY

6.13.1 Introduction

In addition to freeze/thaw durability, there are many factors that influence the durability of shotcrete. These factors include:

a) The quality of the coarse and fine aggregates;
b) The petrographic character of aggregates;
c) The soil and groundwater to which the shotcrete is exposed; and
d) Whether the shotcrete is exposed to chlorides.

a) **Aggregate quality**
   The aggregates should be free from excessive amounts of deleterious substances such as clay lumps; low-density granular materials; and flat and elongated particles. In addition, depending on the exposure conditions, aggregates should display adequate impact and abrasion resistance. Quantitative guidance in this regard is provided in publications such as CSA A23.1-19 Table 12 Limits for deleterious substances and physical properties of aggregates.

b) **Petrographic character of aggregates**
   The coarse and fine aggregates should be demonstrated to not be susceptible to alkali-aggregate reactivity. Guidance in this regard is provided in publications such as CSA A23.2-27A *Standard practice to identify degree of alkali-reactivity of aggregates and to identify measures to avoid deleterious expansion in concrete.*

c) **Sulphate exposure**
   In sulphate exposure conditions, the degree of exposure can be categorized as *Moderate, Severe, or Very Severe. CSA A23.1-19* (Table 6.3) provides guidance in this regard, as noted in Table 6.6, which is excerpted from this table. The measures that need to be taken to deal with sulphate attack will vary, depending on the severity of sulphate exposure. They will include the use of cements with either moderate sulphate resistance (ASTM Type II, or CSA Type MS), or high sulphate resistance (ASTM Type V or CSA Type HS). Alternatively, combinations of ASTM Type I, or CSA Type GU cements and suitable amounts of supplementary cementing materials, such as fly ash, silica fume, metakaolin, or ground granulated blast furnace slag (GGBFS) can be used, provided they provide satisfactory resistance to expansion in tests such as:

Table 6.6 Requirements for concrete/shotcrete subjected to moderate, severe and very severe sulphate exposure

Class of exposure	Degree of exposure	Water-soluble sulphate (SO_4) in soil sample, %	Sulphate (SO_4) in groundwater samples, mg/L	Maximum water-to-cementing materials ratio	Minimum specified compressive strength (MPa) and age (d) at test
S-1	Very Severe	> 2.0	> 10000	0.40	35 within 56 d
S-2	Severe	0.20–2.0	1500 to 10000	0.45	32 within 56 d
S-3	Moderate (including seawater exposure)	0.10–0.20	150 to 1500	0.50	30 within 56 d

ASTM C1012 *Standard Test Method for Length* Change *of Hydraulic-Cement Mortars Exposed to Sulphate Solution,* or

CSA A3004-C8 *Test Method for Determination of Sulphate Resistance of Mortar Bars Exposed to Sulphate Solution* (in CSA, 2018).

In addition, the concrete/shotcrete mixtures should meet with limits on the maximum allowable water/cementing materials ratio and minimum compressive strength at 56 days, as detailed in CSA A23.1-Table 2 and shown in Table 6.6

Note that where concrete/shotcrete is exposed to soil or groundwater conditions where both sulphates and chlorides are present, ASTM Type V or CSA Type HS cements should not be used. These types of cements, with low tricalcium aluminate (C_3A) contents are poor at inhibiting chloride ion intrusion into the concrete/shotcrete, and this can be detrimental with respect to corrosion of embedded reinforcing steel and other metal items. Rather, in such circumstances, ASTM Type I or CSA Type GU cements, in conjunction with suitable addition rates of supplementary cementing materials should be used, so that both sulphate resistance and enhanced resistance to chloride-ion penetration can be provided. This approach has been adopted in potash mines in Canada, where both sulphates and chlorides are present. It also applies to concrete/shotcrete structures exposed to seawater. CSA A23.1-19 provides good guidance relating to these matters.

d) **Chloride exposure**

The durability issue of most concern in reinforced concrete/shotcrete is chloride-induced corrosion of reinforcing steel and other embedded metal items (e.g. anchors, bolts and structural steel elements such as lattice girders and H-Sections). Chloride ions from sources such as deicing chemicals (sodium and/or calcium chloride), seawater, or airborne seawater spray, can with time migrate through the concrete/shotcrete to the depth of the reinforcing steel and destroy the protective oxide film, making the steel vulnerable to corrosion, subject to the availability of oxygen and water (reinforcing steel does not corrode in dry concrete/shotcrete). There are two main consequences of corrosion of reinforcing steel in concrete/shotcrete. First, the products of corrosion of reinforcing steel occupy a volume several times larger than the original steel and this exerts expansive stresses within the concrete/shotcrete. If sufficient corrosion product is able to develop, it can result in cracking, delamination and eventual spalling of the cover concrete/shotcrete. Second, the corrosion process reduces the cross-sectional area of the steel, reducing its load-carrying capacity. If remedial measures are not implemented in a timely manner, the structural capacity of the reinforced concrete/ shotcrete structure could be compromised (Broomfield, 2006; Bentur et al., 1997).

Chloride ion penetration occurs predominantly through ionic diffusion and is governed by *Fick's Second Law of Diffusion* (Jolin et al., 2015; Life-365, 2018). The time to initiation of chloride ion induced corrosion is influenced by many factors, including:

a) The quality of the concrete/shotcrete (primarily a function of the water/cementing materials ratio and hence compressive strength; the lower the water/cementing materials ratio, the more difficult it is for the chlorides to migrate through the concrete/shotcrete) (Bolduc et al., 2010).

b) Whether supplementary cementing materials such as fly ash, silica fume, metakaolin or GGBFS are used in the concrete/shotcrete mix design; supplementary cementing materials are beneficial in reducing the rate of chloride ion ingress. This is well demonstrated (Zhang et al., 2016), (Bolduc et al., 2010) in tests such as ASTM C1543 *Standard Test Method for Determining the Penetration of Chloride Ion into Concrete by Ponding and ASTM C1202 Standard Test Method for Electrical Indication of Concrete's Ability to Resist Chloride Ion Penetration (so-called Rapid Chloride Penetration- RCP test)*, or the US Navy Specification UFGS 03 31 29-3 *Ionic Migration Test* (USAC/NAVFAC/AFCESA/ NASA, 2012b).

   i) Whether chemical admixtures containing chlorides were added to the shotcrete; admixtures containing chlorides are now typically not used in reinforced shotcrete construction in North America, except where special circumstances warrant their use. For example, in shotcrete linings in halite or potash mines, where chlorides are often added to the mix water to inhibit substrate dissolution by fresh water in the mix. Also, chlorides are sometimes added to the mix water added at the nozzle in dry-mix shotcrete applied to permafrost ground. They are added to rapidly accelerate the setting time and early-age strength development of the shotcrete before freeze-back from the permafrost; reinforcing steel corrosion is inhibited in below-freezing temperatures (Dufour, 2000).

ii) The depth of cover to the reinforcing steel; low design or as-built shotcrete cover shortens the time for chlorides to reach the reinforcing steel.

iii) The presence of cracks in the shotcrete; cracks provide a localized path for chlorides to migrate rapidly to the reinforcing steel; the wider the cracks, the more rapid the chloride penetration.

vi) The type of reinforcing steel used. Conventional *Black Steel* is most susceptible to chloride ion-induced corrosion. Treatment of *Black Steel* with galvanic coatings will delay the time to onset of corrosion. Epoxy coatings will also delay the time to onset of corrosion in reinforced cast-in-place concrete but are not recommended for use in shotcrete, as there is evidence that the shotcrete application process can damage some types of epoxy coatings, creating local *holidays* (chipping type defects), which diminishes the effectiveness of the epoxy coating. Higher chrome steels, such as MMFX and stainless steel are much more resistant to chloride-ion-induced corrosion and are now being used in marine environments and other aggressive chloride exposure conditions.

6.14 TRANSPORT PROPERTIES

6.14.1 Introduction

The durability of concrete and shotcrete is fundamentally influenced by its transport properties. There are a range of different parameters that have been used to define the transport mechanisms in concrete and shotcrete. Bolduc and Jolin (2010) roughly divided the transport mechanisms into three categories:

a) **Permeability**: the movement of fluid (liquid or gas) resulting from a pressure. While the term permeability is widely used to describe the ingress of fluids into concrete, strictly speaking a pressure must be involved to use this term. A number of different types of water permeability tests have been developed by different agencies to measure the permeability of concrete (e.g. *U.S. Army Corps of Engineers Test CRD-C48-92*), but none of them are standardized by an official standards organization like ASTM or CSA.

b) **Ionic diffusion:** the movement of ionic species resulting from a concentration gradient. Thermodynamic principles dictate that equilibrium must be established when a system is unstable. Thus, for example, when concrete is immersed in seawater with a high concentration of chloride salts, the chloride concentration in the concrete pore solution is lower than in the seawater. Consequently, the chloride ions will migrate into the concrete pores through the pore solution until equilibrium is established. There are a number of different tests that have been developed to measure ionic diffusion of chlorides and other ionic species in concrete. These include the *ASTM C1543 Standard Test Method for Determining the Penetration of Chloride Ion into Concrete by Ponding*, and the *ASTM C1556 Standard Test Method for Determining the Apparent Chloride Diffusion Coefficient of Cementitious Mixtures by Bulk Diffusion*. While useful, these tests are laborious and time-consuming. It can take months to generate test data. Consequently, test methods have been developed which can more rapidly provide indirect measures of chloride diffusion into concrete. These include the *ASTM C1202 Standard Test Method for Electrical Indication of Concrete's Ability to Resist Chloride Ion Penetration* (the so-called RCPT test) and a modified version of this ionic migration test, the *US Navy Specification UFGS 03 31 29-3*. This latter test method was developed, in part, for input into the "Stadium" Service Life Prediction model for reinforced concrete structures subjected to exposure from chlorides and other aggressive ionic species (Bolduc et al., 2010).

c) **Capillary absorption:** suction of water resulting from the surface tension exerted in the capillary porosity. When a capillary tube is immersed in water, the water level rises from surface tension forces. Similarly, if a non-saturated concrete is immersed in water, the capillary pores within the concrete act as a series of tubes and the capillary voids slowly fill with water.

There are a number of different test methods that have been developed to measure capillary absorption in concrete. These include the *ASTM C642 Standard Test Method for Density, Absorption and Volume of Permeable Voids in Hardened Concrete* and *ASTM C1585 Standard Test Method for Measurement of Rate of Absorption of Water by Hydraulic Cement Concretes*.

6.14.2 Shotcrete transport properties study at Laval University

A research study was carried out at Université Laval in Quebec to examine the transport properties of different types of wet and dry-mix shotcretes, with a view to evaluating the potential service life of reinforced shotcrete structures in chloride exposure environments (Bolduc, et al., 2010). Transport properties tests conducted included:

a) Boiled Water Absorption (BWA) and Volume of Permeable Voids (VPV) tests to ASTM C642
b) Rapid Chloride Penetration Test (RCPT) to ASTM C1202
c) Ionic Migration Test (IMT) to determine diffusion coefficients to USACE/NAVFAC/AFCESA/NASA Specification UFGS 03 31 29-3 (2012b) (for input into the Stadium Service Life Prediction Model).

Shotcrete mixture design variables evaluated included:

a) Three different aggregate gradations: ACI 506 Grading No.1 (mortar-like mixes); ACI 506 Grading No. 2 (more concrete like mixes with 10 mm maximum size coarse aggregate) and Ministry of Transportation Quebec (MTQ) grading, which is intermediate between ACI 506 Grading No.1 and No.2 gradings. Figure 6.23 shows actual aggregate gradations for the ACI Grading No.1 and No.2 mixes and MTQ mixes, compared to the ACI 506 Grading No.1 and No.2 gradation limits.
b) Mixtures with water/cementing materials ratios ranging between 0.35 and 0.64.
c) Mixtures with different types of binders; Type GU Portland cement only and mixes with fly ash or silica fume addition.

In addition, unconfined compressive strengths at 28 days were determined on cores extracted from shotcrete test panels.

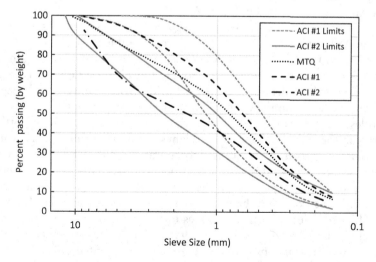

Figure 6.23 Aggregate gradations compared to ACI 506 Grading No. 1 and No. 2 limits.

Table 6.7 provides details of the various wet and dry-mix shotcretes evaluated in this study.

Table 6.8 provides results of unconfined compressive strength at 28 days, together with RCPT (Coulomb) and Diffusion Coefficient test results.

Table 6.9 provides test results for values of Boiled Water Absorption, Volume of Permeable Voids and Bulk Density to ASTM C642.

A number of interesting findings were made in this research study. Firstly, with respect to Boiled Water Absorption (BWA) values, it was shown that aggregate gradation influences BWA results insofar as it influences the paste content of the mix designs. This is well illustrated in Figure 6.24 where it is demonstrated that there is a general correlation between BWA and the Water/Cementing Materials Ratio for mixtures with similar aggregate gradations. The finer aggregate gradation (more mortar-like mixes) requires a higher paste content to coat the finer size aggregate particles. Water absorption occurs predominantly in the paste phase of the mix (unless porous aggregates are used). Hence, note the strong correlation between BWA and Paste Content for a given W/CM ratio in Figure 6.24.

An interesting observation that can be made from these findings is that some engineers/contractors have in the past attempted to reduce values of BWA to meet specification requirements by increasing the cementing materials content of shotcrete mixes in the mistaken belief that this would reduce BWA values. Increasing the cementing material content increases the paste content, which in turn increases BWA values. The most effective approach to reducing BWA values is to use a coarser (more concrete-like) aggregate gradation, which in turn reduces the required paste content for the mix.

Secondly, the Université Laval's research examined chloride ingress into the different wet and dry-mix shotcretes produced using the ASTM C1202 Rapid Chloride Penetration Test (RCPT). Test results are provided in Table 6.8 and graphically illustrated in Figure 6.25.

These test results can be evaluated against the classification system provided in ASTM C1202, which is reproduced in Table 6.10.

The ASTM C1202 test measures the charge passed in coulombs (amperes x seconds) in 6 hours and relates this to the chloride penetrability of the mix. The higher values denote a higher chloride penetrability and hence an expected reduced durability in reinforced shotcrete structures exposed to chlorides. Of note is the observation that the shotcrete mix with Portland cement as the only binder had the highest coulomb value (5471), with a *High* chloride penetrability rating. Incorporation of fly ash in the shotcrete reduced the coulomb value (2725) to produce a *Moderate* chloride penetrability rating. By contrast, all the shotcrete mixes which incorporated silica fume (with one exception) had *Low* to *Very Low* chloride penetrability ratings. This reduction of coulomb values for mixes incorporating supplementary cementing materials such as fly ash and silica fume is well known in the concrete industry and has been extensively documented (ACI 234). It is attributed in part to reductions which occur in the permeability of the paste

Table 6.7 Mixture designs of the study by Bolduc et al., 2010

Mix	Description	Process	Aggregate gradation	W/Cm	Binder content, kg/m³	Aggregate content, kg/m³	Paste volume, %
CD1	Type GU, 10% silica fume	Dry	MTQ	0.35	511	1604	34.7
				0.54	385	1648	33.4
CD2	Type GU, 10% silica fume, predampened	Dry	MTQ	0.49	415	1633	34.0
				0.57	392	1608	35.2
CD3	Type GU, 10% silica fume synthetic fibres, powdered AEA	Dry	MTQ	0.37	505	1662	35.3
				0.51	423	1663	35.5
CD4	Type GU, no SCM's	Dry	MTQ	0.44	437	1703	33.2
CD5	Type GU, 25% fly ash	Dry	MTQ	0.41	451	1724	33.4
MD1	Type GU, 10% silica fume	Dry	ACI#1	0.2	522	1594	39.1
				0.64	395	1596	38.3
MD2	Type GU, 12% silica fume	Dry	ACI#1	0.44	508	1527	39.1
				0.53	447	1525	38.4
MD4	Type GU, 12% silica fume Synthetic fibres, powdered AEA	Dry	ACI#1	0.47	460	1603	36.8
CW1	Type MS, 8% silica fume naphtalene HRWRA 4ml/kg Cm	Wet	ACI#2	0.42	405	1744	30.2
CW2	Type MS, 8% silica fume naphtalene HRWRA 12ml/kg Cm	Wet	ACI#2	0.47	372	1809	29.6
MW1	Type GU, 12% silica fume naphtalene HRWRA 10ml/kg Cm	Wet	ACI#1	0.55	433	1493	37.9

Table 6.8 Unconfined compressive strength, RCPT and OH⁻ diffusion coefficient test results

Mix	Consistency	UCS[1] 28d, MPa	RCPT[2], C	OH-diffusion coefficient, $\times 10^{-11}$ m^2/s
CD1	Dry	68.3	431	1.64
	Wet	55.4	922	3.21
CD2	Dry	59.1	830	3.54
	Wet	50.0	1300	4.66
CD3	Dry	52.2	435	1.45
	Wet	39.5	1418	3.48
CD4	In between	48.2	5471	13.60
CD5	In between	53.8	2725	3.76
MD1	Dry	52.5	1119	2.54
	Wet	42.5	2043	5.05
MD2	Dry	75.3	234	0.88
	Wet	54.8	1036	3.51
MD4	Wet	51.7	666	1.56
CW1	—	61.4	689	2.69
CW2	—	53.6	713	2.13
MW1	—	53.4	862	2.95

[1] UCS: Unconfined Compressive Strength.
[2] RCPT: Rapid Chloride Penetration Test.

Table 6.9 Boiled absorption, volume of permeable voids and bulk density

Mix	Consistency	BWA[1], %	Volume of permeable Voids, %	Bulk density (dry), kg/m^3
CD1	Dry	5.0	11.4	2 290
	Wet	6.8	15.0	2 200
CD2	Dry	6.4	14.2	2 230
	Wet	7.7	16.6	2 170
CD3	Dry	6.0	13.3	2 190
	Wet	7.5	15.9	2 120
CD4	Dry	5.7	13.0	2 260
CD5	Dry	5.7	13.0	2 270
MD1	Dry	7.9	17.1	2 150
	Wet	9.4	19.6	2 080
MD2	Dry	6.5	14.4	2 210
	Wet	8.8	18.6	2 120
MD4	Wet	7.2	15.5	2 150
CW1	—	4.8	11.2	2 320
CW2	—	5.1	11.8	2 290
MW1	—	9.1	19.2	2 110

[1] BWA: Boiled Water Absorption.

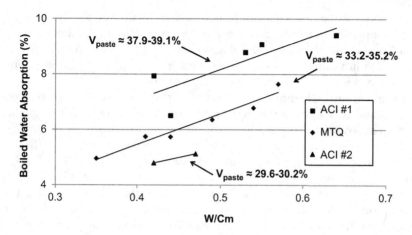

Figure 6.24 Relationship between BWA and W/CM for mixtures with different aggregate gradations and paste contents.

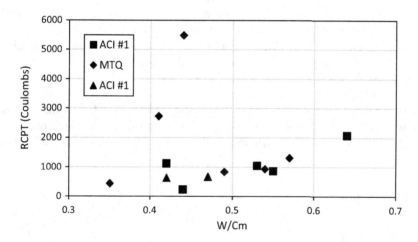

Figure 6.25 Relationship between RCPT and W/CM from Bolduc et al., 2010.

Table 6.10 ASTM C1202 classification system

Charge passed, coulombs	Chloride ion penetrability
>4000	High
2000–4000	Moderate
1000–2000	Low
100–1000	Very low
<100	Negligible

due to pozzolanic reactions, but primarily to reductions in the hydroxyl ion (OH-) concentration in the concrete pore solution. The current flow (ampere) and hence coulomb values are reduced as the hydroxyl ion concentration is reduced. Silica fume is a *superpozzolan* and dramatically reduces the amount of hydroxyl ion available to facilitate current flow.

Examination of Figure 6.31 shows that there is a correlation between W/CM and RCPT (coulomb) test results for the mixtures containing silica fume. The lower the W/CM, the lower the coulomb value.

Thirdly, the Université Laval study determined the OH⁻ Diffusion Coefficient of the different shotcrete mixtures using the Ionic Migration Test referred to above. This test is a modified version of the ASTM C1202 RCPT test and produces values needed for input into the *Stadium* Service Life Prediction Model. The procedure and theoretical background to this Ionic Migration Test can be found in a paper by Samson et al (Samson et al., 2008). Test results are shown in Table 6.8. This test produces similar comparative data to the RCPT test in that it also shows that the highest diffusion coefficients occur in the mix with cement as the only binder, followed by the mix with fly ash and then lowest diffusion coefficients in the mixes incorporating silica fume. Figure 6.26 shows the correlation between the RCPT and Ionic Migration (OH⁻ Diffusion Coefficient) test results.

In 1987 Morgan et al (Morgan et al., 1987) published suggested Quality Indicators for Shotcrete based on ASTM C642 values for Volume of Permeable Voids (VPV) and Boiled Water Absorption (BWA), as shown in Table 6.11. This table was developed based on examination of the results of tests in numerous research and development projects and field applications of wet and dry-mix shotcretes. It was found that the ASTM C642 test was able to identify shotcretes which were deficient (low compressive strength,

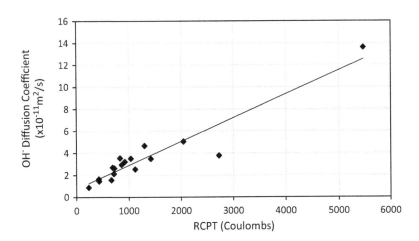

Figure 6.26 RCPT vs OH⁻ diffusion coefficient from Bolduc et al., 2010.

Table 6.11 Morgan's suggested quality indicators for shotcrete based on ASTM C642

Sprayed concrete quality	Permeable void volume, %	Boiled absorption, %
Excellent	< 14	< 6
Good	14–17	6–8
Fair	17–19	8–9
Marginal	> 19	> 9

excessively permeable, or susceptible to leaching and deterioration in aggressive exposure environments) as a result of factors such as:

a) Improper consolidation, caused by shooting with insufficient impacting velocity, or too acute angles to the receiving surface,
b) Lean mixtures with an insufficient cementing materials content,
c) Excessive accelerator addition resulting in a weak, porous cement hydrate structure.

Bolduc et al (Bolduc et al., 2010) examined the relationship between RCPT test values and BWA values for the different shotcrete mixtures. In order to do this, they plotted the data from these two very different tests against the ASTM C1202 Classification system for RCPT test values and suggested Quality Indicators for BWA proposed by Morgan (Morgan et al., 1987). This data is shown in Figure 6.27.

The correlation between the RCPT and BWA parameters is low. This is not surprising, in that the two tests measure different phenomena. The RCPT test

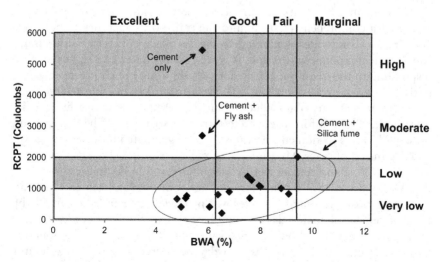

Figure 6.27 Relationship between RCPT and BWA.

is an ionic diffusion test and measures current flow in coulombs and is highly influenced by the reductions in hydroxyl ions (OH^-) caused by the addition of pozzolanic materials like fly ash and silica fume. By contrast, the ASTM C642 test measures capillary absorption in the shotcrete and is much less influenced by the addition of pozzolanic materials, compared to the RCPT test. The net result of these differences between the two test methods is that there can be poor correlations between the ASTM C1202 classification system (High, Moderate, Low, Very Low, Negligible, as shown in Table 6.10) and Morgan Quality Indicators for Shotcrete (Excellent, Good, Fair, Marginal, as shown in Table 6.11) for the ASTM C642 test.

The above observations beg the question: Which are the most appropriate performance parameters to use in a shotcrete specification for the production of durable shotcrete? It is suggested that the answer to this question depends on the specific shotcrete application and exposure environment. For example, if shotcrete is to be used in a reinforced structure exposed to a chloride environment, such as a marine structure, or bridge exposed to chlorides from deicing chemicals, then the specification of performance parameters based on either the ASTM C1202 RCPT test (Coulombs), or Ionic Diffusion Test (Diffusion Coefficient), would be appropriate. By contrast, if the shotcrete is to be used in a tunnel or mine, or freshwater retaining structure, where no chlorides (or any other aggressive chemical species are present), then specification of limits based on BWA in the ASTM C642 test would be appropriate for the production of durable shotcrete. A study by Power (Power, 2014) offers some more insight on the subject of shotcrete service-life.

6.14.3 Shotcrete transport properties study by Zhang et al.

In 2016, Zhang, Morgan and Mindess (Zhang et al., 2016) published the results of a comprehensive study into the transport properties of both wet and dry-mix shotcretes compared to cast-in-place concretes with similar water/cementing materials ratios. This study was undertaken with a view to responding to the question: "How does the durability of shotcrete compare to that of cast-in-place concrete?". The test methodologies selected included tests which generated data which could be input into service life prediction models for reinforced concrete/shotcrete structures. The information presented in this section concentrates on data generated for actual shot wet and dry-mix shotcretes. Mixture design variables included mixes made with a Type GU Portland cement as the only binder and mixes with substitution of 20% fly ash or 8.7% silica fume by mass of Portland cement. In addition, each of the wet-mix shotcretes was produced with and without 5% by mass of cementing materials of a liquid alkali-free accelerator added at the nozzle. In the dry-mix shotcrete, mixes were produced with and without 3% by mass of cementing materials of a dry powdered alkali-free accelerator preblended in with the dry-bagged materials.

Table 6.12 provides the as-batched mixture proportions for the different wet-mix shotcretes. Table 6.13 shows the calculated dry-mix shotcrete mixture proportions.

Fresh shotcrete properties were tested according to the ACI 506R Guide and are summarized in Table 6.14. Properties tested included slump, air content before and after shooting and setting time for accelerated mixes. Note that the shotcrete mixes were intentionally not air-entrained in this study. Also note that the as-batched slump ranged from 80 to 120 mm for the wet-mix shotcretes without accelerator, but slump was increased to 180 to 220 mm for mixes with shotcrete accelerator addition at the nozzle. This is current standard practice in industry in order to facilitate uniform dispersion of the shotcrete accelerator through the mix at the nozzle. The increase in slump was achieved by increasing the dosage rate of high-range water-reducing admixture; the W/CM ratio was not changed.

The dry-mix shotcrete was supplied in bulk bin bags which were discharged into a predampener, before discharge into a rotary dry-mix gun, with water addition at the nozzle to produce the required applied shotcrete consistency. Fresh shotcrete properties (air content as-shot and setting time) are shown in Table 6.15.

The hardened shotcrete was tested on cores extracted from shot test panels for:

a) Compressive strength at 7 and 28 days
b) Boiled Water Absorption (BWA) and Volume of Permeable Voids (VPV) to ASTM C 642
c) Rapid Chloride Penetration Test (Coulombs) to ASTM C1202
d) Ionic Migration in accordance with the US Navy Specification UFGS 03 31 29-3, from which Coefficients of Diffusion, Effective Coefficient of Diffusion, Tortuosity were calculated
e) Water Absorption/Drying Test to ASTM C1792, from which Permeability (K) values were calculated.

Results of all these tests on the wet and dry-mix shotcretes are provided in the sections, which follow.

a) Compressive strength

Compressive strength test results at 7 and 28 days are shown in Table 6.16.

All mixtures achieved compressive strengths in excess of 40 MPa at 28 days, with the exception of the silica fume wet-mix shotcrete with 5% accelerator addition at the nozzle, and the Portland cement dry-mix shotcretes with and without 3% accelerator. As a general observation, the mixes with accelerator addition (with two minor exceptions) produced lower compressive strengths at 7 and 28 days than mixes without accelerator. This is consistent with general findings in the field and is as expected. Also, (with one

Table 6.12 As-batched wet-mix shotcrete mixture proportions

Mixture No.	Mixture description	Placement method	Mixture ID	As-batched mixture proportions for 1.0 m³								
				Cement (Type GU), kg	Fly ash, kg	Silica fume, kg	Coarse aggregate (10 mm, SSD), kg	Fine aggregate, SSD, kg	Water, L	High-range water-reducing admixture, L	Total mass, kg	w/cm
A3	Portland cement	Shot wet-mix	C-Wet-Mix-Shot	445	0	0	425	1273	179	0.533	2322	0.40
A4	Portland cement	Shot wet-mix 5% accelerator	C-Wet-Mix-Shot-5%	443	0	0	423	1267	179	0.530	2313	0.40
B3	Fly ash modified	Shot wet-mix	FA-Wet-Mix-Shot	351	86	0	418	1252	176	0	2284	0.40
B4	Fly ash modified	Shot wet-mix 5% accelerator	FA-Wet-Mix-Shot-5%	349	86	0	416	1246	176	0.633	2274	0.40
C3	Silica fume modified	Shot wet-mix	SF-Wet-Mix-Shot	404	0	39	422	1265	178	1.285	2310	0.40
C4	Silica fume modified	Shot wet-mix 5% accelerator	SF-Wet-Mix-Shot-5%	400	0	38	418	1253	177	2.036	2287	0.40

Notes: 1 kg/m3 = 1.68556 lb/yd³; 1 L/m³ = 29.5 fl oz/yd³.

Table 6.13 Calculated dry-mix shotcrete mixture proportions

							Calculated mixture proportions for 1.0 m³				
Mixture No.	Mixture description	Placement method	Mixture ID	Cement (Type GU), kg	Fly ash, kg	Silica fume, kg	Coarse aggregate (10 mm, SSD), kg	Fine aggregate, SSD, kg	Estimated water, L	Total mass, kg	Estimated w/cm	Air content, as-shot, %
A5	Portland cement	Shot dry-mix	C-Dry-mix-shot	450	0	0	430	1290	180	2351	0.40	3.20
A6	Portland cement	Shot dry-mix 3% accelerator	C-Dry-mix-shot-3%	450	0	0	430	1290	180	2351	0.40	4.20
B5	Fly ash modified	Shot dry-mix	FA-dry-mix-shot	360	90	0	430	1290	180	2351	0.40	2.60
B6	Fly ash modified	Shot dry-mix 3% accelerator	FA-dry-mix-shot-3%	360	90	0	430	1290	180	2351	0.40	4.10
C5	Silica fume modified	Shot dry-mix	SF-dry-mix-shot	410	0	40	430	1290	180	2351	0.40	4.10
C6	Silica fume modified	Shot dry-mix 3% accelerator	SF-dry-mix-shot-3%	410	0	40	430	1290	180	2351	0.40	2.60

Table 6.14 Wet-mix shotcrete fresh properties

Mixture No.	Mixture description	Placement method	Mixture ID	Air content, % (as-batched)	Air content, % (as-shot)	Slump mm	Initial set, h:mins	Final set, h:mins	w/cm	Shotcrete temperature, °C	Air temperature, °C
A3	Portland cement	Shot wet-mix	C-wet-mix-shot	4.50	3..20	120	N/A	N/A	0..40	15	7
A4	Portland cement	Shot wet-mix 5% accelerator	C-wet-mix-shot-5%	5..90	3..60	190	12 min	1:20	0..40	14	9
B3	Fly ash modified	Shot wet-mix	FA-wet-mix-shot	5..40	3..50	80	N/A	N/A	0..40	14	7
B4	Fly ash modified	Shot wet-mix 5% accelerator	FA-wet-mix-shot-5%	5..60	3..90	180	32 min	2:0	0..40	13	8
C3	Silica fume modified	Shot wet-mix	SF-wet-mix-shot	5..10	3..40	100	N/A	N/A	0..40	15	7
C4	Silica fume modified	Shot wet-mix 5% accelerator	SF-wet-mix-shot-5%	6..60	4.00	220	10 min	1:15	0..40	13	8

Table 6.15 Dry-mix shotcrete fresh properties

Mix. No	Mix. description	Placement method	Mixture ID	Air content, % (as-shot)	Initial set, h:mins	Final set, h:mins	Shotcrete temperature, °C	Air temperature, °C
A5	Portland cement	Shot dry-mix	C-dry-mix-shot	3.20	Not available	3:25	14	10
A6	Portland cement	Shot dry-mix 3% accelerator	C-dry-mix-shot-3%	4.20	0:6	0:16	16	10
B5	Fly ash modified	Shot dry-mix	FA-dry-mix-shot	2.60	Not available	3:25	14	10
B6	Fly ash modified	Shot dry-mix 3% accelerator	FA-dry-mix	4.10	0:6	0:38	16	12
C5	Silica fume	Shot dry-mix	SF-dry-mix-Shot	4.10	Not available	3:30	14	10
C6	Silica fume modified	Shot dry-mix 3% accelerator	SF-dry-mix-Shot-3%	2.60	0:5	0:15	14	12

Table 6.16 Wet and dry-mix shotcretes compressive strength

Mixture ID	Compressive strength	
	7 days, MPa	28 days, MPa
C-wet-mix-shot	38.5	47.1
FA-wet-mix-shot	39.7	44.9
SF-wet-mix-shot	38.1	51.5
C-wet-mix-shot-5%	31.5	49.9
FA-wet-mix-shot-5%	37.5	41.9
SF-wet-mix-shot-5%	29.4	38.1
C-dry-mix-shot	29.5	34.9
FA-dry-mix-shot	32.2	52.9
SF-dry-mix-shot	45.0	64.3
C-dry-mix-shot-3%	24.6	35.9
FA-dry-mix-shot-3%	26.6	43.5
SF-dry-mix-shot-3%	30.3	47.9

exception) the mixes with silica fume produced the highest compressive strengths at 7 and 28 days. This is also consistent with general findings in the field and is as expected.

b) Boiled water absorption and volume of permeable voids

Results of boiled water absorption and volume of permeable voids to ASTM C1202 are shown in Table 6.17.

Table 6.17 Boiled water absorption and volume of permeable voids to ASTM C1202

Boiled Absorption	Shot wet-mix shotcrete, %	Shot wet-mix shotcrete with 5% accelerator, %	Dry-mix shotcrete, %	Dry-mix shotcrete with 3% accelerator, %
Cement	5.4	6.8	5.9	6.3
Fly ash	5.3	6.3	4.7	5.9
Silica fume	4.9	5.2	3.5	5.6
Volume of permeable voids	Shot wet-mix shotcrete, %	Shot wet-mix shotcrete with 5% accelerator, %	Dry-mix shotcrete, %	Dry-mix shotcrete with 3% accelerator, %
Cement	12.2	14.8	13.1	13.9
Fly ash	11.9	14.0	10.7	13.2
Silica fume	11.0	11.2	8.4	12.5

From review of this data, it is clear that all the wet and dry-mix shotcretes tested had values of boiled water absorption and volume of permeable that would fall within the "Good" to "Excellent" range according to the Quality Indicators suggested by Morgan (Morgan et al., 1987). It is also apparent that the addition of supplementary materials (fly ash and silica fume) reduced the values of Boiled Water Absorption and Volume of Permeable Voids, with the silica fume being most effective. Conversely, the addition of accelerators in both the wet and dry-mix shotcretes increased the values of Boiled Water Absorption and Volume of Permeable Voids. This is consistent with general findings in the field and is as expected.

c) Rapid chloride penetration test

Results of the rapid chloride penetration test to ASTM C1202, in coulombs, are provided in Table 6.18.

From review of these data, it is apparent that the incorporation of supplementary cementing materials (fly ash and silica fume) has a very beneficial effect in reducing the coulomb values. This is particularly true for both wet and dry-mix shotcretes with silica fume, where ASTM C1202 would rate the mixes as having "Very Low" Chloride Penetrability. For the mixtures with fly ash ASTM C1202 would rate the mixes as having "Very Low" to "Low" Chloride Penetrability. By contrast, nearly all the wet and dry-mix shotcretes made with Portland cement as the only binder had only "Moderate" Chloride Penetrability. It is also apparent that the addition of accelerators increased the coulomb values compared to like mixes without accelerators, for both wet and dry-mix shotcretes.

d) Ionic migration test results

As mentioned previously ionic migration tests were conducted in accordance with the USACE/NAVFAC/AFCESA/NASA Specification UFGS 03 31 29-3, 2012b. It is a modified version of the ASTM C1202 Rapid Chloride Penetration Test Method in that it employs a larger testing chamber (150 mm diameter) that provides a more stable environment. In addition, Na(OH) solutions are placed in both the upstream and downstream

Table 6.18 Rapid chloride penetration test results (coulombs)

Coulombs	Shot wet-mix shotcrete	Shot wet-mix shotcrete with 5% accelerator	Dry-mix shotcrete	Dry-mix shotcrete with 3% accelerator
Cement	2047	2937	1582	2274
Fly ash	912	1259	637	752
Silica fume	305	269	250	295

chambers to stabilize the Cl⁻ and other ionic species. The measured values in current (milliamps) are input into *Stadium* model and the rate of diffusion is calculated for each chemical species based on Fick's Second Law of Diffusion (Samson et al., 2008). In addition, a water absorption/drying test (which is now ASTM C1585) is incorporated in this USACE/NAVFAC/AFCESA/NASA (2012a) Specification to calculate Permeability (K) values. The *Stadium* Model is then used for Service Life Prediction calculations.

Calculated parameters from these test methods include:

- Coefficient of Diffusion: Diff [OH⁻] (10^{-11} m² /s);
- Effective Coefficient of Diffusion: Diff [OH⁻] × VPV % (10^{-11} m²/s);
- Tortuosity;
- Permeability, K 10^{-22} m².

Test results for these parameters for both the wet and dry-mix shotcretes studied are provided in Table 6.19.

The general trends observed in the ASTM C642 and ASTM C1202 tests are also observed in the test results shown in Table 6.19. In brief, there is a reduction in the Coefficient of Diffusion, Effective Coefficient of Diffusion and Permeability K, and increase in Tortuosity in mixes incorporating

Table 6.19 Results for ionic migration and water absorption/drying test

Mixture ID	Coefficient of diffusion, Diff[OH⁻] (10^{-11}m²/s)	Effective coefficient of diffusion, Diff[OH⁻] × VPV% (10^{-11} m²/s)	Tortuosity	K, permeability, 10^{-22} m²
C-wet-mix-shot	10.37	1.27	51.8	4.84
FA-wet-mix-shot	7.35	0.87	71.9	4.76
SF-wet-mix-shot	5.7	0.63	92.6	2.66
C-wet-mix-shot-5%	11.45	1.69	46.1	5.02
FA-wet-mix-shot-5%	10.36	1.45	61.0	4.97
SF-wet-mix-shot-5%	5.04	0.56	104.2	2.69
C-dry-mix-shot	12.01	1.57	43.9	3.3
FA-dry-mix-shot	6.77	0.72	78.1	2.88
SF-dry-mix-shot	5.19	0.44	102.0	1.57
C-dry-mix-shot-3%	8.94	1.24	58.8	2.83
FA-dry-mix-shot-3%	5.97	0.79	88.5	1.45
SF-dry-mix-shot-3%	3.38	0.42	156.3	1.29

supplementary cementing materials (fly ash and silica fume), with silica fume being most effective. Conversely, there is an increase in the Coefficient of Diffusion, Effective Coefficient of Diffusion and Permeability K, and decrease in Tortuosity for like mixes incorporating accelerators. When these parameters are input into the Stadium Service Life Prediction Model it demonstrates that longer Service Life can be expected with wet and dry-mix shotcrete mixtures incorporating supplementary cementing materials, in particular for mixes with silica fume. Conversely, the incorporation of accelerators in the mix shortens service life.

6.14.4 Summary

In summary, from a long-term durability and service life prediction perspective, an understanding of the transport properties is important in concrete and shotcrete mixture design selection and quality assurance/quality control. Given that there are a complex array of transport phenomena (e.g. permeability, ionic diffusion, capillary absorption) that can affect the durability and service life of concrete and shotcrete structures and that one or more of these transport phenomena can play a role in different environmental exposure conditions, for major projects it is best to conduct an array of transport tests, as was done in the Université Laval (Bolduc et al., 2010) and Zhang et al. (2016) studies in order to optimize mixture design selection and construction processes. This chapter provides valuable guidance on what is achievable and should be of assistance to the design engineer in preparation of suitable shotcrete specifications for different types of environmental exposure conditions.

Finally, with respect to the question: "How does the durability of shotcrete compare to that of cast-in-place concrete", the study by Zhang et al (Zhang et al., 2016) demonstrates that properly applied shotcretes can provide equivalent or superior transport properties and hence durability and service life to that of comparable cast-in-place concretes. Details of this comparison can be found in the paper by Zhang et al (Zhang et al., 2016).

REFERENCES

ACI 234. 2006. *Guide for the Use of Silica Fume in Concrete*. Farmington Hills, Michigan, American Concrete Institute. 63 p.

ACI 506.1R-21. 2021. *Guide to Fiber Reinforced Shotcrete*. American Concrete Institute. 20 p.

ACI 506R. 2016. *Guide to Shotcrete*. Farmington Hills, Michigan, American Concrete Institute. 52 p.

ACI CODE-318-19. 2019. *Building Code Requirements for Structural Concrete and Commentary*. American Concrete Institute. https://doi.org/10.14359/51716937

ACI CT. 2018. *Concrete Terminology*. Farmington Hills, American Concrete Institute. Michigan. 80 p.

ACI-506.2-13(18). 2013. reapproved 2018. *Specification for Shotcrete*. American Concrete Institute. 12 p.

Aitcin, P-C. 1999. *Demystifying Autogenous Shrinkage. Concrete International*. Vol. 21. No. 11. November. 54–56.

American Shotcrete Association. 2015. *Position Statement #4*. Watertight Shotcrete for Swimming Pools.

Armelin, H. S. 1997. *Rebound and toughening mechanisms in steel fiber reinforced dry-mix shotcrete*, Doctoral Thesis, University of British Columbia, Department of Civil Engineering.

Armelin, H. S., Banthia, N., Morgan, D. R. and Steeves, C. 1997. Rebound in Dry-mix Shotcrete. *Concrete International*. Vol. 19. No. 9. September. 54–60.

ASTM C231. 2017. *Standard Test Method for Air Content of Freshly Mixed Concrete by the Pressure Method*. 10p. ASTM International. https://doi.org/10.1520/C0231_C0231M-17A

ASTM C1012. 2018. *Standard Test Method for Length Change of Hydraulic-Cement Mortars Exposed to a Sulfate Solution*. 9p. ASTM International. https://doi.org/10.1520/C1012_C1012M-18B

ASTM C1018. *Standard Test Method for Flexural Toughness and First Crack Strength of Fiber Reinforced Concrete Using Beam with Third Point Loading* (Now discontinued and replaced with ASTM C1609).

ASTM C1117-89. 1994. *Standard Test Method for Time of Setting of Shotcrete Mixtures by Penetration Resistance*.

ASTM C1140. *Practice for Preparing and Testing Specimens from Shotcrete Test Panels*.

ASTM C116-90. 1990. *Test Method for Compressive Strength of Concrete Using Portions of Beams Broken in Flexure (Withdrawn 1999)*.

ASTM C1202. 2019. *Standard Test Method for Electrical Indication of Concrete's Ability to Resist Chloride Ion Penetration*. ASTM International. 8 p. https://doi.org/10.1520/C1202-19

ASTM C1202. *Standard Test Method for Electrical Determination of Concrete's Ability to Resist Chloride Ion Penetration*.

ASTM C1399. *Standard Test Method for Obtaining Average Residual Strength of Fiber-Reinforced Concrete*.

ASTM C1543. *Standard Test Method for Determination of Chloride Ion Penetration into Concrete by Ponding*.

ASTM C1550. *Standard Test Method for Flexural Toughness of Fiber-Reinforced Concrete (Using Centrally Loaded Round Panel)*.

ASTM C1556. *Standard Test Method for Determination of the Apparent Chloride Diffusion Coefficient of Cement Mixtures by Bulk Diffusion*.

ASTM C1579. 2021. *Standard Test Method for Evaluating Plastic Shrinkage Cracking of Restrained Fiber Reinforced Concrete (Using a Steel Form Insert)*. 7p. ASTM International. https://doi.org/10.1520/C1579-21

ASTM C1585. *Standard Test Method for Measurement of Rate of Absorption of Water by Hydraulic Cement Concretes*.

ASTM C1604. *Standard Test Method for Obtaining and Testing Drilled Cores of Shotcrete*.

ASTM C1609. *Standard Test Method for Flexural Performance of Fiber Reinforced Concrete (Using Beam with Third Point Loading)*.

ASTM C1792. *Standard Test Method for Measurement of Mass Loss versus Time for One-Dimensional Drying of Saturated Concretes.*

ASTM C403/C403M-99. *Standard Test Method for Time of Setting of Concrete Mixtures by Penetration Resistance.*

ASTM C42. *Standard Test Method for Obtaining and Testing Drilled Cores and Sawed Beams of Concrete.*

ASTM C642. 2013. *Standard Test Method for Density, Absorption and Voids in Hardened Concrete.* ASTM International. 3 p. https://doi.org/10.1520/c0642-13.

ASTM C666. 2015. *Standard Test Method for Resistance of Concrete to Rapid Freezing and Thawing.* ASTM International. 7 p. https://doi.org/10.1520/C0666_C0666M-15

ASTM C672. 2012. *Standard Test Method for Scaling Resistance of Concrete Surfaces Exposed to Deicing Chemicals.* ASTM International. 7 p.

ASTM C78. *Standard Test Method for Flexural Strength of Concrete (Using Simple Beam with Third Pont Loading).*

Austin, S. and Robins, P. 1995. *Sprayed Concrete, Properties, Design and Application.* Whittles Publishing Services. 382 p.

Australian Shotcrete Society. 2010. *Shotcreting in Australia.* Concrete Society of Australia. Second ed. 84 p.

Austrian Concrete Society. 2013. *Sprayed Concrete Guidelines.*

Barton, N. and Grimstad, E. 2014. *Q System Application in NMT and NATM and the Consequences of Overbreak.* Sandjeford, Norway, Seventh International Conference on Sprayed Concrete. 33–49.

Beaupré, D. 1994. *Rheology of High Performance Shotcrete,* Ph.D. Thesis, University of British Columbia, Vancouver, BC, Canada, 250 p.

Beaupré, D., Dufour, J.-F., Lamontagne, A and Pigeon M. 1996. Powdered Air-Entraining Admixture in Dry-Mix Shotcrete. *Proceedings of the ACI/SCA International Conference on Sprayed Concrete/Shotcrete, Sprayed Concrete Technology for the 21st Century,* Edinburgh, Scotland, September 1996, 153–162.

Beaupré, D. and Jolin, M. 2002. Efficiency of Shotcrete Accelerator: A Fundamental Approach. *Proceedings of the Conference on Shotcrete for Underground Support IX,* 99–111.

Bentur, A., Berke, N. and Diamond, S. 1997. *Steel Corrosion in Concrete: Fundamentals and Civil Engineering Practice.* E& FN Spon. 201 p.

Bernard, E.S. 2002. Correlations in the Behavior of Fibre Reinforced Shotcrete Beam and Panel Specimens, *Materials and Structures, RILEM.* Vol. 35. April. 156–164.

Bernard, S. and Geltinger, C. 2007. Determination of Early-Age Compressive Strength for FRS. *Shotcrete Magazine* Fall 2007. 22–27.

Bloem, D. L. 1965. *Concrete Strength Measurements-Cores Versus Cylinders. Proceedings ASTM.* Vol. 65. 668–696.

Bolduc L.-S. and Jolin, M. 2010. Shotcrete Boiled Water Absorption. Shotcrete Magazine Winter 2010. 12–17.

Bolduc, L.-S., Jolin, M. and Bissonnette, B. 2010. Evaluating the Service Life of Shotcrete. Shotcrete, Elements of a System. Edited by Bernard, Taylor and Francis Group, 57–63.

Broomfield, J. P. 2006. *Corrosion of Steel in Concrete: Understanding, Investigation and Repair*. CRC Press, Taylor & Francis Group. 2nd edition. 296 p.

Campbell, K. 1999. *Plastic Shrinkage Cracking in Dry-Mix Shotcrete*, Masters Thesis, University of British Columbia, Civil Engineering Department.

Clements, M. J. K., Jenkins, P. A. and Malmgren, L. 2004. Hydro-scaling-an Overview of a Young Technology. *Shotcrete: More Engineering Developments*. Edited by Bernard, A. A. Balkema, London, 89–96.

CSA. (2018). *A3000 Cementitious materials compendium*. Canadian Standards Association. 253 p.

CSA. (2019). *A23.1/A23.2 Concrete materials and methods of concrete construction/Test methods and standard practices for concrete*. Canadian Standards Association. 690 p.

Dufour, J-F. 1996. *Effects of Air-Entraining Admixtures on the Durability of Dry-Mix Shotcretes*, Masters Thesis, Laval University, Quebec. 176 p.

Dufour, J-F. 2000. Performance of Dry-Mix Shotcrete in Permafrost Environment. *Shotcrete Magazine* August 2000. 28–31.

Dufour, J-F. 2008. Can Dry-Mix Shotcrete be Air Entrained? *Shotcrete Magazine* Fall 2008. 28–30.

Dufour, J-F., Reny, S. and Vezina, D. 2006. State-of-the-Art Specifications for Shotcrete Rehabilitation Projects. *Shotcrete Magazine*. Vol. 8. No. 4. Fall 2006. 4–11.

European Standard EN 14488-3. 2006. *Testing Sprayed Concrete: Flexural strengths (first peak, ultimate, and residual) of fibre reinforced beam specimens*.

European Standard EN 14488-5. 2006. *Testing Sprayed Concrete: Determination of energy absorption capacity of fibre reinforced slab specimens*.

Forrest, M. P., Morgan, D. R., Obermeyer, J. R., Parker, P. L. and LaMoreaux, D. D. 1996. Seismic Retrofit of LittleRock Dam. *Concrete International*. Vol. 17. No. 11. 24–29.

Gagnon, A. and Jolin, M. 2018. A New Approach for Fibre Reinforced Shotcrete under Dynamic Loading. *8th International Symposium on Sprayed Concrete*, Trondheim, Norway, 2018.

Gilbride, P., Morgan, D. R. and Bremner, T.W. 1988. Deterioration and Rehabilitation of Berth Faces in Tidal Zones at the Port of Saint John. *American Concrete Institute, Concrete in Marine Environment, SP-109*, 96–102.

Gilbride, P., Morgan, D. R. and Bremner, T. W. 1996. Performance of Shotcrete Repairs to Berth Faces at the Port of Saint John, New Brunswick. *Third CANMET/ACI International Conference on Performance of Concrete in Marine Environment*, St. Andrews-by-the-Sea, New Brunswick, Canada, August 1996, 61–72.

Gryzbowski, M. and Shah, S. P. 1990. Shrinkage Cracking in Fiber Reinforced Concrete. *ACI Materials Journal*. Vol. 87. 138–148.

Hanskat, C. 2014. Shotcrete Placed in Multiple Layers does NOT Create Cold Joints. *Shotcrete Magazine* Spring 2014. 40–41.

International Concrete Repair Institute (ICRI) Technical Guideline 310.2R-2013. 2013. *Selecting and Specifying Concrete Surface Preparation for Sealers, Coatings, Polymer Overlay and Concrete Repair*, 48 p.

Jolin, M. 1999. *Mechanism of Placement and Stability of Dry Process Shotcrete*, Dept. of Civil Engineering, University of British Columbia, Vancouver, BC, Canada, 166 p.

Jolin, M. and Beaupré, D. 2003. *Understanding Wet-Mix Shotcrete Mix Design, Specifications and Placement*. Shotcrete Magazine Summer 2003. 6–12.

Jolin, M., Beaupré, D., Pigeon, M. and Lamontagne, A. 1997. Use of Set Accelerating Admixtures in Dry-Mix Shotcrete, *Journal of Materials in Civil Engineering*. Vol. 9. No. 4. 180–184. https://doi.org/10.1061/(asce)0899-1561(1997)9:4(180)

Jolin, M., Melo, F., Bissonnette, B., Power, P. and Demmard, D. 2015. *Evaluation of Wet-Mix Shotcrete Containing Set-Accelerator and Service Life Prediction, Shotcrete for Underground Support XII, Singapore*. Engineering Conferences International, 14 p.

Juilland, P., Gallucci, E. and Lindhar, B. 2011. Effect of aluminium-sulphate ratio of alkali free accelerator on the shotcrete performance. *Sprayed Concrete Symposium*, 226–231.

Lamontagne, A., Pigeon, M. and Beaupré, D. 1996. Use of Air-Entraining Admixture in Dry-Mix Shotcrete. *ACI Materials Journals*. Vol. 93. No. 1. 69–74.

Life-365. 2018. *Service Life Prediction Model*, Version 2.2.3, September 2018. Life-365 Consortium Illinois, 88 p.

Litvin, A. and Shideler, J. J. 1966. *Laboratory Study of Shotcrete*. Detroit, Shotcreting, American Concrete Institute, 165–184.

Menu, B., Jacob-Vaillancourt, T., Jolin, M. and Bissonnette, B. (2020). Influence of Curing Methods on Moisture Loss and Drying Shrinkage of Shotcrete at Early Age. *ACI Materials Journalx* Vol. 117. No. 4. https://doi.org/10.14359/51724624

Morgan, D. R. 1973. *Effect of Lignin-Based Admixtures on Time Dependent Volume Changes in Concrete*, Ph.D. Thesis, University of New South Wales, Sydney, NSW, Australia, 352 p.

Morgan, D. R. 1975. Effects of Chemical Admixtures on Creep and Shrinkage in Concrete. *Workshop on the Use of Chemical Admixtures in Concrete*, University of New South Wales, Sydney, NSW, Australia, December 1975, 113–148.

Morgan, D. R. 1989. Freeze-Thaw Durability of Shotcrete. *Concrete International*. Vol. 11. No. 8. August 1989. 86–93.

Morgan, D. R. 1991. Freeze-Thaw Durability of Steel and Polypropylene Reinforced Shotcrete: A Review, SP-126. *CANMET/ACI International Conference on Durability of Concrete*, 901–911.

Morgan, D. R. 2008. Shotcrete: A Versatile Construction Solution. *Shotcrete Magazine* Fall 2008. 32–33.

Morgan, D. R. and Chan, C. 2001. Understanding and Controlling Shrinkage and Cracking in Shotcrete. *Shotcrete Magazine* Vol. 3. No. 2. Spring 2001. 26–30.

Morgan, D. R., Chen, L. and Beaupré, B. 1995. Toughness of Fibre Reinforced Shotcrete. In the *Proceedings of the Shotcrete for Underground Support VII*, Telfs, Austria, June 11–15, 1995, 66–87.

Morgan, D. R., Heere, R., Chan, C., Buffenbarger, J. K. and Tomita, R. 2001. Evaluation of Shrinkage Reducing Admixtures in Wet and Dry-Mix Shotcrete, Edited by Bernard, E.S., *Shotcrete: Engineering Developments, Proceedings of the International Conference on Engineering Developments in Shotcrete*.

Morgan, D. R., Kirkness, A. J., McAskill, N. and Duke, N. 1988. Freeze-thaw Durability of Wet-Mix and Dry-Mix Shotcretes with Silica Fume and Steel Fibres. *Cement, Concrete and Aggregates*. Vol. 10. No. 2. Winter 1988. 96–102.

Morgan, D. R., McAskill, N. and Heere, R. 1999. Determination of Early-Age Compressive Strength of Shotcrete. *International Conference on Sprayed Concrete*, Gol, Norway, September 1999, 26–29.

Morgan, D. R., McAskill, N., Neill, J. and Duke, N. F. 1987. Evaluation of Silica Fume Shotcrete. *Proceedings of the International Workshop on Condensed Silica Fume in Concrete*, Montreal, Canada, 34 p.

Morgan, D. R. and Neill, J. 1991. Durability of Shotcrete Rehabilitation Treatments of Bridges. *Transportation Association of Canada Conference*, Winnipeg, Manitoba, September 1991, 15–19.

Morgan, D. R., Zhang, L. and Pildysh, M. 2017. New Hemp Based Fiber Enhances Wet-Mix Shotcrete Performance. *Shotcrete Magazine* Spring 2017. 36–45.

Neubert, B. and Manns, W. 1993. Mechanical-Technological Properties of Shotcrete with Accelerating Admixtures. *International Conference on Sprayed Concrete*, Norwegian Concrete Association, Fagerness, Norway, 258–270.

Neville, A. M. 1996. *Properties of Concrete*, John Wiley & Sons Inc. Fourth ed. 844 p.

Parker, H. W. 1976. *Field-Oriented Investigation of Conventional and Experimental Shotcrete for Tunnels*, Ph.D. Thesis, University of Illinois at Urbana-Champaign, 628 p.

Parker, H. W. 1999. Early Developments of Shotcrete and Steel Fiber Shotcrete. *Shotcrete for Underground Support XIII*, Edited by Celistino, T. B. and Parker, H. W., Sao Paulo, Brazil, ASCE, 241–258.

Power, P. 2014. *Predicting the service life of shotcrete: investigation on the transport properties of various shotcrete mixes*, M.Sc. Thesis, Civil and Water Engineering Department, Université Laval, Quebec, Canada. 176p.

Radomski, S. M., Morgan, D. R., Zhang, L. and Graham, D. 2019. Structural Modifications to Hydroelectric Turbine Draft Tube Ceiling. *Shotcrete Magazine* Summer, 2019. 22–34.

Reading, T. J. 1981. Durability of Shotcrete. *Concrete International: Design and Construction*. Vol. 3. No. 1. January. 27–33.

Rispin, M. 2005. Reentry into a Shotcreted Underground Heading. *Shotcrete Magazine* Spring 2005. 26–30.

RTC. 2019. *Guideline on the Applicability of Fibre-Reinforced Shotcrete for Ground Support in Mines*. Rock Tech Centre – MIGS III – WP 24, 1–53.

Samson, E., Marchand, J., Henocq, P. and Beausejour, P. 2008. Recent Advances in the Determination of Ionic Diffusion Coefficients Using Migration Test Results. *RILEM Proceedings 58-CONMOD*, Edited by Schlangen, E. and de Schutter, G., Delft, the Netherlands, 65–78.

Schrader, E and Kaden, R. 1987. *Durability of Shotcrete, Concrete Durability SP-100*. American Concrete Institute. 1071–1101.

Talbot, C., Pigeon, M, Beaupré, D. and Morgan, D. R. 1994. Influence of Surface Preparation on Long Term Bonding of Shotcrete. *ACI Materials Journal*. Vol. 91. No. 6. November–December. 560–566.

US Army Corps of Engineers. 1992. *CRD-C48-92 Standard Test Method for Water Permeability of Concrete*, 4 p.

USACE/NAVFAC/AFCESA/NASA. 2012a. *Specification UFGS-03 31 20 (August 2012)*, Division 03-Concrete, Section 03 31 29 Marine Concrete, 67 p.

USACE/NAVFAC/AFCESA/NASA. 2012b. *Specification UFGS 03 31 29-3*, Ionic Migration Test.

Wolsiefer, J. and Morgan, D. R. 1993. Silica Fume in Shotcrete. *Concrete International.* Vol. 15. No. 4. April. 35–39.

Yurdakul, E. and Reider, K-A. 2015. Effect of Pozzolan-Based Rheology Control Agent as a Replacement for Silica Fume. Shotcrete Magazine Spring 2015. 26–31.

Zhang, L. 2012. Air Content in Shotcrete: As-Shot Versus As-Batched. *Shotcrete Magazine* Winter 2012. 50–54.

Zhang, L., Morgan, D. R. and Mindess, S. 2016. Comparative Evaluation of the Transport Properties of Shotcrete Compared to Cast-in-Place Concrete. *ACI Materials Journal.* Vol. 113. No. 1–6. 373–384.

Chapter 7

Shotcrete research and development

7.1 INTRODUCTION

The last 30 years have seen many interesting innovations in the field of shotcrete technology, mainly involving improved equipment, novel mix designs and new concrete chemical admixtures. The use of dry-mix shotcrete for ground support in mining has increased exponentially, and applications of wet-mix shotcrete have expanded to include tunnels, ground support, new structures, infrastructure rehabilitation, and more. This success can be directly attributed to these innovations and the resultant enhancements in the quality of the shotcrete produced, the increased robustness and flexibility of the methods, and the greater variety of applications now currently possible. Of course, all this has generated additional expectations and even enhanced performance requirements for shotcrete in terms of durability, quality control and mix design characteristics.

It is well known that quality shotcrete requires a combination of adequate airflow velocity, proper material proportions, and appropriate nozzle handling. On top of all the basic concrete technology notions, pneumatic application of concrete brings about new challenges relating to material losses through rebound or fall-outs, build-up thickness, and compaction and encapsulation of reinforcement and embedments. Many factors related to the *spraying parameters* (process selected, air velocity, shooting angle, orientation and thickness) and *mix design parameters* (cement content, silica fume content, water content, aggregate gradation, etc.) impact shotcrete placement (Armelin and Banthia, 1997; Jolin et al., 2001). Since 1997, the *Shotcrete Laboratory* at Université Laval has been actively involved in education and fundamental research and developments in shotcrete. The following paragraphs present some of the key results and applications emerging from these research efforts for both dry- and wet-mix shotcretes as a way to illustrate the importance given to the *placement process* itself in shotcrete research.

7.2 DRY-MIX SHOTCRETE

Since the dry-mix shotcrete process is widely used in Eastern Canada to repair infrastructure damaged by frost and deicing salts and reinforcing steel corrosion, the subject has received considerable attention at Université Laval's concrete research laboratory. Important topics investigated include the effects of set accelerating admixtures on shotcrete durability, the levels of protection against frost damage and deicing chemical scaling offered by air-entraining admixtures, and the effect of encapsulation quality of reinforcing bars on structural performance.

7.2.1 Use of set accelerators

Tests were carried out to study the influence of set accelerating admixtures on the durability of dry-mix shotcrete. A total of 27 mixtures were shot using two different types of cements (ASTM Type I cement with silica fume as a partial cement replacement and ASTM Type III cement) and five different types of accelerator at various dosages. Half the mixtures were shot with a liquid air-entraining admixture. The aim was to confirm earlier test results showing the positive effect of air entrainment on the frost durability of dry-mix shotcrete (Lamontagne et al., 1996). In addition to setting time determination, the hardened shotcrete was assessed for air-void characteristics, compressive strength, drying shrinkage, rapid freeze-thaw resistance, and deicer salt scaling resistance (Jolin et al., 1997). Key results from these studies indicate that the mixture's general behaviour is primarily a function of the chemical family of the set accelerator used, and to a lesser extent the dosage of the admixture itself. In this study, carbonate-based and aluminate-based powdered admixtures were used. While the initial and final setting times were greatly reduced for the mixes with carbonate-based accelerators, the resulting 28-day compressive strength and deicer salt scaling resistance were diminished by as much as 50% and 90%, respectively (Figure 7.1). On the other hand, the aluminate-based accelerator showed a reduction in initial set only, with strength development less affected. In this case, 28-day compressive strengths were reduced by only 12% and deicer salt scaling resistance by 30%. In all cases, the presence of an air-entraining admixture in the mix significantly improved freeze-thaw resistance in the presence of deicing salt.

7.2.2 Use of powdered air-entraining admixture

As noted above, a former method for entraining an appropriate air-void system in dry-mix shotcrete was to add a *liquid* air-entraining admixture into a water tank used for water addition at the nozzle. This technique is extremely efficient for improving the freeze-thaw durability of dry-mix shotcrete (particularly in the presence of deicing salt) and is still in use

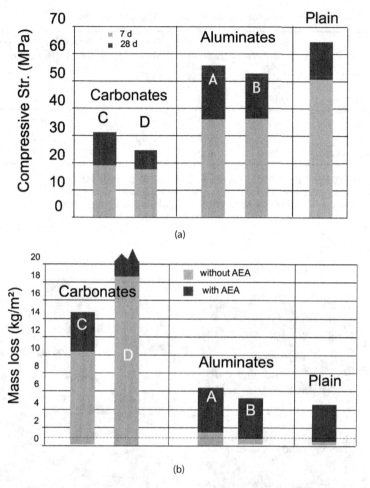

Figure 7.1 Effect of set accelerating admixtures' chemical family on (a) compressive strength (ASTM C1604) and (b) mass loss during a deicer-salt surface scaling test (freezing-thawing). (ASTM C672.)

in some areas of the industry (Beaupré et al., 1996; Lamontagne et al., 1996). However, this method has some disadvantages. For instance, the amount of air-entraining admixture added to the spraying water can be difficult to control on site and varies as the nozzleman changes the spraying consistency. To bypass these disadvantages, a study was conducted to verify the effectiveness of *powdered* air-entraining admixtures for increasing the frost durability of dry-mix shotcrete. Fortunately, the powdered form can be pre-bagged with the other oven-dried materials (cementing materials, sand, coarse aggregates, and fibres). The air-entraining powder dosage can therefore be adjusted in a controlled

Table 7.1 Dry-mix shotcrete with air-entraining admixtures

Mixture	Comp. str. at 28 days ASTM C42 (MPa)	Air content (%)	Spacing factor (μm)	Deicer salt scaling (surface losses after 50 cycles) ASTM C672 (kg/m²)
		ASTM C457		
Plain[1]	28	4.7	415	8.8
Liquid AEA[2]	33	6.3	185	0.3
Powder AEA[3]	38	6.2	101	0.1

[1] Cement: 450 kg/m³, sand: 1500 kg/m³, coarse aggregate (10–2.5 mm): 265 kg/m³
[2] Plain cement, with 20 ml of liquid air-entraining admixtures per litre of shooting water
[3] Plain cement, with 1.2% of powdered air-entraining admixtures by mass of cement

Deicer salt scaling specimen (ASTM C672)

Air void characterization specimen (ASTM C457)

Air-entrained

Non air-entrained

Figure 7.2 Left: Air-void characterization specimen (ASTM C457). Right: Deicer salt scaling resistance specimen (ASTM C 672) after 50 freeze-thaw cycles. Top: Air-entrained shotcrete mixture. Bottom: Non-air-entrained shotcrete mixture.

manner. At the proper dosage, results showed that powdered air-entraining admixture produces an excellent air-void system, which in turn gives a dry-mix shotcrete mixture good resistance to freeze-thaw cycles and deicer salt scaling (Beaupré et al., 1996). Table 7.1 and Figure 7.2 present some results demonstrating the effects of both liquid and powdered admixtures on the deicer salt scaling resistance of dry-mix shotcrete (Beaupré et al., 1996).

Through other research projects, the use of air-entraining admixture in dry-mix shotcrete in conjunction with silica fume was found to allow for further rebound reduction while improving reinforcement encapsulation. This positive outcome has more to do with the effect of the air-entrainment agent (AEA) on the water surface tension; hence, the rheological properties at high shear rates of fresh shotcrete mixtures during placement (Jolin et al., 2001).

7.2.3 Improving shotcrete quality and reducing rebound

Anyone who has spent time placing different mix designs using the dry-mix shotcrete process will readily support this statement: all dry-mix shotcretes do not behave the same during placement. Indeed, they will show different rebound rates, varying maximum build-up thicknesses and even different potential for reinforcement encapsulation. Keeping in mind how the placement of dry-mix shotcrete takes place, i.e. a large number of individual aggregates of all sizes – more or less covered with cement paste – traveling at high velocity towards the receiving surface, these different behaviours are not surprising.

A very interesting study on the fundamental mechanisms behind dry-mix shotcrete rebound was published by Armelin and Banthia (1998a, b). They analysed the kinetic energy of traveling aggregates as influenced by various parameters (aggregate size, mixture design, shooting consistency, etc.) and the substrate properties, to assemble what to this day is still regarded as the basis for all models used to predict rebound. The basic approach of this model evaluates the importance of all the elements of spraying shotcrete, from the details of the mixture design, along with the nozzleman's technique and to the selection, and operation of the equipment.

7.2.3.1 Aggregate size distribution

It turns out that an important mixture design parameter that deserves more attention is the composition of the aggregate phase. Since aggregate makes up as much as 80% of the mix volume, and considering that rebound is mainly composed of aggregates, the aggregate phase has a substantial impact on the amount of rebound exhibited by a dry-mix shotcrete. In a research project by Jolin and Beaupré (2004), the investigation focused on the effect of the particle size distribution of the entire aggregate phase on the total amount of rebound.

Keeping the same dry-mix equipment setup and a constant binder/aggregate ratio in the original mix, five different aggregate size distributions were investigated to find the optimal distribution for minimal rebound in dry-mix shotcrete. The binder/aggregate ratio was kept constant at 1:4 (by mass),

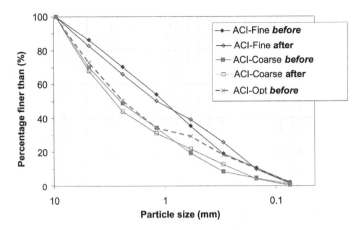

Figure 7.3 Particle size distribution of various mixtures.

Note that the tendency of *in-place gradations* to flatten between 1 mm and 0.6 mm was also produced in the *ACI-Optimal* before shooting.

using a normal Portland cement with 8% replacement by mass of silica fume as the binder. The maximum aggregate size was fixed at 10 mm.

The first mixtures shot were called *ACI-Fine* and *ACI-Coarse*, which meet ACI committee 506 recommendations for Gradation No. 2 (ACI 506R-16). The trick in this project was that the next aggregate gradation selected, *ACI-Optimal*, was designed to mimic the *in-place* particle size distributions of the other previous ones (see Figure 7.3).

Although detailed results (rebound, in-place composition, and mechanical properties) are presented by Jolin and Beaupré (2004), the most interesting parameter is the equivalent rebound calculated from the shooting sessions. Indeed, while *ACI-Fine* and *ACI-Coarse* had rebound values of 28.5% and 27.7%, respectively, the *ACI-Opt* saw its rebound value dropping to 24.6%. It shows that *ACI-Opt* would be a good choice as far as rebound is concerned. However, for engineers, the crucial question remains of how to characterize the particle size distribution.

Many approaches have been put forward to characterize aggregates and particle size distribution (Holtz and Kovacs, 1981; Fuller and Thompson, 1907). Some refer to unique values, maximum aggregate size, mean aggregate size, etc., while others suggest calculations involving mesh size, fineness modulus, sand/coarse aggregate ratio, etc. Going back to the basics of Fuller's approach, it was decided to use a formulation proposed by Funk and Dinger (1994), which fits a particle size distribution and yields a simple characteristic variable, *n*:

$$\text{Cumulative percent finer } (\%) = \frac{D^n - D_s^n}{D_l^n - D_s^n} \quad \text{(Funk and Dinger, 1994)}$$

where D is the particle size, D_S is the smallest particle size (80 μm), D_L is the largest particle size (10 mm), and n is the distribution modulus. The curve fitting is simply done using a least-squares method with the particle size distribution data points. This calculation yielded n values for ACI-*Fine* and ACI-*Coarse* of 0.12 and 0.47, respectively, and an n value of 0.36 for *ACI-Opt*. What is interesting is that there is a theoretical value of n (obtained analytically) optimized for *lowest void content*, that is, $n = 0.37$ (Funk and Dinger, 1994). The match between the theoretical value n for highest packing density of the aggregate phase and the practical optimum value of n obtained for lowest rebound makes the proposed optimization approach very valuable for future research and for shotcrete mix design with variable aggregate contents.

7.2.3.2 Rebound and non-traditional materials

Concrete can be a valuable asset when it comes to dealing with post-consumed materials. The use of these alternative materials as replacements for cement or aggregates in concrete is a great way to deal with two sustainability issues. It provides a solution to the increasing generation of waste materials as it represents a cheap and efficient way to give many products normally sent directly to landfills a second life. It also lowers the need for provision of natural resources in concrete. However, when using new ingredients with significantly different properties than those of traditional constituents, fresh and hardened properties of concrete/shotcrete must be carefully studied.

Some of these alternative materials were evaluated as potential replacement ingredients in dry-mix shotcrete mixtures in Université Laval's Shotcrete Laboratory (Fily-Paré, 2015; Fily-Paré and Jolin, 2013; Gagnon, Fily-Paré and Jolin, 2016). The key concept in these studies was to look away from conventional cement replacements and to instead focus on alternative materials that could potentially enhance dry-mix shotcrete placement in order to further reduce rebound losses.

Powdered glass is one of the post-consumer materials that have been tested in dry-mix shotcrete mixtures (Fily-Paré, 2015; Fily-Paré and Jolin, 2013). Glass bottles are widely used in North America, but there has not been much interest in finding them a second life, sending most of the collected glass to landfills – less than 30% of the collected glass is actually recycled and the rest is discarded. However, crushing glass into powder is a way to create a new ingredient for concrete and shotcrete, offering a more sustainable future for these used glass bottles.

The use of 20% of glass powder (GP) as a cement replacement in shotcrete has shown very interesting results when combined with 10% silica fume (SF) addition. In general, the fine particles (1–100 μm) of GP allowed for a higher water content in the dry-mix shotcrete without creating stability issues once on the receiving surface. This is of great interest as it improves the plasticity of the material, resulting in a lower rebound and a better reinforcing bar

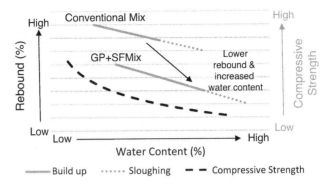

Figure 7.4 Behaviour of dry-mix shotcrete containing glass powder and silica fume as cement replacement.

encasement (ACI 506R-16, 2016; Beaupré and Jolin, 2001). Unfortunately, this increase in water to binder ratio (w/b) impacts negatively on the mechanical strength and the overall service life of the structure (Figure 7.4).

Nevertheless, some very novel observations regarding shotcrete rheology were made during the placement of GP-shotcrete. They can possibly be explained either by a shear thinning or thixotropic behaviour created by the GP in the cement paste (ACI 238.2T, 2014), which allowed for easy placement while maintaining stability on a vertical surface. This type of behaviour was also observed with shotcrete mixtures containing magnesium aluminium silicate (MAS) with or without silica fume (SF) (Gagnon, 2017).

Other waste materials were tested in dry-mix shotcrete mixtures as replacements for natural aggregates (Gagnon, 2017; Gagnon et al., 2016). For example, plastic aggregates produced from collected plastic containers crushed into small particles were evaluated (Figure 7.5). Although plastic can normally be recycled in a sustainable way, the plastic used in this research came from a portion of the waste plastic stream that cannot be properly sorted in the plant, making it unsuitable for recycling.

Rubber aggregates made from shredded used tires were also tested. Consumed in large quantities every year, there are still not many ways to provide value for rubber tires after their initial life. Therefore, rubber powders produced from discarded rubber tires have become available in high volumes and are particularly cheap.

Both these alternative aggregates have presented serious workability issues in the case of cast-in-place concrete (Nacif et al., 2013; Saika and Brito, 2012). This is why the dry-mix process is the most suitable method in which to use these products since workability is only required for the shortest time during spraying. Processed waste plastic and rubber materials were tested in mixtures at 20% replacement of the total *volume* of aggregates as a substitute for sand (Figure 7.6). The results of this study showed, as expected, a reduction in mechanical strength due to the relatively poor

Figure 7.5 Plastic aggregates (1–5 mm) from crushed plastic containers.

(a)   (b)

Figure 7.6 Substitution of 20% of natural aggregates by plastic (a) and rubber (b).

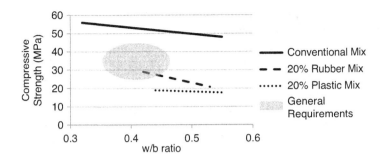

Figure 7.7 Strength behaviour of dry-mix shotcrete containing rubber and plastic aggregates as sand replacement.

mechanical properties of these new aggregates. However, the quality of the shotcrete could still be considered sufficient for use in many applications considering the large replacement rate used and the potential for optimization of the mixtures (Figure 7.7). Because of their low stiffness (modulus of elasticity), plastic and rubber aggregates could also have some potential for use in ground support applications where a higher deformability and energy absorption capacity is sometimes sought.

Even though the rubber aggregates did not have any notable influence on the rebound behaviour whatsoever when using the dry-mix shotcrete application process, they showed unexpected behaviour in the plastic (fresh) shotcrete: It yielded a very soft or wet consistency while maintaining a very high cohesion (similar to that seen with powdered glass), but while leading to a higher water-binder ratio. Also, the mixture quite obviously generated little to no dust during the spraying, even at a low water content when using prebagged oven-dry material and a hydromix nozzle. This effect was attributed to improved mixing in the nozzle created by the rubber particles bouncing against the hose or some electrostatic action of the fine rubber particles. This interesting behaviour is quite unusual in dry-mix shotcrete and could have great potential in design of dry-mix shotcretes for use in confined spaces such as tunnels and mines where reduction of dust is valuable.

Whether it is glass, plastic or rubber, the introduction of these materials as cement or aggregate replacement in a sustainable approach challenges the way we have designed shotcrete for many years. Reinventing shotcrete mixtures design with such ingredients will help us reconcile our needs to build and maintain quality structures and our environmental obligations.

7.3 WET-MIX SHOTCRETE

The placement of high-strength wet-mix shotcrete is sometimes complicated by the compromise required between pumpability and shootability. At the pump, a relatively fluid, easily pumped concrete is required, whereas at the nozzle, a stiffer material that neither sags nor sloughs on the wall is desired. Often, the simplest solution to deal with this dichotomy is to add a set accelerator at the nozzle and/or adapt the application schedule to allow sufficient time for initial stiffening of the first layer of in-place material before the next layer is applied. However, due to stringent quality requirements for modern shotcretes, limiting the amount of accelerator to what is strictly required for stability and early strength is by far the better working method. A solution to tackle this apparent paradox was put forward by Denis Beaupré in the course of his Doctoral research work at the University of British Columbia (Beaupré, 1994) and is often presented as the concept of *Temporary High Initial Air Content Concept* (Jolin and Beaupré, 2000). This approach is described below along with other interesting improvements in wet-mix shotcrete pumping and placement procedures.

7.3.1 Pumping wet-mix shotcrete: High initial air content

The *High Initial Air Content Concept* is a very clever yet simple approach whereby fresh concrete fluidity is increased to meet *pumpability* requirements by introducing large amounts of entrained air bubbles (as much as 10%–12% air content) instead of relying solely on water reducers and plasticizers to provide the required workability (slump). During spraying, large amounts of air are lost due to the compaction process. Lower fluidity and reduced slump are instantaneously obtained by loss of air as the shotcrete hits the receiving surface, thus improving the *sprayability* (resistance to sagging, sloughing and fall-out) of the shotcrete (Figure 7.8). Air loss upon impact is known as the *slump killing* effect. This shotcrete production method has now been used in a wide range of civil shotcrete applications over the past 30 years, with great success.

Implementation of this concept is simple. Instead of adjusting the plasticizer content to produce a 75 to 100 mm slump at the pump, its content is reduced so as to produce a 25 to 50 mm slump. The air-entraining admixture is then incorporated during batching to produce the slump required for easy pumping, typically between 75 mm and 100 mm. It is noteworthy that the slump killing effect works best when the initial air content at the pump is high, typically between 10% and 12%. This high air content falls to between 3% and 6% after placement due to the compacting effect, thus avoiding the negative effect of high air content on compressive strength. Table 7.2 shows a typical mix design for a high-performance air-entrained shotcrete, and Table 7.3 shows some test results obtained with this mixture.

7.3.2 Pumping wet-mix shotcrete: Effect of paste content and mixture design

Although the *High Initial Air Content* concept is now used around the globe, it is only recently that a clear understanding of the mechanisms behind the

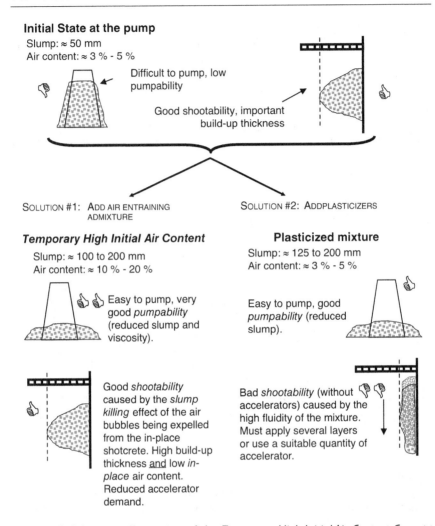

Figure 7.8 Schematic illustration of the *Temporary High Initial Air Content Concept.*

improved pumpability of such high air-content shotcretes has been brought to light by Burns (Jolin et al., 2009). When trying to understand exactly what happens in the hoses, Burns found that the air bubbles where easily dissolved into the cement paste under the normal operating pressures found in concrete pumping. Through pumping a dozen different wet-mix concretes, it was found that the ability to pump, or not, was significantly influenced by the paste content in the mixture design (Table 7.4). Indeed, only small modification of the total *paste content* for a given mix design would make it pumpable. Considering that the aggregates relative proportion remained constant and that the water/binder ratio was also maintained constant, it is difficult, looking at the first columns of Table 7.4, to

Table 7.2 Typical wet-mix shotcrete composition using *temporary high initial air content*

Ingredient	Quantity for 1 m³
Cement	400 kg
Silica fume	40 kg
Sand	1110 kg
Coarse aggregate (max 10 mm)	460 kg
Water	180 kg (w/cm = 0.41)
Water reducer	1500 ml
Superplasticizer	5000 ml
Air-entraining admixture	2500 ml

Table 7.3 Example of test results obtained on the mix described in Table 7.3

Slump before pumping	220 mm
Air content in fresh concrete before pumping	17 %
Air content in hardened in-place shotcrete	5.3 %
Compressive strength (28 d)	48 MPa

Table 7.4 Experimental results of pumpability test

Mixture*	Binder content kg/m³	Air content (before pumping) %	Pumpability	Real paste content**
A	392	13	NO	33.2
A-mod1	405	13	Blocked-2 strokes	34.2
A-mod2	415	13	Pumpable	35.1
B	406	7	NO	31.8
B-mod	445	7	Pumpable	35.1
C	438	3	NO	33.1
C-mod	465	3	Pumpable	35.1
C	403	13	NO	33.8
C-mod	420	13	Pumpable	35.2
D	400	13	NO	33.8
D-mod	415	13	Pumpable	35.1

* All water/binder ratios are of 0.41 –slump for all mixtures 75–100 mm (3–4 in.).
** Volume of paste in the concrete under pressure.

understand the key parameters that made a mixture pumpable or not (Note: all mixes would pump in a 50 mm internal diameter hose; the challenge in this study was pumpability when going down to a 38 mm internal diameter hose). A careful examination of the results reported in Table 7.4 as well as a comprehensive analysis of the laboratory observations and available literature led the authors to derive what is called the *Real Paste Concept* defined as the *amount of paste (%) present in the concrete while under pressure* (last column of Table 7.4). Therefore, it is a *volumetric interpretation* of the paste content as the material is under pressure (Jolin et al., 2009). It is interesting to note that the actual paste volume changes as pressure is applied to the concrete since the dissolving air volume diminishes to negligible values. Therefore, as pressure increases, the paste content becomes equivalent to the volume of binder material and water.

As can be seen, it appears that a value of *Real Paste Content* of 35.1% is a minimum value below which a mixture is not pumpable (with the particular aggregates used and a 38 mm internal diameter hose). The implications of this finding are significant; it not only shows the importance of providing a sufficient amount of paste to coat all of the aggregates and lubricate the inner wall of the pumping hoses, but it more interestingly demonstrates that there is a threshold value for the *real paste content* below which pumping is not possible. Combined with previous research, it can be further affirmed that this threshold value will change with the aggregate gradation and the hose diameter (Kaplan et al., 2005; Jolin et al., 2006). The *real paste content* calculated by Burns is the first time we have an actual value and a calculation method to start optimizing wet-mix shotcrete mixture designs for pumping. This facilitates a better selection of aggregates size and proportions so as to minimize the amount of paste required to fill the aggregate's skeleton to fill in order to maximize the amount of paste available for lubricating the inside of the hoses.

7.3.3 Placing wet-mix shotcrete

Although the provisions of air in the plastic (fresh) shotcrete is certainly a useful approach to facilitate pumping and placement, most wet-mix shotcretes found in underground applications require the use of some kind of set accelerating admixture added at the nozzle to provide suitable shootability and rapid setting and early strength development characteristics. Indeed, workers' safety nearly always mandates that some mechanical strength develops in the seconds and minutes following placement in order to prevent dangerous and sometimes deadly fallouts of the freshly placed shotcrete. It is therefore important to investigate how the set-accelerating admixture is distributed in the fresh wet-mix shotcrete (since it is added only at the nozzle) and how it performs in the moments following placement.

Actual distribution of the set accelerator in the in-place shotcrete mass has rarely been studied. The need arises, however, to examine this issue when

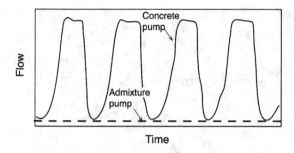

Figure 7.9 Concrete pump flow and additive pump flow.

evaluating set times on wet-mix shotcretes, where it has been noted in practice that measurements can vary considerably depending on the precise location of the test on the shotcrete surface. This is usually explained by uneven distribution of the accelerating admixture in the in-place shotcrete, due to the intermittent or pulsating nature of most pumping operations and the regular feed of set accelerator at the nozzle. Problems can also arise when the entry point of the admixture at the nozzle is poorly designed (Millette, 2011).

As shown in Figure 7.9, a typical dual-piston pump produces a pulsating flow, in contrast to the regular stream from the additive pump that feeds the accelerator to the nozzle. In these circumstances, a non-uniform dispersion of the accelerator in the in-place wet shotcrete should normally be expected. It should be noted however that pump manufacturers have managed to greatly reduce the variation of the concrete flow at the nozzle over the years. However, perfect coordination of concrete and admixture flow at the nozzle is a rare encounter in the industry and is only found in special pumping systems where the admixture pump control is imbedded in the shotcrete pump controls.

To determine the degree to which the different flow rates generate a non-uniform dispersion of accelerator, an evaluation method was developed to allow visual observation of the accelerator dispersion in the matrix. The approach was to introduce a product that showed a distinction between high and low accelerator concentration areas. Thus, the accelerating admixture was replaced with a phosphorous solution. Under a high emission UV light, the phosphorous particles are excited and produce a glowing tint.

A small-scale trial was first conducted on conventional concrete samples. A visual inspection was performed, and as shown in Figure 7.10, initial results revealed a significant and easily perceived difference in coloration produced by the phosphorous solution.

In Figure 7.10, equal amounts of solution were incorporated in approximately 2.5 kg of concrete. The samples in Figure 7.10a were minimally mixed, whereas the samples in Figure 7.10b were thoroughly hand-mixed.

A large-scale test was conducted in the Université Laval laboratory. A dual-piston shotcrete pump was used to produce a pulsating stream of

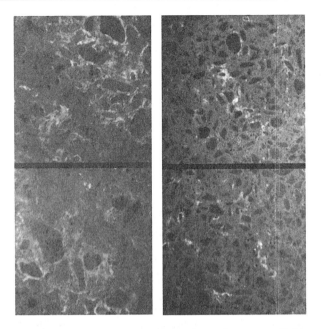

Figure 7.10 Dispersion of accelerator: non-uniform dispersion (left) and uniform dispersion (right).

shotcrete at the nozzle, and a typical additive pump was used to produce a constant feed of the substituted phosphorous solution. The phosphorous solution was dosed at 5% by mass of cement (typical accelerator dosage). A visual inspection and an image analysis of various sections of a test panel revealed a less than uniform dispersion of the substituted product throughout the entire 50 kg of the sample (Figure 7.11). Further investigation is needed on this subject as various combinations of shotcrete and accelerator pumps could be tested to evaluate the influence of equipment type on the uniformity of accelerator dispersion. In parallel, nozzle configuration and particularly the accelerator addition port configuration should be studied, as feed-back from expert observers on various job sites around the world identifies this configuration as also being critical for adequate delivery of accelerator in the shotcrete stream.

7.3.4 Set accelerator dosage

Set accelerators are usually designed not only for their effect on shotcrete setting time and early strength development but also for their effect on long-term physical properties. In fact, the type and dosage of accelerator used have proven to be equally crucial, as briefly explained below (Bessette et al., 2001).

Figure 7.12 presents results on the strength development of seven accelerated wet-mix shotcretes and one plain shotcrete. Compressive strengths at 4,

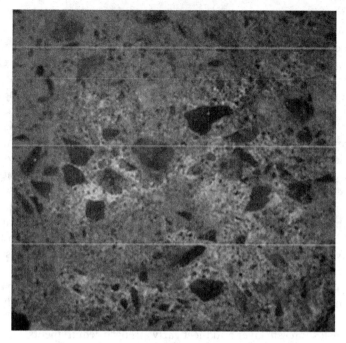

Figure 7.11 Distribution of a phosphorus solution (in replacement of accelerator) in wet-mix shotcrete produced using full-scale equipment.

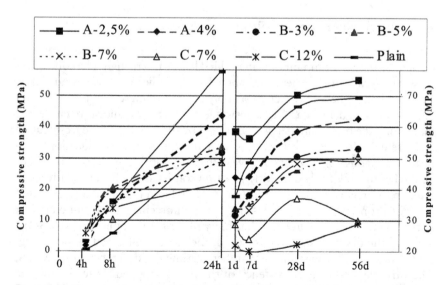

Figure 7.12 Compressive strengths of wet-mix shotcretes containing set accelerator.

8, and 24 hours were measured using the end beam test (Heere and Morgan, 2002), while strengths at 7, 28 and 56 days were measured on cores taken from shotcrete panels. All accelerating admixtures increased the early-age compressive strength at 4 and 8 hours compared to the plain shotcrete. For example, increases in early strength development on the order of 200% were obtained with products A and B at 8 hours. However, compressive strength results at 28 and 56 days showed substantial reductions for some mixtures compared to the plain mixture (up to 55% reduction for C-12%). It was apparent that final strength is highly dependent on the type and dosage of accelerating admixture. The resulting recommendations were, therefore used to identify the optimal amount of set accelerator addition in a wet-mix shotcrete mixture to produce the required short-term effects (setting time, build-up thickness, and early age strength development), along with an acceptable long-term strength performance. Effects on absorption and drying shrinkage, which indicated increases of as much as 100% and 50%, respectively, were also measured. More details regarding these tests can be found in Bessette et al. (2001) and Beaupré and Jolin (2002).

It is therefore crucial to not only select the right accelerator (compatibility with cement and other admixtures, early strength development, shelf life, etc.) but also to restrict the dosage to only the amount required to insure a stable fresh shotcrete layer and meet early strength requirements. Use of this approach, along with the proper equipment (shotcrete pump, accelerator dispensing pump and nozzle configuration) would result in higher quality in-place wet-mix shotcrete throughout the industry.

7.4 SHOTCRETE PLACEMENT

7.4.1 Encapsulation of reinforcement

Although fresh dry-mix shotcrete consistency depends on many parameters, the key factor is the amount of water added by the nozzleman. The conclusion of several years of experience combined with earlier research (Studebaker, 1939) is that the best approach is to apply dry-mix shotcrete at its *wettest stable consistency*, defined as "the consistency at which the moisture content is maximum, the maximum being determined by the stability of the fresh gunite (shotcrete)." However, observations at many job sites and education/certification sessions for nozzlemen reveal that dry-mix shotcrete is sometimes applied with a relatively dry (stiff) shooting consistency, which may adversely affect reinforcement encapsulation, increase rebound, and modify expected in-place properties. Proper encasement of reinforcement with shotcrete is a critical issue for the quality and durability of shotcrete application (CCS-4).

Using the dry-mix shotcrete method, the same pre-bagged material presented in Table 7.5 was shot a number of times at different *consistencies*. The variables were the consistency of the freshly applied shotcrete and the experience of the nozzleman. Nozzleman experience varied widely from an

Table 7.5 Pre-mix proportions

Material	Proportion*
Type 10 cement with 8% silica fume	450 kg/m³
Fine aggregates (sand)	1510 kg/m³
Coarse aggregates (10–2.5 mm)	235 kg/m³
Synthetic fibres	1.0 kg/m³
Powdered AEA	As required

* Proportions reported for an assumed w/cm equal to 0.4.

ACI certified (15-year experience) nozzleman, a shotcrete researcher (Ph.D. in shotcrete technology) with limited shotcreting experience (less than 500 hours), and an individual with no shotcreting experience. Each was asked to shoot several panels at different consistencies. The experienced nozzleman adjusted the spraying consistency (amount of water added at the nozzle) for the inexperienced nozzleman prior to application. The following paragraph describes the method to evaluate shooting consistency (Beaupré and Jolin, 2001).

Three days after shooting, the sixteen (16) test panels shot by the different nozzlemen were saw cut perpendicular to the reinforcement in preparation for observation of the reinforcement encapsulation. Figure 7.13 shows the test panel used and examples of reinforcement encasement evaluation specimens. Each panel yielded 16 individual evaluation locations.

As expected, results show that nozzleman experience is of prime importance in the production of good quality reinforcement encapsulation. The second key observation is that, along with nozzleman experience, shooting consistency is of crucial importance. There are therefore two important

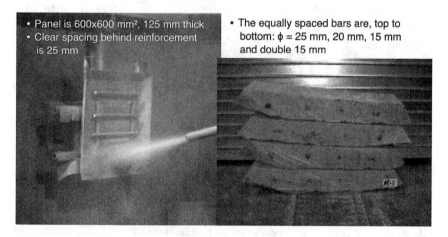

Figure 7.13 Test panel used with typical sawn specimens.

requirements to obtain a good quality dry-mix shotcrete application in terms of reinforcement encapsulation (given the use of proper equipment that is set and operated by an experienced crew): adequate shooting technique (here, nozzleman experience) and sufficiently fresh plastic shotcrete (here, shooting consistency).

Figure 7.14 shows examples from six different panels. Nozzleman experience and shooting consistency are indicated in each picture. It is evident that a beginner had a very difficult time embedding reinforcement, even given adequate shooting consistency, and that even an experienced nozzleman might find it difficult to fully encase the reinforcement if the shooting consistency was not adequately adjusted.

Next, considering the two conditions for good rebar encapsulation (shooting consistency and nozzleman experience), further observations on the encapsulation test panels were made to verify whether defect types found were related to these conditions. Albeit a simple, arguably subjective visual examination was conducted, two interesting observations were made. Although many defect types can be identified in a specimen used to assess reinforcement encasement quality, this study focused here on the quality of shotcrete immediately behind the reinforcement, and uncovered two major defect categories: voids behind the reinforcement (Figure 7.14 d, e, and f) and entrapped rebound behind the reinforcement (Figure 7.14 c, e, and f). Overall observations on the 16 panels led to the following conclusions: (i) poor nozzling technique alone (given adequate consistency) generally results in trapped rebound behind the majority of reinforcing bars and (ii) high shooting consistency (stiffer mixtures), given proper nozzling technique, favours voids behind the reinforcement due to the lack of plasticity in the mixture. Clearly, other defect types were observed as well, but a general trend appeared sufficiently evident for reporting here.

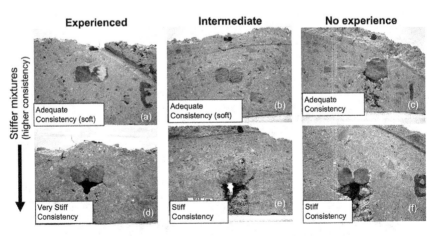

Figure 7.14 Six examples of reinforcement encasement quality as a function of shooting consistency and nozzleman experience.

Samples similar to those shown in Figures 7.13 and 7.14 were later used in a reinforcement corrosion study (Gagnon et al., 2004), which tested the quality of the applied shotcrete material itself as well as the encapsulation quality for its ability to protect against corrosion initiation. From the observations, the conclusion is that correctly applied shotcrete offers equivalent or superior corrosion protection to that of similar strength conventional concrete.

7.4.2 Encapsulation quality and structural performance

Proper reinforcement encapsulation is a concern amongst structural engineers who must work with limited specific guidelines for shotcrete. Indeed, imperfections behind reinforcing bars (or any other obstacles) are reported in cases of excessive use of set-accelerating admixtures or with unskilled nozzlemen. To address such concerns, past research has mainly focused on optimal mixture consistencies and best nozzle handling techniques to obtain perfect encapsulation (Crom, 1981; Jolin et al., 2002). While improvements in rheology of the mixtures and nozzleman skills have limited the creation of imperfections behind reinforcement, the main issue has remained unresolved for decades: What actions must be taken if voids do appear? The reliability and applicability of various encapsulation quality evaluation systems has been subject to continuous debate from industry experts. It has generally been suggested that accounting for the impact of the voids' size on the bond strength of shotcrete to the bars would be more useful.

Early studies confirmed the assumption that small, scattered voids would not have considerable negative effects (Gagnon et al., 2004), and publication in recent years of a *Visual Shotcrete Core Quality Evaluation* document (ACI 506.6T-17) combined with the *Acceptance Criteria for Shotcrete* chapter in the *Guide for the Evaluation of Shotcrete* (ACI 506.4-19) from the American Concrete Institute reiterate that perfect encapsulation of reinforcement is not to be expected. This invites the engineer to use his judgement regarding what is acceptable, based on the specifics of the job at hand and the expected outcome. However, a complete tool for the design and evaluation of reinforced shotcrete structures has yet to be offered. To examine this issue, an extensive experimental investigation was conducted in which complex bond test specimens were built with different qualities of reinforcing bar encapsulation (Basso-Trujillo et al., 2018a). The effect of the voids' geometry and length on bond performance of the bars was studied. The *slope of the load–slip curve*, *ultimate load* and *failure mode* were analysed. A unique approach was pursued in this research: regular shotcrete specimens of varying quality of encapsulation were produced and thoroughly tested for (pull-out) bond strength and encapsulation quality (Figure 7.15). Comparing sprayed and cast-in-place specimens, it was found that the *slope of the load–slip curve* was always *stiffer* for shotcreted specimens provided optimal air flow velocity was used for shotcrete compaction.

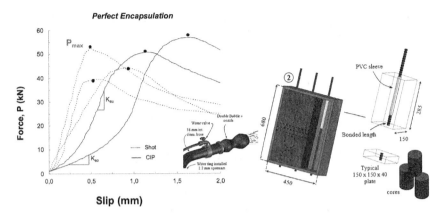

Figure 7.15 Pull-out tests performed on shotcrete and cast-in-place shotcrete.

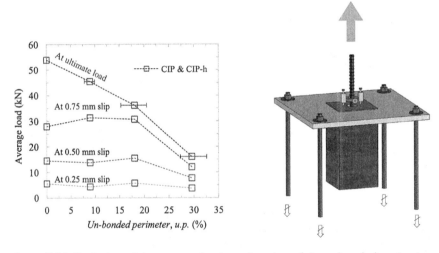

Figure 7.16 Evolution of the average load as a function of the unbonded perimeter.

The most noteworthy results of this part of the research project are the existence of a threshold value at around an equivalent unbonded perimeter of 20% of the bar perimeter. Indeed, although there is a gradual reduction of the ultimate load, the load that corresponds to a 0.25 mm and 0.75 mm bar slip (common criteria used in such a test) remains constant up to that 20% value (Figure 7.16). It was also shown that the height of the defect behind the bar does not seem to have an effect (Basso et al., 2018b).

In addition, reinforcing bars with artificial voids encased with a cast-in-place shotcrete mixture were created in order to precisely know their geometry and location. These were prepared to be tested under the Beam-End Tests (ASTM A944-10) testing method; a testing procedure that generates a stress field around the bar that reflects more closely what is found in reality

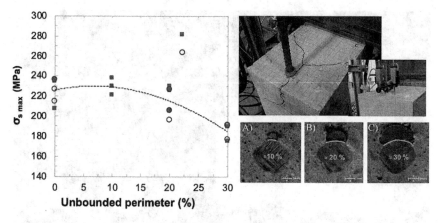

Figure 7.17 Results from the End-Beam test (ASTM A944).

and that yields the information required to conduct proper *reinforcing bar development length* calculations (ACI 318-19, CSA A23.3-2019).

This End-Beam test (ASTM A944) allowed generation of even more interesting information since the stress at failure around the bar and the failure mode are much more representative of what is found, for example, for a reinforcing bar located at the bottom (tensile) side of a reinforced concrete beam (Figure 7.17). Coupled with finite element modelling (FEM) that specifically incorporated details of the bar-concrete bond area, the results further validated that a void with an unbonded perimeter of approximately 20% of the bar's perimeter sets the limit at which bond strength begins to decrease drastically (Basso-Trujillo et al., 2018a; Basso-Trujillo et al., 2018b), as initially indicated by Gagnon et al. (2004). Independent of the bar's diameter, beyond that 20% unbonded perimeter limit, a change from a splitting failure mode to a pull-out failure mode seems to be favoured, indicating a rapid degradation of the bond behaviour. Further analyses will help engineers reliably assess the bond strength of reinforcing bars by the visual examination of cores and determine if corrective design measures are required (Basso-Trujillo et al., 2021).

7.4.3 Shotcrete placement – spray

Further development of knowledge on shotcrete greatly depends on our comprehension of the material *placement process*, particularly for the reduction of rebound and control of the *in-place* material composition. In spite of considerable advances in shotcrete mix design development in the past few decades, many aspects of the placement process are still not clearly understood.

Most of our understanding on the rebound phenomenon relies today on the work of Armelin (Armelin and Banthia, 1998a, b), who successfully modelled the different impact phases for a *single* aggregate on a fresh

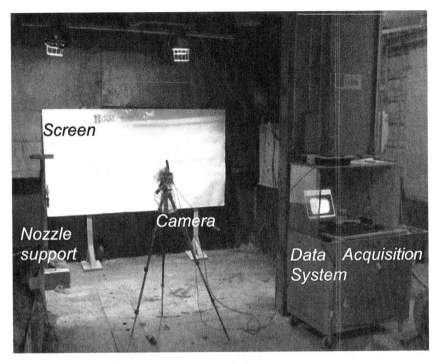

Figure 7.18 Experimental set-up for capturing high-speed images for velocity measurements.

concrete substrate. His study demonstrated the key role of the energy (mass and velocity) of the incoming particles on the amount of rebound.

It was subsequently decided to further investigate the placement process for shotcrete from the concrete transport in the hose and the shotcrete spraying at the nozzle, to the study of the material impact on the receiving surface. This led to the development of a novel research approach using a high-speed camera (see Figure 7.18), a project led by Ginouse during his thesis study (Ginouse and Jolin, 2014). The 1250 frames per second capacity camera was positioned perpendicular to the screen and the concrete spray. The white screen helped to ensure a satisfactory contrast to discern particles in the spray when the post-treatment assessment on captured images was done. When shotcreting, the nozzle was put on a static support and kept motionless to avoid effects due to movement of the nozzle. Images were then post-processed with a specialized software to track the particles image by image. With the data acquired, the particle velocity profiles and spray limits were defined.

Amongst the numerous innovative testing methods and significant results presented in this work, two of the most interesting findings can be seen in Figures 7.19 and 7.20.

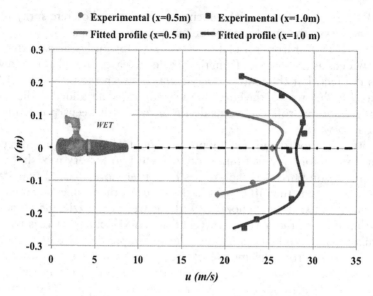

Figure 7.19 Experimental and fitted velocity profiles u(y) obtained at 0.5 and 1.0 meter from the wet-mix nozzle outlet. (From Ginouse and Jolin, 2015.)

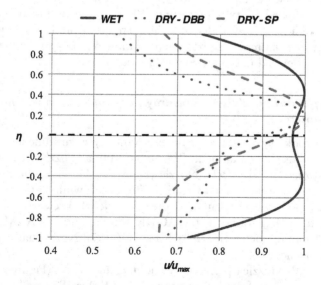

Figure 7.20 Normalized axial velocity profiles obtained for the three shotcrete nozzles considered. (From Ginouse and Jolin, 2015.)

In Figure 7.19, the material velocity of a wet-mix shotcrete spray is followed as it exits the nozzle and values are reported for two positions: at 0.5 m and at 1.0 meter from the exit of the nozzle. Obviously, the pattern of the spray widens as the distance from the nozzle increases, but what is noteworthy is the fact that the material *accelerates* between the 0.5 m and 1.0 m marker. In other words, the effect of the compressed air added at the nozzle has an important role even outside the nozzle as it keeps projecting the material forward.

Figure 7.20 reports the velocity profiles obtained (at 1.0 m) for three different nozzles (one for wet-mix shotcrete and two for dry-mix shotcrete). For comparison purposes, the profiles have been normalized. What stands out in the figure is the differences in the *shape* of the profiles between dry-mix and wet-mix shotcrete nozzles. With the wet-mix nozzle, the shape suggests that most of the particles travel at similar velocities whereas with the dry-mix nozzles the material ejected shows a rapid decrease of velocity as we move away from the middle of the spray axis. Keeping in mind the importance of the velocity (energy) of the particles as they hit the surface for the control of rebound, the shape of the curves in Figure 7.20 somehow intuitively explains the higher amount of rebound found in dry-mix shotcrete where only the particles travelling near the centre of the flow curve have the high impact velocity required to limit rebound.

These two figures are only a small example of the significant contributions of Ginouse to our understanding of how shotcrete is projected out of the nozzle and how it gets placed on the receiving surface. In fact, this knowledge allowed for two interesting follow-up research projects, one on the design of a new type of dry-mix shotcrete nozzle and one on the effect of the wet-mix shotcrete nozzle configuration on spray velocities. These studies are described in the following sub-sections.

7.4.3.1 Effect of nozzle type on spray performances in wet-mix shotcrete

The study took place in a controlled laboratory environment using conventional industrial equipment. Two conventional nozzles, the so-called ACME Nozzle and the 1978 Nozzle (Figure 7.21), were put to the test. Those nozzles present some interesting differences: while both air rings are similar (8 holes), the air plenum of the 1978 Nozzle is clearly thinner and narrower than that found in the ACME Nozzle, and the ACME Nozzle has a 19.1 mm diameter air inlet whereas the 1978 Nozzle has a 12.7 mm diameter air inlet.

Moreover, the nozzle tip presents noticeable differences (Figure 7.22). The ACME Nozzle tip (referred to as a long nozzle tip) is 193 mm long and has a 31 mm diameter outlet, whereas the 1978 Nozzle tip (referred to as a short nozzle tip) is 130 mm long and has a 36 mm diameter outlet. The ACME Nozzle tip is therefore longer and more tapered than the 1978 Nozzle tip.

Figure 7.21 Tested nozzles during experiments – 1978 (left) and ACME (right). (taken from Bérubé, 2018.)

Figure 7.22 Close-up of the nozzle tips.

Furthermore, these two nozzle tips have different rigidity due to their thicknesses and the type of rubber used; the long nozzle tip is stiffer.

The first trials of the project brought to light interesting differences in the concrete spray pattern produced by the two nozzles. Table 7.6 presents the spray characteristics at a distance of 1.0 meter from the nozzle outlet for the two nozzles and for two different airflows.

As shown in Table 7.6, particles in the spray produced by the ACME Nozzle travel around 50% faster than in the 1978 nozzle spray for both airflows. Moreover, the ACME spray pattern is narrower than the 1978 nozzle spray pattern. There is an interesting observation: the nozzle (body and

Table 7.6 Spray characteristics for the two nozzles

Characteristics	ACME		1978	
Airflow (CFM)	150	200	150	200
Vmax (m/s)	24.0	23.5	16.0	16.9
Angle (°)	28.2	27.2	49.6	52.0

Table 7.7 Maximum velocity for each nozzle configuration

Body	Tip	V_{max} (m/s)	
		150 CFM	200 CFM
ACME	Long	24.0	23.5
	Short	18.5	23.0
1978	Long	19.5	22.4
	Short	16.0	16.9

nozzle tip) has a noticeable effect on the particles velocities and spray limits. To explore further, the nozzle tips were switched. This way, the long nozzle tip was put on the 1978 Nozzle body, and the short nozzle tip was put on the ACME Nozzle body. Table 7.7 presents details of the experimental programme and the results obtained with each nozzle configuration.

From a theoretical rebound point of view, the best configuration achievable considering the particle velocities is the ACME Nozzle body combined with the long nozzle tip. Both for 150 and 200 CFM airflow volumes, particles are travelling around 24 m/s. The worst configuration would be the 1978 Nozzle body combined with the short nozzle tip. Particles travel around 16–17 m/s whatever the airflow used.

The short nozzle tip produced lower velocities, both for the ACME nozzle and 1978 nozzle bodies at 150 CFM. But, at 200 CFM, particle speed with the ACME nozzle is high, whereas the 1978 nozzle particle velocities are still slow. It is worth noting that, at 200 CFM, a good nozzle body (ACME) combined with extra airflow helps to reduce the bad effects of the short nozzle tip.

This brief study showed the importance of choosing both the right nozzle body and the right nozzle tip in order to ensure optimal placement conditions in wet-mix shotcrete (Siccadi et al., 2020). Moreover, it seems that increasing the airflow will not always necessarily increase particle velocities, probably because of turbulence effects. Cutting the end off the nozzle tip makes it easier for the nozzleman to manipulate the nozzle and is sometimes seen on construction sites. However, in most conditions, such practice is not recommended as it will lead to a reduction in shotcrete impacting velocity and placement quality and overall shotcrete performance.

7.4.3.2 Nozzle design

A number of developments and improvements seen in the dry-mix shotcrete industry over the past few decades have mostly arisen through improvements in mixture designs and admixture efficiency. Unfortunately, few studies have focused on the modelling and optimization of some of the most important aspects of shotcrete placement: the acceleration of the material through the nozzle and its subsequent travelling towards and impacting on the receiving surface.

In parallel, there has been a multiplication over the past decade in supply of high-tech concrete mixtures which come with particular challenges. Ultra-High-Performance Fibre Reinforced Concrete (UHPFRC) allows reduced application thicknesses while offering exceptional durability and mechanical properties. However, the small amount of water needed in the mix creates dust and homogeneity issues, and the absence of coarse aggregates eliminates the self-cleaning effect occurring in the hose (Reny and Jolin, 2011). Ultra-high early strength shotcrete based on calcium aluminate (CAC) cement, or sulfoaluminate (CSA) cement (Oberlink and Jewell, 2015; Lemay et al., 2014; Reny and Ginouse, 2014) used, for example, in mining or emergency repairs offer very rapid early strength gain, but again can cause dust control and homogeneity issues as the material cannot be predampened in any way.

Finally, although losses due to rebound are not a new topic, a recent study has highlighted and quantified the magnitude of this phenomenon from economical and environmental points of view. In a mine, a rebound reduction from 21% to 11% may reduce the emission of CO_2 eq. by as much as 14%, while creating overall savings of 9% (Gagnon, 2017).

The current situation is that the traditional nozzle equipment available for dry-mix shotcrete seems to no longer be fully adapted to tackle modern shotcreting requirements, namely being able to shoot all types of shotcretewhile minimizing losses due to rebound and insuring a dense and homogenous in-place shotcrete.

One can wonder what the main drawbacks are for existing nozzles. ACI 506R-16 recommends the use of a short nozzle along with predampening for oven-dry material (see Figure 8.1). This indirectly brings attention to the limited wetting and mixing performance of the short nozzle configuration itself. In many cases, however, predampening is avoided because it requires an operator and a machine in addition to the basic setup. Many dry-mix shotcrete teams will instead use a hydro-mix nozzle where water is added 2 to 3 metres before the exit point (see Figure 8.6), providing a longer wetting and mixing period. However, as mentioned earlier, high-tech concrete mixes do not allow for predampening (lack of cleaning effect of the coarse aggregates and/or ultra-rapid setting). Hence, the need for a research project where an improved *short nozzle configuration* (without predampening) had to be designed.

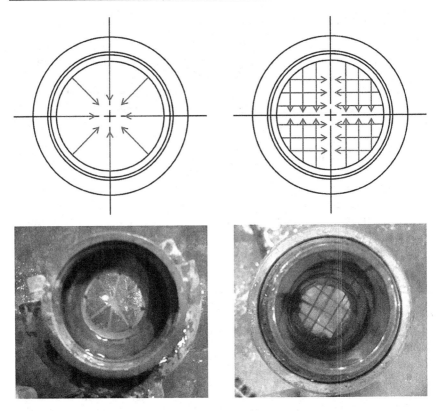

Figure 7.23 Traditional water ring (left) and improved water ring (right) (water pressure is low for the picture: not showing the atomization effect).

In a traditional water ring, concrete wetting is achieved by a unique set of concentric water jets as shown on Figure 7.23. The water is introduced through a small number (usually 8) of relatively large diameter holes. The disadvantage of the traditional water ring is that water covers a small area of the section through which the dry material passes. Moreover, the relatively large water holes do not always allow for the high-water pressure needed to reach the centre of the ring. If the pressure is insufficient, water is deflected from its path towards the inner surface of the hose by the material passing through the ring. In the worst case, it leads to an absence of wetting for a part of the spayed concrete, a phenomenon well known by nozzlemen, which is a source of dust and inhomogeneity in the in-place concrete.

Using the research on spray patterns and rebound conducted by Ginouse (see above), the idea was twofold: design a nozzle that would allow for proper wetting of high tech dry-mix shotcrete (in a short nozzle configuration without predampening) and that would also allow for reduced rebound losses and dust emissions by better controlling the spray pattern velocities (Siccardi, 2018).

To achieve this, the water addition method was completely revised. Instead of having a single row of concentric water jets, holes were positioned on multiple rows, creating a grid pattern and several water screens. Furthermore, water atomization comes into play using high water pressure and very small diameter holes. Finally, the high-pressure water jets grid shears the material travelling inside the water ring. This enhanced water addition method thus becomes part of the mixing action in the process.

The optimization process was not limited to the water ring alone; the nozzle tip received attention as well. Instead of being a passive mixing element relying on turbulence alone, the emphasis was put on the use of an external energy source to act on the concrete spray pattern. By adding air at the periphery of the nozzle tip, the velocity spray pattern tends to be more uniform, which leads to a better concrete placement and limits losses due to rebound (Figure 7.24).

This research project was considered a great success (Jolin et al., 2020a & b). Indeed, once the first prototype was completed, it was possible to shoot UHPFRC using only this short nozzle with oven-dry materials. The enhanced equipment helped decrease rebound by up to 50% while increasing the strength obtained by 50%. Finally, comparative testing revealed a significant decrease of as much as 90% in dust emission compared to using regular dry-mix shotcrete nozzles.

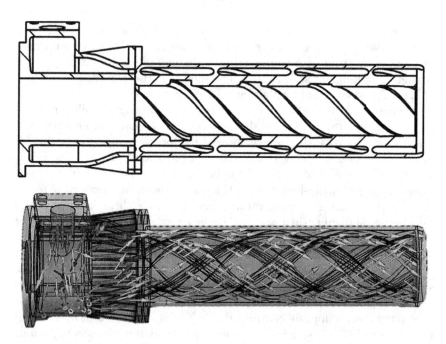

Figure 7.24 Schematic of the nozzle tip with addition of air on the periphery.

These promising and outstanding results led to further research funding being obtained to support ongoing research efforts aimed at creating equipment that better serves the dry-mix shotcrete process. This new approach in nozzle design will undoubtedly help promote the use of dry-mix shotcrete, and shotcrete in general, as improvements in rebound reduction, dust control and in-place quality are all key elements.

7.5 DEVELOPMENT AND ASSESSMENT OF A HIGH SLAG SHOTCRETE MIX

The first author was involved in 2018/2019 in a three-phase research and development program to optimize a 70% slag content wet-mix shotcrete mixture design for construction of heavily reinforced mass shotcrete walls for underground stations on a Metro line in Toronto, Canada, and demonstrate that the mix was:

a) suitable for pumping, shooting and finishing for such construction, and

b) could satisfy all the specified plastic and hardened shotcrete performance requirements for a CSA A23.1 Class C-1 Exposure category (i.e. *structurally reinforced concrete exposed to chlorides with or without freezing and thawing conditions*).

Phase 1 was a largely bench-top study, which looked at the rheology of a number of different mixes using vane shear testing, and the thermal signature and setting time of the mixes using isothermal calorimetry. Compressive strength development at 1, 7, 28 and 56 days was also recorded.

In the Phase Two study, a plain control mix with a blend of 50% of a Type GU cement and 50% of a Type GUb cement containing 8% silica fume as the binder, and three mixes with 30% Type GUb cement containing 8% silica fume and 70% slag, which showed the most promising performance in the Phase One study, were selected for evaluation. All three slag mixes selected also contained a colloidal nano silica and two of the mixes contained a natural hemp-based fibre. The plastic shotcrete mixes were tested for slump, air content, temperature, rheology (in a shear vane test) and thickness to sloughing (in a so-called *beehive* test). The thermal signature of three of the four mixes was tested in 1.0 m cube semi-adiabatic tests. Thermal test results are shown in Figure 7.25

The project specification called for the peak temperature in the core of the structural elements to not exceed 70°C. The plain control shotcrete mix reached a peak temperature of 90°C and was clearly not suitable for mass shotcrete construction. By contrast, the 70% slag mixes had peak temperatures below 67°C and satisfied the project specification requirements. All four mixes were then evaluated for pumpability, shootability and finishability in

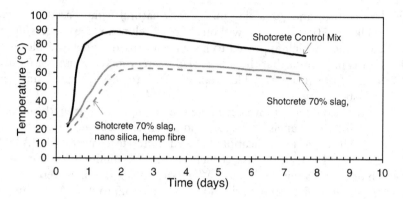

Figure 7.25 Semi-adiabatic cube exotherm test results.

(Graph courtesy Lloyd Keller.)

full scale tests with ready-mix shotcrete supply. Shotcrete was applied to 2.4 m high reinforced shotcrete walls. Plastic shotcrete properties recorded included: slump, air content and temperature at the point of discharge into the shotcrete pump, after pumping, and as-shot. The shotcrete was batched at air contents in the 6.8% to 8.8 % range, to take advantage of the *slump killer* effect that is realized from air-content reduction from impact of the shotcrete on the receiving surface. Test results are shown in Table 7.8

While all four mixes pumped and shot well, the best resistance to slough-ing (in the *beehive* test) occurred in the two mixes with the natural hemp-based fibre. Also, it was found that the 70% slag mix without fibre did not perform well during finishing operations. After shooting, all four mixes were trimmed back to the shooting wires with a cutting rod, followed by closing the surface with a wood darby and then steel trowel finished. While

Table 7.8 Plastic shotcrete test results

Trial		At discharge into pump			Pumped			Shot		
		Slump, mm	Air, %	Temp, °C	Slump, mm	Air, %	Temp, °C	Slump, mm	Air, %	Temp, °C
I	Shotcrete control	85	8.8	25.5	55	8.8	28.6	15	4.2	28.1
2	70% slag	90	6.8	23	55	6.8	29.0	40	3.9	26.3
3	70% slag, + fibre	65	8.1	21.6	40	7.8	29.4	30	4.3	27.7
4	70% slag, + fibre, +accel.	75	7.9	19.1	55	6.9	26.0	40	3.7	25.2

the plain control and 70% slag mixes with natural hemp-based fibre finished well, the 70% slag mix without fibre developed some *blisters* in the finished surface, which appeared to have been caused by delayed bleeding. Clearly it is important that these high slag content mixes contain a natural hydrophilic fibre to control bleeding, in order to provide good finishing characteristics.

The hardened shotcrete was evaluated for compressive strength of cores extracted from test panels at 1, 7, 28 and 56 days. Test results are shown in Table 7.9. The project specification required shotcrete to meet a CSA A23.1-19 Class C-1 Exposure Class, which requires a minimum compressive strength of 35 MPa within 56 days. While the 70% slag mixes were slow in early age compressive strength development (only 3.3 to 4.4 MPa at an age of 1 day), by 7 days, compressive strengths were already in excess of 35 MPa.

In addition, the durability characteristics of the plain control and 70% slag mixes were evaluated in the following tests:

    a) Parameters of the air-void system in the hardened sprayed shotcrete (ASTM C457);

    b) Permeability in the ASTM C642 Boiled Absorption and Volume of Permeable Voids test;

    c) Chloride permeability in the ASTM C1202 Rapid Chloride Permeability (RCP) test; and

    d) Drying shrinkage in the CSA A23.2-21C length change at 28 days test.

All four shotcrete mixes were properly air entrained and satisfied the requirements of CSA A23.1 for freeze/thaw durable concrete of >3.0% air-content and air-void spacing factor of <0.260 mm in the hardened shotcrete. In the ASTM C642 test, the Boiled Absorption in the four mixes was in the 3.7% to 5.5% range, which would place them in the *Excellent* category according to the criteria developed by Morgan, (Morgan et al., 1987) shown in Table 6.9. The corresponding Volume of Permeable Voids values in the four mixes were in the 8.3 to 12.0% range, which would also place them in the *Excellent* category. In the RCP test, the plain control mix had a charge passed of 1004 coulombs at 91 days, which would place it in the

Table 7.9 Phase Two study compressive strength test results

Trial		Average compressive strength, MPa			
		1 day	7 days	28 days	56 days
1	Shotcrete control	27.9	45.2	54.1	57.0
2	70% slag	4.4	38.7	48.7	52.1
3	70% slag, +fibre	3.7	35.7	46.8	48.3
4	70% slag, +fibre, +accelerator	3.3	43.3	55.1	55.5

Table 7.10 Phase Two study drying shrinkage test results

Shotcrete Mix no.	Shrinkage, %				
	1 day	4 days	7 days	14 days	28 days
1	−0.007	−0.021	−0.027	−0.036	−0.044
2	−0.002	−0.006	−0.008	−0.014	−0.024
3	0.002	−0.005	−0.008	−0.014	−0.025
4	−0.003	−0.008	−0.011	−0.020	−0.032

Notes: CSA A23.1 defines low shrinkage concrete as having less than 0.04% shrinkage at 28 days.

Low Chloride Ion Permeability rating according to the criteria provided in ASTM C1202. The three high-volume slag mixes had values in the 252 to 322 coulombs range at 91 days, which would place them in the *Very Low Chloride Ion Permeability* rating. These chloride ion permeability test results are well below the maximum of 1500 coulombs at 91 days required by CSA A23.1-19 for a Class C-1 Exposure concrete.

Finally, the drying shrinkage characteristics of shotcrete prisms cut from test panels was evaluated in tests conducted following the method detailed in CSA A23.2-21C, except that measurement studs in the ends of the prisms were installed by drilling and epoxy grouting, rather than by being cast in moulds as done with cast concrete. Test results for drying shrinkage at 28 days are shown in Table 7.10. CSA A23.1 defines *Low Shrinkage Concrete* as concrete with a length change of < 0.04% at 28 days. Clearly the 70% slag mixes have very low length change values, which would place them in this *Low Shrinkage Concrete* category. This is a very exciting finding for the shotcrete industry, where control of drying shrinkage-induced cracking has long been an issue that needs to be dealt with. Feedback from the field where these 70% slag mixes (with natural fibres) are being used in mass structural shotcrete walls and other elements, is that they are being very effective in mitigating both plastic shrinkage cracking in the plastic shotcrete and drying shrinkage cracking in the hardened shotcrete.

Based on the results of the Phase Two study, Mix 3 was selected for use in the Phase Three study. The Phase Three study was used to evaluate the performance of the selected 70% slag mix with hemp-based fibre in construction of full-scale mock-up sections of a heavily reinforced, underground station wall. Two sections were evaluated, one comprising the middle part of the wall and the other comprising an upper part of the wall. Each section had dimensions of 2.5 m high × 3.9 m long × 1.3 m thick, and in addition to horizontal reinforcing bars, had six layers of 30M vertical reinforcing steel bars with many of them being double lapped. Figure 7.26 shows the constructed mock-up ready for shooting. The mock-up was used to not only qualify the 70% slag shotcrete mixture, but also to qualify the shotcrete contractor, six nozzlemen and crew to work on underground station

Figure 7.26 Mock-up with rebar installed ready for shooting.

construction of mass shotcrete structural walls, using the *hybrid* wet-mix shotcrete construction process.

The mock-up construction process basically followed the procedures outlined in Section 9.10 on *hybrid* shotcrete construction. Bench gun shooting commenced at the bottom corners of the mock-up, building up the first bench. Two blowpipe operators worked in tandem with the nozzleman, one working in front of the nozzlemen, blowing away rebound and any build-up of overspray on rebar and embedments about to be shot. The second blowpipe operator worked behind the nozzleman, blowing off any accumulations of shotcrete from the back rows of reinforcing steel bars so that the indentations on the bars were visible to the nozzleman shooting the next bench. Two configurations of 30M bars were shot: one with the bars lapped side-by-side and the other with the bars fixed back-to-back, relative to the nozzleman's shooting orientation. Two vibrator operators followed behind the blowpipe operators. They used stiff rod-like immersion vibrators that could penetrate right to the back of the wall (Note: On actual underground station construction projects, a stiff vibrator with an L-hook on the end has also been used where needed to facilitate vibrating behind embedments like waterstops and utility boxes). Figure 7.27 shows a vibrator operator at work.

The nozzlemen systematically inserted the nozzle through the outer layer of reinforcing steel bars to maximize impact velocity at the back of the wall.

Figure 7.27 Insertion of stiff rod vibrator in mock-up wall construction.

High shotcrete impact was the prime means of consolidating the shotcrete and getting encasement of the bars. Internal vibration with the stiff rod vibrators was a supplemental method used to achieve full consolidation and wrap around bars and embedments in the shotcreted walls. The mock-ups were built up in about three 0.8 m high lifts. No sagging or sloughing occurred and the shotcrete finished well to produce an attractive smooth surface appearance, free of any blemishes, acceptable to the architect. After being allowed to cure for several days, the back form was stripped and other than for a *few bugholes* from the supplemental vibration used, the stripped formed face was free of any defects.

Cores were drilled and *windows* diamond wire saw cut from the mock-up at six locations: one from each section shot by six different nozzlemen. Figure 7.28 shows three windows cut in one part of the mock-up. Note the smooth finished surface appearance with a tooled control joint.

Figure 7.29a shows a view of one slab removed from a window where the front vertical bars were lapped side-by-side relative to the nozzleman's shooting orientation. Fig 7.29b shows a slab with the front vertical bars lapped back-to-back. The removed slabs are free of any voids or defects and the encapsulation of reinforcing steel is excellent.

The heat exotherm was recorded at the core of the mock-up and at the finished surface. This data, together with a record of the prevailing ambient

Figure 7.28 Windows cut in mock-up.

(a)   (b)

Figure 7.29 Slab diamond wire saw cut from section of mock-up and note the excellent rebar encapsulation: (a) with back-to-back positioning outer vertical rebar and (b) with side-by-side outer vertical bars.

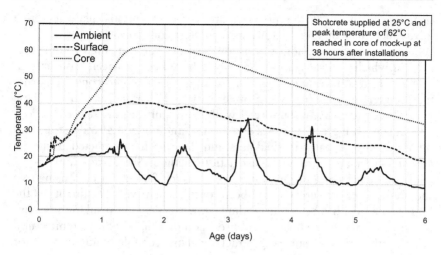

Figure 7.30 Heat exotherm in mock-up in core and finished shotcrete surface. (Graph courtesy Lloyd Keller.)

temperature is shown in Figure 7.30. The shotcrete was supplied at a temperature of 25°C at the point of discharge into the shotcrete pump and the peak temperature in the core reached 62°C after 38 hours, well below the maximum 70°C permitted. The temperature differential between the core and the finished surface was a maximum of 16°C, well below the maximum 20°C required by CSA A23.1-19 and the project specifications.

Quality control testing on samples extracted from shot test panels produced the following test results:

- Compressive strength: 3 days: 14.8 MPa; 7 days: 29.6 MPa; 28 days: 45.9 MPa; 56 days: 50.7 MPa.
- Hardened air-void spacing factor: 220 μm
- Rapid chloride permeability at 28 days: 461 coulombs
- Boiled absorption: 5.5% and volume of permeable voids: 12.0%
- Drying shrinkage at 28 days: 0.025%

To summarize, the ready-mix supplied 70% slag mix with a natural hemp-based fibre supplied to the mock-up pumped, shot and finished well with no sagging or sloughing, using the *hybrid* shotcrete construction process. Extracted slabs from the mock-up all showed excellent shotcrete consolidation and encapsulation of reinforcing steel and embedments. The nozzlemen who shot the mock-up were qualified to shoot heavily reinforced mass shotcrete walls in underground stations in Ontario. The mixture supplied met all the specified plastic and hardened shotcrete performance requirements and satisfied the requirements of CSA A23.1-19 for a Class C-1 Exposure concrete. Of particular benefit was the low heat of hydration and low drying shrinkage of the 70% slag mix compared to a conventional plain shotcrete mix, which made it suitable for mass shotcrete construction.

Slightly modified versions of this low heat of hydration, high volume slag mix (in which natural hemp-based fibres have been replaced with natural cellulose fibres) have since been used with great success to construct structural shotcrete walls in underground stations in Toronto, Ontario. These mass shotcrete, heavily reinforced walls with embedments (electrical conduit, curtainwall grouting tubes and vertical and horizontal waterstops) are often 1.3 m or greater in thickness and have been constructed using the *hybrid* (shoot and vibrate) construction method. Shotcrete supply is by ready-mix trucks and production rates of up to 220 m3 per day (using two shotcrete pumps and crews) have been routinely achieved. The quality of the finished product has been outstanding, with excellent encapsulation of reinforcing steel and embedments and provision of a high-quality architectural finish, with very little shrinkage cracking. This technology augurs well for the future of the structural shotcrete industry.

7.6 CONCLUSIONS

This chapter offers a brief glimpse of the vast amount of R&D information available in a highly complex field. Obvious from the few research projects reported here, shotcrete is more than just a placement method; it is a rich and exciting industry where ideas and innovation can take place in a number of ways. But more than anything, it is a field where the research must be firmly anchored in the trade that is shotcrete. It is hoped that this chapter will inspire more people to get involved in the field of shotcrete research.

This chapter would not be complete without acknowledging the contribution, through great effort and hard work, of numerous undergraduate and graduate students at Université Laval to these and many other research projects. If you have ever held a nozzle in your hand or shovelled rebound, and they all have!, you can appreciate their level of dedication in conducting research projects in this field using life-size equipment.

REFERENCES

ACI 238.2T. 2014. *Concrete Thixotropy*. American Concrete Institute. 6p.
ACI CODE-318. 2019. *Building Code Requirements for Structural Concrete and Commentary*. American Concrete Institute. 624p.
ACI 506.4R. 2019. *Guide for the Evaluation of Shotcrete*. American Concrete Institute. 18p.
ACI 506.6T. 2017. *Visual Shotcrete Core Quality Evaluation Technote*. American Concrete Institute. 4p.

ACI 506R. 2016. *Guide to Shotcrete.* American Concrete Institute. 52p.

Armelin, H. and Banthia, N. 1997. Predicting the Flexural Postcracking Performance of Steel Fibre Reinforced Concrete from the Pullout of Single Fibres. *ACI Materials Journal.* Vol. 94. No. 1. 18–31.

Armelin, H. and Banthia, N. 1998a. Mechanics of Aggregate Rebound in Shotcrete Part I. *Materials and Structures.* Vol. 31. No. 206. 91–120.

Armelin, H. and Banthia, N.1998b. Mechanics of Aggregate Rebound in Shotcrete Part II. *Materials and Structures.* Vol. 31. No. 207. 195–202.

ASTM A944. 2015. *Standard Test Method for Comparing Bond Strength of Steel Reinforcing Bars to Concrete Using Beam-End Specimens.* 4 p. ASTM International. https://doi.org/10.1520/A0944-10R15

ASTM C457. 2016. *Standard Test Method for Microscopical Determination of Parameters of the Air-Void System in Hardened Concrete.* 7 p. ASTM International. https://doi.org/10.1520/C0457_C0457M-16

ASTM C642. 2013b. *Standard Test Method for Density, Absorption and Voids in Hardened Concrete.* 3p. ASTM International. https://doi.org/10.1520/C0642-13

ASTM C672. 2012. *Standard Test Method for Scaling Resistance of Concrete Surfaces Exposed to Deicing Chemicals.* 7 p. ASTM International.

ASTM C1202. 2019b. *Standard Test Method for Electrical Indication of Concrete's Ability to Resist Chloride Ion Penetration.* 8p. ASTM International. https://doi.org/10.1520/C1012_C1012M-18B

Basso-Trujillo, P., Jolin, M., Massicotte, B. and Bissonnette, B. 2018a. Bond strength of reinforcing bars encased with shotcrete. *Construction and Building Materials.* Vol. 169. doi: 10.1016/j.conbuildmat.2018.02.218.

Basso-Trujillo, P., Jolin, M., Massicotte, B. and Bissonnette, B. 2018b. Bond strength of reinforcing bars with varying encapsulation qualities. *ACI Structural Journal.* Vol. 115. No. 6. doi: https://doi.org/10.14359/51702415.

Basso Trujillo, P., Massicotte, B., Bissonnette, B. and Jolin, M. 2021. *Shotcrete Modification Factors for the Development Length Equation. ACI Structural Journal.* Vol. 118. No. 3. 305–314. https://doi.org/10.14359/51730539

Beaupré, D. 1994. *Rheology of High-Performance Shotcrete,* Thesis in Civil Engineering, University of British Columbia, Vancouver, BC, Canada.

Beaupré, D. and Jolin, M. 2001. Effect of Shotcrete Consistency and Nozzleman Experience on Reinforcement Encasement Quality. *Shotcrete Magazine, American Shotcrete Association.* Vol. 3. No. 4. 20–23.

Beaupré, D. and Jolin, M. 2002. Efficiency of shotcrete accelerator: A fundamental approach. *Proceedings of the Conference on Shotcrete for Underground Support IX,* Kyoto, November 18–20, 99–111.

Beaupré, D., Lamontagne, A., Pigeon, M. and Dufour, J.-F. 1996. Powder Air-Entraining Admixture in Dry-Mix Shotcrete. *ACI/SCA International Conference on Sprayed Concrete/Shotcrete,* 3–7.

Bérubé, S. 2018. *Study of shotcrete nozzles: effect on velocities and mass distribution patterns (in French),* M.Sc. thesis, Université Laval, 150 p.

Bessette, M.-O., Beaupré, D., Jolin, M. and Guay, J. 2001. Accelerated Wet Process Shotcrete. *The Proceeding of Concrete under Severe Conditions Conference,* Edited by Banthia & Gjørv, Vancouver, Canada, 1255–1262.

CCS-4. 2020. *Shotcrete for the Craftsman.* American Concrete Institute. 92p.

Crom, T.R. 1981. Dry-Mix Shotcrete Nozzling. *ACI Concrete International.* Vol. 3. No.1. 80–93.

CSA A23.3. 2014. *Design of Concrete Structures*. Canadian Standard Association.

CSA. 2019b. *A23.1/A23.2 Concrete materials and methods of concrete construction/Test methods and standard practices for concrete*. 690p. Canadian Standards Association.

Fily-Paré, I. 2015. *Revalorisation du verre en béton projeté: Étude sur le remplacement partiel du ciment par de la poudre de verre en béton projeté par voie sèche*, M.Sc. thesis In *Département de Génie Civil et de Génie des Eaux*, Université Laval, Québec City, Canada.

Fily-Paré, I. and Jolin, M. 2013. The use of recycled glass in shotcrete. *Shotcrete Magazine, American Shotcrete Association*. Vol. 15. No. 4. 3 p.

Fuller, W. B. and Thompson. S. E. 1907. The Laws of proportioning concrete. *Transactions of the American Society of Civil Engineers*. Vol. 33. No. 2. 223–298. https://doi.org/10.1061/TACEAT.0001979

Funk, J. E. and Dinger, D.R. 1994. *Predictive Process Control of Crowded Particulate Suspensions*. Boston, Springer. https://doi.org/10.1007/978-1-4615-3118-0

Gagnon, A. 2017. *Développement de mélanges de béton projeté à valeurs environnementales ajoutées*, M.Sc. Thesis *Département de génie civil et de génie des eaux*, Université Laval, 116 p.

Gagnon, A., Fily-Paré, I. and Jolin, M. 2016. *Rethinking Shotcrete Mixture Design Through Sustainable Ingredients*. *Shotcrete Magazine Fall 2016*. 28–31.

Gagnon, F., Jolin, M. and Beaupré, D. 2004. Determination of criteria for the acceptance of shotcrete for Certification. *Second Int. Conf. on Engineering Developments in Shotcrete*, Cairns, Queensland, Australia, October 4, 2004, 175–182.

Ginouse, N. and Jolin, M. 2014. Characterization of placement phenomenon in wet sprayed concrete. *Proceedings of the 7th International Symposium on Sprayed Concrete: Modern Use of Wet Mix Sprayed Concrete for Underground Support*. 2014, Sandefjord, Norway, 173–183.

Ginouse, N. and Jolin, M. 2015. Investigation of spray pattern in shotcrete applications. *Construction and Building Materials*. Vol. 93. 966–972.

Heere, R. and Morgan, D. R. 2002. Determination of Early-Age Compression Strength of Shotcrete. *Shotcrete Magazine, American Shotcrete Association* Spring 2002. 28–31.

Holtz, R.D. and Kovacs, W.D. 1981. *An Introduction to Geotechnical Engineering*. Prentice Hall, 808 p.

Jolin, M. and Beaupré, D. 2000. Temporary high initial air content wet process. *Shotcrete Magazine, American Shotcrete Association*. Vol. 2. 22–23.

Jolin, M. and Beaupré, D. 2004. Effect of the Particle Size Distribution in Dry-Process Shotcrete. *ACI Material Journal*. Vol. 101. No. 2. 131–35.

Jolin, M., Beaupré, D. and Mindess, S. 2001. Rheology of dry-mix shotcrete. *Concrete Science and Engineering* December 2001. 195–201.

Jolin, M., Beaupré, D. and Mindess, S. 2002. Quality Control of Dry-mix Shotcrete during Construction. *Concrete International*. Vol. 24. No. 10. 69–74.

Jolin, M., Beaupré, D., Pigeon, M. and Lamontagne, A. 1997. Use of Set Accelerating Admixtures in Dry-Mix Shotcrete. *Journal of Materials in Civil Engineering*. Vol. 9. No. 4. 180–184. 10.1061/(asce)0899-1561(1997)9:4(180)

Jolin, M., Burns, D. and Bissonnette, B. 2009. Understanding the pumpability of concrete. *Shotcrete for Underground Support XI*, Davos, Switzerland, March 2009.

Jolin, M., Chapdelaine, F., Gagnon, F. and Beaupré, D. 2006. Pumping concrete: a fundamental and practical approach. *Shotcrete for Underground Support X*, Whistler, British Columbia, Canada.

Jolin, M., Siccardi, P., Gagnon, A. and Jacob-Vaillancourt, T. 2020a. *Shotcrete Nozzle Assembly and Stream Controlling Device Therefor* (CA2020050214) Canadian Intellectual Property Office.

Jolin, M., Siccardi, P., Gagnon, A. and Jacob-Vaillancourt, T. 2020b. *Shotcrete Nozzle Assembly* (CA2020050213) Canadian Intellectual Property Office.

Kaplan, D., Larrard, F. D. and Sedran, T. 2005. Design of Concrete Pumping Circuit. *ACI Materials Journal*. Vol. 102. No. 2. 110–117.

Lamontagne, A., Pigeon, M. and Beaupré, D. 1996. Use of Air-Entraining Admixture in Dry-Mix Shotcrete. *ACI Materials Journals*. Vol. 93. No. 1. 69–74.

Lemay, J. -D., Jolin, M. and Gaggné, R. 2014. *Ultra rapid strength development in dry-mix shotcrete for ultra rapid support in challenging mining conditions. Deep Mining Conference*, Edited by Hudyma, M. & Potvin, Y., Sudbury, Canada.

Millette, D. 2011. *Using Accelerator for Shotcreting. Shotcrete Magazine, American Shotcrete Association* Spring 2011. 36–39.

Morgan, D. R., Neill, J., McAskill, N. and Duke, N. 1987. Evaluation of silica fume shotcrete. *International Workshop on Condensed Silica Fume in Concrete*.

Nacif, G. L., Panzera, T. H., Strecker, K., Christoforo, A. L. and Paine, K. 2013. *Investigations on cementitious composites based on rubber particle waste additions*, Materials Research. Vol. 16. No. 2. 259–268. doi: 10.1590/S1516-14392012005 000177.

Oberlink, A. and Jewell, R. 2015. Rapidly Deployable Shotcrete System. *Shotcrete Magazine, American Shotcrete Association* Spring 2015. 38–43.

Reny, S. and Ginouse, N. 2014. *Development of a rapid strength gain dry-mix shotcrete using calcium sulfo-aluminate cement for mining and tunneling applications, Deep Mining 2014: 7th International Conference on Deep and High Stress Mining, Australian Centre for Geomechanics*, Edited by Hudyma, M. & Potvin, Y., 281–290

Reny, S. and Jolin, M. 2011. *Improve Your Shotcrete: Use Coarse Aggregates!* Shotcrete Magazine, American Shotcrete Association Winter 2011. 26–28.

Saika, N. and Brito, J. D., 2012. Use of Plastic Waste as Aggregate in Cement Mortar and Concrete Preparation: A Review. *Construction and Building Materials*. Vol. 34. September. 385–401.

Siccadi, P., Laradh, A., Bérubé, S. and Jolin, M. 2020., The Influence of the Nozzle Tip on Shotcrete Spray Performance. *Shotcrete Magazine, American Shotcrete Association* Spring 2020. 16–19.

Siccardi, P. 2018. *Influence de la lance en projection de béton: homogénéité et rebond*, M.Sc. Thesis, Université Laval, Québec City, Canada, 153 p.

Studebaker, C. H. 1939. *Report on Gunite at Arrowrock Dam*, U.S. Bureau of Reclamation Memorandum, 66 p.

Chapter 8

Shotcrete equipment

8.1 INTRODUCTION

Selecting the right equipment for shotcrete placement is paramount in achieving high-quality applications. There are many equipment configurations possible for applying dry-mix shotcrete and wet-mix shotcrete; in fact, an entire book could probably be dedicated only to the equipment used for shotcreting. While a lot of information can be found on individual pieces of equipment from different suppliers, it is more difficult to find information on how to assemble them and put them to work towards high-quality shotcrete production. It thus seems more appropriate to concentrate in this chapter on the critical elements related to shotcrete equipment *selection* for both processes.

The first part of the chapter focuses on the dry-mix shotcrete process, especially on the challenges of properly transporting the material through the delivery hose and then the key portion where water is added and blended in with the dry constituent materials at the nozzle.

The second part of the chapter concentrates on the wet-mix shotcrete process and particularly on the requirements for properly accelerating and spraying the material out of the nozzle, and on the challenges of assuring proper dispersion of the set-accelerator in the nozzle, when used, in the wet-mix shotcrete process.

8.2 DRY-MIX SHOTCRETE

Dry-mix shotcrete is defined as *shotcrete in which most of the mixing water is added at the nozzle* (ACI CT-18, 2018). Indeed, this process consists of conveying the dry components of a shotcrete mixture down a delivery hose where it goes through a nozzle assembly where water is added to the mixture before exiting at high velocity and traveling towards the spraying surface (see Figure 8.1). The definition uses the words *"most of the water"* since the shotcrete material can either be batched on site using aggregates in

DOI: 10.1201/9780429169946-9

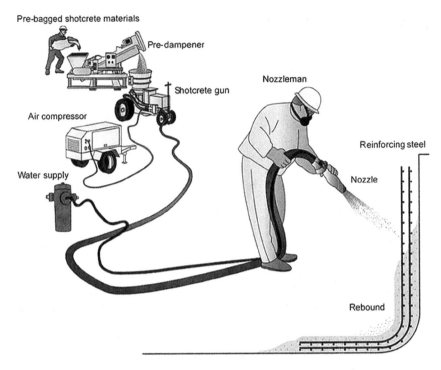

Figure 8.1 Schematics of a typical dry-mix shotcrete equipment layout.

their natural moisture state (i.e. containing some water) or as a prebagged formula containing oven-dry aggregates (i.e. negligible moisture content) that should undergo some *predampening* prior to its introduction into the shotcrete gun. It should be stressed that when naturally moist aggregates or predampening is used, the water content of the dry-mix shotcrete material *prior* to its introduction into the gun is relatively low, giving the material an earth-like consistency. If pressed into the palm of the hand, the material should form an easily breakable clump, without leaving any moisture on the skin. This is best achieved by using natural aggregates with 3%–6% moisture content (ACI CCS-4, 2020), or by tuning the predampener to provide this earth-like consistency. Too much water in the dry-mix shotcrete mixture before going into the gun will create clumps and hinder the uniform flow of material into the gun or the hose and eventually create plugs. Too little moisture in the mix will in turn create more dust (both at the gun and at the nozzle) and more rebound. It should be pointed out that in cases where the use of a predampener is difficult, a *hydromix nozzle* can be used instead when prebagged oven-dry material is used (see Section 8.2.3). It should also be mentioned that it is considered unacceptable to use prebagged oven-dry material without predampening (through a predampener or a hydromix nozzle) as it makes the placement of a properly mixed and homogeneous shotcrete too challenging (ACI 506R-16, 2016).

Assuming the right mix design has been selected (see Chapter 5) and that a properly trained and certified shotcrete nozzleman is standing at the end of the hose holding the nozzle, all that is needed is the proper equipment to convey the predampened material to the nozzle and the right type of nozzle to ensure proper mixing of water and placement. To be more precise, the objective is to make sure that the water added at the nozzle gets to be properly mixed with the dry material passing through the hose at high velocity. This does not only require having a constant flow of material and water at the nozzle, but also having sufficient water pressure and a properly designed nozzle to optimize the distribution of water into the predampened material stream. The next sections take a closer look at these equipment requirements.

8.2.1 Conveying material through the hose

The first step is to convey the dry-mix shotcrete material all the way to the end of the hose. This is usually done using a *shotcrete gun*: a device that meters and transfers the dry material into a pressurized hose where the air stream then transports it to the nozzle. There are two types of dry-mix shotcrete guns; pressure vessels and continuous feed rotary guns (ACI CCS-4, 2020; Bridger, 2017). While the former are the oldest in the industry, they are less popular today, probably due to their size and relatively complex operation. The continuous feed rotary guns have replaced most of these older machines; they work by using a rotating airlock principle where small volumes of dry material are metered into the conveying hose. Two configurations are available depending on the manufacturers, identified as the *rotary barrel type gun* or the *rotary bowl-type gun*, because of the shape of the rotary feed system (see Figure 8.2).

The idea is that although material is introduced intermittently into the hose at the gun, because of the rotation of the barrel or bowl, the length of the hose and the friction between the material and the inside of the hose, all these factors even out the material delivery to a homogeneous and non-pulsating flow of dry material as it reaches the nozzle. This is an essential aspect of quality dry-mix shotcrete work, since it is the only way the nozzleman can properly control the amount of water added at the nozzle. This means the dry-mix shotcrete gun must be selected to suit the nature of the work and be operated properly. The size of the rotor (barrel or bowl) must be selected to fit the hose size (25 mm, 37.5 mm or, more generally, 50 mm inside diameter for hand-nozzling) and the production rate. For example, a full-size barrel rotor which is good for up to 6 m^3/h production rate would not work well with a smaller hose diameter on a small repair job where the nozzleman has to apply relatively thin layers of

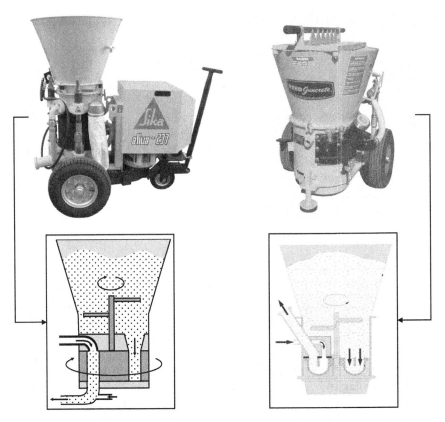

Figure 8.2 Continuous feed guns (a) rotary barrel type and (b) rotary bowl type. (Photo on left courtesy of Sika and photo on right courtesy of Reed Shotcrete Equipment.)

shotcrete. A longer delivery distance and larger hose diameter will require a larger air compressor to achieve proper material velocity at the nozzle. Manufacturers usually supply tables or graphs to properly combine rotor size, hose size and the required minimum air compressor output (m³/min or CFM) for their equipment. Examples of such selection tables are provided in Figures 8.3 and 8.4.

While a steady flow of material can readily be achieved by careful selection of the shotcrete equipment, when trouble arises, it is often the airflow (m³/min or CFM) itself that is deficient. Indeed, the volume of air per unit of time produced by the air compressor is used not only to "push" the material down the hose, but is also often used to run an air motor on the gun itself, one or two vibrators on the gun hopper, and, depending on the job site, may also be used for other tasks such as air blowing surfaces dry during shooting. In such cases, the air compressor size requirement (m³/min or CFM) can therefore be significantly larger than that illustrated in Figure 8.3.

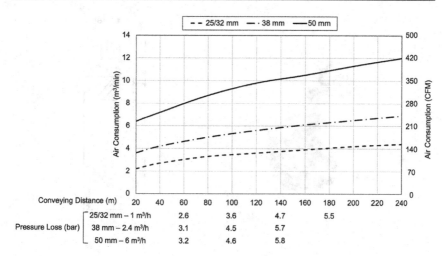

| 25/32 mm | - - - 38 mm | 50 mm |

Figure 8.3 Compressor output requirements.

(Graph adapted from Aliva, 2016; courtesy of Sika.)

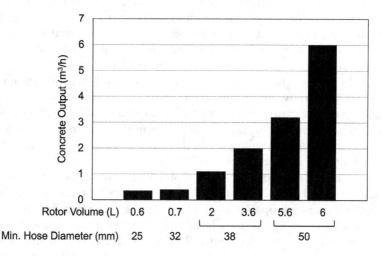

Figure 8.4 Minimum hose size and typical output for different barrel-type continuous feed guns.

(Graph adapted from Aliva, 2016; courtesy of Sika.)

8.2.2 Water addition

There is probably nothing more infuriating to a nozzleman than to have to continuously adjust the water valve at the nozzle in order to try to maintain the desired consistency of the fresh dry-mix shotcrete being placed. The fact is, in most cases where this happens, the problem has to do with the delivery

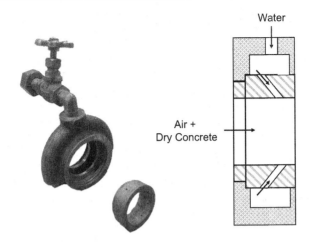

Figure 8.5 Examples of water rings.

of water at the nozzle. To clearly understand the situation, one must visualize the inside of the nozzle where the water ring is placed (see Figure 8.5); there must be enough water coming into the hose at a *sufficiently high pressure* to help create a curtain of water jet that the dry material will traverse, distributing the water in the material stream as evenly as possible.

The most common misconception when trouble arises with water addition at the nozzle is to assume that it is a problem with the *amount* of water available (waterflow, litre/min), while most of the time the problem lies with the water *pressure* (bar). Nonetheless, running out of sufficient water addition at the nozzle, or not having sufficient pressure to force water into the hose at the nozzle, will result in the same unwanted situation; the dry-mix shotcrete exiting the nozzle will be insufficiently or only partially wetted, and most likely one or more holes in the water ring will become plugged by sand and cement particles from the dry-material stream. While stopping shotcreting operations to clean out the water ring may temporarily fix the problem, it will only last until the water pressure or flow drops again, even if only momentarily, allowing sand and cement particles to enter the water ring again. This is the reason why most publications on the subject strongly encourage nozzleman to use a booster pump on the water line to provide a suitable water pressure at the nozzle (ACI CCS-4, 2020; Yoggy et al., 1995).

The situation described where water pressure is insufficient is particularly critical when using a hydromix nozzle, i.e. a nozzle body where the water-ring is located up to 3 m before the exit of the hose (Figure 8.6). This hydromix nozzle is often used as a pre-dampening system as it helps reduce dust emissions and rebound. Indeed, as seen in Figure 8.6, with such a layout, the air pressure found in the hose at the point of water entry is higher than what is found for a conventional "short" dry-mix shotcrete nozzle. A water

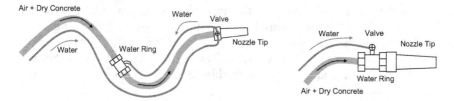

Figure 8.6 Hydromix nozzle and standard dry-mix shotcrete nozzle.

booster pump with sufficient pressure is quite important in order to not only maintain positive discharge of water towards the inside of the hose but to also create sufficient turbulence to maximize water distribution throughout the dry-material stream.

8.2.3 Dry-mix shotcrete nozzle

The dry-mix shotcrete nozzle body contains a water ring and the nozzle tip. While details regarding the water ring have been discussed in the previous section, much still needs to be said about the nozzle tip (see Figure 8.7). Indeed, the nozzle tip is usually made of some sort of rubber, plastic or metal attached to the nozzle body. It characteristically has an exit diameter slightly smaller than that of the hose in order to impart final acceleration of the material to the receiving surface. It is also the device used to create turbulence to promote as much integral mixing of the water in the dry material stream as possible. Nozzle tips come in different shapes and sizes (see Figure 8.7) with some generating more turbulence than others. Some are designed to provide a more tightly controlled stream of material exiting the nozzle, i.e. provide a more *rifling* type of action, with a higher impacting velocity. In general, the longer the nozzle, the tighter the material stream

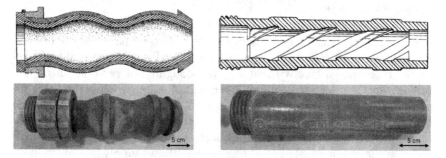

Figure 8.7 Typical nozzle tips for dry-mix shotcrete.

(Spirolet schematic (left): Breunsbach, M. C. (1972). US3743187A. U. S. P. Office. Spirolet Corporation; Double-bubble schematic (right): Mccormack, L. E. (1954). US2690901A. U. S. P. Office. Gunite Concrete and Construction Company.)

exiting the nozzle and the higher the impacting velocity, and the shorter the nozzle tip, the wider the material stream and the lower the impacting velocity. In general, longer shotcrete nozzles are used for shooting thicker, more heavily reinforced shotcrete walls and other structural elements. Shorter nozzles are more commonly used in thinner shotcrete elements and finish coats.

While the development of nozzles (tips and body) over the past few decades has not been quite as active as it has been for other dry-mix shotcrete equipment components, recent advances in development of a high-pressure water ring and double-walled nozzle tip have brought the focus back onto this essential component of dry-mix shotcrete equipment (see Section 7.4.3.2). Based on the results of research published on shotcrete velocity profiles and their effects on rebound (Ginouse and Jolin, 2014), it is expected that we will see more developments in this field, which should ultimately result in dry-mix shotcretes generating much lower rebound and overspray in the near future.

8.3 WET-MIX SHOTCRETE

Wet-mix shotcrete is defined as a *shotcrete in which the ingredients, including water, are mixed before introduction into the delivery hose* (ACI CT-18, 2018). To someone new to the shotcrete world, this process will appear more intuitive than the dry-mix shotcrete process. Indeed, wet-mix shotcrete consists of preparing a fully mixed fresh concrete mixture and discharging it into a shotcrete pump. The pump conveys the material to the end of the hose, where the attached nozzle is equipped with an *air ring* that introduces compressed air into the stream, spraying the pumped material out of the nozzle at high velocity towards the receiving surface (see Figure 8.8). With this process, the nozzleman controls the amount of compressed air introduced at the nozzle (as opposed to controlling the water added at the nozzle in the dry-mix shotcrete process).

The main challenge in conventional wet-mix shotcrete production is to overcome the apparent contradiction of having to prepare a shotcrete mix that will allow it to be easily pumped and yet adhere to and build-up well on the receiving surface without sagging, sloughing or fall-out. This is the reason why the selection of the shotcrete mixture design as per the guidance provided in Chapter 6 is so important. A distinction also needs to be made between plain wet-mix shotcrete applications and applications that require the addition of an accelerator at the nozzle. Because the accelerator is introduced at the nozzle in wet-mix shotcrete, this allows supply of a much more workable mix to the pump (slumps in the range of 180–220 mm are common), but will, at the same time, require a shotcrete pumping system that minimizes, and ideally eliminates, the surging or pulsating of material flow

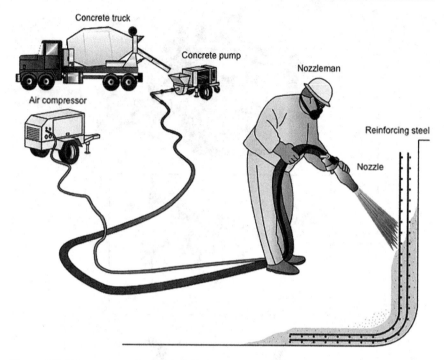

Figure 8.8 Schematics of a typical wet-mix shotcrete layout.

at the nozzle in order to have distribution of the accelerator as uniform as possible in the *in-place* shotcrete. This is unfortunately easier said than done. Wet-mix shotcrete applications with accelerator addition at the nozzle, which have resulted in layered shotcrete or inconsistent setting time of the shotcrete over the sprayed surface, are still encountered on job sites. The next sections provide guidance on the selection of suitable equipment for the production of quality wet-mix shotcrete.

8.3.1 Pump

A lot could be said about shotcrete pumps given all the different models available on the market. While some small repair applications may use small rotor/stator or peristaltic (a.k.a. squeeze pumps) to convey the material down the line, most shotcrete applications today rely on pumps with pistons and a swing tube configuration to pump the shotcrete. Although such pumps are very popular and available in various sizes, the challenge in selecting the pump is to make sure its size is suitable for the job at hand (see Figure 8.9). Indeed, smaller repair jobs will probably need a pump that allows for a lower output (say 5–10 m³/h) and smaller output hose diameter (typically 37.5 mm inside hose diameter). Medium to large size jobs will

Figure 8.9 Wet-mix shotcrete pumps.

(Top photos courtesy Reed Shotcrete Equipment; bottom photo courtesy Putzmeister America Shotcrete Technology.)

have pumps that have output rates of 10–15 m³/h and above and require a larger hose inside diameter (typically 50 mm inside hose diameter).

One should however realize that typical hand-held nozzle work using a maximum internal diameter hose size of 50 mm will seldom exceed a 10–12 m³/h production rate (Schallom, 2009). By contrast, when placement takes place from a man basket or a swing stage for example and the wet-mix shotcrete hose is tied to it so the nozzleman "only" has to direct the nozzle (as opposed to supporting its weight as well), the production rate may be increased to 15–18 m³/h. It should, however, be cautioned that the selection of a large concrete pump is generally not the answer to increased production. In fact, too large a pump can be difficult to use for shotcreting by hand if its output flow cannot be reduced to a level the nozzleman is comfortable with handling, and this can reduce productivity by creating shotcrete thicknesses above specified requirements, increase rate of material losses, as well as causing potential safety issues. Higher output will require the use of remote-control hydraulic placement arms and larger hose diameters (50 mm inside diameter and above) along with a larger air compressor for air supply to the nozzle.

Another important aspect to consider in the selection of a pump for shotcreting is its capacity to push relatively low workability fresh shotcrete through the hose, i.e. its maximum hydraulic (and hence concrete face) pressure. While most concrete pumps will provide up to 70 bar (1015 psi) of pressure, pumps designed for shotcrete will as much as double the available pressure in order to enable proper movement of the fresh shotcrete in the hose, even when the workability is low. These shotcrete pumps are also designed to minimize the surging or the pause of material at the nozzle when the swing valve changes between cylinders during pumping; this is done not only to reduce stress on the nozzleman and the equipment, but also in shotcrete with accelerator addition at the nozzle, to maximize uniform accelerator distribution in the shotcrete stream (see Section 8.3.4).

8.3.2 Reducers and hoses

While the selection of reducers and hoses may seem to be of less importance than other aspects of wet-mix shotcrete placement equipment, it is often an important item which can make the difference between a successful pumping operation and one that is plagued by blockages. Obviously, the pressure required by the pump to convey the material down the hose towards the nozzle will vary greatly depending on the mixture design and its workability, but it will also depend on the reducer type and hose layout. The nature of the movement of concrete under pressure means that it moves as a plug in the hose, requiring the presence of a lubricating layer on its outer edge against the hose inside surface (Jolin et al., 2006; Kaplan et al., 2005). Also, given this plug-like movement, a reduction in hose diameter will require changes in the fresh shotcrete material where the aggregates rearrange themselves during pumping making more paste available to the outer surface of the line for lubrication. This explains why most of the blockages which occur during concrete pumping occur at the reducer near the pump (Jolin et al., 2009). Moreover, a fact often overlooked is that steel pipes generate about a third (or even less) of the friction of a rubber hose (Kultgen, 2016). Of course, a lot will depend on the wet-mix shotcrete mixture design itself as well as proper lubricating of the line prior to introduction of shotcrete into the system, but nonetheless it is possible to formulate a few recommendations for the selection of reducers and hoses:

- Use long, straight reducers at the exit from the pump. Typically, a 125 mm diameter pump outlet should be reduced to a 50 mm diameter hose over about a 1.5 m to 2 m length. Short elbow-reducers often found in conventional concrete pumping should be avoided;
- As pumping distances increase, use steel pipe to get as close to the point of placement as possible before switching to rubber hose;
- Given that larger diameter hoses generate less friction, it is possible for even longer pumping distances to pump in larger diameter steel pipe (typically 100 mm diameter) and place the reducer and rubber hose closer to the point of placement; and
- In all cases, make sure that the pressure rating of all the equipment, and especially the pipes, hoses and couplings, is adequate for the concrete/shotcrete pump used; concrete/shotcrete face pressure can vary widely depending on the pump selected.

8.3.3 Nozzle

Apart from the research reported in Chapter 7, there has been very limited active R&D on the subject of nozzles in wet-mix shotcrete. Although the perception is that because wet-mix shotcrete is already fully mixed before it is placed in the pump, the action of the nozzle is of less importance; this could not be further from reality (Bridger, 2006). Indeed, in the very short distance from where the shotcrete arrives at the air ring and gets accelerated and exits the nozzle tip (see Figure 8.10), a lot can happen. It is important to make sure that the air ring is clean and that all of the holes are free of hardened paste. The material exiting the nozzle must be sufficiently broken down and properly accelerated so it reaches the receiving surface and consolidates adequately. The use of a nozzle body with an inadequately sized air plenum, or nozzle body with a single-entry point for the air in the material stream, should be completely avoided.

The nozzle tip itself is of importance. Many nozzlemen will tell you of their preferred nozzle tip for a particular type of shotcrete application. In general, a shorter nozzle tip provides less exit velocity and longer nozzle tips with a tighter opening size will, on the other hand, create increased velocity. The reducing diameter shape of the nozzle tip is designed to control both the velocity and the spray pattern of the shotcrete material (Duckworth, 2010). The nature of the work and the available space for working will dictate which nozzle works best to achieve optimal compaction. It should be noted that the nozzle tip of a wet-mix shotcrete nozzle is a wear part; as the thickness decreases and flexibility increases due to the abrasion wear from passage of fresh shotcrete, it reduces the effectiveness of the nozzle tip and can

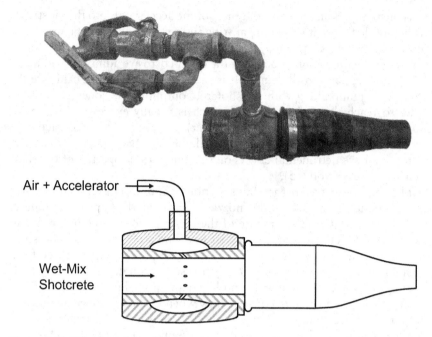

Figure 8.10 Wet-mix shotcrete nozzle.

eventually lead to a poorly controlled spray pattern and shotcrete consolidation problems.

An important element with respect to the wet-mix shotcrete nozzle is the diameter of the hose utilized to convey air from the air compressor to the nozzle. Indeed, this is often overlooked. The typical size of an air hose found on most North American job sites (19 mm diameter) is considered to generally be smaller than optimal for hand-held nozzling. It creates too much air-flow resistance, not feeding the nozzle with a sufficient volume of air to enable optimal dispersion of the shotcrete material (spraying) and compaction on the receiving surface. It is therefore recommended to use a minimum 25 mm diameter air hose to promote good material velocity at the exit from the nozzle (Duckworth, 2017). Of course, as for the size of the air compressor, the capacity (m^3/min or CFM) may need to be increased as the air hose diameter or the distance from the receiving surface increases.

8.3.4 The use of accelerators

The addition of liquid accelerator at the nozzle has to be done on site using an *accelerator pump* that discharges the admixture directly at the nozzle. This pump has to be sufficiently precise to deal with relatively low flow volumes (from 1 litre/min and up) and reliable enough to provide sufficient and constant pressure to force the entry of the accelerator into the air stream at the nozzle before it enters the air-ring inside the nozzle (see Figure 8.10). Most accelerator pumps today are peristaltic pumps which have the advantage of eliminating contact between the often-corrosive admixtures and any metal moving parts in the pump. It is mandatory to properly calibrate the accelerator pump along with the shotcrete output of the concrete pump in order to reach the desired dosage, which is usually expressed in litres of admixture per kilogram of cement (binder) in the technical manufacturer's data sheets (Zhang, 2012; Radomski et al., 2019). Overdosage of the accelerator can have detrimental effects on the long-term properties of the shotcrete (refer to Section 6.5).

It has been discussed before, but selection of appropriate equipment when an accelerator is added at the nozzle is particularly important. Indeed, because of the intermittent nature of the concrete flow at the pump due to the swing valve changing from cylinder to cylinder every few seconds, some surging is manifested at the nozzle. The intensity of this surging can go from a complete stop of concrete flow for up to a second (in the case of short hose length, low workability concrete and less than optimal pump construction), to only a slight reduction of concrete flow when the hose is long enough, and the pump has been built for shotcrete application (shorter travel distance and time for the swing valve and fast cylinder response for rapid pressure uptake in the hose). Strictly speaking, some surging is not a problem when spraying *without* using an accelerator because the wet-mix shotcrete is already completely mixed (note that too much surging will have a negative impact on equipment wear and nozzleman fatigue and can lead to safety concerns). However, surging during placement while *using* an accelerator introduced at the nozzle can create an unwanted situation that can have serious consequences for the quality of the in-place shotcrete and overall safety. Indeed, it is a simple problem of hydraulics: when shotcrete passes through the nozzle, it is the moment where the pressure inside the nozzle is the highest, therefore the time where the accelerator flow in the airstream is the lowest. Inversely, when surging occurs and the shotcrete flow reduces (or even momentarily stops), it is the moment where the pressure inside the nozzle is the lowest and therefore the accelerator flow in the airstream the highest (refer to Section 7.3.3). The result is that in some cases, still witnessed too often today, the nozzleman unwantedly "*paints*" a layer of accelerator onto the receiving surface in-between shotcrete strokes, not only creating poor bond between shotcrete layers, but also creating non-uniform setting and strength development of the shotcrete. This can lead to a potential safety hazards, particularly in the case of overhead wet-mix shotcrete applications.

Another potential source of improper dispersion of the accelerator in the in-place shotcrete is the use of a poorly designed nozzle, where the accelerator port is placed directly on the air plenum instead of being placed on the air inlet. Experience shows that this will also lead to an uneven distribution of accelerator and, again, non-uniform setting and strength development of the shotcrete.

In summary, it is important to select a suitable pump, accelerating dispensing system, and nozzle type (in addition to having an appropriate shotcrete mixture design and consistency) to produce a high-quality shotcrete with uniform dispersion of accelerator throughout the mix and satisfactory plastic and hardened properties.

REFERENCES

ACI CCS-4. 2020. *Shotcrete for the Craftsman*. American Concrete Institute. 92 p.

ACI 506R-16. 2016. *Guide to Shotcrete*. American Concrete Institute. 52 p.

ACI CT-18. 2018. *Concrete Terminology*. American Concrete Institute. 80 p.

Aliva. 2016. *Aliva 257 Top – Concrete spraying machine, User Manual*, Operating manual, 2016 Sika Schweiz AG. Aliva Equipment, 86 p.

Bridger, P. 2006. Wet-Mix Shotcrete Nozzles. *Shotcrete Magazine, American Shotcrete Association* Winter 2006. 32 p.

Bridger, P. 2017. The History of Shotcrete Equipment. *Shotcrete Magazine, American Shotcrete Association* Fall 2017. 34–37.

Duckworth, O. 2010. Are You Using the Right Wet-Mix Nozzle. *Shotcrete Magazine, American Shotcrete Association* Spring 2010. 36–39.

Duckworth, O. 2017. Trouble in the Air: Common Air System Errors Influence Shotcrete Quality. *Shotcrete Magazine, American Shotcrete Association* Winter 2017. 68–70.

Ginouse, N. and Jolin, M. 2014. Effect of Equipment on Spray Velocity Distribution in Shotcrete Applications. *Construction and Building Materials*. Vol. 70. 362–369.

Jolin, M., Chapdelaine, F., Gagnon, F. and Beaupré, D. 2006. Pumping Concrete: A Fundamental and Practical Approach. *Shotcrete for Underground Support X – Proceedings of the Tenth International Conference on Shotcrete for Underground Support*, 215: 334–347. American Society of Civil Engineers (ASCE). doi: 10.1061/40885(215)28.

Jolin, M., Burns, D. and Bissonnette, B. 2009. Understanding the Pumpability of Concrete. *Conference on Shotcrete for Underground Support XI*, Davos, Switzerland, March 2009.

Kaplan, D., De Larrard, F. and Sedran, T. 2005 Design of Concrete Pumping Circuit. *ACI Materials Journal*. Vol. 102. No. 2. 110–117.

Kultgen, A. 2016. Steel Pipe: More Volume, Less Cost. Shotcrete Magazine, American Shotcrete Association Fall, 2016. 32–34.

Radomski, S. M., Morgan, D. R., Zhang, L. and Graham, D. 2019. Structural Modifications to Hydroelectrical Turbine Draft Tube Ceiling. *Shotcrete Magazine. American Shotcrete Association*. Summer 2019. 22–34.

Schallom, R. 2009. What You Need to Know Before Selecting a Wet-Mix Shotcrete Pump. *Shotcrete Magazine, American Shotcrete Association* Summer 2009. 6–8.

Zhang, L., 2012. Accelerator Dosing Pump Calibration and Verification. *Shotcrete Magazine, American Shotcrete Association* Summer 2012. 2–4.

Yoggy, G., Schallom, R. and Mooney, M. 1995. *The Theory and Practice of Dry Shotcrete for Underground Mines*. NORCAT – Norther Centre for Advanced Technology. 67 p.

Chapter 9

Shotcrete application

9.1 INTRODUCTION

The American Concrete Institute *CT-18 Concrete Terminology* defines shotcrete as *Concrete placed by a high-velocity pneumatic projection from a nozzle*. In the dry-mix shotcrete process, the preblended shotcrete materials are conveyed by the shotcrete *gun* down a suitably sized hose by compressed air. For most equipment, mixing water is added through a water ring in the nozzle and mixing takes place in the nozzle and on the receiving surface through nozzle manipulation. It was recognized by Carl Akeley in 1908 that it is important that the shotcrete be applied at sufficient impacting velocity to achieve high-quality in-place compaction. Figure 9.1 shows a nozzleman applying dry-mix shotcrete (*gunite*) for construction of a water storage facility in Pittsburgh in 1919 (Yoggy, 2000). The same basic principles developed for quality dry-mix shotcrete construction in the early 1900s have changed little in the over 120 years since invention of the process and still apply today.

In the wet-mix shotcrete process, the mixing water is added to the shotcrete materials during batching (just like conventional concrete) and the resulting concrete-like mixture is discharged into a shotcrete pump. The pump conveys the shotcrete mix at high pressure (up to 17 MPa) down a high-pressure hose to the nozzle where air is added to pneumatically project the shotcrete at high impacting velocity onto the receiving surface. Note that the ACI definition for shotcrete does not include other methods for projecting concrete or mortar onto a receiving surface, such as *centrifugal placed concrete* (Morgan et al., 2010).

The sections which follow comment on things that need to be done on a typical structural shotcrete project before shotcrete application can proceed. These include surface preparation, design and installation of formwork and scaffolding (where appropriate), fixing and setting of reinforcing steel and anchors, setting up for control of alignment and tolerance, joint construction details and protection of adjacent surfaces. This is followed by a description of the shotcrete crew and their responsibilities. Details are

DOI: 10.1201/9780429169946-10

Figure 9.1 Dry-mix shotcrete application in water reservoir in Pittsburgh in 1919.

provided regarding the correct placement methods for both the dry- and wet-mix shotcrete processes. Included are descriptions of the bench shooting method and layer shooting method, as well as correct methods to properly encapsulate reinforcing steel and other inclusions in the shotcrete. Finally, sections are provided describing different types of shotcrete finish achievable and last, but not least, protection and curing measures that should be adopted during and after shotcrete application.

9.2 SURFACE PREPARATION

In most infrastructure repair and rehabilitation cases, the shotcrete will be applied to existing prepared concrete surfaces, although in some structures, such as historic masonry structures, it may also be applied to brick or stone masonry. Irrespective of the substrate medium, proper preparation of the substrate surface prior to the application of shotcrete is critical for integral bond of the shotcrete to the substrate. The bond must be sound in both the short and long term (Talbot et al., 1995). For concrete, a minimum tensile bond strength of 1.0 MPa is often specified (Reny, 2013), although the Canadian Standards Association (CSA A23.1) permits a minimum bond strength of 0.9 MPa and the American Concrete Institute (ACI 506R-16, 2016) states that *properly applied shotcrete with sufficient consolidation on a properly prepared substrate usually develops a bond strength of over* 145 psi (1.0 MPa).

The International Concrete Repair Institute (ICRI 310.2R-2013) provides guidance regarding different types of methods that can be used to prepare substrate concrete surfaces for repair. They also provide examples of the different types of Concrete Surface Profiles (CSPs) that can be produced using these different methods (see Section 6.10). The U.S. Department of the Interior Bureau of Reclamation also provides valuable advice regarding *Best Practices for Preparing Concrete Surfaces Prior to Repairs and Overlays* (Bissonnette et al., 2012).

There are various means of preparing existing substrate concrete surfaces prior to shotcrete application. These include:

a) High-pressure water blasting (sometimes referred to as hydrodemolition or hydromilling)
b) Wet grit blasting
c) Sand Blasting
d) Steel shot blasting
e) Chipping with light-duty (not more than 7 kg) chipping hammers
f) Mechanical removal with scabblers, bush-hammers or scarifiers
g) Grinding
h) Diamond wire saw cutting to remove slabs of concrete, followed by use of one of the above methods to roughen the cut concrete surface.

There are pros and cons to each of these methods. The following is a brief discussion of the relative merits and limitations of these various procedures.

Where practical and economically feasible, high-pressure water blasting at pressures around 3.5 times the compressive strength of the concrete is probably the best method of removing surface concrete to provide a sound, roughened substrate surface well suited to optimal shotcrete bond, e.g. for a concrete with a 40 MPa compressive strength, the water pressure should be about 140 MPa. *Hydromilling* must, however, be followed with lower pressure water washing (typically 30 MPa or more) to remove any residual laitance or slurry from the hydro blasting process and leave a clean substrate. The International Concrete Repair Institute provides more details regarding the use of this method in their publication ICRI 310.3R-2014, 2014 *Guidelines for the Preparation of Concrete Surfaces for Repair Using Hydrodemolition Methods.*

Heavy-duty sand blasting can be a technically and cost-effective method for preparing concrete and other types of substrates for shotcrete application. Figure 9.2 shows application of a wet-mix steel fibre-reinforced shotcrete to the upstream face of the Littlerock Dam in California, as part of a major seismic retrofit of this structure. The substrate concrete was prepared by heavy-duty sand blasting to meet a specified surface roughness profile with a minimum of three 5 mm peak to valley measurements over a 150 mm

Figure 9.2 Wet-mix steel fibre-reinforced shotcrete application to upstream face of Littlerock Dam in California.

length, or five 4 mm peak to valley measurements over a 150 mm length. Details regarding the method of measuring the profile and typical recorded values are provided in a paper by Forrest et al (Forrest et al., 1995).

Wet grit blasting can achieve results similar to heavy-duty sand blasting but is more suited to use in closed spaces where the dust from dry sand blasting would not be acceptable, e.g. inside culverts or bridge box girder structures. The main advantages of both sand blasting and wet grit blasting are that they leave the substrate in a condition ready for shotcrete application, other than for the need to presaturate the substrate with potable water and allow it to dry back to a saturated surface dry (SSD) condition prior to shotcrete application.

Steel shot blasting can be used on horizontal concrete surfaces to prepare the substrate with a suitably roughened surface texture. It should, however, be followed up with water pressure blasting (minimum 30-MPa pressure) to remove any *bruised* surface concrete from the shot blasting process. Such water pressure blasting is also an effective means of bringing the concrete to an SSD condition.

Where considerable thicknesses of substrate concrete need to be removed, such as in removal of concrete around corroded reinforcing steel, or removal of concrete damaged by frost action or alkali-aggregate reactivity, the use of hand-held light-duty chipping hammers can be effective. Such hammers should not exceed 7 kg in mass, as heavier duty chipping hammers can cause cracking and damage to the substrate concrete. The use of machine-mounted concrete breakers should be avoided as they can cause major damage to the substrate concrete. Concrete removal with light-duty chipping hammers should always be followed by water pressure blasting to remove the *bruised* layer from the chipping process.

Mechanical concrete removal devices, such as scabblers, bush hammers and scarifiers are sometimes used to prepare substrate concrete surfaces, particularly where greater thicknesses of concrete are required to be removed than can be achieved with sand blasting or wet grit blasting. These devices can be used to prepare concrete substrates to different specified surface roughness profiles. ICRI (ICRI 310.2R-2013, 2013) provides examples of different types of surface roughness profiles that can be achieved. CSP in the range of No. 6 to No. 9 are commonly specified for shotcrete repairs. Such mechanical removal processes should always be followed by water pressure blasting (minimum 30 MPa pressure) to remove concrete *bruised* by the mechanical removal devices.

Grinding has been used by some contractors to remove defective surface concrete (e.g. concrete weakened by early-age carbonation). While it can be effective in removing such weakened surface concrete, it usually results in an excessively smooth surface and should be followed up by one of the above water, sand or wet grit blasting, or mechanical removal processes to achieve a suitable surface roughness profile.

In patch-type repairs, the procedures detailed in the ACI RAP Bulletin 6 should be used in preparation of substrate concrete prior to shotcrete application. In particular, the prepared cavity should be generally square or rectangular in shape. The edges of the patch area should be saw cut perpendicular to the surface to a depth of about 15 to 20 mm in order to avoid *featheredging* of the shotcrete repair material. In the C-SHRP study on durability of shotcrete repairs to highway bridges previously referred to (Morgan and Neill, 1991), tapered shotcrete patch repairs were found to have resulted in peeling-type delaminations at the edges of patches.

Where corrosion of the reinforcing steel exists, concrete removal should continue along the reinforcing steel and any adjacent areas with evidence of corrosion-induced damage until sound concrete and corrosion-free reinforcing steel is reached. The International Concrete Repair Institute (ICRI 310.1R-2008, 2008) provides guidance regarding *Surface Preparation for the Repair of Concrete Resulting from Reinforcing Steel Corrosion*. Corroded reinforcing steel should be undercut to at least the diameter of the bar, or 20 mm, whichever is greater. This is required in order to enable full encapsulation of the reinforcing steel in the patch area with new shotcrete. The shotcrete builds up from behind the bars to envelop them during shooting; if the clearance behind the bar is too low, this encapsulation process can be compromised, and *shadows* or voids can form behind the bars. Proper preparation is illustrated in Figure 9.3 which follows.

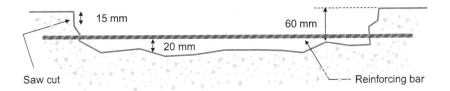

Figure 9.3 Schematic of corroded reinforcing steel area prepared for shotcreting.

9.2.1 Bonding agents

In cast-in-place concrete repairs, bonding agents such as wet-to-dry epoxies, latex polymers or latex modified cementitious slurries, or plain Portland-cement-based slurries are often used to bond the repair concrete to the substrate material. The question is often asked as to whether such bonding agents should be used in shotcrete repair applications. The answer is a definitive "NO!" (Reny, 2013). The shotcrete application process, when properly applied, results in excellent bond to the substrate. The cement paste is driven into the roughened substrate surface at a high impacting velocity resulting in optimal bond. Figure 9.4 provides a good example of the intimate bond to a substrate concrete achieved with the shotcrete process.

For shotcrete, after removal and roughening of the substrate concrete using one of the methods described above, the correct substrate preparation

Figure 9.4 Shotcrete bond to substrate concrete in a core extracted for tensile bond strength testing.

(Photo courtesy Randle Emmrich and Marcus H von der Hofen.)

procedure is to pre-saturate the substrate concrete with potable water and then allow it to dry back to a Saturated Surface Dry (SSD) condition immediately prior to shotcrete application. If dry-back to SSD is too slow, oil-free compressed air applied through a blow-pipe can be used to accelerate the dry-back process. If the substrate dries back excessively, fogging sprays with potable water can be used to bring the substrate back to an SSD condition.

Shotcrete should not be applied to a bone-dry substrate surface, as this can suck moisture out at the bond interface and result in reduced shotcrete bond strength. Even more importantly, shotcrete should not be applied to a substrate with free liquid water on the surface, as this can result in a high water/cement ratio at the critical bond interface and drastically reduce bond strengths. A major infrastructure retrofit project where the contractor sprayed down the prepared substrate concrete surface with water immediately prior to shotcrete application and failed to meet the specified 1.0 MPa tensile bond strength has been reported and documented. Many of the tensile bond test cores failed during coring and those that remained intact struggled to reach 0.5 MPa and the contractor lost a contract for a million-dollar project.

Some design engineers have specified the use of bonding agents such as wet-to-dry epoxies, or latex modified slurries in shotcrete repairs. While such systems can be made to work with formed cast-in-place concrete repairs, or concrete overlays, they are totally unsuitable for shotcrete repairs. Not only are they not needed, but they can result in failures. If the material is not sufficiently *tacky* at the time of shotcrete application, it can result in shotcrete sloughing off vertical and/or overhead surfaces. If the contractor waits too long and the bonding agent sets or dries out before shotcrete application, it can act as a debonding agent. The first author witnessed such failure in shotcrete applied to a wet-to-dry epoxy bonding agent on the sides and soffits of beams in a marine pier retrofit project. The design engineer was persuaded to remove the requirement for a bonding agent from the project specifications and the shotcrete remedial work then proceeded well with shotcrete directly applied to a suitably prepared SSD concrete substrate surface.

9.3 FORMWORK AND SCAFFOLDING

While much shotcrete is applied to soil or rock, or in infrastructure rehabilitation to prepared concrete or masonry substrate surfaces, it can also be applied to a wide range of different types of formwork. Formwork types include:

a) Rigid sealed plywood forms (the same as used in cast-in-place concrete construction);
b) Wooden board forms (sometimes used when the architect wants the stripped face of the shotcrete to show a board-form finish);

c) Plywood forms with polyurethane or other types of textured form liners, where special architectural finishes, such as stamped concrete type patterns, or artificial rock type appearances are required;
d) Glass fibre-reinforced moulds with sprayed latex rubber linings to produce special shotcrete sculptures (e.g. Centre Street Bridge Calgary shotcrete lions [Kroman et al., 2002]);
e) Expanded metal lath (as in bobsleigh and luge track construction [ASA, 2008]);
f) Rigid steel forms, or structural steel beams, columns or other elements;
g) Air supported, polyurethane foam lined forms, as in inflated dome construction (Zweifel, 2010); and
h) Flexible forms composed of a rebar armature to create the desired shape, with a plastic scrim cloth fixed with ties to the armature (as in hollow artificial rock construction and construction of ventilation seals in mines).

The sections which follow elaborate on some of these different types of formwork. Discussion is also provided regarding scaffolding considerations, where appropriate.

By far the most common type of formwork used in structural shotcrete construction is rigid sealed plywood forms. Steel forms are also sometimes used. Single-sided forms are used in construction of structural walls, pilasters, columns, header beams and other types of structural elements. Heights of such forms can range from as little as one metre (e.g. in planter box construction), to up to 12 m or more in two to three-story high structural shotcrete walls. Figure 9.5 shows a good example of steel formwork erected for construction of a high wall with structural wet-mix shotcrete for the 2010 Winter Olympics Preparation Centre in Surrey, British Columbia (ASA, 2010). Figure 9.6 shows a view of the completed high wall.

While there is no formwork pressure on such forms during shotcrete construction (such as would be exerted by plastic concrete in formed, cast-in-place-concrete construction), it is important that the forms be adequately braced against tipping over, as well as being braced against a *toppling* (tipping forward) type of failure, as shown in Figure 9.5. Design calculations for formwork bracing should include resistance to wind gusts, as well as forces that could be exerted by the mass of the reinforcing steel and freshly applied shotcrete *toppling*. Over the entire spraying surface, the actual forces applied by the impacting shotcrete during shotcrete placement are relatively small and can generally be ignored. A study on the subject at Université Laval recorded maximum forces in normal spraying conditions of 100 N and 200 N for the dry-mix and wet-mix shotcrete process, respectively (Gagnon and Jolin, 2007).

Zynda (Zynda, 2008) provides good examples of a variety of different types of projects constructed with single-sided plywood forms. For load-bearing structural elements such as beams, the forms need to be braced or

Figure 9.5 Single-sided steel formwork and scaffolding erected for construction of a 12.2 m high structural shotcrete wall for the 2010 Winter Olympics Preparation Centre in Surrey, British Columbia.

(Photo courtesy T. Ross King, Consolidated Shotcrete Inc.)

shored so that no deflection occurs under the dead load of the plastic shotcrete. The shotcrete needs to develop the compressive strength specified by the structural engineer before any formwork removal. Also, beams should be re-shored after formwork removal for the period specified by the structural engineer. For most low walls, while technically the forms could be removed as soon as the shotcrete has reached final set, in practice the forms are typically left in place for at least a couple of days before formwork removal, in order to help protect the shotcrete from damage during formwork stripping.

A variety of different techniques can be used for forming and shooting pilasters and columns. In addition to the back form, some contractors like to erect side forms on either side of the column or pilaster. Such work generally needs to be carried out with the use of a blowpipe, such that rebound is continuously blown out of the wall or pilaster during shooting. Other contractors prefer to place a form on only one side of the column or pilaster and use a vertical shooting wire to define the other edge of the element. The potential for entrapment of rebound is reduced with this method. For columns or pilasters with multiple layers of steel and/or dense reinforcement, some contractors will dispense with side forms altogether and use shooting

Figure 9.6 View of completed structural shotcrete wall for 2010 Winter Olympics Preparation Centre in Surrey, British Columbia.

(Photo courtesy T. Ross King, Consolidated Shotcrete Inc.)

wires to define the edges of the elements. Round free-standing columns have also been shot without the use of any formwork, using shooting wires only to control line and grade. Irrespective of the method of forming, it is usually desirable to use a blow pipe to remove excess rebound and overspray when shooting columns and pilasters. In addition, in more heavily reinforced elements, the judicious use of an immersion (pencil) vibrator may be needed to provide full encapsulation of the reinforcing steel with shotcrete.

An example of the use of expanded metal lath as formwork in construction of a bobsleigh/luge track at the Whistler Sliding Centre, for the 2010 Winter Olympic Games is provided in Section 10.7. In such cases, shotcrete is typically applied to both sides of the metal lath. Expanded metal lath has also been widely used for construction of tunnel portal canopies, and in mining in construction of bulkheads and ventilation seals in drifts and other underground openings. The lath is fixed to reinforcing steel and other elements (e.g. lattice girders, rock bolts, steel sets), and is typically shot from both sides and becomes completely encased in the shotcrete. This provides additional reinforcement to the structure. Section 10.5 provides a description of the use of air-supported forms for construction of structures such as domes.

With respect to scaffolding, it is important that it be designed, erected, inspected and tagged in conformance with the requirements of the local authorities having jurisdiction. Scaffolding should be wide enough to allow the nozzleman to be positioned at the optimal shooting distance from the work and enable workers such as the hose dragger, blow pipe operator and finishers to pass by the nozzleman without interfering with the shooting operations. All scaffolding should have back braces to protect the nozzleman from getting blown off the scaffold in the event of an uncontrolled release of a plug at the shotcrete nozzle. Many jurisdictions also require the installation of *toe boards* on the scaffold planks to protect workers below from accidentally falling tools and other objects. Figure 9.7 provides an example of a shotcrete scaffold with back braces and *toe boards*. *Housekeeping* is important and labourers should continuously remove rebound and cuttings and trimmings from finishing operations from the scaffold boards to provide a safe working environment for the shotcrete crew.

When the form is stripped it provides an immediate quality control indicator of the adequacy of the shotcreting operation. Well placed shotcrete should be blemish free without any voids, rock pockets (entrapped rebound) or *shadows* (porous zones) behind reinforcing steel. *Shadows* should not be confused with a slightly darker colour that sometimes appears in the stripped shotcrete surface behind the location of reinforcing steel. Coring at such

Figure 9.7 Typical shotcrete scaffold with back braces and *toe boards*.

(Photo courtesy American Shotcrete Association.)

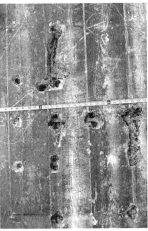

Figure 9.8 Voids and *shadows* behind a poorly shot swimming pool wall.

darker-coloured locations has demonstrated that the shotcrete was sound and dense, and the imaging of the rebar locations was attributable to subtle variations in the paste content in the shotcrete matrix behind the back layer of reinforcing steel arising from the shooting process. By contrast, Figure 9.8 shows a poorly shot swimming pool wall with serious voids and *shadows* behind the back layer of reinforcing steel.

9.4 REINFORCEMENT

Unreinforced shotcrete (like unreinforced concrete) has low tensile strength compared to its compressive strength (only about 12% to 15%). It thus requires reinforcement to carry tensile and shear loads and limit the development and width and depth of cracking from restrained drying shrinkage, autogenous shrinkage and differential thermal stresses.

A variety of different types of reinforcement have been used in shotcrete construction. These include:

a) Welded wire mesh fabric (and occasionally woven *chicken wire* mesh has been used in some ground support and mining applications, but it is generally not recommended);
b) Conventional reinforcing steel bars (as used in reinforced concrete design and construction);
c) Steel fibre reinforcement (including black steel and stainless steel fibres);
d) Macro synthetic fibre reinforcement (including polypropylene, polyethylene, carbon and polyvinyl acetate fibres);
e) Expanded metal lath (such as *Stayform*);

f) Glass fibre/resin bars; and

g) Glass fibre reinforcement (usually chopped strand added at the nozzle).

The above types of reinforcement may be used alone, or in combination with one or more other types of reinforcement. For example, in bobsleigh/luge track construction, both conventional reinforcing steel bars and expanded metal lath constitute part of the track reinforcement (together with the steel cooling pipes). In some mining applications with severe ground deformation characteristics, steel fibre reinforcement (or macrosynthetic fibre reinforcement) in conjunction with welded wire mesh fabric and reinforcing steel *ladders* (or steel lattice girders) are used with the shotcrete to provide ground support.

The following is a brief review of the major reasons for and areas of usage and *pros and cons* of the above types of reinforcement.

9.4.1 Welded wire mesh

As far back as the early 1900s wire mesh fabric was used to limit the development and width and depth of cracking in dry-mix shotcrete from restrained drying shrinkage and differential thermal stresses. Depending on the size and spacing of the wires in the mesh, it also provided some limited structural reinforcement (ability to carry tensile and shear forces). Welded wire mesh is still used today, but on many projects (particularly in tunnelling and mining and some ground support applications) it has been replaced with steel or macro synthetic fibre reinforcement.

Welded wire mesh is best suited for use in relatively thin shotcrete applications (30 to 75 mm). In thicker applications, conventional reinforcing steel is generally better suited for use. Different sizes (spacing and diameter) of mesh reinforcement have been used in shotcrete, depending on the specifics of the application. Mesh spacings ranging from 152 mm × 152 mm to as little as 51 mm × 51 mm have been used. Wire diameters have ranged from 4.88 mm (US 6 gauge) to 3.40 mm (US 10 gauge), although other wire diameters have also been used. Table 9.1 shows the sizes of different types of welded wire mesh fabric commonly used in shotcrete.

The mesh is best supplied in sheet stock, rather than rolls, as sheet stock is more easily installed to line and grade and tolerance. The stiffer (4.88 mm

Table 9.1 Welded wire mesh fabric sizes

Nominal size	Metric designation	US designation
152 mm × 152 mm 4.88/4.88 mm diameter	152 × 152 MW18.7 × MW18.7	6 × 6 6/6
102 mm × 102 mm 4.11/4.11 mm diameter	102 × 102 MW13.3 × MW13.3	4 × 4 8/8
51 mm × 51 mm 3.40/3.40 mm diameter	51 × 51 MW9.1/MW9.1	2 × 2 10/10

diameter wire) mesh is best suited to installation on flat surfaces, such as walls and canal linings. The more pliable (4.11 mm diameter) wire is better suited to installation on irregular surfaces, such as blasted rock in slope stabilization and tunnelling and mining applications. The very pliable small size (3.40 mm diameter) closely spaced (51 mm × 51 mm) wire mesh is best suited for use in thin applications (30 to 50 mm thick), such as small patch repairs and thin bonded coatings to structural steel elements.

It is important that mesh be properly secured to anchor bars, pins or other reinforcing steel such that it does not move or vibrate excessively during shooting, as this can result in voids around the mesh and shotcrete delamination. In addition, the mesh should be properly *chaired* off the substrate to which the shotcrete will be applied, so that the shotcrete can build from behind the mesh during shooting to fully encapsulate the mesh. If this is not done, voids or *shadows* (porous zones) can develop behind the mesh. In overhead applications (such as in tunnelling and mining) the mesh should be secured to rock bolts or pins at sufficiently close spacings such that the mesh does not sag under the weight of the freshly applied shotcrete in the event that bond to the substrate is lost. (Effective bond can be lost at, or immediately behind the shotcrete/substrate interface in shotcrete application, particularly in ground conditions such as loose soils, wet clays and slaking ground.)

ACI 506R Guide to Shotcrete (ACI 506R-16, 2016) recommends that when mesh sheets intersect that they be lapped by at least 1.5 spaces in each direction, but in no case should the wires be spaced less than 50 mm apart. Where more than one sheet of mesh intersects at a joint, the excess mesh should be cut out, so that the nozzleman does not have to shoot through an area of excessively congested steel wires. The mesh should be securely tied using 1.3 mm diameter (16 gauge) or heavier tie wire, but large knots of tie wire, which could interfere with shooting operations should be avoided. From the above, it is apparent that the nozzleman faces more challenges the smaller the spaces between the wires in the mesh. Thus, the specification of closely spaced (51 mm × 51 mm) wire mesh should be used with caution.

9.4.2 Reinforcing steel bars

Shotcreting is a method of placing concrete and so the same principles that apply for reinforced concrete design also apply to structural shotcrete, but with some differences with respect to reinforcing steel installation. Reinforcing steel bars provide an obstruction to the shotcrete material stream during shotcrete placement and so bars should be designed and placed to provide the least possible interference with the shotcrete stream. In particular, it is recommended that:

a) The use of bundled bars should be avoided. The clearance between individual bars should be at least three times the maximum size of the largest aggregate particle in the shotcrete mixture.

b) Where possible, direct contact of reinforcing bars in lapped splices should be minimized. Non-contact splices with spacings of at least three times the diameter of the largest bar are preferred. Where contact lap splices are unavoidable, splice bars should preferably be placed back-to-back, rather than side-by-side, relative the orientation of the shotcrete stream, to better facilitate full encapsulation of the bars with shotcrete. *Cranked* contact splice bars are sometimes used in such applications to keep the vertical bars properly positioned in the thickness of the wall. (Note that there are exceptions to these recommendations; in hybrid shotcrete construction, for instance, where there is very heavy reinforcing steel congestion, and walls 1.0 m or greater in thickness, shotcrete application is followed by supplemental consolidation with immersion vibrators. Contractors will often prefer to have contact lap splices with rebar, in order to create more open *"windows"* for the nozzlemen to be able to insert the nozzle through during shooting. See Section 9.10.5 on hybrid shotcrete construction.)

c) More frequent securing of intersecting reinforcing bars (compared to reinforced cast-in-place-concrete construction) is required, in order to minimize vibration and the potential for movement of the bars during shotcrete placement. Some specifications require all intersecting steel bars to be rigidly tied to one another and to their anchors with 1.3 mm diameter (16 gauge) or heavier gauge tie wire. Large knots of tie wire should be avoided as they can impede the shotcrete stream, creating *shadows*.

d) When multiple layers of rebar are required to be installed overhead, common practice is to install the first layer of steel, connecting it to the anchors, and then apply shotcrete to cover this layer of rebar, allowing it to set before installing and shooting the next layer of rebar, and so on. In this way, indefinite thicknesses of reinforced shotcrete can be applied overhead (Morgan et al., 2006; Radomski et al., 2019). This same approach can be used if necessary, for construction of very heavily reinforced walls or other elements, with multiple layers of reinforcing steel.

Earlier versions of the ACI 506R Guide to Shotcrete suggested that the maximum size of rebar in shotcrete installations be limited to 15 mm diameter (15 M bars). However, while it is more challenging to properly encase larger diameter bars (and other inclusions, such as steel and plastic pipes), extensive practical experience during the past several decades in California and elsewhere has demonstrated that proper mix-design and experienced nozzlemen with proper training and skills can consistently thoroughly encapsulate 30 mm diameter (30M) and even larger size rebar. Warner reports that individual bars as large as 43 mm in diameter have been successfully encapsulated with shotcrete in seismic retrofit work in California (Warner, 2001).

It requires special shooting technique, such as shooting from either side of the bars, to prevent the formation of shadows or voids behind the bars. With multiple layers of rebar (in structural elements such as in pilasters, columns and shear walls), nozzlemen will often insert the nozzle tip inside the outermost layers of rebar, in order to achieve good compaction in the back layers of rebar. The outermost layers of rebar should be positioned to facilitate this process.

On most structural shotcrete projects, the nozzlemen are usually required to shoot mock-ups of the most congested reinforcing details on the project. After the shotcrete has set and gained sufficient compressive strength, the forms are stripped from the mock-ups and the stripped face examined. The mock-ups are then cored and/or diamond saw or diamond wire cut to examine the adequacy of shotcrete encapsulation of the reinforcing steel. Nozzlemen are only permitted to shoot on the project after demonstrating satisfactory mock-up construction. Figure 9.9 shows an example of a mock-up of a heavily reinforced wall connection ready for shotcreting. Figure 9.10 shows a diamond saw cut section from a heavily reinforced seismic wall/column connection. It demonstrates excellent encapsulation of the reinforcing steel with shotcrete.

Figure 9.9 Mock-up of a heavily reinforced wall ready for shooting.

(Photo courtesy Johnson Western Gunite.)

Figure 9.10 Diamond wire cut section from a heavily reinforced wall.

(Photo courtesy T. Ross King, Consolidated Shotcrete Inc.)

9.4.3 Fibre reinforcement

Section 4.6 describes the various types of discrete fibre reinforcement that can be used in shotcrete. Fibres are primarily used as an alternative to mesh reinforcement in shotcrete. They provide a number of useful attributes to the shotcrete, including:

a) Fibres help control cracking (plastic and drying shrinkage and differential thermal stress-induced cracking) (ACI 506.1R-21, 2021);
b) Fibres provide the shotcrete with toughness, i.e. for shotcrete support, the ability to continue to carry load after cracking (Morgan et al., 1989, 1995; Morgan and Heere, 2000; Morgan et al., 1999; RTC, 2019);
c) Enhance the impact resistance of shotcrete (ACI 506.1R-21, 2021); and
d) Microsynthetic fibres provide substantial enhancement of resistance to thermal explosive spalling in shotcrete (and concrete) exposed to high-temperature fires (Tatnall, 2002; ACI 506.1R-21, 2021).

A major advantage of the use of fibres is that the reinforcement is already in the mixture being shot. Time does not have to be spent installing mesh and this can result in significant cost savings. With suitable shotcrete mixture designs, not much has to be changed in the shotcrete application process for either the wet or dry-mix shotcrete processes. Also, as discussed in Chapter 12 on Ground Support with shotcrete, major cost savings can be achieved with fibre-reinforced shotcretes, compared to mesh-reinforced shotcretes by not having to fill in the irregularities behind the mesh in installations on irregular rock surfaces (drill and blasted rock).

There are, however, some precautions that need to be adopted when using fibre reinforcement. With wet-mix shotcrete, the grates should always be kept on the pump hopper, so that any fibre balls produced during the batching and mixing process do not get into the pumping system. Fibre balls can cause blockages in the pump line, or at the nozzle, and can be hazardous for the nozzleman and shotcrete crew. Steel fibres can cause increased wear on the pumping system and rubber hoses should be regularly checked for any indications of excessive wear.

With dry-mix steel fibre-reinforced shotcretes, increased rates of wear can be found in the rubber wear pads in rotary guns. Some contractors have used harder polymer wear pads in such applications in order to obtain extended service life from the pads. Also, proper setting and tightening of the wear pads in the shotcrete gun is crucial. If this is not properly done, steel fibres can get into the gap between the wear pad and machined bowl in the gun. If this happens, the steel fibres will very rapidly gouge the wear pads and render them useless. Also, the flatness of the machined bowl in the gun should be regularly checked for tolerance. If it starts to become bowed or dished with usage, it should be removed and re-machined to meet tolerance specifications. If this is not done, rubber wear pads will wear out very rapidly when using steel fibre-reinforced shotcrete.

Most synthetic fibres have a specific gravity of less than 1.0 and will thus float in water. This can be problematic in applications in tunnels and mines with both wet and dry-mix shotcretes, where fibre rebound can float in water in drainage ditches and cause blockages at sump pumps, unless special measures are taken to protect against this situation. e.g. installation of screens at sump pumps, with frequent cleaning of such screens.

With steel fibre-reinforced shotcrete left in the natural as-shot state, without any surface finishing, some steel fibres will be left protruding from the as-shot surface. This can be problematic in some applications, such as mines that use equipment with trailing electric cables. Such cables can experience increased rates of wear from contact with protruding fibres (Duffield, 1999). Also, protruding steel fibres can cause scratches to the skin of miners brushing up against shotcreted walls and scratches can lead to infections. This situation can be mitigated by applying a plain shotcrete finish coat in areas of concern and finishing it to a relatively smooth surface using hand trowels.

9.4.4 Expanded metal lath

Expanded metal lath is a useful adjunct to the shotcrete process. It can be used as an alternative to conventional plywood or other types of forms.

It is particularly useful in construction of structures where the shotcrete can be applied from both sides of the lath, such that it becomes an integral part of the reinforcing in the shotcrete structure. Examples of its use include:

a) Bulkheads in construction of structural shotcrete walls and other structural shotcrete elements;
b) Construction of tunnel portals, in conjunction with the use of lattice girders and conventional reinforcing steel. See Figure 9.11 (Hart, 2008);
c) Construction of backfill barricades and ventilation seals in mines;
d) Repair of curved structures such as bulk storage silos (Hart, 2008); and
e) Construction of complex curved structures such as bobsleigh/luge tracks and water chutes in water parks. See Section 10.7 (ASA, 2008).

One proprietary version of the product is made from US 26-gauge galvanized sheet steel, with the *herringbone*-shaped openings designed to be of such dimensions that there is only minimal loss of mortar and paste penetrating the openings during shooting (Hart, 2008). This particular product is typically supplied in 685 mm × 2464 mm sheets with a series of 20 mm deep V-ribs spaced at 98 mm on centre. The V-ribs provide two useful

Figure 9.11 Tunnel portal construction using expanded metal lath as integral formwork/ reinforcing.
(Photos courtesy Amico, Alabama Metal Industries Inc.)

Figure 9.12 Expanded metal lath designed for use in shotcrete construction. (Photo courtesy Lihe (John) Zhang, LZhang Consulting & Testing Ltd.)

functions. Firstly, they provide the expanded metal lath steel sheets with rigidity, which is beneficial in handling and erection of the sheets, and in helping to control line and grade and tolerance of the installation. Secondly, the V-ribs provide *chairing* of the expanded metal lath off reinforcing steel bars, such that the shotcrete impacting the lath can build from behind to fully encapsulate the bars (ASA, 2008). Figure 9.12 shows a picture of this expanded metal lath, designed specifically for use in shotcrete construction.

9.4.5 Glass fibre reinforcement

Glass fibre reinforcement comes in two different forms:

a) Glass fibre/resin reinforcing bars (as an alternative to reinforcing steel bars)
b) Chopped glass strand, added to the shotcrete during the shooting process (as an alternative to steel fibre or synthetic fibre reinforcement).

Glass fibre/resin reinforcing bars have been used in lieu of conventional reinforcing steel bars in reinforced shotcrete construction in aggressive exposure environments, such as marine environments and other locations with high chloride exposure, such as potash or halide mines. They have also been used as rock bolts and forepoling reinforcement in mining applications, such as extraction drives where shotcrete-supported openings are mined as part of the ore recovery process. Glass/resin bars are much more conducive to this process than steel anchors and bars.

Some contractors in Canada specializing in repair of wastewater and sewer lines and manholes use glass fibre reinforcement in wet-mix shotcrete, in lieu of steel or synthetic fibres. The glass fibre is supplied in rovings and a special chopper gun is used to add the fibres to the mix during the shooting process. Higher than conventional (steel or synthetic fibre) fibre reinforcement addition rates can be achieved using this process, and the system has provided a good track record of performance in these aggressive exposure environments.

9.5 ANCHORS

Anchors are routinely used in shotcrete construction to support or space the reinforcement and help provide control over line and grade. A wide variety of anchor types are used, depending on the substrate material and other considerations. Examples of different types of anchor installations follow:

a) In shotcrete ground support applications, such as in rock slope stabilization and underground support in tunnels and mines, drilled and grouted rock bolts are commonly used to secure steel wire mesh fabric and other reinforcing elements such as lattice girders and steel bar *ladders*. Friction anchors, such as *split sets* or expansion anchor bolts are also sometimes used for such purposes. With mesh installation, if the rock bolt spacing is too wide, special shotcrete pins are also often used to help secure the mesh and prevent it from excessive vibration or movement (sagging) during shotcrete placement.

b) As previously mentioned, steel or macrosynthetic fibre reinforcement is now commonly used in lieu of wire mesh in many ground support and other applications (see Section 4.6). Special devices such as *bow-tie* plates are used to connect the fibre-reinforced shotcrete to the anchor bolts. Figure 9.13 shows a schematic of an anchor bolt commonly used in British Columbia with fibre-reinforced shotcrete for rock slope stabilization and underground support applications.

c) In infrastructure rehabilitation and seismic retrofit projects, anchor bolts are used to attach the reinforcement to concrete or masonry surfaces. A range of different types of anchor bolts are used, including self-drilling fasteners, expansion anchor bolts and drilled and grouted steel dowels or *ready-rod*. Different types of grouts are used to grout such anchors, including simple Portland cement grouts, special rapid setting cementitious grouts, polyester resins and epoxy resins.

d) In shotcrete rehabilitation of dams and other concrete structures, extensive use has been made of drilled L-Bar reinforcing bars grouted with high alumina cement-based rapid setting and strength gain anchoring capsules. The *sausage-like* dry capsules, properly sized for the diameter of the drilled hole into which they will be inserted, are

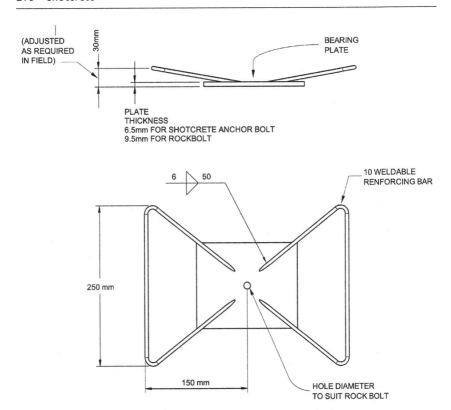

Figure 9.13 Bow-tie anchor plate used to connect fibre-reinforced shotcrete to rock bolts.

briefly dipped in a water bath to saturate them and activate the grout, before being inserted into the hole. After capsule insertion, the steel anchor bar is hammered into the hole to set it. Pull-out testing has demonstrated excellent bond strength development of such anchoring capsules. Figure 9.14 shows L-Bar anchors installed with anchoring capsules in seismic retrofit of the downstream spillway face of a dam in British Columbia.

e) Reinforcement can be anchored to structural steel using a variety of different techniques, including mechanical clips, self-tapping screws and welded nuts or other devices. The anchoring method used should, however, not interfere with the structural capacity of the structural steel element.

With grouted anchors, care should be exercised to ensure that the grouting material used is compatible with the substrate material into which the anchor will be installed. Proof load testing should be used to verify that

Figure 9.14 L-Bar Anchors installed with cementitious anchoring capsules in dam in British Columbia.

(Photo courtesy Mazin Ezzet, Wood PLC.)

the minimum specified pull-out loads are met. Also, particularly in overhead installations, the anchors should not lose load capacity as a result of creep or other factors. Experience has shown that water-based cementitious grouts tend to perform better than polymer resins in anchoring steel dowels into clay brick masonry in seismic retrofit of historic masonry structures. Also, some polymer resins have not provided satisfactory pull-out loads for anchors installed in wet rock conditions in tunnels and mines.

9.6 ALIGNMENT CONTROL AND TOLERANCE

In shotcrete applications, control of line and grade is achieved by the use of devices such as shooting wires (also called *ground wires*), high-tension prestressing steel rods (also called *pencil rods*), plastic screed pipes, guide strips, depth gauges, or open formwork. In addition, in relatively rough shotcrete applications, such as rock slope stabilization, or ground support in tunnels and mines, depth probes are sometimes used to check shotcrete thickness. The sections which follow elaborate on the use of these various devices.

9.6.1 Shooting wires

Shooting wires typically consist of high-strength steel wires, typically 0.8 to 1.0 mm in diameter that are set using some type of tensioning device. Turnbuckles set beyond the area being shotcreted are sometimes used to tension the wires. They are useful in that should the wires lose any tension during the shotcrete application process; the turnbuckles can be used to retighten the shooting wires. Shooting wires are easily set to control line and grade and are widely used where control of finish and tolerance is important. They are also useful in that the *covercrete* (depth of shotcrete cover to the outermost layers of rebar) can be easily measured and checked prior to shotcrete application. In vertical walls, a series of parallel ground wires are typically set horizontally about 600 to 900 mm apart to provide screed guides for shotcrete cutting and finishing. In complex structures with very tight tolerances, shooting wires can be set at closer spacings.

A good nozzleman will shoot to just cover the shooting wires, and when the shotcrete has stiffened sufficiently, the finishers will trim the shotcrete with cutting rods back to the depth of the shooting wires. Any low spots are filled with a flash coat of fresh shotcrete, followed by re-cutting, closing the surface with a *darby*, and floating and/or trowelling the shotcrete to provide the specified surface finish. Once satisfied that the specified line and grade and tolerance have been achieved, the shooting wires are removed, and final surface finishing operations completed. With a competent shotcrete and finishing crew, an end-product superior to a formed, cast-in-place-concrete can be achieved. The finished shotcrete surface is completely free of the *bugholes* (entrapped air voids), pour lines, form panel marks and form tie holes evident in stripped formed cast-in-place-concrete construction.

In addition to setting shooting wires horizontally on elements such as vertical walls and beams, shooting wires are often placed vertically to define the edges of structural elements such as columns, pilasters and the ends of walls. Sometimes one side of the structural element may be formed with conventional sealed form plywood. In structural elements with multiple layers of reinforcing, or a heavy congestion of reinforcing steel, the contractor may prefer to dispense with edge formwork altogether and use shooting wires only to define vertical edges. This provides the nozzleman with more open access to shooting to encase the reinforcing steel from different angles and reduces the potential for rebound entrapment.

9.6.2 Guide strips

Guide strips, often with chamfered edges, can be used to define the edges of shotcrete construction. They can be made from wood lath or form plywood. They can be linear or curved.

9.6.3 Curved surfaces

Control of line and grade and tolerance on curved surfaces can be achieved using devices such as pencil rods or stiff plastic conduit pipe. Pencil rods are typically 5 mm diameter high-tension prestressing steel rods. When bent, they form a perfect arc. They can be tied off to provide an arc meeting a specified radius. Figure 9.15 shows a pencil rod installed on a curved bridge column, ready for shotcreting. Pencil rods have also been used in construction of curved architectural features in buildings and other structures and in rehabilitation of buttress dams with curved barrel vaults.

Stiff plastic conduit pipe has been widely used as screed pipe for control of line and grade and tolerance for curved structures such as circular water tanks, tunnel shafts (Zhang et al., 2018) and bobsleigh/luge tracks (ASA, 2008). Similar to pencil rods, when bent it forms a perfect arc. Figure 9.16 shows plastic conduit pipe installed on a mock-up for shotcrete construction of the Alpensia Sliding Centre bobsleigh/luge track for the 2018 Winter Olympics at PyeongChang in South Korea. The plastic conduit

Figure 9.15 Pencil rod installed to define curved wall profile.

(Photo courtesy Ryan Regier, HC Matcon Inc.)

Figure 9.16 Plastic conduit screed pipe installed on mock-up of bobsleigh/luge track at Alpensia Sliding Centre for 2018 Winter Olympics at Pyeongchang, Korea.

screed pipe was tied to the outer layer of reinforcing steel to very exacting tolerances using plastic clip ties. After the shotcrete had been placed, screeded and finished, the plastic clip tires were cut, and the ties and screed pipe removed. Wet-mix shotcrete material was hand placed to fill the void left by the screed pipe as part of the final finishing operations. The same method was used for construction of the 2010 Whistler Winter Olympics bobsleigh/luge track (ASA, 2008) and the Beijing 2022 Winter Olympics bobsleigh/luge track. In structures with less exacting tolerances, structures with multiple curvatures, such as skate parks, can be constructed using curved guide strips.

9.6.4 Depth gauges and depth probes

Depth gauges are metal or plastic devices installed perpendicular to the substrate that defines the thickness to which the shotcrete should be applied. They are usually left embedded in the shotcrete after shooting. They may, however, have to be cut back after shotcrete placement, so that they do not protrude into the *covercrete* zone. Otherwise, they could provide a conduit for moisture to penetrate through to the reinforcing steel.

Depth probes are devices that are used to check the thickness of the freshly applied shotcrete before it takes initial set. They can be as simple as a washer welded to a piece of rebar with a pointed end at the specified minimum shotcrete thickness. When pushed into the plastic shotcrete, the imprint of the washer should be visible on the exposed shotcrete surface. If it is not, this indicates that the shotcrete is of less than adequate thickness at the probed location. This method is quite widely used in mines to check shotcrete thickness, with the probe fixed to a scaling bar.

9.7 JOINTS

There are various types of joints that are required in the shotcrete construction process. These include the following types of joints:

a) Joints between layers of shotcrete, when the bench shooting method with a top-down finish coat is used.
b) Joints between layers, when the layer shooting method is used;
c) Construction joints, either vertical or horizontal (and occasionally inclined), which define the perimeters of the shot area;
d) Restrained shrinkage crack control joints; and
e) Architectural reveals to provide a joint-like appearance to a shotcrete installation.

The sections which follow elaborate briefly on the design and construction of these various types of joints.

9.7.1 Joints between layers of shotcrete

When the bench shooting method with a top-down finish coat is used, the bench shot layer is typically applied to just cover the outer layer of rebar. This shotcrete is typically trimmed with cutting rods or trowels to remove any high spots or sloughed material and then allowed to stiffen sufficiently before application of the top-down finish coat, which is applied by the layer shooting method. When the layer shooting method is used, each successive shotcrete layer can be applied to either a still fresh previous shotcrete layer, that has stiffened sufficiently so that the composite layers of shotcrete do not sag or slough (fall out), or to a layer of shotcrete that has already set and hardened. One of the advantages of the shotcrete process, compared to cast-in-place-concrete construction, is that when the substrate to which the shotcrete is to be applied has been properly prepared, shotcrete application in multiple layers does not create *cold joints (Hanskat, 2014)*.

When layer shooting against freshly applied shotcrete, surface preparation methods should involve techniques such as:

a) Trim the shotcrete with a cutting rod; this leaves a flat, relatively open textured surface that is well suited to application of the next layer of shotcrete.
b) Use a stiff-bristle broom to remove any loose overspray or smooth surface sheen (laitance) and leave a roughened surface texture.

c) Irrespective of the method used, the existing shotcrete layer should be in a damp state at the time of application of the next layer of shotcrete. If the shotcrete has started to dry back excessively, it should be dampened with a fogging device (the mist produced by a 20-MPa water pressure sprayer is useful in this regard). The use of water hoses which result in liquid water running down the surface of the fresh shotcrete should be avoided, as in addition to washing paste out of the freshly shot surface, excess surface water at the time of application of the next lift of shotcrete can result in a high water/cement ratio and hence reduced bond strength at the interface between shotcrete layers.

When layer shooting against an existing shotcrete that has already set and hardened (shotcrete may be hours, days, or even weeks old), surface preparation techniques should involve methods such as:

a) Clean the existing hardened shotcrete layer to remove any hardened overspray, dust, dirt or other contaminants using methods such as high-pressure water blasting (minimum 35-MPa water pressure), wet-grit blasting, or dry sand blasting. (Note: simply washing down the shotcrete surface with a fire hose does not provide adequate cleaning.)

b) The above cleaning procedures should leave a suitably textured surface finish. It is not recommended that shotcrete be applied to smooth steel trowelled shotcrete surface finishes, or stripped form-ply finishes (Morgan and Neil, 1991).

c) Bring the existing shotcrete to a Saturated Surface Dry (SSD) condition at the time of application of the next lift of shotcrete. This provides optimal bonding conditions for the next layer of shotcrete. Too dry a substrate shotcrete at the time of application of the next shotcrete layer can desiccate the freshly applied shotcrete at the bond interface and diminish bond strength. Also, avoid having excess free surface water on the substrate shotcrete at the time of application of the next layer of shotcrete. This can result in a very high water/cement ratio at the critical bond interface and markedly diminish bond strength. The practice of wetting down the existing shotcrete substrate immediately before fresh shotcrete application, with the water added at the water ring at the nozzle in dry-mix shotcrete application, or with a garden hose in wet-mix shotcrete application, should not be permitted.

In summary, if the preparation procedures described above are followed, then there should be no *cold joints* between layers of shotcrete. In cores extracted through the shotcrete layers, the shotcrete should appear homogeneous and it should be difficult to even determine whether the shotcrete was applied in layers.

9.7.2 Construction joints

Construction joints are used to define the edges of a shotcreted area. They can be vertical or horizontal (or occasionally inclined). There are various types of construction joints. They can be created by shooting up against a form board set at right angles or inclined at 45 degrees to the orientation of the shotcrete as applied. Alternatively, they can be created without the use of edge form boards by shooting to vertically or horizontally set shooting wires and then cutting back the freshly placed shotcrete to a 90 degree, or 45-degree edge, depending on the design requirements.

For example, in construction of vertical structural walls for in-ground parking structures, the horizontal construction joint at the top of the wall, for each parking level, is typically cut back at 90 degrees, so that the subsequent cast-in-place-concrete reinforced structural slab can bear on the top of the structural shotcrete wall. By contrast, in permanent structural soil nail wall construction, the horizontal joints at the top and bottom of the shotcrete lifts are typically either shot against form boards oriented at 45 degrees, or the fresh shotcrete is cut back to 45 degrees. This is done in order to minimize the potential for entrapment of rebound, which could occur in 90-degree joints. Figure 9.17 shows an example of a 45-degree edge form

Figure 9.17 45-degree horizontal joint in soil nail wall construction.

(Photo courtesy Nicholson Construction Company.)

board set for construction of a horizontal construction joint in a soil nail wall construction.

When cutting back freshly applied shotcrete to create a 45-degree edge, best practice is to cut a top vertical edge about 20 mm deep. This provides a sharp, well-defined edge to the 45-degree inclined construction joint and prevents the formation of tapered edges. Note that long thin tapered edges should be avoided in shotcrete construction, as they can lead to peeling type delaminations with time (Morgan and Neil, 1991).

The question is sometimes asked by structural engineers as to whether shotcrete applied to a 45-degree construction joint will provide a plane of weakness at this location. This issue was systematically studied by Trottier and others at Dalhousie University in Halifax, Nova Scotia (Trottier et al., 2002). In tests conducted using the *South African Water Bed* test method (Kirsten, 1992) in which anchored shotcrete panels are tested to destruction in flexure, they compared the performance of:

a) Plain shotcrete panels, with and without a 45-degree construction joint against;
b) Panels reinforced with welded wire mesh (102 mm × 102 mm–4.1 mm/4.1 mm gauge) with and without a 45-degree construction joint;
c) Panels reinforced with steel fibres with and without a 45-degree construction joint; and
d) Panels reinforced with macrosynthetic fibres with and without a 45-degree construction joint.

They found that the presence of construction joints did not have any detrimental effect on the load-carrying capacity or cracking behaviour of plain, steel fibre or macrosynthetic fibre-reinforced shotcretes. There was some detrimental effect on the cracking behaviour of the mesh-reinforced shotcrete panel, and this was attributed to overlapping of mesh at the joint location, affecting the quality of shotcrete consolidation at the joint location. They concluded that (apart from the issue of overlapping mesh), provided there was proper fabrication and preparation of the joint itself, no particular precautions were required to provide equivalent performance between panels, with and without construction joints.

9.7.3 Shrinkage crack control joints

As in cast-in-place reinforced concrete structural walls, control joints are often specified by the design engineer/architect to provide control over the location of drying shrinkage-induced cracks. There are various ways of creating such shrinkage crack control joints, including tooling grooves into the freshly placed shotcrete, or diamond saw cutting the shotcrete *covercrete* shortly after the shotcrete has attained final set. Depending on the thickness of the wall, and the reinforcing steel configuration, such initiatives may,

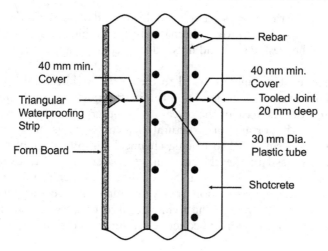

Figure 9.18 Cross-section of a shrinkage crack control joint in a thick structural wall.

however, not be sufficient to cause all the shrinkage cracks to occur at joint locations. Steps taken by engineers and contractors to mitigate this issue include measures to intentionally weaken the cross-section of the wall at location of joints by practices such as:

a) Where permitted by the structural design, cut alternative horizontal reinforcing steel bars at the joint locations;
b) Set triangular wood or polymer strips against the formwork at the location of joints (Some contractors use water-reactive polyurethane strips for this purpose, as they can help provide a waterproofing function at the joints); and
c) In thick structural walls, with two or more layers of reinforcing steel, fix appropriately sized stiff plastic conduit in the middle of the thickness of the wall.

Figure 9.18 shows a cross-section of a shrinkage crack control joint in a thick structural wall with a double row of reinforcing steel, with a triangular wood strip at the back of the wall, plastic conduit insert in the middle of the wall and tooled groove in the front of the wall. There is a much higher probability of shrinkage cracks occurring at such a joint location, than at a wall which only has a tooled groove or diamond saw-cut in the *covercrete*.

9.7.4 Architectural reveals

Architects sometimes specify the use of architectural reveals to break up the appearance of a flat finished wall. These can be produced by setting slightly tapered wood reveal strips in the exposed surface and shooting to carefully encase these strips. After a suitable period of setting and hardening, the reveal strips are removed. Alternatively, the architectural reveals can be tooled into the freshly shot and finished surface using appropriately shaped finishing tools.

Irrespective of the method used to create the architectural reveals, the design should take care to not compromise the thickness of the protective *covercrete* from the base of the reveal to the outermost layer of rebar. This is particularly important for structural elements such as bridge piers and abutment walls subjected to deicing chemical run-off or spray, or marine structures exposed to the chlorides in sea water. There are examples in Canada (Morgan and Neil, 1991), where the use of architectural reveals in reinforced concrete construction of elevated highway structures, with compromised cover at the base of the architectural reveals, resulted in premature reinforcing steel corrosion and concrete spalling and delamination.

9.8 PROTECTION OF ADJACENT SURFACES

Shotcreting is a pneumatic application process and so there are always return air currents with the material exiting from the shotcrete nozzle. These return air currents carry with them fine particulate matter in the form of a vapour or mist containing cementitious material, and coarser material referred to as *overspray* which contains both cementitious material and fine sand particles. In addition, there is *rebound* material, which is comprised primarily of coarser aggregate particles and some mortar (sand plus cementitious material). Mist, overspray and rebound are thus a fundamental part of the shotcrete process and need to be understood and properly dealt with in order to provide a successful shotcrete project. Proper protection of adjacent surfaces is one important issue that needs to be dealt with.

For example, in shotcrete repair of buildings and structures, adjacent elements such as doors, windows, painted concrete walls, or other building components need to be protected against damage from impact from rebound, and coatings from cementitious mists and overspray. Contractors use techniques such as temporary coverings of such elements with plywood, heavy-duty polyethylene sheets, drop cloths, etc. In shotcrete installations in large civil engineering infrastructure such as dams, spillways, locks and canal linings, contractors may elect to not provide any special protection to adjacent surfaces, but rather use methods such as water pressure blasting (minimum 35 MPa), wet-grit blasting, or sand blasting to remove any accumulations of overspray from the shotcrete application process.

In multilayer shotcrete construction it is important to recognize that shotcrete overspray will accumulate on both adjacent *yet-to-be-shot* surfaces, as well as the adjacent just shot surface. A thin film of overspray on the adjacent *yet-to-be-shot* surface should not be an issue, provided that the overspray is still fresh (plastic and not yet dried out and hardened) at the time of shotcrete application, and the build-up of overspray is not too thick (as can occur at corners or obstacles). If the overspray has dried out and hardened, or is too thick, it must be removed prior to application of the next layer of shotcrete. This can be done using the methods referred to above, i.e. water pressure blasting, wet-grit blasting or sand blasting. If this is not done, it can result in the formation of a weakened porous layer at the critical bond interface between the shotcrete layers. This can be particularly problematic with certain types of polymer-modified shotcretes in hydraulic or marine structures, where water migrating along this porous interface between shotcrete layers can result in a serious degradation of bond strength between shotcrete layers.

Finally, it should be recognized that the development of overspray and rebound is considerably more pronounced in dry-mix shotcrete compared to wet-mix shotcrete (Wolsiefer and Morgan, 1993). Also, in windy environmental conditions, wind can blow fines out of the shotcrete stream emerging from the nozzle. Dry-mix shotcrete is more susceptible to this situation than wet-mix shotcrete. Thus, in windy conditions, special attention needs to be paid to protection of adjacent elements. If too windy, shotcrete operations should be terminated. (It can get expensive to have to pay for washing or repainting of cars parked in an adjacent parking lot.)

9.9 SHOTCRETE CREW

ACI 506R Guide to Shotcrete (ACI 506R-16, 2016) provides a detailed description of the composition and duties of the various members of a shotcrete crew for hand placement of shotcrete. A typical shotcrete crew consists of a foreman, nozzleman, nozzleman assistant, blowpipe operator, finishers, labourers, pump operator for wet-mix shotcrete and *gun* operator for dry-mix shotcrete. In addition, in complex structural shotcrete projects, a shotcrete engineer may be employed to supervise the project. The size of the crew will vary depending on the nature and size of the project. For example, in a simple shotcrete slope stabilization project, where the shotcrete is left in a natural as-shot finish, a shotcrete crew of only three people may suffice (nozzleman, nozzleman assistant, pump operator). By contrast, in a complex project with high finishing demands, a shotcrete crew of as many as 14 people may be required. For example, in construction of a bobsleigh/luge track, the shotcrete team may be comprised of a superintendent engineer, foreman, nozzleman, relief nozzleman, nozzleman assistant, blow pipe operator, vibrator operator, as many as six finishers and a pump operator. In addition, a quality control technician would be required to test every truck load of shotcrete for plastic properties (shotcrete slump, air content and temperature) and monitor production of test panels for hardened shotcrete tests (compressive strength, boiled absorption and volume of permeable voids). In addition, the Owner would likely retain a qualified Shotcrete Inspector to monitor the work and provide a Quality Assurance (QA) report. Such Shotcrete

Inspectors are often provided with authority to stop the work and have the shotcrete contractor take corrective actions if any non-conformances to the project specifications are encountered during shotcrete construction.

9.9.1 Nozzleman

It is important that the shotcrete crew operate as a team, with each member being well trained in their specific duties. The most important member in the team is the shotcrete nozzleman. The nozzleman provides leadership and direction for the crew. It is the nozzleman's responsibility to ensure that the surface preparation, formwork and scaffolding, reinforcement, alignment control, provision for joints and protection of adjacent surfaces are all satisfactory prior to application of any shotcrete. In addition, for wet-mix shotcrete the nozzleman should check that the shotcrete delivered is of the specified type, slump, air content, temperature and age, prior to discharge into the shotcrete pump. For dry-mix shotcrete, the nozzleman should check that the correct mixture has been provided and that it has been satisfactorily predampened prior to discharge into the shotcrete gun. The nozzleman should also be prepared to shut down the project if environmentally unsuitable conditions occur, such as excessively hot or cold ambient or substrate temperatures, high winds, or rain. Once satisfied that all the preceding items are satisfactory, the nozzleman can then proceed with shotcrete placement. The nozzleman's prime responsibilities are to place the shotcrete with proper consolidation to the specified line and grade and thickness with full encapsulation of the reinforcing steel and embedments. Requirements for proper shotcrete placement are dealt with in the sections which follow.

9.9.2 Nozzleman's assistant and blowpipe operator

The prime role of the nozzleman's assistant is to manoeuvre the hose such that the nozzleman can concentrate on proper shotcrete placement. This is particularly important in the wet-mix shotcrete placement method, where the hose is quite heavy and the nozzleman cannot shoot correctly if trying to drag the hose at the same time. The nozzleman's assistant is often a nozzleman-in-training and may relieve the nozzleman for short periods and shoot areas without congested reinforcing under the direct supervision of the nozzleman. In addition, in areas with less congested reinforcing steel, the nozzleman's assistant may also double up as a blowpipe operator. In areas of congested reinforcing steel, a dedicated blowpipe operator will be required. The blowpipe operator works in tandem with the nozzleman, blowing out rebound and build-up of overspray in advance in the area in which the nozzleman is about to place shotcrete. In applications with a very heavy reinforcing steel configuration, a dedicated vibrator operator may be required to insert a vibrator to provide the final shotcrete encasement of the reinforcing steel and embedments (e.g. in encasing reinforcing steel and

Figure 9.19 Consolidation of shotcrete in invert of a bobsleigh/luge track using a pencil vibrator.

cooling pipes in the invert, cove and header beam areas in a bobsleigh/luge track). Figure 9.19 shows the use of a pencil vibrator in consolidation of wet-mix shotcrete in construction of the invert of the bobsleigh/luge track for the Beijing 2022 Winter Olympics.

9.9.3 Finishers and labourers

While much shotcrete is left in its natural as-shot surface finish appearance and does not require the use of finishers (e.g. slope stabilization, ground support in tunnels and mines), nearly all reinforced structural shotcrete elements require finishing (e.g. walls, pilasters, columns, sides and soffits of beams and slabs, hydraulic structures such as swimming pools, canal linings, dams, spillways, water tanks etc.). On small projects, one or two finishers may suffice to provide the required surface finish. However, on a high-volume shotcrete production project, or complex curvature projects, such as a skate park, or bobsleigh/luge track, with high finishing tolerance requirements, six or more finishers may be required to keep up with the nozzleman. There is normally a lead finisher, who trims the shotcrete to line and grade with a cutting rod (screed). The type of finish specified (see Section 9.11) will dictate the operations required by the finishing crew. Where textured surface finishes are specified, finishers will typically close and smooth the rodded surface using a wood *darby*, followed by finishing with wood, rubber or sponge floats, or sometimes a light broom finish, depending on the roughness required in the finished surface texture. Where smooth surface finishes are specified, final finishing is typically done with magnesium or steel trowels.

Labourers are required for a variety of functions, including shovelling up and disposing of rebound and cuttings and trimmings from finishing operations. They also typically assist the crew in shotcrete equipment layout, cleaning out the shotcrete hoses and nozzle at the end of the shift and generally keeping the shotcrete site in a safe and clean condition. Labourers are an entry-level position in the shotcrete crew, and as a career path, can advance to become finishers or shotcrete nozzlemen, and eventually shotcrete foremen, or even managers of shotcrete contracting companies. A number of successful shotcrete contracting companies in North America are now run by persons who have followed this career path.

9.9.4 Shotcrete supply equipment operators

In the wet-mix shotcrete system, the pump operator is an important member of the shotcrete crew. The pump operator is responsible for delivery of a steady supply of shotcrete to the nozzleman at the required rate, free to the extent possible of objects such as large rocks, scale detached from the fins of ready-mix concrete trucks, or fibre balls, which could result in blockages in the shotcrete reducers, hose or nozzle (Hence, the importance of keeping the screen on the top of the pump hopper at all times). One of the most important duties of the pump operator is to maintain direct communication with the shotcrete nozzleman at all times, so that there can be instant shut-down of pumping and reversal of pressure in the line in the event that a blockage occurs. Another important duty of the pump operator is to monitor the consistency (slump) of the shotcrete being discharged from the shotcrete supply equipment (ready mix truck, mobile batcher unit, or transmixer) and either ask for adjustments to be made to the workability of the mix (e.g. by superplasticizer addition on site), if permitted by the project specifications, or reject the load if the mix becomes too stiff, and/or old. Note: ACI 506-16 requires shotcrete to be used within 90 minutes of batching, unless special measures are taken to retard the mix.

In the dry-mix shotcrete process the shotcrete the *gun* operator is responsible for supplying a steady stream of properly predampened material (if required, about 3 to 4% moisture content) to the nozzleman. The *gun* operator will usually operate the predampener and make sure that the bowl on the gun is kept full and that the feed barrel in the gun rotates at the correct speed, so that the nozzleman does not experience surges in materials supply. Surges would make it difficult for the nozzleman to consistently control the amount of water added at the nozzle to maintain the correct consistency (wetness) of the shotcrete being ejected onto the receiving surface. The *gun* operator is also responsible for the set-up, maintenance and cleanliness of the shotcrete gun and supply hoses and ancillary equipment (clamps, air hoses, and whip checks on air hoses). As with the wet-mix shotcrete process, direct communication between the *gun* operator and nozzleman is important, so that the dry-mix shotcrete gun and air compressor can be shut down instantaneously in the event of a blockage in the materials supply line or nozzle.

9.10 SHOTCRETE PLACEMENT

A seminal publication by T. Crom (Crom, 1981) provides detailed guidance regarding optimal procedures for hand nozzling application of dry-mix shotcrete. Subsequent publications such as:

a) ACI 506R-16 Guide to Shotcrete (ACI 506R-16, 2016);
b) ACI CCP-60 Certification, Shotcrete Nozzleman Craftsman Workbook (ACI CCP-60.1-20, 2020); and
c) AASHTO-AGC-ARTBA Joint Committee Task Force 37 Guide Specification for Shotcrete Repair of Highway Bridges (AASHTO-AGC-ARTBA, 1998)

provide comprehensive guidance regarding correct methods for placement of both wet and dry-mix shotcrete using hand nozzling. The EFNARC European Specification for Sprayed Concrete, Guideline for Specifiers and Contractors (EFNARC, 1999) provides guidance on placement methods for both wet and dry-mix shotcretes using both hand placement and remote control (*robotic*) placement methods. The sections, which follow, elaborate on the recommendations in these publications, augmented by the experience of the authors from their involvement in hundreds of different shotcrete projects over a four-decade period.

9.10.1 Bench shooting

As mentioned in Section 9.1, there are basically two different methods for shotcrete placement: bench shooting and layer shooting. The bench shooting method is typically used in construction of relatively thick (150 mm to 500 mm) structural shotcrete walls and like elements. The bench shooting method is also used in construction of mass shotcrete walls, with thicknesses in excess of 1.0 m. In this case, it is often used in conjunction with the "*hybrid*" (shoot and vibrate) method. The elements are shot to the full thickness in a single pass. The nozzleman normally starts shooting in a corner, creating a 45-degree sloped surface both within the plane of the wall and at right angles to the wall. The nozzleman shoots continuously at right angles to this 45-degree slope, advancing the shotcreted face. The important point to note is that the fresh shotcrete is continuously impacting at

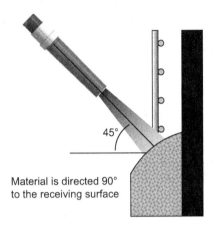

45°

Material is directed 90°
to the receiving surface

Figure 9.20 Schematic of the bench shooting method.

Figure 9.21 Bench shot structural shotcrete wall.

(or close to) 90 degrees to the surface being shotcreted. This facilitates optimal shotcrete consolidation. Figure 9.20 shows a schematic of the bench shooting method. Figure. 9.21 shows a photograph of a bench shot structural shotcrete wall.

This 45-degree slope is very beneficial in that it enables rebound materials to roll down the slope, and with the aid of the blowpipe operator, be removed and not become entrapped in the shotcreted wall. The height of the bench will vary, depending on factors such as the thickness of the wall, the consistency (slump) of the shotcrete, and factors which affect the rate of stiffening and setting of the shotcrete, such as the shotcrete and ambient temperatures. Bench heights ranging from 600 mm to 1000 mm are common, although greater heights are possible with more rapidly setting shotcretes with accelerators. The important factor is that the shotcrete should not be benched to an excessive height, which results in sagging and/or sloughing. The nozzleman proceeds to bench shoot the first lift of shotcrete along the length of the wall. The blowpipe operator works in tandem with the nozzleman, keeping the area where the nozzleman is about to shoot clean by blowing out rebound and any accumulations of overspray on rebar or any other inclusions in the shotcreted wall (plastic conduit, waterstop, anchors, grout tubes, etc.).

After the first bench lift has stiffened sufficiently, the nozzleman then stacks the second lift on the first lift, repeating the process until the full height of the wall for the day's shift has been constructed. It is important to not stack successive lifts on top of the previous lift too rapidly (before they have stiffened and set sufficiently), or sagging and/or sloughing (fall-out) can occur. Sloughing is usually immediately obvious, and the affected shotcrete can be cut out while still plastic and re-shot. Sagging is more insidious and may not be immediately obvious. Figure 9.22 shows an example of a stripped structural shotcrete wall with a large sag below reinforcing steel. The sag only became evident on stripping of the back shotcrete form. It was not evident in the finished shotcrete face where it was likely covered by a final *flash* coat. It was remediated by cutting out the affected hardened shotcrete area and reshooting.

9.10.2 Layer shooting

The layer shooting method can be used to build the full thickness of a wall or other elements by shooting a series of relatively thin (25 to 50 mm) layers of shotcrete with the shotcrete impacting at (or close to) right angles (90 degrees) to the receiving surface. The layer shooting method is less commonly used than the bench shooting method but does have applications where it performs well. An example is shotcrete encasement of wrapped prestressing steel in construction of circular water tanks, as described in Section 10.6. It lends itself well to robotic shotcreting operations for such construction.

Probably the most common use of the layer shooting method is the application of the final finish coat of *covercrete* shotcrete to a bench shot wall or other structural elements. The final finish coat is usually shot using the same shotcrete mix and application equipment as used in shooting the bench, but with the mix shot at right angles at a greater distance from the receiving surface, with more rapid movement of the nozzle to build up the required shotcrete thickness. Figure 9.23 shows a finish coat application to a bench shot wall. While it is possible to bench shoot a wall to the full thickness and

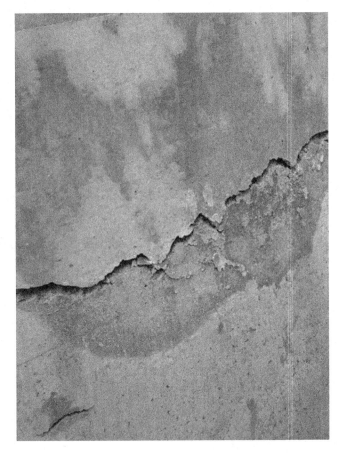

Figure 9.22 Example of a sag in the stripped back face of a shotcrete wall bench shot too high too rapidly.

(Photo courtesy Lihe (John) Zhang, LZhang Consulting & Testing Ltd.)

finish it without using a finish coat, the advantage of using the finish coat method of shotcrete construction is that the base shotcrete layer will have already stiffened such that it is not likely to be disturbed by surface finishing operations. Also, if architecturally required, pigmented shotcrete can be used in the finish coat. Note in Figure 9.23 how the finish coat layer is shot from the top down. This is so that overspray and trimmings from the finishing operations do not mar the surface finish.

The question is sometimes asked as to how thick a shotcrete element can be constructed using the layer shooting method for vertical and overhead shotcrete applications. There is conceptually actually no limit to how thick the shotcrete can be applied. The shotcrete can be built up in layers to any prescribed thickness, providing the previous layer is allowed to stiffen and set sufficiently prior to application of the next layer of shotcrete. In one

Figure 9.23 Layer shooting of a finish coat to a bench shot structural shotcrete wall.

(Photo courtesy T. Ross King, Consolidated Shotcrete Inc.)

hydroelectric project in British Columbia, the reinforced shotcrete was required to be built up to a total thickness of 1.5 m overhead in a transition from a rectangular water pressure rock tunnel to a circular steel penstock (Ripley et al., 1998). In retrofit of a hydroelectric turbine draft tube ceiling in a project in Washington state, steel fibre-reinforced shotcrete was built up overhead in 100 mm thick layers to a total thickness of 2.0 m (Radomski et al., 2019) – see *Section 11.11, Dams and Hydraulic Structures*. In a mining project in Saskatchewan, in which the first author was involved, an emergency water cut-off plug 3 m high, 6 m wide and 10 m long was constructed using continuous wet-mix shotcrete application.

9.10.3 Shooting technique

One of the most important considerations in shotcrete application is that the shotcrete should be applied at sufficiently high impacting velocity to achieve full consolidation of the shotcrete. This is achieved by:

a) Orient the nozzle at as close as possible to right angles (90 degrees) to the receiving surface. For overhead shooting, using a *clock analogy*, a shotcrete nozzle stream orientation ranging from about 11 am to 1 pm would be considered to be acceptable. Orientations more acute than 10 am or 2 pm would be much too acute and result in less than optimal consolidation, a large increase in rebound and a phenomenon known as *rolling*. For vertical shooting, a similar *clock analogy* can be applied, with the clock rotated through 90 degrees. Shooting angles should not be too acute, either side-to-side, or up-and-down. *Rolling* is visually evident as an uneven wavy-textured surface with rolls, or folds of poorly compacted shotcrete. *Rolling* is particularly pronounced when a nozzleman applies the shotcrete at angles approaching 45 degrees from the receiving surface. Rolling is sometimes found in robotically applied shotcrete in underground mining applications, when the remote control nozzleman orients the nozzle at the end of the shotcrete boom at too acute an angle from the rock surface, in order to reduce the chances of being struck by rebounding coarse aggregate particles.

b) Position the nozzle at a suitable distance from the receiving surface to achieve optimal shotcrete consolidation. The question is sometimes asked: *What is a suitable distance?*

There is no single answer to this question. The optimal distance of the nozzle from the receiving surface is usually between 600 mm and 1.8 m, but will vary depending on a variety of factors, including:

1) The type and size of the shotcrete delivery equipment, including the diameter of the shotcrete and air hoses. Handheld materials hoses may be 38 to 50 mm in diameter, whereas robotic application hoses are commonly 65 mm in diameter.

2) The volume of air and quantity of material being delivered to the shotcrete nozzle. As a general rule, the greater the volume of air and materials being delivered to the nozzle, the further away the nozzle will have to be held from the receiving surface.

3) The type and configuration of the shotcrete nozzle. Hand-held shorter rubber-tipped nozzles need to be held much closer to the receiving surface than long stiff plastic or steel *rifling* type nozzles, often used in robotic shotcrete applications. For intricate hand shooting of multiple layers of congested reinforcing steel, the nozzle may have to be held only 300mm away from the receiving surface. By contrast, in robotic shooting of vertical and overhead surfaces in tunnel and mining applications, a *rifling* nozzle may be positioned as much as 2.0 m (EFNARC, 1999) or even more from the receiving surface.

An experienced nozzleman will very quickly find the optimal distance at which to position the nozzle. If the nozzle is placed too close to the receiving surface, the impacting velocity will be too great and freshly placed shotcrete will tend to be displaced (dug-out) by the arriving shotcrete stream. This phenomenon is sometimes referred to as *scalloping*. An experienced nozzleman will back off until *scalloping* stops and then knows that optimal consolidation is being achieved for the shotcreting system being utilized. Inexperienced nozzlemen sometimes either back off too far, or start shooting at too great a distance from the receiving surface and consequently produce poorly consolidated shotcrete which can be porous, with high permeability and reduced compressive strength. The ASTM C642 test for Boiled Absorption and Volume of Permeable Voids will very quickly identify poorly consolidated shotcrete.

There is a difference in the nozzling technique used in the dry-mix shotcrete process, compared to the wet-mix shotcrete process. In the dry-mix shotcrete process, the nozzleman typically applies the shotcrete using an overlapping concentric circular motion (Crom, 1981). This action promotes the production of uniform quality shotcrete, as it enables some *mixing* of the shotcrete on the receiving surface (blends wetter and drier materials exiting from the nozzle as a result of unwanted surges in the dry-mix shotcrete materials supply to the nozzle). It also facilitates the application of a more uniform thickness of shotcrete in a pass, without irregular lumps or clumps of materials being built up at any one place on the receiving surface. Figure 9.24 shows a schematic of dry-mix shotcrete placement using this circular motion.

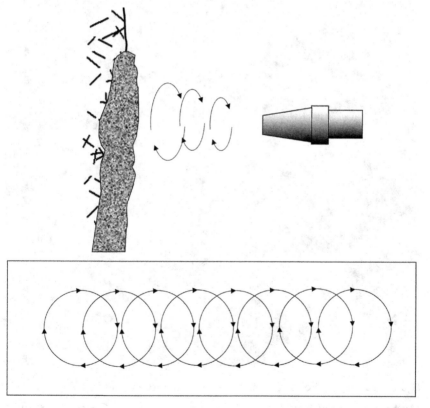

Figure 9.24 Dry-mix shotcrete placement using a circular motion.

By contrast, in shooting using the wet-mix shotcrete process, the shotcrete material exiting the nozzle is all of the same uniform consistency and so the concentric circular motion used in the dry-mix shotcrete process is generally not needed. The nozzleman tends to use more of a sweeping type of motion to place bulk shotcrete and encapsulate reinforcing steel and other embedments. In the wet-mix shotcrete process, there is typically a considerably greater volume of shotcrete exiting the nozzle than in the dry-mix shotcrete process and so the nozzleman has to continuously move the nozzle rapidly to prevent irregular clumps of material from being built up at any one place. An experienced nozzleman should be able to shoot to shooting wires and produce a fairly flat surface with minimal trimmings when cut with a cutting rod. Figure 9.25 shows a nozzleman bench shooting using the wet-mix shotcrete process.

Figure 9.25 Bench shooting using the wet-mix shotcrete process.

(Authorized reprint from ACI 506R-16, courtesy American Concrete Institute.)

There are, however, some situations where a circular motion may be used when applying wet-mix shotcrete. Firstly, when hand shooting a *flash coat* surface finish, the nozzleman will tend to step back from the work a bit and apply the relatively thin (30 mm to 50 mm thick) final coat using a circular motion. This facilitates shooting of a flatter surface finish layer and reduces the amount of surface cutting and trimming operations required. Secondly, with remote control robotic shooting, the nozzle mounted on the manipulator arm often has a built-in automated circular motion. There is a large volume of shotcrete being discharged through the nozzle with such robotic placement methods and the nozzle needs to be moving constantly to prevent irregular clumps of material from being built up and produce a relatively smooth as-shot surface finish. The automated circular nozzle movement facilitates this process. Figure 9.26 shows robotic placement of wet-mix shotcrete using such a system.

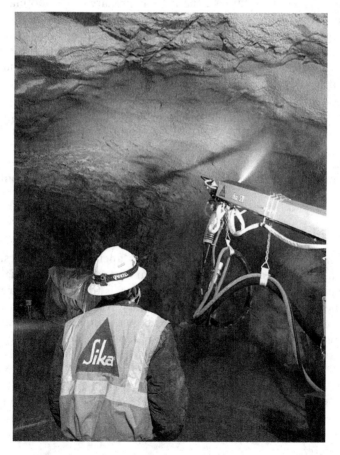

Figure 9.26 Robotic placement of wet-mix shotcrete.

(photo courtesy Sika.)

Horizontal surfaces are usually best constructed using conventional cast-in-place concrete construction methods. There are, however, some applications where contractors prefer to shoot horizontal surfaces for logistics and economic reasons. Examples of this include shooting the floors of swimming pools and spas, and the *inverts* (floors) of some tunnels and other underground structures, as an integral part of the shotcrete construction. The publications by Crom (Crom, 1981) and ACI 506R Guide to Shotcrete (ACI 506R-16, 2016) provide guidance on the correct methods to be used in shooting horizontal surfaces. In construction of such structures, the shooting sequence adopted is very important. The nozzleman usually starts by shooting a *cove* at the wall/floor interface. This is done such that rebound and overspray from shooting the walls does not accumulate in this critical *cove* area.

After shooting of the walls (and also overhead surfaces in tunnels and other underground structures), the floor is prepared for shooting. In construction of swimming pools and spas on grade, shotcrete is usually applied to a compacted gravel bed, and floor preparation may involve either removing, or redistributing rebound, such that it does not intrude into the thickness of the structural slab. By contrast, for hard rock tunnelling applications, the engineer will sometimes require the excavated rock invert to be cleaned of all overspray and rebound from shooting of the tunnel walls and *back* (ceiling) such that strong bond can be achieved between the prepared rock and invert shotcrete (Ripley et al., 1998). Rebound is generated in shooting horizontal surfaces and an experienced nozzleman will use a shooting sequence which prevents the accumulation of pockets of rebound from incorporation in the shotcrete layer. Judicious use of a blow pipe can help in this regard.

9.10.4 Encasing reinforcing steel and embedments

Reinforcing steel and embedments such as anchors, grout tubes, water-stops, pipes and plastic conduit provide an obstacle to the material stream being ejected from the nozzle. The good news is that with proper training and experience, a qualified nozzleman can provide excellent encapsulation of reinforcing steel and embedments with shotcrete. Most structural shotcrete projects require preconstruction mock-ups to be shot, with reinforcing steel and embedments which represent the most congested details expected to be encountered on the project. Figure 9.27 shows a heavily reinforced mock-up of a shear wall for a high-rise building being shot with wet-mix shotcrete. Subsequent coring and diamond saw cutting will clearly identify whether the mock-up is free of porous zones and voids of incomplete consolidation and reinforcing steel and embedments are fully encased with shotcrete.

Figure 9.28 shows an example of a core extracted from the mock-up shown in the Figure 9.27. There was excellent encapsulation of the reinforcing

Figure 9.27 Wet-mix shotcrete being applied in a heavily reinforced mock-up for a shear wall for a high-rise building.

(Photo courtesy T. Ross King, Consolidated Shotcrete Inc.)

Figure 9.28 Core extracted from a heavily reinforced shotcrete mock-up; note excellent shotcrete encasement of reinforcing steel.

(Photo courtesy T. Ross King, Consolidated Shotcrete Inc.)

steel with shotcrete and the nozzleman and crew were qualified to work on the project.

Publications such as those by Crom (Crom, 1981) and CCS-4 *Shotcrete for the Craftsman (ACI, CCS-4, 2020)* provide good guidance on important considerations and procedures that should be implemented in order to provide full encasement of reinforcing steel and embedments with quality shotcrete, free of defects. The sections which follow elaborate briefly on some of these considerations and procedures.

There are three prime considerations in achieving full encasement of reinforcing steel and embedments with shotcrete. The first is that the shotcrete should be applied with a sufficiently high impacting velocity. The second is that the shotcrete should have sufficient plasticity such that it can flow around and fully envelop the bars or embedments. The third is that the shotcrete should have proper shooting orientation (as discussed in Section 9.10.3). A deficiency in any one of these factors can result in the creation of *shadows* (porous zones) and voids behind the rebar or embedments. When applied with sufficiently high impacting velocity, shotcrete should not build up on the face of the rebar or embedment. The deformations on rebar should be visible at all times during the shooting process until the shotcrete builds up from behind to fully encase the rebar or embedment. With respect to plasticity, the shotcrete should be applied at the *wettest stable consistency*. This is the consistency (slump in wet-mix shotcrete), at which the shotcrete will readily flow around the rebar and embedments during shooting, but not be so wet that the shotcrete sags and/or sloughs after application. If the shotcrete is shot at too stiff a consistency (low slump in wet-mix shotcrete), it will not flow readily around the rebar or embedments. Slumps of 40 mm or less are not conducive to proper encapsulation of rebar or embedments, particularly with larger diameter (20 mm or more) rebar and embedments. These phenomena have been well demonstrated in laboratory studies conducted at Université Laval (see Chapter 7).

There are basically three ways to increase the impacting velocity. The first is to select a nozzle type that is conducive to producing a high impacting velocity stream. The second is to increase the volume of air supplied to the nozzle in the wet-mix process and gun in the dry-mix process. The third is to move the nozzle closer into the work. With respect to plasticity, in dry-mix shotcrete application, the nozzleman controls the amount of water added at the water ring at the nozzle and can readily fine-tune the mix to be at the *wettest stable consistency* during shooting. In wet-mix shotcrete the nozzleman needs to continuously monitor the consistency of the mix during shooting. If the mix becomes too stiff, the nozzleman should stop shooting, and either reject the load, or have the slump adjusted to produce a suitable consistency.

Larger diameter rebar and embedments require special shooting techniques to provide full encapsulation. Shotcrete needs to be applied from

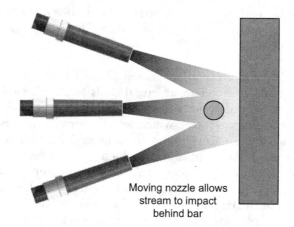

Moving nozzle allows
stream to impact
behind bar

Figure 9.29 Shooting technique for large diameter bars.

both sides of the bars so that a void does not develop behind the rebar. This requires frequent movement of the nozzle by the nozzleman. Figure 9.29 shows a schematic of this process.

9.10.5 Hybrid shotcrete

Hybrid Shotcrete refers to a process in which wet-mix shotcrete placed by pneumatic projection from a nozzle at a high impacting velocity to achieve compaction is followed by supplemental consolidation by mechanical vibration using immersion vibrators. While the ACI 506R-16 Guide to Shotcrete and ACI 506.2-13 Specification for Shotcrete make no reference to this supplemental consolidation process with shotcrete, it has in fact been used by many shotcrete contractors over several decades for applications such as the following where it is difficult, or not possible to achieve full consolidation without supplemental consolidation with immersion vibrators:

a) In very heavily reinforced structural elements (walls, pilasters, columns, beams, copings, etc.) where the configuration of the reinforcing steel is such that it is not possible to achieve full shotcrete consolidation and encapsulation of the reinforcing steel by the shotcrete process alone;

b) In walls and other structural elements with embedments, such as steel H-sections, congested plastic conduit for electrical outlets and/or curtain wall grouting, and electrical outlet boxes, where it is difficult to obtain complete consolidation around the embedded items by the shotcrete process alone; and

c) In projects with vertical and/or horizontal polyvinyl chloride (PVC) waterstops, which are notoriously difficult to fully encase using shotcreting alone.

The *hybrid shotcrete* process has proven to be particularly beneficial for construction of mass shotcrete structural walls and other elements. Thick structural shotcrete walls and beams with multiple layers of closely spaced large-diameter reinforcing steel, which would normally not be considered suitable for construction using the shotcrete process, are now being successfully constructed on large underground Metro station projects, using this *hybrid shotcrete* construction process. An excellent example of this is work now being carried out in Toronto, Canada on large underground Metro stations (some of the largest underground stations in North America). The following paragraphs provide an outline of this work.

Many of the walls in these underground stations are 1.3 m or greater in thickness and contained multiple layers of closely spaced 30M and 35M reinforcing steel bars. Congestion is particularly severe in the lower parts of the walls where vertical starter bars were parallel spiced. This work necessitated the development of low heat of hydration shotcrete mixes, which would not be subject to damage from excessive peak temperatures and differential thermal stresses from the thermal gradient between the core and the finished shotcrete surface. Because of the congestion in the walls from most of the elements listed in items a), b) and c) above, in development of the Thermal Control Plan (TCP), the contractor elected to not use cooling pipes, because of the additional congestion and difficulties that this would bring. Instead, they elected to meet the TCP requirements using a low heat of hydration shotcrete with 70% slag replacement for Portland cement. While such high slag contents have been regularly used in cast-in-place concretes in the Toronto area, there was no precedence for the use of 70% slag mixes in shotcrete in Canada. Consequently, a detailed research and development program was carried out to optimize a shotcrete mixture design which would be suitable for the work. Details of development of such a mix are provided in Section 7.5.

An example of the construction of mass shotcrete underground station walls in a Toronto metro station using the *hybrid* wet-mix shotcrete construction process is provided in Section 10.3.

9.11 FINISHING

For many shotcrete projects, such as rock slope stabilization and underground support in tunnels and mines, the shotcrete is left in its natural *as-shot* state and finishing is not specified or required. The as-shot surface appearance will depend primarily on the gradation of the aggregates used in the shotcrete mixture design. Shotcrete made with ACI 506 Gradation

No.1 aggregate produces essentially a mortar mix with 5 mm maximum size aggregate and leaves the least rough as-shot surface appearance. By contrast, the more commonly used ACI 506 Gradation No. 2 aggregate blend has a nominal 10 mm maximum size aggregate and leaves a rougher textured surface appearance, because of the deeper *craters* left by the impacting larger sized aggregate particles. Shotcrete with a nominal 14 mm maximum size (which is commonly used in structural shotcrete wall construction), will leave an even rougher surface and is normally covered with a finished surface coat. Figure 9.30 shows a typical ACI 506 Gradation No. 2 as-shot surface finish.

It should be noted that a natural as-shot surface finish, in spite of its inherent roughness, still provides a good finish, from both a structural and durability perspective. In fact, ACI CCS-4(2020) suggests that for many applications it is the preferred finish, in that it is not susceptible to damage from improper finishing operations.

Most shotcrete used for structural applications, seismic retrofit, infrastructure rehabilitation, swimming pools and spas and architectural applications is finished for reasons such as:

a) Control over line and grade and tolerance (typically equivalent to, or even superior to formed cast-in-place-concrete construction);
b) Functional reasons (e.g. smooth surface finish in hydraulic structures to minimize potential for cavitation erosion induced damage);

Figure 9.30 As-shot surface appearance for shotcrete with ACI 506 Gradation No.2 aggregate blend.

c) Aesthetic reasons (e.g. plain flat surface finish, suitable for paint application in in-ground parking structures); and

d) Architectural reasons (e.g. simulated natural rockscapes in highway retaining walls, zooscapes, and water features).

The sections which follow briefly examine some of the different types of surface finish that can be achieved, and the methods used to create them. Most common are plain, flat shotcrete walls, pilasters, columns and other structural elements. After shooting to line and grade, using devices such as guide wires and/or wood edge forms, the finishers wait until the shotcrete has stiffened sufficiently before commencing with finishing operations. If a finish coat is not being used and the shotcrete has been shot to its full thickness, the finishers will cut and trim the shotcrete to its final line and grade using cutting rods (sharp-edged screeds). The use of cutting rods with levelling bubbles can aid in this process, as it reduces the number and spacing of shooting wires needed to be installed. The nozzleman slightly overshoots the shotcrete and the finisher then scores it with the cutting rod to the required thickness and verticality, followed by cutting away excess shotcrete to the base of the scored grooves.

Figure 9.31 shows a finisher trimming the shotcrete to line and grade using a cutting rod. This leaves an open textured surface finish. If the wall or other structural element is to be covered with other surface finishes such as drywall, then specifications often require the elements to be left in the open-textured *rodded finish*. More common, however, is closing and smoothing the rodded finish using a *darby*. Figure 9.32 shows a finisher closing and smoothing the rodded surface with a darby. The use of darbys is preferable for this purpose, as it provides better control over line and grade and tolerance than shorter wood floats.

Following finishing with the darby, the specified final surface finish texture is applied. A range of different types of surface finishes can be applied. Smoothest surface finishes are achieved by steel trowels. Steel trowel finishing is often specified for hydraulic structures, such as dam spillways, water intake structures and draft tubes where very tight surface finish tolerances are specified to minimize the potential for cavitation erosion induced damage (ACI 210R, 1993) and (ACI 210.1R, 1994). Steel trowel finishes are also often specified for hydraulic structures such as water pressure tunnels, aqueducts and syphons, where very smooth surface finishes are required to produce low *Reynold's Numbers* and thus minimize water flow resistance and maximize water flow output (Town, 2004). Steel trowel finishes are also often specified for structures such as skate parks, where smooth surface finishes are required to provide the skateboarders with improved *rideability* and protection against injury from abrasion when falling. Figure 10.37 shows a steel trowelled shotcrete finish in the Metro Skate Park in Burnaby, British Columbia (EcoSmart, 2004).

Figure 9.31 Cutting and trimming a structural shotcrete wall using a cutting rod.

Steel trowel finishes are, however, generally not necessarily the preferred finish for architectural shotcrete walls and other elements. For walls in in-ground parking structures and other structures that are to be painted, architects generally prefer to have some texture in the finished surface so that the paint will adhere better. This can be achieved using a magnesium trowel, or if an even more textured surface finish is required, a wood float finish, or light-textured broom or sponge finish can be applied. Such more textured surface finishes are also often specified for walls and other elements that will not be painted. Compared to very smooth steel trowel finishes, they tend to be more aesthetically pleasing in that they do not highlight the appearance of features such as any plastic or restrained drying shrinkage cracks, and subtle undulations from hand finishing operations. Figure 9.33 shows a light broom textured finish being applied to the Whistler Sliding Centre bobsleigh/luge track. In this case, the broom

Figure 9.32 Closing and smoothing a rodded finish using a darby.
(Photo courtesy Shaun Radomski.)

textured surface finish was specified to provide better bond of the sliding
ice to the shotcrete track.

Even rougher surface finish textures are sometimes specified for various
types of architectural structures, such as artificial rockscapes and water
features. Cutting and carving, imprinting with crumpled aluminum foil
and finishing with soft rubber floats, or sponge floats are some of the techniques that can be used to produce rougher textured surface finishes.
Examples of such work are presented in Chapter 16 on Architectural
Shotcrete.

9.12 PROTECTION AND CURING

On completion of finishing, it is important to protect the shotcrete from
rapidly drying out, as this can cause plastic shrinkage cracking and/or *crazing* (fine pattern cracking in the hardened shotcrete surface). This can be
accomplished by using techniques such as erection of wind breaks and sunshades, fogging/misting, or spray application of evaporation retarders to the
finished shotcrete surface.

Figure 9.33 Light broom finish application to Whistler Sliding Centre bobsleigh/luge track.

As soon as the shotcrete has taken a hard set, it should be cured. Curing is best achieved with moist curing using methods such as:

a) Wrap the shotcrete repairs in wet burlap covered with a plastic sheet, or use a presaturated plastic-coated non-woven synthetic fabric;
b) Where conditions permit, install sprinklers or soaker hoses to keep the shotcrete continuously wet for the specified period; and
c) Maintain wet curing for at least 7 days.

With wet curing, it is important to keep the shotcrete continuously wet and avoid procedures which allow the shotcrete to undergo cycles of wetting and drying during the curing process.

Figure 9.34 shows an example of fogging the freshly applied steel fibre-reinforced, silica fume wet-mix shotcrete during seismic retrofit of the Littlerock Dam in Southern California, using a 20-MPa water pressure sprayer. After the shotcrete had attained final set, it was covered with pre-saturated plastic-coated synthetic fabric curing blankets. Soaker hoses were turned on and the shotcrete was kept continuously wet for 7 days. With this rigorous approach to wet curing, on completion of the project the shotcrete was found to be essentially free of plastic and drying shrinkage cracking, in spite of ambient temperatures during shotcrete application often rising above 40°C during summer months (Forrest et al., 1995).

Figure 9.34 Fogging and wet curing the upstream face of the Littlerock Dam in Southern California.

By contrast, Figure 9.35 shows an example of a wet-mix, fibre-reinforced shotcrete retaining wall being constructed at a dam project in Northern California that was not adequately protected against drying after shotcrete application. This westerly facing retaining wall was subjected intense heat from solar radiation in the afternoon (shotcrete surface temperatures well in excess of 40°C). The specification called for fogging and misting after shotcrete application until such time as the shotcrete had attained final set, followed by continuous wet curing for 7 days. The contractor simply wet down the hardened shotcrete surface intermittently with a water hose and the shotcrete experienced cycles of wetting and drying. This attempt at wet curing proved to be totally inadequate and severe pattern cracking developed as shown in Figure 9.35, The work was rejected and had to be redone. The second time round, rigorous attention was paid to the specified wet curing procedures and a satisfactory, largely crack-free product was produced.

Where moist curing is not suitable because of logistical or other constraints, spray-on curing compounds can be used. They are less desirable than moist curing, as they do not provide the additional water that shotcrete needs for optimal hydration and minimizing the potential for autogenous and drying shrinkage-induced cracking (Aitcin, 1999). They are, however considerably better than providing no curing protection at all. When used, they should be applied at twice the coverage rate at which they would be used in concrete flatwork, as they tend to flow down vertical surfaces, thus reducing the effective coverage rate.

Figure 9.35 Cracking in an inadequately wet-cured retaining wall at a project in Northern California.

In addition to wet curing, or the use of spray-on curing compounds, the shotcrete should be protected against adverse thermal effects. ACI 506R (ACI 506R-16, 2016) recommends that in hot weather conditions shotcrete application should be suspended if ambient temperatures rise above 35°C. There are however some areas in North America where ambient temperatures rise above 35°C most days during summer months. In such conditions, additional protection measures need to be adopted, such as installation of sun shields and wind breaks, use of ice during wet-mix shotcrete batching, to lower the supplied shotcrete temperature, and carrying out shooting during night shifts.

In cold weather conditions, ACI 506R (ACI 506R-16, 2016) recommends that work should be suspended if the substrate temperature is below 5°C and/or the ambient temperature is forecast to fall below 5°C, unless suitable cold weather protection measures are undertaken. For example, in Edmonton and Calgary in Alberta, shotcrete construction of major structures has proceeded throughout the winter by constructing suitable heated enclosures with wet curing. Work has typically only been suspended when ambient temperatures fall below –20°C. (It simply gets too difficult to maintain shotcrete supply under such conditions.)

During shotcrete construction of the bobsleigh/luge track for the Beijing 2022 Winter Olympics, all shotcrete application, finishing and wet curing was conducted inside six travelling tents, in which the temperature and humidity was controlled. In summer, the tents provided protection against

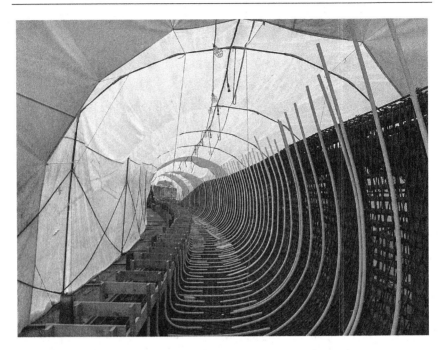

Figure 9.36 Travelling tent used for environmental control during the shotcrete construction of the bobsleigh/luge tracks for the Whistler 2010 Winter Olympics.

the drying effects of wind and solar radiation and shutdowns in construction because of rain. In winter, the tents provided protection against wind and snow and freezing in the heated enclosures. This enabled shotcrete construction to proceed throughout the year in a project with harsh environmental conditions and a tight schedule. Figure 9.36 an example of a tent used on the Whistler 2010 Olympics project.

In addition to the above protection measures, consideration should also be given to the effects of wind and rain. Shotcrete work should be terminated during periods of high winds. Not only can high winds cause separation of materials in the shotcrete stream as shotcrete is ejected from the nozzle (dry-mix shotcrete can be particularly vulnerable to this condition), but it can also result in excessive build-up of overspray down-wind of where the shotcrete is being deposited. If not removed, and allowed to harden, such overspray can create a porous layer which can adversely affect the quality of bond of the shotcrete to the substrate or subsequent layers of shotcrete. With respect to rain, as discussed in Section 9.2, best bond is achieved in shotcrete applied to a substrate in the saturated surface dry (SSD) condition. If rain results in free surface water flowing down the substrate surface, then installation of tarpaulins or other protective measures should be implemented, or the work should be terminated. Also, rainwater running down the surface of freshly applied shotcrete can wash out the cement paste, compromising finishing operations and the quality of the finished surface.

REFERENCES

AASHTO-AGC-ARTBA Joint Committee Task Force 37 Report. 1998. *Guide Specifications for Shotcrete Repair of Highway Bridges*, American Association of State Highway and Transportation Officials, 101 p.

ACI 210.1R. 1994. *Compendium of Case Histories on Repair of erosion-Damaged Concrete in hydraulic Structures (reapproved 1999)*. American Concrete Institute. 33 p.

ACI 210R. 1993. *Erosion of Concrete in Hydraulic Structures*. American Concrete Institute. 24 p.

ACI 506.1R-21. 2021. *Guide to Fiber Reinforced Shotcrete*. American Concrete Institute. 20 p.

ACI 506.2-13. 2013. *Specification for Shotcrete*. American Concrete Institute. 12 p.

ACI 506R-16. 2016. *Guide to Shotcre*te. American Concrete Institute. 40 p.

ACI, CCS-4. 2020. *Shotcrete for the Craftsman*. American Concrete Institute. 92 p.

ACI CCP-60.1-20. 2020. *Craftsman Workbook for ACI Certification of Shotcrete Nozzlemen*. American Concrete Institute. 122 p.

ACI CT-18. 2018b. *Concrete Terminology*. American Concrete Institute. 80.

ACI RAP-6. 2005. *Vertical and Overhead Spall Repair by Hand Application*. American Concrete Institute. 5 p.

Aitcin, P.-C. 1999. Demystifying Autogenous Shrinkage. *Concrete International*. Vol. 21. No. 11. November. 54–56.

ASA. 2008. Whistler Sliding Center, 2007 Outstanding Infrastructure Project. *Shotcrete Magazine. American Shotcrete Association* Summer 2008. 37–41.

ASA. 2010. Olympic Games Preparation Center, 2009 Outstanding Architectural Project. *Shotcrete Magazine. American Shotcrete Association* Spring 2010. 6–8.

ASTM C642. 2013c. *Standard Test Method for Density, Absorption and Voids in Hardened Concrete*. 3p. ASTM International. https://doi.org/10.1520/C0642-13.

Bissonnette, B., Vaysburd, A. M. and von Fay, K. F. 2012. Best Practices for Preparing Concrete Surfaces Prior to Repairs and Overlays. *U.S. Department of the Interior Bureau of Reclamation Report. No.MERL 12–17*. 61 p.

Crom, T. R. 1981. Dry Mix Shotcrete Nozzling. *Concrete International*. Vol. 3. No. 1. January. 80–93.

CSA. 2019c. *A23.1/A23.2 Concrete materials and methods of concrete construction/Test methods and standard practices for concrete*. 690p. Canadian Standards Association.

Duffield, S. 1999. Shotcrete Applications at Northparkes E26 Mine. *Shotcrete Magazine. American Shotcrete Association* August 1999. 18–24.

EcoSmart. 2004. *Use of EcoSmart Concrete for the Metro Skate Park, Burnaby, BC, Construction Report*. EcoSmart. Vancouver. British Columbia. November 2004. 19 p.

EFNARC. 1999. *Guidelines for specifiers and contractors*. European specification for Sprayed Concrete. 31 p.

Forrest, M. P., Morgan, D. R., Obermeyer, J. R., Parker, P. L. and LaMoreaux, D. D. 1995. Seismic Retrofit of Littlerock Dam. *ACI Concrete International*. Vol. 18. No. 3. March. 24–29.

Gagnon, F. and Jolin, M. 2007. Dynamic Forces during Shotcreting Operations. *Shotcrete Magazine. American Shotcrete Association* Summer 2007. 26–28.

Hanskat, C. S. 2014. Shotcrete Placed in Multiple Layers does Not Create Cold Joints. *Shotcrete Magazine. American Shotcrete Association* Spring 2014. 40–41.

Hart, E. 2008. Expanded Metal Sheet Forming. *Shotcrete Magazine. American Shotcrete Association* Summer 2008. 8–9.

ICRI 310.1R-2008. 2008. *Guideline for Surface Preparation for the Repair of Deteriorated Concrete Resulting from Reinforcing Steel Corrosion*. International Concrete Repair Institute. 12 p.

ICRI 310.2R-2013. 2013. *Selecting and Specifying Concrete Surface Preparation for Sealers, Coatings, Polymer Overlays and Concrete Repair*. International Concrete Repair Institute. 48 p.

ICRI 310.3R-2014. 2014. *Guideline for the Preparation of Concrete Surfaces for Repair Using Hydrodemolition Methods*. International Concrete Repair Institute. 28 p.

Kirsten, H. A. D. 1992. Comparative efficiency and ultimate strength of mesh and fibre reinforced shotcrete as determined from full-scale bending tests. *Journal of The South African Institute of Mining and Metallurgy*. Vol. 92. No. 11/12. November/December. 303–323.

Kroman, J., Morgan, D. R. and Simpson, L. 2002. Shotcrete Lions for Calgary's Centre Street Bridge. *Shotcrete Magazine. American Shotcrete Association* Winter 2002. 4–8.

Morgan, D. R., Chen, L. and Beaupré, D. 1995. Toughness of Fibre Reinforced Shotcrete. *Shotcrete for Underground Support VII*. edited by Klapperich, H., Potler, R. & Willocq, J. Telfs, Austria, American Society of Civil Engineers, 66–87.

Morgan, D. R. and Heere, R. 2000. Evolution of Fiber Reinforced Shotcrete. *Shotcrete Magazine. American Shotcrete Association* Spring 2000. 8–11.

Morgan, D. R., Heere, R., Chan, C. and McAskill, N. 1999. Comparative Evaluation of System Ductility of Mesh and Fire Reinforced Shotcretes. *Shotcrete for Underground Support VII. American Society of Civil Engineers*. edited by Celistino, T.B. & Parker, H.W., Campos do Jordao, Brazil. 216–239.

Morgan, D. R., Kazakoff, K. and Ibrahim, H. 2006. Seismic Retrofit of a Concrete Immersed Tube Tunnel with Reinforced Shotcrete. *Shotcrete for Underground Support X. American Society of Civil Engineers*. edited by Morgan, D.R. and Parker, H.W. Whistler. B.C. 270–284.

Morgan, D.R., Loevlie, K. and Kwong, N. 2010. Centrifugal Sprayed Concrete for Lining Horizontal Pipes and Culverts and Vertical Shafts. *Shotcrete: Elements of a System*, Edited by Bernard, S., Taylor and Francis Group. 225–232.

Morgan, D. R., McAskill, N., Richardson, B. W. and Zellers, R. C. 1989. *A Comparative Evaluation of Plain, Polypropylene Fiber, Steel Fiber and Wire Mesh Reinforced Shotcretes*. Transportation Research Record 1226. Transportation Research Board. National Research Council. Washington. DC. 78–87.

Morgan, D. R. and Neil, J. 1991. Durability of Shotcrete Rehabilitation Treatments of Bridges in Canada. *Transportation Association of Canada Annual Conference*, Winnipeg. Manitoba, September 1991, 14–19. Republished in *Shotcrete: A*

Compilation of Papers. American Shotcrete Association. editor D.R. Morgan. 269–306.

Radomski, S. M., Morgan, D. R., Zhang, L. and Graham, D. 2019. Structural Modifications to Hydroelectrical Turbine Draft Tube Ceiling. *Shotcrete Magazine. American Shotcrete Association* Summer 2019. 22–34.

Reny, S. 2013. Surface Preparation for Shotcrete Repair. *Shotcrete Magazine. American Shotcrete Association* Spring 2013. 28–30.

Ripley, B. D., Rapp, P. A. and Morgan, D. R. 1998. *Shotcrete Design, Construction and Quality Assurance for the Stave Falls Tunnels*. Tunnelling Association of Canada. 141–156.

RTC. 2019. *Guideline on the Applicability of Fibre-Reinforced Shotcrete for Ground Support in Mines*. Rock Tech Centre – MIGS III – WP 24. 53 p.

Talbot, C., Pigeon, M., Beaupré, D. and Morgan, D.R. 1995. Influence of Surface Preparation on Long-Term Bonding of Shotcrete. *ACI Materials Journal*. Vol. 91. No. 6. November. 560–566.

Tatnall, P.C. 2002. Shotcrete in Fires: Effects of Fibers on Explosive Spalling. *Shotcrete Magazine. American Shotcrete Association* Fall 2002. 10–12.

Town, R. 2004. Restoring the Century-Old Wachusett Aqueduct. *Shotcrete Magazine. American Shotcrete Association* Summer 2004. 16–18.

Trottier, J. -F., Forgeron, D. and Mahoney, M. 2002. Influence of Construction Joints in Wet-Mix Shotcrete Panels. *Shotcrete Magazine. American Shotcrete Association* Fall 2002. 26–30.

Warner, J. 2001. Dealing with Reinforcing. Shotcrete Magazine. *American Shotcrete Association* Winter 2001. 24–26.

Wolsiefer, J and Morgan, D. R. 1993. Silica Fume in Shotcrete. *Concrete International*. Vol. 15. No. 4. April 1993. 34–39.

Yoggy, G. D. 2000. The History of Shotcrete, Part I of a Three Part Series. Shotcrete Magazine. American Shotcrete Association Fall 2000. 28–29.

Zhang, L., Morgan, D. R., Walter, T., McInnes, B., Rule, A. and Mitchell, A. 2018. Shaft Lining with Dry-Mix Shotcrete. *Shotcrete Magazine. American Shotcrete Association* Summer 2018. 48–56.

Zweifel, C. 2010. Shotcrete Domes, A Model of Sustainability. *Shotcrete Magazine. American Shotcrete Association* Fall 2010. 31–33.

Zynda, C. 2008. *Forming for Shotcrete. Shotcrete Magazine. American Shotcrete Association* Summer 2008. 14–15.

Chapter 10

Buildings and structures

10.1 INTRODUCTION

Shotcrete has a long history of use for construction of various structural components in buildings and structures. In early years, the dry-mix shotcrete (*gunite*) process was used for applications such as encasement of structural steel columns and beams and steel stacks to provide fire protection and/or protection from corrosion. Such shotcrete was typically reinforced with wire mesh chaired off the structural steel elements. Figure 10.1, for example, shows a steel kiln stack wrapped with mesh and vertical and horizontal band rods in preparation for application of dry-mix shotcrete (*gunite)* at St. Mary's Cement Co. plant in Ontario, Canada in 1926. The reinforced shotcrete was applied to the steel kiln stacks to make them structurally self-supporting (and thus do away with guy ropes), as well as extend their service life (Lind, 1926).

The impetus for true *structural shotcrete* construction, where structural elements with reinforcing steel were constructed using shotcrete, in lieu of conventional cast-in-place concrete construction, arose from the results of earthquakes in California (Warner, 2004). As a result of a school fire in Los Angeles in the 1920s the Los Angeles School Board mandated that all future school buildings be constructed with masonry. However, masonry of the day was typically not reinforced and the Long Beach earthquake which occurred in 1933 resulted in severe damage or destruction of several hundred school buildings. As a consequence, the California State Legislature passed an act requiring seismic retrofit of all remaining school buildings. This was a major task and engineers and contractors rapidly found that the most expeditious and economical means to undertake this task, included strengthening elements such as masonry walls and pilasters by installing anchors in the masonry, connected to vertical and horizontal reinforcing steel, which was then encased in shotcrete. Warner (Warner, 2004) provides a review of the history of use of shotcrete in seismic retrofit in California from the 1930s to the 1990s.

With the development of the wet-mix shotcrete process in the 1960s, and its increased use in the 1970s, structural shotcrete quality improved and construction became more reliable and economical. Contractors bidding

Figure 10.1 Steel kiln stacks ready for shotcreting at St. Mary's Cement Co. plant in Ontario, Canada in 1926.

(Photo courtesy Chris Zynda.)

projects increasingly started to ask the question: *Should I form and pour or shoot?* The state-of-the-art of structural shotcrete design and construction has now advanced to the extent that in many of the major cities in Western North America (particularly in California, Washington State, British Columbia and Alberta) and now increasingly elsewhere in North America, wet-mix shotcrete has become the preferred means of construction of permanent deep foundation exterior structural walls, pilasters and even interior structural elements such as shear walls and elevator walls. Such preferences arise from the reduction or even elimination of formwork. Exterior structural walls and pilasters are often constructed without any formwork and interior walls can be constructed with single-sided formwork. This not only saves on materials costs but also typically accelerates the construction schedule, with attendant cost savings.

In addition to structural walls and pilasters, shotcrete has found use in a number of other types of structural applications, including:

a) Construction of complex curvature structures that do not lend themselves well to forming, such as domes and shells (Briggs and Poole, 2006, Ragen and Briggs, 2008;South, 2009; Zynda, 2009; Zweifel, 2010; Flanagan, 2015);

b) Prestressed water tanks (Balck, 1999; Hanskat, 2010; Hanskat, 2011);

c) Bobsleigh/luge tracks (Shotcrete Magazine, 2008); and

d) Skate parks (Tremere, 2000; EcoSmart, 2004; Leone, 2011).

The sections which follow provide some examples of the above types of structural shotcrete applications.

10.2 STRUCTURAL SHOTCRETE WALLS AND OTHER ELEMENTS

In construction of many high-rise buildings in the large cities in Western North America city planning departments require the developers to provide in-ground parking for the residents, users and visitors to the buildings. This commonly results in a requirement for four to as many as eight floors of in-ground parking, some as much as 30 m deep below street level. As described in Chapter 12, the deep excavations are often shored with either temporary passive soil-nailed reinforced shotcrete faced linings or stressed tie-back reinforced shotcrete linings. Once the excavation and shoring is completed to its full depth, construction of the permanent shotcrete walls can then proceed. Figure 10.2 shows an example of a stressed tie-back shotcrete shored deep foundation ready for construction of perimeter walls and other structural elements.

Conventionally, after placement of the slab-on-grade, the perimeter reinforced concrete walls and pilasters would be constructed using formed cast-in-place concrete construction. This would be followed by forming and construction of the lowest level suspended reinforced concrete slab and ramps and this process would be repeated one floor level at a time, until reaching street level. Such construction, however, requires the use of either single-sided, or in some cases double-sided formwork. Supply and installation of formwork is a substantial materials and time cost item in such construction. Owners, engineers and contractors have found that substantial materials and time cost savings can be realized (particularly in congested city sites, with limited lay-down areas for formwork and high demand on crane time) by constructing perimeter walls and other elements with reinforced wet-mix shotcrete, in lieu of formed, cast-in-place concrete methods. The use of shotcrete minimizes or even eliminates the need for formwork.

Figure 10.2 Stressed tie-back shotcrete shored deep excavation ready for construction of perimeter walls.

(Photo courtesy T. Ross King, Consolidated Shotcrete Inc.)

The same reinforcing steel details can be used as in conventional formed, cast-in-place-concrete construction, but with some modifications to make the fixed steel better suited to encapsulation with shotcrete. For example:

a) The use of bundled bars, which make it more difficult for the nozzleman to achieve full consolidation around the reinforcing steel should be avoided;

b) Contact lap splices should be avoided if possible. If unavoidable, bars should preferably be lapped back to back, rather than side by side, relative to the shooting orientation;

c) Where multiple layers of reinforcement are required, the outermost layers should be sufficiently open to allow the nozzle clear unobstructed access to the innermost layers of bars; and

d) Intersecting reinforcing steel bars should be rigidly tied to one another and to their anchors with 1.3 mm or heavier gauge tie wire and adequately chaired and supported to minimize vibration during shotcrete placement. However, large knots of tie wire, that could impede the shotcrete stream and create voids, should be avoided.

ACI 506R-16 provides good guidance on the best methods for placing and fixing reinforcing steel in order to make it suitable for encapsulation with shotcrete. For example, the clearance between bars should be at least three times the maximum aggregate size, or three times the bar diameter, whichever is greater.

Figure 10.3 Start of bench gun shooting of a structural shotcrete wall with suitably fixed reinforcing steel.

Figure 10.3 shows a structural shotcrete wall with reinforcing steel suitably fixed for shotcrete encapsulation. Shotcrete is being placed by the *bench
shooting* method by the nozzleman, working in conjunction with a blowpipe operator who continuously removes any rebound and excessive overspray from the work area in advance of shotcrete placement. A detailed
description of the bench shooting method is provided in Chapter 9. Shooting
wires are installed to define the final line and grade for the walls. Before
shooting, the cover between the back layer of rebar and shored wall and
front layer of rebar and shooting wires is checked. The nozzleman bench
shoots to just encase the outer layer of rebar. Any high spots of shotcrete are
removed with cutting rods or trowels. The walls are typically benched in
about 0.75 m high lifts, with each lift of shotcrete being allowed to stiffen
sufficiently before the nozzleman stacks the next lift. This process is repeated
until the full height of the wall has been shot.

After the benched shotcrete has stiffened sufficiently, it is trimmed with a
cutting rod or trowel, and/or broomed with a stiff bristle broom to remove
any uneven or loose material and laitance. The final lift of *covercrete* is then
applied from the top down using the layer shooting method. The shotcrete
is trimmed to the final line and grade with cutting rods and the final finishing treatments applied. Figure 10.4 shows top-down construction of the
final *covercrete* layer in a structural shotcrete wall.

Finishing usually encompasses closing the rodded surface texture with a
bull float or derby, followed by trowelling with a steel or magnesium trowel.
The final surface texture specified by the architect can then be applied.

Figure 10.4 Top-down construction of final *covercrete* shotcrete layer in structural shotcrete wall.

(Photo courtesy T. Ross King, Consolidated Shotcrete inc.)

Control joints for shrinkage cracking control are installed with special joint-
ing tools at this stage. Final surface textures specified can range from smooth
steel or magnesium trowel finishes to more textured finishes such as wood
or rubber float finishes or even light broom textured finishes. In-ground
parking lots are often painted with white paints to improve visibility and
more textured finishes are generally preferred in such applications for better
long-term paint adherence. They are generally more aesthetically pleasing
than formed cast-in-place-concrete walls in that they are free of form lines,
pour lines, *bugholes* and filled form-tie holes. Figure 10.5 shows a good
example of a finished structural shotcrete wall.

    In construction of permanent structural shotcrete walls, it is important
that adequate protection and curing be provided. In cold weather conditions, heated enclosures are commonly built to heat the substrate and protect the shotcrete from low ambient temperatures. For example, in a number
of large shotcrete wall construction projects in Alberta the use of heated
enclosures has allowed shotcrete construction to proceed year-round, with
exterior ambient temperatures falling as low as –20°C in winter months. At
temperatures lower than this shotcreting is usually terminated because of
the dangers of shotcrete freezing and blockages in boom pumps and shotcrete hoses.

Figure 10.5 Finished structural shotcrete wall.

(Photo courtesy T. Ross King, Consolidated Shotcrete Inc.)

In hot weather conditions, shade screens and wind barriers are often used to protect the freshly placed and finished shotcrete from heating from solar radiation and excessive rates of evaporation. The best means of protecting the shotcrete against drying shrinkage cracking is wet curing (Morgan and Chan, 2001). Many structural shotcrete specifications require wet curing for a minimum of 7 days after shotcrete placement, using methods such as:

a) Saturated plastic-covered burlap or coated fabrics kept continuously wet with soaker hoses; and
b) Fogging and misting devices or soaker hoses.

Where wet curing is not considered suitable, spray-on curing compounds can be used. They do, however, not provide the external source of moisture which is so important in mitigating the potentially damaging effects of autogenous desiccation (plastic shrinkage cracking and crazing) (Aitcin, 1999) and should be considered a second-best alternative to wet curing.

In structural shotcrete projects, provision of a suitable specification, with enforcement through a thorough Quality Assurance (QA) and Quality Control (QC) inspection and testing program is important. Attached in Appendix A is a generic *Guide Specification for Structural Shotcrete*

Table 10.1 Structural shotcrete performance requirements

Test description	Test method	Age, days	Specified requirements
Maximum water/cementitious materials ratio		—	0.45
Air content – as-shot	ASTM C231, or CSA A23.2-4C	—	4 ± 1%
Slump at discharge into pump	ASTM C143, or CSA A23.2-5C	—	65 ± 25 mm
Minimum compressive strength	ASTM C1604, or CSA A23.2-14C	7 28	20 MPa 30 MPa

developed by Morgan and Totten (Morgan and Totten, 2008) which can easily be adapted for most structural shotcrete projects. It details requirements for QA and QC and provides typical recommended shotcrete performance requirements, as summarized in Table 10.1. The structural engineer can, of course, specify higher compressive strengths, if required for structural purposes. The specification of compressive strengths lower than 30 MPa at 28 days is, however, not recommended, as lower strength shotcretes, with leaner cementing materials contents, may not provide the required adhesion and cohesion shooting characteristics.

10.3 MASS SHOTCRETE

ACI Concrete Terminology Standard (CT-18) defines mass concrete as *any volume of structural concrete in which a combination of dimensions of the members being cast, boundary conditions, the characteristics of the concrete mixture, and the ambient condition can lead to undesirable thermal stresses, cracking, deleterious chemical reactions, or reduction in the long-term strength as a result of elevated concrete temperature due to heat from hydration.*

CSA A23.1:19 Annex T provides detailed guidance regarding mass concrete and states: *For practical purposes, mass concrete placements are commonly identified as placements where the minimum dimension is large, such as 1 m thick or greater.*

Until recently, shotcrete was not often placed in thicknesses which exceeded 1 m and so concerns relating to mass concrete placements were seldom an issue. This has, however, recently changed and the first author has recently been involved in several projects where wet-mix shotcrete walls and other structural elements with least dimensions in the 1.0 to 2.0 m thickness range have been constructed. This has necessitated the development of a new range of special low heat of hydration structural shotcrete mixtures.

In addition, depending on project specifics, measures such as the following have been implemented:

a) Installation of cooling pipes (such as used in mass concrete construction);
b) Construction of the shotcrete in multiple lifts (allowing for heat dissipation between lifts);
c) Development of Thermal Control Plans (TCP's), in conjunction with preconstruction adiabatic and/or semi-adiabatic testing and thermal modelling; and
d) Rigorous thermal monitoring, with detailed requirements for protective measures, such as the timing and removal of thermal insulation blankets.

Zhang et al. (2021) provide a good case history example of the thermal design and construction of a large 1.0 m thick mass shotcrete structural wall for a wastewater treatment plant in Vancouver, British Columbia. The project specification called for a peak temperature in the wall to not exceed 60°C and the thermal differential between the centre and surface of the wall to not exceed 20°C. These requirements were met in mock-up testing by:

e) Use of a low heat of hydration mass shotcrete with 40% ground granulated blast-furnace slag, in conjunction with,
f) Installation of plastic cooling pipes at 1.0 m spacing with cooling provided by city tap water with a temperature of 13.7°C.

In addition, cut sections through the mock-up demonstrated excellent encapsulation of the reinforcing steel and plastic cooling pipes. The cooling pipes were not damaged by the shotcrete impacting process. Figure 10.6 provides a view of the mass shotcrete wall under construction.

Seventy-two (72) cubic metres of shotcrete was supplied to the project and the wall was shot and finished in a 10½ hour shift. The peak temperature in the centre of the wall was 60°C, which met the specified performance requirement and was very close to the peak temperature predicted by thermal modelling using the 3-dimensional Finite Element Modelling (3D-FEM) B4Cast thermal modelling program. The thermal differential between the interior and formed face of the wall was less than 20°C, which met the specified performance requirement. The thermal differential between the centre and finished face of the wall, however, peaked at 25°C after 50 hours. This was attributed to a delay in installation of the thermal blankets. See thermal measurements in Figure 10.7.

As a consequence, a thermal stress analysis was conducted using the 3D-FEM program and it was determined that the thermal stress vs. tensile strength ratio was 59%, which is less than 75% at which the potential for thermal cracking is considered high. Subsequent visual examination of the finished shotcrete surface revealed no evidence of thermal cracking. Zhang concluded the paper with detailed recommendations for a thermal control plan for construction of mass shotcrete walls and other elements.

Figure 10.6 Mass shotcrete wall under construction.

(Photo courtesy Lihe (John) Zhang, LZhang Consulting & Testing Ltd.)

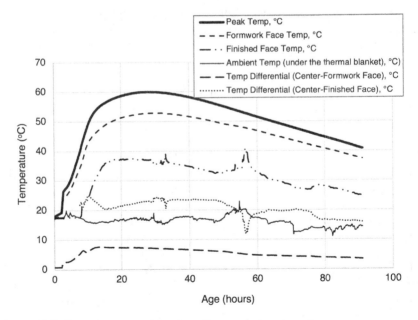

Figure 10.7 Temperature monitoring of mass shotcrete wall.

(Graph courtesy Lihe (John) Zhang, LZhang Consulting & Testing Ltd.)

10.4 SEISMIC RETROFIT WITH STRUCTURAL SHOTCRETE

As mentioned in Section 10.1, seismic retrofit with structural shotcrete had its origins in California in the 1930s and has since been used for many thousands of buildings and infrastructure in North America and around the world. Examples of such seismic retrofit work include the following:

a) Brick masonry schools, hospitals and commercial and residential buildings (Warner, 2004; Morgan and Zhang, 2009);
b) Heritage stone masonry government and civic buildings (Woodhead and Morgan, 1983; von der Hofen, 2004);
c) Seismically deficient reinforced concrete sports stadiums (Kasdi and Totten, 2012); and
d) Immersed tube reinforced concrete undersea tunnels (Morgan et al., 2006).

Brief descriptions of some of these projects follow.

10.4.1 Historic Masonry Building Seismic Retrofit, Vancouver, British Columbia

The Wing Sang Building is the oldest heritage masonry structure in Chinatown in Vancouver, British Columbia. The front (south) building was first built by a Chinese immigrant, Yip Sang, as a two-story brick struc-ture in 1889, with a third floor being added in 1901. His import business thrived, as did his family, and in 1912 he built a back (north) six-storey brick masonry building to house his four wives and 23 children. Over the years the buildings deteriorated, being of simple brick masonry construction with interior timber framing and flooring, which were highly deficient by modern seismic standards. It would have been a simple solution to demol-ish and replace the buildings with a modern high-rise tower. However, in the late 2000s a successful Vancouver realtor, with a penchant for historic structures preservation purchased the property and seismically retrofitted it as his offices and an art gallery. Figure 10.8 shows a view of the façade of the south building during retrofit. Morgan and Zhang (Morgan and Zhang, 2009) provide a detailed description of the seismic retrofit carried out on this building.

Reinforced shotcrete was used to strengthen all the exterior walls and the parapet in the north building and exterior and interior walls in the south building. In addition to installing new internal bracing and reinforced con-crete floors, a major component of the seismic retrofit was tying back all the exterior brick masonry to a new reinforced shotcrete wall and pilaster sys-tem. Figure 10.9 shows a typical wall and pilaster section detail in the north building exterior wall. Figure 10.10 shows shooting of a wall using the bench shooting technique.

Figure 10.8 Wing Sang building south façade.

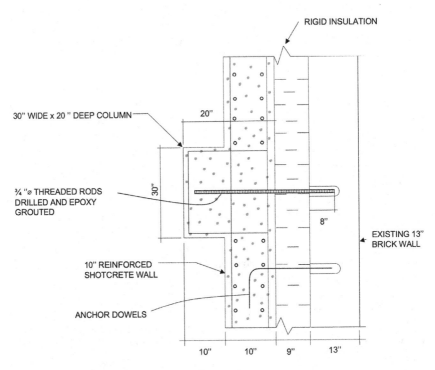

Figure 10.9 Typical wall and pilaster section detail.

Figure 10.10 Shooting an exterior wall using the bench shooting technique.

10.4.2 Heritage stone masonry buildings

Like unreinforced brick masonry buildings, most heritage stone masonry buildings are seriously seismically deficient by modern seismic standards. Reinforced shotcrete with anchors connecting the stone masonry to new interior structural shotcrete walls, pilasters and other structural elements, has been widely used to seismically strengthen heritage stone masonry buildings. In Vancouver, BC, such methods were used in the early 1980s to seismically retrofit the Carnegie Library, which was built in 1903. It now serves as a community centre. Similar methods were also used in the early 1980 to seismically retrofit the heritage stone masonry post office clock tower in Vancouver, BC, which was built in 1909 (Woodhead and Morgan, 1983).

10.4.3 Sports stadium seismic retrofit

In 1923 the California Memorial Stadium was built at the University of California in Berkeley. This 63,000 person capacity stadium was modelled on the Colosseum in Rome. It had deteriorated with time and was considered to be seismically at risk, as it sits directly on the Hayward Earthquake Fault. In 2006, the stadium was included on the National Register of Historic Places. The stadium was in critical need of a seismic retrofit and upgrade to modern standards. In the retrofit carried out in 2011–2012, the majority of the existing structure was demolished and reconstructed. However, the outer

Figure 10.11 General view of existing historic walls at California Memorial Stadium during demolition and excavation work.

(Photo courtesy Johnson Western Gunite.)

perimeter wall had to remain in place to protect this historic landmark. Structural reinforced shotcrete played a large role in the seismic retrofit of the stadium (Kasdi and Totten, 2012). Figure 10.11 shows a general view of the stadium historic walls during demolition and excavation activities.

Initially, the seismic retrofit to the walls was specified to be carried out using formed, cast-in-place concrete. However, a value engineering proposal by the contractor to use structural wet-mix shotcrete in lieu of cast concrete was accepted by the owner, as it resulted in significant cost savings as well as allowing for completion of the project on a tight time schedule. A heavily reinforced shotcrete layer was applied to the existing walls in thicknesses varying from 127 mm to as much as 914 mm. In addition, on seeing the efficiency and quality of the shotcrete alternative, the engineer and owner allowed the scope of structural shotcrete work to be expanded to include construction of new shear walls, retaining walls, a loading dock building and miscellaneous interior walls.

The seismic retrofit work required a dense configuration of large diameter reinforcing steel (up to 32M size) in structural elements such as walls, pilasters and columns. Consequently, all nozzlemen approved to shoot on the project had to demonstrate in preconstruction mock-up testing that they had the ability to properly encase the most congested reinforcing steel details to be encountered on the project.

Figure 10.12 Shotcrete cores extracted from test panel mock-up. Note excellent encapsulation of reinforcing steel with shotcrete and absence of voids.

(Photo courtesy Johnson Western Gunite.)

Full-depth cores were recovered from the test panels. Figure 10.12 shows an example of cores extracted from one preconstruction test panel. Seven of the eight nozzlemen who shot preconstruction test panels passed the test and were approved to shoot on the project. Note the excellent encasement of the reinforcing steel. This requires a high level of skill on the part of the shotcrete nozzleman and crew. In addition to the use of a blow-pipe to remove rebound and build-up of overspray in shooting areas, small diameter pencil vibrators were judiciously used to facilitate complete encapsulation of the reinforcing steel with the plastic shotcrete and eliminate voids.

Figure 10.13 Existing historic shotcrete wall after seismic retrofit with reinforced shotcrete.

(Photo courtesy Johnson Western Gunite.)

Figure 10.13 shows a view of a completed section of the seismic retrofit of the historic wall. In places the reinforced shotcrete wall was up to
12.2 m high. Shotcrete mixture designs were developed which allowed the
shotcrete to be applied in up to 300 mm high lifts. Once the shotcrete had
set sufficiently the next lift was applied, until the full height of the wall was
reached. The shotcrete was applied in one layer of *scratch coat* from the
bottom to the top. The final finish coat was later applied from the top
down and provided with a steel trowel finish, as shown in Figure 10.13.
The shotcrete mixture design specified had a design 28-day compressive
strength of 48 MPa and had a cement content of 450 kg/m^3 and fly ash
content of 80 kg/m^3.

10.4.4 Immersed tube tunnel seismic retrofit

The George Massey Tunnel is an immersed precast concrete tube tunnel
under the South Arm of the Fraser River near Vancouver, British Columbia.
It was constructed in the early 1960s to take road traffic on Highway 99
connecting Vancouver to the I-5 Interstate Highway to Seattle and beyond
in the US. Figure 10.14 shows a typical cross-section of the tunnel. The

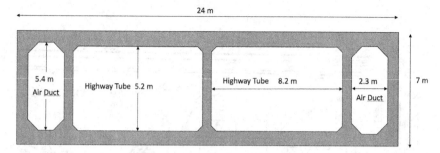

24 m

5.4 m
Air Duct

Highway Tube 5.2 m

Highway Tube   8.2 m

2.3 m
Air Duct

7 m

Figure 10.14 Cross-section of sunken precast concrete tunnel segment.
(Drawing courtesy COWI NA Ltd.)

629 m long tunnel carries four lanes of traffic in two split running tunnels, each 8.2 m wide and 5.2 m high. There are fresh air ducts 2.3 m wide by 5.4 m high on each side of the sunken box tubes. Structural analysis in the early 2000s found that the tunnel was seismically deficient by current seismic standards and was vulnerable to breaching in the event of an earthquake of sufficient magnitude (Morgan et al., 2006).

The British Columbia Ministry of Transportation decided to carry out seismic retrofit of this tunnel using a combination of reinforced concrete and steel plates to strengthen the floor and soffits of the running tunnels. In the fresh air ducts, however, they decided to construct bonded and anchored heavily reinforced beams in the soffits of the air ducts, using shotcrete. Shotcrete was selected, in lieu of cast-in-place concrete for this application, because of the superior bond it has been found to provide in overhead construction. Figure 10.15 provides a detail of the reinforced shotcrete design used in the air ducts. The design details included the use of 3 layers of shotcrete, each 100 mm thick, with each layer reinforced with 20M rebars at 150 mm on centre longitudinally and 15M rebars at 250 mm on centre transversely. The bars were tied to 20M L-Bars anchored into the soffit of the air duct. The precast concrete air duct soffits were prepared to a suitably roughened surface texture by hydromilling prior to installation of the L-Bar anchors and first layer of reinforcing steel. Figure 10.16 shows a view of the installed anchors and first layer of reinforcing steel ready for shotcreting.

The original project specifications were written based on the assumption that wet-mix shotcrete would be used. The shotcrete contractor, however, requested that the work be allowed to be performed using the dry-mix shotcrete process. This request was largely based on the considerable distances the shotcrete had to be conveyed to the point of placement (up to 400 m), and the considerable slick line and hose clean-up efforts that this would require on a daily basis if wet-mix shotcrete was used. This change to dry-mix shotcrete was approved and the contractor supplied the shotcrete in preblended 1000 kg bulk bin bags. Figure 10.17 shows a bulk bin bag of

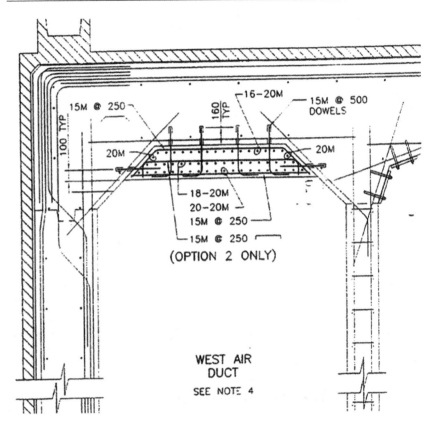

Figure 10.15 Details of reinforced shotcrete in air duct.
(Drawing courtesy COWI NA Ltd.)

dry-mix shotcrete suspended above the hopper of a predampener, with discharge of the dampened material into a rotary barrel dry-mix gun.

After the first layer of rebar was installed the first 100 mm thick layer of shotcrete was applied. Once inspected and approved, a second layer of rebar was installed and the second lift of 100 mm thick shotcrete was applied. This process was repeated for the third layer of rebar, but with the final lift of shotcrete being trimmed to shooting wires with a cutting screed and finished with steel trowels and a light brush finish to provide a finish tolerance not exceeding 10 mm under a 3 m straightedge. (Control of finish tolerance was important because of airflow requirements in the fresh air ducts.) Figure 10.18 shows a nozzleman applying the final lift of shotcrete overhead. Shooting wires were used for control of line and grade.

Moist curing with pressurized soaker hoses was used for curing the first and second shotcrete lifts. A spray-on curing compound was used for curing the final finished shotcrete lift. Also note that the substrate concrete and first

Figure 10.16 Air duct soffit with anchors and first layer of reinforcing steel installed, ready for shotcreting.

Figure 10.17 Discharge of dry-mix shotcrete from bulk bin bag into predampener and then into a rotary barrel dry-mix gun.

Figure 10.18 Nozzleman applying finishing layer of shotcrete overhead.

Table 10.2 Specified requirements and actual average performance for dry-mix shotcrete

Parameter	Specific requirement
Cement	CSA Type GU
Supplementary cementing materials	Fly ash and silica fume
Combined coarse and fine aggregate gradation	ACI 506 Gradation No. 2
Micro-synthetic fibre	1 kg/m³
Compressive strength on cores	Min 40 MPa at 28 days (actual average: 55.0 MPa)
ASTM C642 boiled absorption	Max 8% at 7 days (actual average: 5.6%)
ASTM C642 volume of permeable voids	Max 17% at 7 days (actual average: 12.4%)
Tensile bond strength to substrate Concrete and between shotcrete layers	Min 1.0 MPa at 28 days (actual average: 2.0 MPa)

and second lifts of shotcrete were required to be in a saturated surface dry (SSD) condition at the time of application of fresh shotcrete, in order to maximize bond.

Table 10.2 shows the specified dry-mix shotcrete performance requirements, together with average test results achieved during quality control testing on the project. The shotcrete readily satisfied all the specified performance requirements (Morgan et al., 2006).

10.4.5 Littlerock Dam, California Seismic Retrofit

In 1994, a major seismic retrofit program was carried out on the Littlerock Dam in southern California. This multiple-arch dam provides vital water supply for both the Palmdale Water District and the Littlerock Creek Irrigation District. Its location just 2.4 km south of the San-Andreas fault raised concerns about the adequacy of the dam and its stability in the event of an earthquake. To provide seismic strengthening, air-entrained, silica fume modified, steel fibre-reinforced, wet-mix shotcrete was applied at a nominal thickness of 100 mm over a 4500 m² surface area of the upstream face together with installation of over 3400 grouted anchors (Forrest et al., 1996). Table 10.3 shows the shotcrete mixture design used and the specified shotcrete performance requirements. Figure 10.19 shows the shotcrete work in progress.

Quality control testing indicated excellent shotcrete performance (compressive strength, bond pull-off strength, consolidation, toughness, boiled absorption and volume of permeable voids) which conformed to all the specified performance requirements. Details of test results are provided in the paper by Forrest et al. (1996). On completion of the project, the shotcrete was observed to be essentially crack-free, in spite of the work being completed in a desert climate, where the ambient temperatures frequently rose as high as 40°C during the daytime, and by project end fell below 0°C

Table 10.3 Littlerock Dam shotcrete mixture design and performance requirements

Material	Mixture proportions, kg/m³
Portland cement, Type II	405
Silica fume	41
Coarse aggregate (10 mm) (SSD)	486
Fine aggregate (SSD)	1127
Steel Fibres	60
Water	200L
Water-reducing admixture	0.5L
Superplasticizer	3.0L
Air-entraining admixture	0.8L
Total	2323
Specified performance requirements	
Air content	As-batched: 8–10% at pump As-shot: 4–6%
Compressive strength	Min. 41 MPa at 28 days
Bond pull-off strength	Min. 1.0 MPa at 28 days
ASTM C642	Boiled water absorption: Max. 8% Volume of permeable voids: Max. 17%
ASTM C1018	Min. toughness performance level III

Figure 10.19 Seismic retrofit of Littlerock Dam with steel fibre-reinforced wet-mix shotcrete.

at night. This was attributed in large measure to the rigorous moist curing program that was specified and enforced for the project. The freshly placed shotcrete was protected against drying evaporation by fogging with the mist from water pressure sprayers, as shown in Figure 9.34. As soon as the finished shotcrete had taken a hard set, it was covered with presaturated, plastic-coated, synthetic-fabric curing blankets. Water soaker hoses were used to keep the shotcrete wet for a minimum of seven days. The curing blankets were then reused on newly shot surfaces. The work was successfully completed on time and within budget to the satisfaction of the owner.

10.5 DOMES

Shotcrete lends itself well to the construction of complex curvature structures, such as domes and shells which are time-consuming and difficult to construct using formwork and conventional cast-in-place-concrete construction methods. It is thus not surprising that shotcrete has a long history of use in the construction of such structures. Figure 10.20 shows an example of some 19 domes, 8.8 m in diameter and 4.3 m high constructed in Portugal in 1956 for the government wine storage program (Zynda, 2009). The domes were constructed on inflated spherical rubber membranes and had wall thicknesses tapering from 100 mm at the base to 50 mm at the top. The domes were constructed by application of dry-mix shotcrete from the outside of the inflated membranes and the construction records indicate that

Figure 10.20 Government wine storage tanks constructed in Portugal in 1956.
(Photo courtesy Chris Zynda.)

two tanks were finished each day and that the entire project was completed
in 2.5 months.

Shotcrete dome construction technology has come a long way since the
1950s. There are now a number of companies in North America and worldwide specializing in the design and construction of shotcrete domes. In 1976,
the idea of building a concrete shell dome with inflated forms using shotcrete was added to by two brothers, David and Barry South. The two built a
32 m diameter by 10.5 m tall dome used for potato storage in Shelley, Idaho
USA (see Figure 10.21). They sprayed shotcrete from the inside of the dome.
This led, in 1990, to the ACI 334 Concrete Shell Design and Construction
committee working on a document that described the means and methods
of the South Brother's construction technique, the *ACI-PCR-334.3-05(2)
Concrete Shell Construction Using Inflated Forms*.

The Souths patented this building method, and it has since been used to
construct literally thousands of domes worldwide. Today, there are several
companies that use the method. Domes as large as 100 m in diameter and
up to 60 m high have now been constructed, using wet-mix shotcrete applied
from the inside of the inflated air form. The advantages of concrete shell
domes built with inflated forms using shotcrete, compared to more conventional types of structures include the following:

a) *Strength*. The doubly curved shape of a dome building is stronger than
   any other type of structural building or element. The inherent strength
   of the dome has been utilized in buildings such as homes, schools,
   churches, swimming pool enclosures, gymnasiums, auditoriums,
   offices and other types of buildings. The inherent strength the dome

Figure 10.21 South's first air-supported membrane reinforced concrete dome
built with shotcrete; 32 m diameter by 10.5 m tall potato storage
located in Shelley, Idaho.

(Photos courtesy South inc.)

shape is such that these buildings can be built to resist hurricanes,
tornadoes, and earthquakes. FEMA (Federal Emergency Management
Agency in the USA) has approved many of these structures for use
as official disaster-resistant buildings. Domes have also been used to
store bulk and liquid material such as cement, grain, coal, sugar, wood
pellets and water. The shape of the dome resists the tremendous internal pressure from the stored material better than any other shape.

b) *Economy.* A dome shape provides the largest floor area and enclosed
volume using the least amount of material of any building shape. This
allows the cost of dome buildings to be competitive compared to other
types of buildings (Zweifel, 2010).

c) *Speed of Construction.* The method of constructing concrete shell
domes with inflated forms using shotcrete is much faster than conventional concrete methods using shored formwork. It offers an enclosed
building environment protected from rain, wind, snow, and cold. The
interior of the air-supported membrane offers an ideal environment
for curing concrete. The surface of concrete is protected from direct
sun and wind exposure and can be kept at a high humidity.

d) *Safety.* The safety record using this technique of building is excellent.
To build these large structures, manlifts are used on level ground to
place the rebar and shotcrete. There are no interior obstructions for
the lifts to work around. The shotcrete is not exposed to wind during construction. There are no heavy lifting or hoisting requirements.

There have been millions of hours worked in this environment applying shotcrete without any serious injuries.

e) *Thermally Efficient.* Many domes are constructed with an applied
layer of polyurethane to the membrane before the shotcrete and reinforcing is placed. This provides an airtight envelope with excellent
R value, and most importantly, the concrete provides thermal mass
to store energy in the building. The energy savings using this type of
construction generally will save 20–35% on heating and cooling costs
compared to conventional buildings.

Some domes are still constructed by shotcrete application from outside the
dome. This process does, however, have some distinct disadvantages relative
to shotcrete application from inside the dome. Such disadvantages include:

a) The shotcrete application is not protected from the prevailing weather
conditions;
b) Rebound does not fall from the work by gravity but has to be removed
with blow pipes; and
c) Shooting and finishing the shotcrete often requires workers to be
clambering on the fixed reinforcing steel, with the challenges that this
represents.

Thus, most modern shotcrete domes are shot from the inside, as described
in the section which follows. Figure 10.22 shows a schematic of a typical

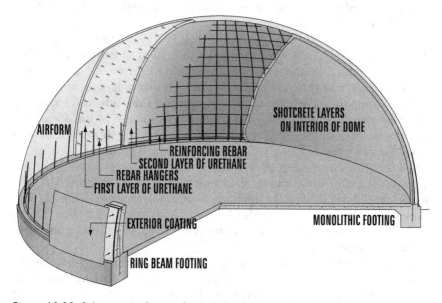

Figure 10.22 Schematic of a reinforced shotcrete dome construction.

(Schematic courtesy Monolithic Dome Institute.)

modern shotcrete dome construction. The steps for construction of a typical shotcrete dome is as follows:

1. A circular reinforced concrete ring foundation beam or concrete mat foundation, with vertical starter bars is first cast on, or in the ground;
2. A vertical stemwall may be added to the foundation, if required to provide the dome with more height. The stemwall may be constructed with typical construction techniques using masonry or reinforced concrete or it may be air formed;
3. A prefabricated fabric form is then attached to the top of the foundation, or stemwall, depending on the type of shape required for the structure;
4. Large blowers inflate the fabric membrane, and it serves both as formwork for the structure and as the final roof membrane (Ragen and Briggs, 2008);
5. Once the form is fully inflated, polyurethane foam is sprayed on the interior side of the form to the required thickness;
6. Special fasteners are embedded in the foam and steel reinforcement is fixed to the fasteners;
7. Wet-mix shotcrete is then applied in a systematic manner in gradually thicker layers until all the reinforcing steel is encased with the required thickness of cover. Thickness gauges are used to control shotcrete thickness; and
8. Shotcrete application can proceed in all types of weather conditions because of the protection provided by the polyurethane-coated inflated membrane.

Figures 10.23 and 10.24 illustrate the various steps of construction. Care has to be exercised during shotcrete application to ensure that a systematic pattern of shotcrete spraying is carried out such that bulges do not develop in the air-supported dome, as any departures from the spherical shape can adversely affect the structural capacity and performance of the dome. The specialty dome design and construction companies doing such work are well versed on this issue and take measures to avoid such problems.

In Figure 10.23, the top photos depict the inflation process of the air-supported form (78 m diameter x 48 high clinker dome in Romania). The bottom left photo depicts the application of a polyurethane foam (22,700 tonnes wood pellet storage in Martinique). The bottom right photo shows reinforcement installed in a bulk storage dome silo; note the large diameter reinforcing regularly used.

The use of shotcrete and inflated forms building technology has yielded structures of enormous size and structural capacity. Figure 10.25 shows an example of wet-mix shotcrete-lined wood pellet storage domes constructed in Selby, UK. Each of the domes is 63 m in diameter and 50 m high and can

Figure 10.23 Different steps involved in the construction of a dome.
(Photos courtesy Dome Technology.)

Figure 10.24 This photo depicts wet-mix shotcrete installation in a bulk storage
dome silo. Note the large diameter reinforcing.

(Photo courtesy Dome Technology.)

Figure 10.25 Drax Power Wood Pellet Storage Dome Silos in Selby, UK.
(Photo courtesy Dome Technology.)

hold up to 80,000 tonnes of biomass. An interesting feature is the unique "tops" for the domes: a specialized design incorporates a 27 m opening at the apex of each dome accommodating panels, which relieve and dissipate pressure should it arise from a dust explosion.

The construction of concrete shells using inflated forms built with shotcrete has great potential in a variety of different applications. State-of-the-art design methods now allow for the construction of new inflated form geometry and new types of construction projects. An example of such a structure is presented in Figure 10.26 where the vertical wall and the dome were constructed entirely with an air form and reinforced shotcrete to complete a 3.8 million litre water tank; proper design of the air form insures the straightness of the vertical walls.

10.6 PRESTRESSED WATER TANKS

Shotcrete has over 100 year's history of use in construction of liquid-containing structures (Yoggy, 2000). Hanskat (2010) provides a review of the use of shotcrete in design and construction of liquid-containing tanks. Tanks constructed include potable water treatment and storage tanks and wastewater and sewage treatment tanks. Hanskat notes that today shotcrete remains a vital part of wrapped, prestressed concrete tanks. In 1942, J.M. Crom in Florida first wrapped high-strength steel wire in a continuous

Figure 10.26 Water tank where vertical wall and dome are entirely constructed using inflated air form and wet-mix shotcrete.

(Photo courtesy Dome Technology.)

spiral around the exterior of cylindrical concrete water tanks, to help maintain the watertightness of the tanks. Dry-mix shotcrete *(gunite)* was then applied to the prestressing steel wires to fully encase them, thus providing fully bonded reinforcing and mechanical and corrosion protection to the wires. Hanskat reports that by 2010 over 9000 wrapped, prestressed tanks of various shapes and sizes had been constructed. The American Concrete Institute (ACI 372R and ACI 373R) and American Water Works Association (AWWA D110 and AWWA D115) provide guidance for the design of circular prestressed concrete structures.

The technology has evolved over the years and designs have been developed in which the use of cast-in-place concrete tank construction has been replaced with shotcrete construction. Balck (1999) presents an example of a now widely used method of tank construction in which a composite shotcrete encased steel shell is wrapped with prestressing strands which in turn are shotcrete encased. Figure 10.27 shows a schematic of such a prestressed composite wall. The steel shell is important in that not only does it act as formwork for subsequent shotcrete application, but it also provides a positive watertight barrier and acts as vertical reinforcement. The construction sequence is briefly as follows:

a) A circular steel shell diaphragm is installed in the reinforced concrete base slab. The steel shell has re-entrant angles to provide a mechanical key for shotcrete encasement;

b) The steel shell diaphragm sheets are continuous and have no horizontal joints. Vertical joints are made watertight by epoxy injection;

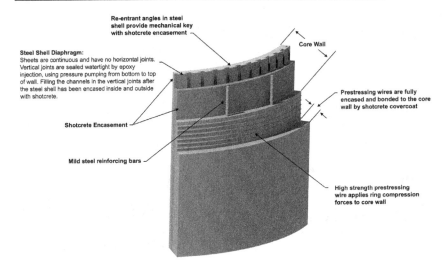

Re-entrant angles in steel
shell provide mechanical key
with shotcrete encasement

Core Wall

Steel Shell Diaphragm:
Sheets are continuous and have no horizontal joints.
Vertical joints are sealed watertight by epoxy
injection, using pressure pumping from bottom to top
of wall. Filling the channels in the vertical joints after
the steel shell has been encased inside and outside
with shotcrete.

Prestressing wires are fully
encased and bonded to the core
wall by shotcrete covercoat

Shotcrete Encasement

Mild steel reinforcing bars

High strength prestressing
wire applies ring compression
forces to core wall

Figure 10.27 Schematic of a prestressed composite wall.

(Photo courtesy CROM LLC.)

   c) Mild reinforcing steel bars are installed vertically and horizontally on the outside of the steel shell and shotcrete is applied to both the inside and outside of the steel shell, as shown in Figure 10.27;

   d) After the shotcrete has developed suitable strength, spiral wrapping of the tank with the continuous prestressing strands proceeds. This provides ring compression forces to the core wall. Sophisticated automated devices have been developed for this wrapping process;

   e) A final layer of shotcrete is then applied to encase and protect the prestressing strands; and

   f) The shotcrete is finished to shooting wires to provide the final line and grade and specified cover and surface finish texture.

Up until the 1990, most prestressed liquid-containing tanks were constructed using the dry-mix shotcrete process. Mixture designs were quite simple: 1 part Portland cement to 3 Parts of an ACI 506 Gradation No.1 Concrete Sand. Shotcrete was built up in thin layers, using the *layer-shooting method*. Shotcrete was applied using hand nozzling, as shown in Figure 10.28.

However, since the 1990s shotcrete application has increasingly been carried out using the wet-mix shotcrete process. This change was in part driven by the lower rebound and markedly greater productivity achievable with the wet-mix shotcrete process. In addition, some contractors have automated the shotcrete application process to further enhance productivity and the uniformity of in-place shotcrete quality. Figure 10.29 shows shotcrete application from a remotely controlled rig which can raise and lower the nozzle as it travels around the tank.

Figure 10.28 Hand application of dry-mix shotcrete to prestressed tendons using the layer shooting method.

(Historical photo courtesy DN Tanks.)

With the change to wet-mix shotcrete came changes in the mixture designs. Up to 20% by mass of cement was replaced with fly ash, air entrainment was added to the shotcrete to enhance freeze-thaw durability and synthetic micofibres were added to help mitigate plastic shrinkage cracking. While structural specifications typically only require about 30 MPa at 28-day compressive strengths, it is not uncommon to find actual compressive strengths as high as 50 MPa, or even more. This is because the cementing materials content required to provide the shotcrete with good shooting characteristics (i.e., adhesion and cohesion properties) and with low rebound results in higher compressive strengths.

10.7 BOBSLEIGH/LUGE TRACKS

Bobsleigh/luge tracks have been around since the early 1900s (The sport was offered at the First Winter Olympics in Chamonix, France, in 1924). The shotcrete construction process lends itself very well to the construction of complex curvature free-form structures such as bobsleigh and luge tracks; hence, most of the world's bobsleigh and luge tracks have been constructed using shotcrete rather than cast-in-place concrete. This is primarily because of the great time and cost challenges faced in trying to construct complex curvature formwork for cast-in-place concrete construction. The first author

Figure 10.29 Remotely controlled shotcrete application to tank wall.
(Photo courtesy CROM LLC.)

has been involved in the shotcrete design and construction optimization for the bobsleigh/luge tracks for the 1988 Winter Olympics in Calgary, Alberta; the 2010 Winter Olympics in Whistler, British Columbia; the Alpina Sliding Centre 2018 Winter Olympics in Pyeongchang, Korea and the track constructed for the Beijing 2022 Winter Olympics. The section which follows briefly describes the design and construction of the Whistler Sliding Centre track which is the fastest track in the world (Shotcrete Magazine, 2008).

The Whistler Sliding Centre track is 1700 m long with some 6500 m² of iced surface. It has 16 curves and contains about 100 km of cooling pipe and required 2000 m³ of shotcrete. The track was constructed in 23 sections having an average length of 75 m each. The vertical height of these sections ranges from 650 mm (in straight sections) to over 3.5 m in high-wall curved sections. At its steepest, the track had a grade of 25%. The track was required

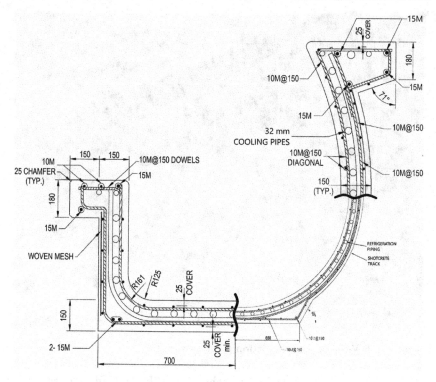

Figure 10.30 Typical cross-section detail for Whistler Sliding Centre track at curved section (not to scale).

(Drawing courtesy Stantec.)

to be constructed to a very exacting surface finish tolerance of 3 mm under a 3 m straightedge. Figure 10.30 shows a cross-sectional view of a curved section of the track.

Construction of the track included the following activities:

a) Erection of a structural steel falsework system and base forms;
b) Installation of a jig assembly to fix the outer layer of reinforcing steel bars at their precise location on the track;
c) Installation of the 32 mm diameter cooling pipes, followed by installation of the interior layer of reinforcing steel;
d) Fixing of the ribbed, expanded metal lath Stay-Form with *V-ribs* to the outer layer of reinforcing steel bars;
e) Installation of upper and lower header beam wood forms;
f) Fixing of temporary plastic screed pipes with plastic form ties to the inner layer of reinforcing steel to provide precise control over finished shotcrete cover thickness, line and grade and tolerance; and application of wet-mix shotcrete.

Figure 10.31 View of the installation prior to shooting.

Figure 10.31 shows a view of the above-described installation, ready for application of shotcrete.

The shotcrete mix design used for the majority of the track construction had the mixture proportions shown in Table 10.4, which follows.

The specified compressive strength was a minimum of 40 MPa at 28 days and actual compressive strengths achieved were consistently between 50 and 60 MPa. Boiled Absorption values in testing to ASTM C642 were consistently below the maximum 8.0% value specified and averaged 6.5%.

Table 10.4 Wet-mix shotcrete mixture proportions for Whistler sliding centre track

Material	kg/m³
Cement, Type GU	420
Fly ash, Type F	65
Coarse aggregate (10 mm)	420
Fine aggregate	1200
Water (based on SSD aggregates)	190
Water-reducing admixture	Yes
Hydration-controlling admixture	Yes
Air-entraining admixture	Yes

Figure 10.32 Shotcrete application to mock-up section of track at Whistler Sliding Centre.

The mixture displayed suitable shooting characteristics, with good adhesion and cohesion, low rebound and good finishing characteristics.

Prior to the construction of the track, the contractor was required to erect and shoot a full-scale mock-up representative of a 7.5 m long section of a high wall. The mock-up provided an opportunity for all parties involved in the track design and construction to fine-tune design and construction details and optimize the shotcrete mixture design, supply, application and finishing. Three mock-ups were constructed as part of the final optimization process. Figure 10.32 shows the third mock-up under construction.

Some important lessons were learned in construction of these mock-ups. Firstly, the use of an expanded metal lath, without *V-ribs* is not recommended. Lath without *V-ribs* is difficult to fix such that it is chaired off the reinforcing steel bars to which it is attached. Having expanded metal lath in direct contact with reinforcing steel bars makes it very difficult to get full encapsulation of the bars with shotcrete. Thus, ribbed expanded metal sheets with the *V-ribs* chairing the sheets off the bars should be used, so that full encapsulation of the bars can be achieved. Figure 10.33 shows a section illustrating this detail. Figure 10.34 shows a cut-out section from the third mock-up. Note the good encapsulation of the reinforcing steel, cooling pipes and V-ribbed lath.

Secondly, the size of the openings in the expanded metal lath should be sufficiently small to minimize the amount of mortar that blows through the

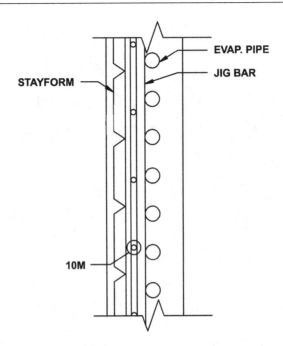

Figure 10.33 Section of mock-up showing lath, reinforcing steel and cooling pipe positioning.

lath during shotcrete application. Otherwise, segregation can occur during shooting, with a porous layer of coarser aggregate being trapped behind the rebar and in front of the lath. The *Stay-Form* ribbed expanded metal lath used was ideally sized to prevent this from happening.

The sequence of shotcrete installation is important in production of a quality final product, and is as detailed below:

a) A first coat of shotcrete is applied to the invert (floor) of the track, leaving the top of the innermost layer of reinforcing steel bars just exposed. Rebound is blown off the invert with blowpipes. After shooting, the shotcrete is further consolidated by insertion of small diameter immersion vibrators (note that it is important to shoot this area first, so that rebound from shooting of the walls does not become trapped in the invert);

b) A first coat of shotcrete is then applied to the coved areas and then upper parts of the walls, leaving the innermost layer of rebar just exposed. Rebound is continuously removed from the work area with blowpipes during shooting. The shotcrete in the coved areas is further consolidated with immersion vibrators;

c) Shotcrete is applied into the upper and lower formed beams and consolidated with immersion vibrators;

Figure 10.34 Cut-out section from mock-up. Note good encapsulation of lath, rebar and cooling pipes with shotcrete.

d) After the shotcrete in the formed beams has stiffened sufficiently, the temporary wood forms are removed and a final coat of shotcrete is applied to the walls, working from the top down. The freshly applied final coat is cut and trimmed to the plastic screed pipes and all rebound and trimmings are removed from the work;

e) A final coat of shotcrete is applied to the floor and is cut, trimmed and finished to the plastic screed pipes. The plastic screed pipes are then removed and the voids they leave are filled with shotcrete. After the second coat has stiffened sufficiently, the entire inside surface of the track is finished to the specified tolerance using bull floats and steel trowels. The shotcrete is then provided with a light broom finish to provide the texture needed for bonding of ice during ice-making on the track; and

Figure 10.35 Completed high-wall section of track at Whistler Sliding Centre.

  f) Days (or even weeks later), the backside of the Stay-Form expanded metal lath is water pressure blasted (20MPa water pressure) to remove any dirt and loose material and an exterior layer of shotcrete is then applied to fully encase the lath.

Because of tight time constraints to get the track completed in time for the 2010 Winter Olympics, shotcrete construction proceeded throughout the year, including during cold, snowy winter months. To enable this to happen, all shotcrete construction was carried out within a traveling tent enclosure, as shown in Figure 9.36. This protected the shotcrete work from the adverse weather effects of wind, direct solar radiation and rain in the summer, and cold temperatures, wind and snow in winter months. After finishing all shotcrete, surfaces were wet cured for a minimum of seven days.

Figure 10.35 shows a completed high-wall section of track. Figure 10.36 shows an aerial night view of the entire track.

10.8 SKATE PARKS

Another substantial area of use of reinforced shotcrete is in construction of skate parks (EcoSmart, 2004; Leone, 2011). While skateparks have been around for over 40 years, the past 15 years have seen an explosion of

Figure 10.36 Aerial night view of Whistler Sliding Centre bobsleigh/luge track.

construction of skateparks in municipal recreation areas, schools and other locations. In early years, skate parks tended to be fairly linear structures and most were constructed with conventional cast-in-place reinforced concrete slabs for horizontal elements and formed, cast-in-place reinforced concrete walls for vertical elements. Recent years have, however, seen rapid increases in the construction of complex curvature structures such as bowls, half-pipes and even full-pipes. While horizontal slab components of skate parks are still usually constructed using conventional cast-in-place concrete construction methods, the complex curvature elements are now almost all constructed with shotcrete. Figure 10.37, which shows a portion of the Metro Skate Park constructed in Burnaby, British Columbia in 2004, is a good example of this. It shows a bowl, half-pipe and full pipe, all constructed with reinforced, structural wet-mix shotcrete.

   Skate boarding had its origins in skating in empty backyard pools and it is thus not surprising that elements of pools are replicated in many modern skate parks (Leone, 2011). Thus, most skate parks are constructed in bowls excavated from the earth, with raised elements being placed on earth-shaped features. Curved wood templates, or plastic or steel pipes, are commonly used to create the required profiles. Wood templates and plastic pipes are normally temporary and are removed after shotcrete has been cut, trimmed and finished to the specified line, grade and tolerance. Galvanized

Figure 10.37 A portion of Metro Skate Park, Burnaby, British Columbia.

Table 10.5 Metro Skate Park, Burnaby, British Columbia wet-mix shotcrete mix design and performance

Parameter	Specified	Actual
Minimum compressive strength	40 MPa at 56 days	Avg. 45 MPa at 28 days
Maximum aggregate size	14 mm	14 mm
Fly ash content (% by mass of cement)	25%	25%
Silica fume content (% by mass of cement)	8%	8%
Hard-Cem	40 kg/m³	40 kg/m³
Synthetic microfiber	1 kg/m³	1 kg/m³
Air content	8% as-delivered	8%
Slump	70 ± 20 mm	70 mm

steel pipes are commonly used to define the transition edge between the top slab and sloped edge of the bowl, and form part of the permanent construction of the bowl.

Skateboarding actually places quite high demands on the concrete or shotcrete, as it generates high abrasion and wear and localized impact forces. Thus, for the Metro Skate Park in Burnaby, British Columbia, the design engineer specified a minimum compressive strength of 40 MPa at 56 days for the wet-mix shotcrete (actual strengths achieved averaged 45 MPa at 28 days). He also specified the incorporation of an integral mineral slag-based hardener, *Hard-Cem* in the wet-mix shotcrete and concrete used on the project. This product has been widely used in Western Canada and now elsewhere in North America to improve the abrasion and wear resistance of industrial floors and other structures. On this project, 40 kg/m³ of sand was replaced with 40 kg/m^3 of the integral hardener in both the shotcrete and concrete mix designs. When recently examined, after over 15 years of service, both the shotcrete and concrete were observed to be displaying excellent abrasion and wear resistance. Table 10.5 provides a summary of the specified shotcrete mixture design and actual average performance values.

REFERENCES

ACI 334.3-05(20). 2020. *Concrete Shell Construction Using Inflated Forms.* American Concrete Institute 13 p.

ACI 372R-13. 2013. *Guide to the Design and Construction of Circular Wire-and Strand-Wrapped Prestressed Concrete Structures.* American Concrete Institute. 31 p.

ACI 373R-97(10). 2010. *Design and Construction of Circular Prestressed Concrete Structures with Circumferential Tendons.* American Concrete Institute. 26 p.

ACI CT-18. 2018c. *Concrete Terminology.* American Concrete Institute. 80.

ACI 506R-16. 2016c. *Guide to Shotcrete.* American Concrete Institute. 52p.

ASTM C642. 2013d. *Standard Test Method for Density, Absorption and Voids in Hardened Concrete.* 3p. ASTM International. https://doi.org/10.1520/C0642-13.

Aitcin, P-C. 1999. Demystifying Autogenous Shrinkage. *Concrete International.* Vol. 21. No. 11. November. 54–56.

AWWA D110-13(R18). 2018. Wire and *Strand Wound Circular Prestressed Concrete Water Tanks.* American Water Works Association. 47 p.

AWWA D115-20. (2020). *Tendon Prestressed Concrete Water Tanks.* American Water Works Association. 74 p.

Balck, L. 1999. Shotcrete and Prestressed Composite Tanks. *Shotcrete Magazine, American Shotcrete Association* November, 1999. 20–21.

Briggs, L. and Poole, R. 2006. Shotcrete Domes: A Versatile Bulk Materials Storage and Architectural Structures Solution. *Shotcrete Magazine, American Shotcrete Association* Summer, 2006. 20–23.

CSA. 2019d. *A23.1/A23.2 Concrete materials and methods of concrete construction/Test methods and standard practices for concrete.* 690p. Canadian Standards Association.

EcoSmart Concrete Project. 2004. *Use of EcoSmart for the Metro Skate Park.* Burnaby, B.C., EcoSmart, November, 2004, 19.

Flanagan, J. 2015. Acoustic Shells. *Shotcrete Magazine, American Shotcrete Association* Winter, 2015. 16–19.

Forrest, M. P., Morgan, D. R., Obermeyer, J. R., Parker, P. L. and LaMoreaux, D. D. 1996. Seismic Retrofit of Littlerock Dam. *Concrete International.* Vol. 18. No. 3. March. 24–29.

Hanskat, C. S. 2010. Shotcrete in Liquid Containing Structures. *Shotcrete Magazine, American Shotcrete Association* Summer, 2010. 24–28.

Hanskat, C. S. 2011. Prestressed Concrete Tanks-Mundane? Or Architectural Gems? *Shotcrete Magazine, American Shotcrete Association* Fall, 2001. 20–23.

von der Hofen, M. 2004. Washington State's Capital Seismic Repair. *Shotcrete Magazine, American Shotcrete Association* Winter, 2004. 4–5.

Kasdi, N., Totten, L. 2012. Seismic Retrofit of California Memorial Stadium. *Shotcrete Magazine, American Shotcrete Association* Fall, 2012. 10–13.

Leone, M. 2011. Skatepark Designs Elevate Shotcrete Craftsmanship. *Shotcrete Magazine, American Shotcrete Association* Winter, 2011. 34–35.

Lind, J. 1926. Guniting Steel Cement Kiln Stacks. *The Canadian Engineer.* Vol. 50. No. 16. April 20, 1926, Republished in Shotcrete Magazine Spring, 2008. 28–30.

Morgan, D. R., Chan, C. 2001. Understanding and Controlling Shrinkage and Cracking in Shotcrete. *Shotcrete Magazine, American Shotcrete Association* Spring, 2001. 26–30.

Morgan, D. R., Kazakoff, K. and Ibrahim, H. 2006. Seismic Retrofit of Immersed Tube Tunnel with Reinforced Shotcrete. *Shotcrete for Underground Support X, Proceedings of the Tenth International Conference on Shotcrete for Underground Support,* Edited by Morgan, D. R. & Parker, H., Whistler, BC, Canada, 2006, 270–284.

Morgan, D. R. and Totten, L. 2008. Guide Specification for Structural Shotcrete Walls. *Shotcrete Magazine, American Shotcrete Association* Winter, 2008, 18–27.

Morgan, D.R., Zhang, L. 2009. Seismic Retrofit of Historic Wing Sang Building. *Shotcrete Magazine, American Shotcrete Association* Winter, 2009, 8–12.

Ragen, E., Briggs, L. 2008. Air Forms for Building Shotcrete Domes. *Shotcrete Magazine, American Shotcrete Association* Summer, 2008, 4–6.

Shotcrete Magazine. 2008. Whistler Sliding Center. *Shotcrete Magazine, American Shotcrete Association* Summer, 2008. 36–41.

South, D.B. 2009. Monolithic Dome School Buildings. *Shotcrete Magazine, American Shotcrete Association* Fall, 2009. 10–12.

Tremere, L. 2000. Shotcrete Used to Construct North America's Largest Skate Park. *Shotcrete Magazine, American Shotcrete Association* Fall, 2000. 14.

Warner, J. 2004. History of Shotcrete in Seismic Retrofit in California. *Shotcrete Magazine, American Shotcrete Association* Winter, 2004. 14–17.

Woodhead, R. & Morgan, D. R. 1983. Block 15 Heritage Redevelopment Seismic Upgrading. *Fourth International Conference on Earthquake Engineering,* Vancouver, B.C., June, 1983, 625–632.

Yoggy, G.D. 2000. The History of Shotcrete: Part I. *Shotcrete Magazine, American Shotcrete Association* Fall, 2000. 28–29.

Zhang, L., Morgan, D. R., Kirk, I., Rolland, A. and Karchewski, R. 2021. *Mass Shotcrete Wall Construction and Thermal Control Plan,* accepted for publication in ACI Materials Journal.

Zweifel, C. 2010. Shotcrete Domes: A Model of Sustainability. *Shotcrete Magazine, American Shotcrete Association* Fall, 2010. 31–33.

Zynda, C. 2009. Airform Industrial Construction. *Shotcrete Magazine, American Shotcrete Association* Winter, 2009 44–47.

Chapter 11

Infrastructure repair and rehabilitation

11.1 INTRODUCTION

Shotcrete has been used for over a century for repair and rehabilitation of infrastructure and buildings. Indeed, as mentioned in Chapter 3, the very first use of shotcrete was in 1907, when Carl Akeley used *gunite* to repair the façade of a building at the Field Columbian Museum in Chicago. The following is a brief listing of some of the areas where shotcrete has been used for infrastructure repair and rehabilitation:

- Bridges and highway infrastructure
- Dams and hydraulic structures
- Marine structures
- Industrial structures
- Buildings and heritage structures
- Tunnels and underground structures
- Culverts, pipes and aqueducts

Case history examples of the use of shotcrete in a number of the above types of projects, drawn mainly from the author's project experience, are provided later in this chapter.

Shotcrete has gained favour over more conventional *form and pour* types of concrete repair on many projects because of its versatile and flexible nature which in many instances can result in considerable cost savings in situations such as the following:

- Where formwork is impractical or can be reduced or eliminated;
- Where access to the work area is difficult;
- Where thin layers or variable thickness is required;
- Where normal concrete casting techniques cannot be employed;
- Where complex curved or irregular shapes need to be constructed; and
- Overhead repair applications.

DOI: 10.1201/9780429169946-13

The sections which follow examine some of the important aspects of shot-crete repair and rehabilitation. These include:

- Evaluation of the cause(s) of the need for repair or rehabilitation;
- Preparation of the substrate surfaces to which the shotcrete will be applied;
- Performance parameters for shotcrete repair systems;
- Materials and mixture design requirements for repair shotcretes;
- Shotcrete batching, mixing and supply;
- Shotcrete application and finishing; and
- Shotcrete protection and curing.

11.2 SHOTCRETE REPAIR PUBLICATIONS

There are scores of publications in the literature pertinent to the topic of shotcrete repair of infrastructure. Taylor (1995) provides an overview on this topic with a list of some 10 pertinent cited publications. Most of Taylor's paper is specific to repair experience in the United Kingdom. Morgan (Morgan, 1997) provides an overview *of Shotcrete Repair of Infrastructure in North America*. He cites some 10 publications pertinent to this topic for projects in Canada and the US. Of particular interest, is the publication by Morgan and Neill (Morgan and Neill, 1991) on the *Durability of Shotcrete Repair of Highway Bridges in Canada*. This paper provided the findings of a Canadian Strategic Highway Research Program (C-SHRP) sponsored study of the performance of shotcrete repairs to some 60 bridges across Canada, from the Pacific to the Atlantic oceans and in most provinces in-between. The shotcrete repairs ranged in age from about 10–30 years. It was found that most of the repairs provided durable performance, but there were some structures where the repairs were less than satisfactory. The cause(s) of such less than satisfactory behaviour were determined and a C-SHRP publication *Recommended Practice for Shotcrete Repair of Highway Bridges* (Transportation Association of Canada, 1992), was prepared. This publication, published in a *Guide Specification* format, provided best practice guidelines for shotcrete repair of highway bridges, but also could be adapted to most types of shotcrete repair with either wet or dry-mix shotcrete.

The C-SHRP initiative was a collaborative programme with the US-SHRP programme and in 1992 a Joint Committee of the American Association of State Highway and Transportation Officials (AASHTO), the Associated General Contractors of America (AGCA) and the American Road and Transportation Builders Association (ARTBA) published the AASHTO-AGC-ARTBA Joint Committee Task Force 37 Report *Guide Specification for Shotcrete Repair of Highway Bridges*. This publication is adapted from the above-referenced C-SHRP report. This guide specification is now widely used throughout North America, not only for shotcrete repair of highway structures but also, with modification as appropriate, for other types of structures.

Useful information is also provided in the ACI RAP Bulletin 6 *Field Guide to Concrete Repair Application Procedures: Vertical and Overhead Spall Repair by Hand Application* (ACI RAP Bulletin 6). While this document is based on hand applied repairs, the sections on substrate preparation prior to repair material application and repair material protection and curing are also pertinent to shotcrete repair.

Also useful is *the Concrete Repair Manual* published jointly by the American Concrete Institute (ACI) and the International Concrete Repair Institute (ICRI), (ACI-ICRI Concrete Repair Manual, 2013). This publication contains many documents helpful to those interested in repair of reinforced concrete structures with shotcrete. Of particular interest are the following documents:

- *ICRI No. 310.1R-2008 Guide for Surface Preparation for the Repair of Deteriorated Concrete Resulting from Reinforcing Steel Corrosion;*
- *ICRI No. 310.2R-2013 Guide for Specifying Concrete Surface Preparation for Sealers, Coatings, Polymer Overlays and Concrete Repairs; and*
- *ICRI No.310.3R-2014 Guide for the Preparation of Concrete Surfaces for Repair Using Hydrodemolition Methods.*

Useful information is also provided in the book *Concrete Repair and Maintenance Illustrated: Problem Analysis; Repair Strategy: Techniques* by Peter Emmons (Emmons, 1993) and in the paper *State-of-the-Art Specifications for Shotcrete Rehabilitation Projects* by Dufour et al. (2006). This latter publication describes how the Ministry of Transportation Quebec (MTQ) shotcrete repair specifications have evolved over the 40 years since shotcrete was first introduced for bridge repair in Quebec and provides recommendations for the production of durable wet-mix and dry-mix shotcrete repairs in aggressive freezing and thawing and deicing chemical exposure environments.

11.3 CAUSES OF THE NEED FOR REPAIR

Much of the infrastructure in North America and elsewhere in the world is aging and deteriorating and in need of repair or rehabilitation. Finding the funds for such remedial works is a multi-billion dollar problem facing governments around the world and authorities are continuously looking for technically sound, cost-effective remedial solutions that will provide durable performance over the design life of the structures. Modern shotcrete technology is well placed to help meet this need.

Existing infrastructure is deteriorating through causes such as:

- **Freeze/thaw damage to concrete:** prior to the 1950s concrete was not air entrained and such concrete is inherently susceptible to cracking, scaling, spalling and ultimately *rubblizing* from exposure to cycles of freezing and thawing and/or exposure to deicing chemicals.
- **Alkali aggregate reactivity (AAR):** A number of the aggregate sources in North America are reactive to the alkalis in Portland cement and external sources of alkalis (CSA A864). Prior to the use of supplementary cementing materials in concrete, such as fly ash, ground granulated blast furnace slag (GGBFS), silica fume, or natural pozzolans, such as calcined metakaolin, concrete made with such aggregates were susceptible to damage from the swelling forces induced by AAR. Such forces can result in cracking, spalling and ultimately *rubblizing* of the concrete. Such cracking also exacerbates frost damage and damage from intrusion of aggressive chemical species, such as chloride ions and/or sulphates, where such chemical species are present.
- **Sulphate attack:** There are a number of places in North America where the naturally occurring soils and/or groundwater have high concentrations of sulphates. Portland cement-based concretes exposed to such conditions are vulnerable to sulphate induced damage. This typically manifests itself in the form of surface cracking and scaling which progressively works its way deeper into the concrete with time. This effect can be mitigated by the use of sulphate resistant cements, and/or the incorporation of suitable supplementary cementing materials (such as fly ash, GGBFS, silica fume, or natural pozzolans).
- **Chloride-induced damage:** Reinforced concrete structures exposed to chlorides in seawater, deicing chemicals, or industrial sources of chlorides are vulnerable to reinforcing steel corrosion-induced damage. Corrosion of the reinforcing steel can lead to cracking, spalling and if left unattended, ultimate failure of a structure. Establishing the chloride ion profile is an important part of any remedial strategy.
- **Abrasion, impact and cavitation erosion:** The surfaces of hydraulic structures, such as downstream faces of dams, spillways, low-level outlet structures and siphons have been damaged by abrasion, impact, and/or cavitation erosion (ACI 210R-93(98) and ACI 207.6-17). It is important to establish the mechanism causing such damage, or repairs could be short-lived. For example, if the mechanism of damage is primarily abrasion erosion, then the use of a repair material with a low water/cementitious materials ratio and high compressive strength is important. If impact from churning boulders in a spillway is of concern, then the repair system would benefit from incorporation of fibre reinforcement in the repair material. If the damage is primarily cavitation erosion induced, then the repair material surface profile and finish

become very important. In addition, mitigative measures might have to be adopted to counteract the conditions giving rise to the development of cavitation forces (ACI 210R-93(98) and ACI 207.6-17).

There are other potential sources of damage to reinforced concrete structures, including fire, structural overload, cyclic loading induced fatigue, delayed ettringite formation, thaumasite attack and others. Suffice to say that it is important to determine and understand the cause(s) of the damage/deterioration affecting the structure, so that an appropriate remedial action can be implemented (Morgan, 1996). For example, there is no point in applying a thin layer of shotcrete to a deteriorating concrete surface if the underlying concrete is not freeze/thaw durable and the depth of frost penetration is likely to progress beyond the depth of the shotcrete overlay. The substrate concrete could continue to develop sub-parallel cracking from freeze/thaw-induced stresses and the repair could fail with the new shotcrete adhered to the failed substrate concrete. Similarly, if a thin layer of shotcrete is used to replace the *covercrete* to reinforcing steel in a structure that has deteriorated from chloride ion-induced corrosion, the repair will likely be short-lived, unless mitigative measures, such as cathodic protection, are implemented. Figure 11.1 shows an example of the shotcrete repair of the Depoe Bay bridge in Oregon, where a flame applied zinc cathodic protection coating was applied to the repair shotcrete to protect the remediated structure from renewed rebar corrosion-induced damage in this heritage

Figure 11.1 Shotcrete repair of Depoe Bay Bridge, Oregon.

structure that had high levels of chlorides at the depth of the rebar, in the substrate concrete.

In summary, before implementing any remedial treatment to a structure, it is important that there be a thorough engineering diagnosis of the likely cause(s) of the damage, so that a suitable repair methodology can be provided. A holistic approach to the assessment should be adopted such that all potentially influencing factors and their interactions are considered. It is only in this way that durable repairs with long service life can be expected (Morgan, 1996).

11.4 PREPARATION OF SUBSTRATE SURFACES

In most infrastructure repair and rehabilitation cases, the shotcrete will be applied to existing prepared concrete surfaces, although in some structures, such as historic structures, it may also be applied to brick or stone masonry. Irrespective of the substrate medium, proper preparation of the substrate surface prior to the application of shotcrete is critical for integral bond of the shotcrete to the substrate. Section 9.2 presents a complete discussion on different methods of substrate preparation before spraying shotcrete.

11.5 PERFORMANCE PARAMETERS FOR SHOTCRETE REPAIR SYSTEMS

The required performance parameters for shotcrete repair systems will depend on the particular structure and exposure conditions. For example, for concrete, the Canadian Standards Association CSA A23.1-19 defines (amongst others) the exposure classes listed in Table 11.1.

The concrete requirements for these various exposure conditions are summarized in Table 11.2.

Table 11.1 CSA A23.1-19 exposure classes

Exposure class	Description
C-1	Structurally reinforced concrete exposed to chlorides with and without freezing and thawing conditions
C-2	Non-structurally reinforced (i.e., plain) concrete exposed to chlorides and freezing and thawing
C-3	Continuously submerged concrete exposed to chlorides but not freezing and thawing
F-1	Concrete exposed to freezing and thawing in a saturated condition, but not to chlorides
F-2	Concrete exposed to freezing and thawing, but not to chlorides
N	Concrete not exposed to freezing and thawing, nor to chlorides

Table 11.2 Performance requirements for concretes with various CSA A23.1-19 exposure conditions

Class of exposure[1]	Maximum w/cm ratio	Minimum specified compressive strength (MPa) and age (d) at test	Air content required[2]	Chloride ion penetrability requirements and age at test Coulombs
C-XL	0.40	50 within 56d	yes	< 1000 within 91 d
C-1	0.40	35 within 56d	yes	< 1500 within 91 d
C-2	0.45	32 at 28 d	yes	—
C-3	0.50	30 at 28 d	no	—
C-4	0.55	25 at 28 d	no	—
F-1	0.50	30 at 28 d	yes	—
F-2	0.55	25 at 28 d	yes	—

[1] See Table 11.1 for a description of classes of exposure.
[2] For air-content requirements, see CSA A23.1, Table 2 and Table 4.

Since shotcrete is essentially a method of placing concrete, in Canada the CSA A23.1-19 *Concrete Materials and Method of Concrete Construction Standards* are also used as a guideline for shotcrete. The American Concrete Institute and other countries standards organizations have similar types of national standards for concrete. There are, however, some differences between the requirements for shotcrete compared to concrete. For example, most shotcrete repair specifications require the shotcrete to have a maximum water/cementing materials ratio (w/cm) not exceeding 0.45. This is because shotcrete mixtures with w/cm in excess of about 0.50 do not have a sufficient cementing materials content for suitable adhesion (to the substrate) and cohesion (in the freshly placed shotcrete) and thus have a susceptibility to sagging and sloughing (fall-out). For CSA A23.1-19 C-1 exposure conditions a maximum 0.40 w/cm would be specified, but a maximum w/cm of 0.45 would be specified for C-2, C-3, F-1 and F-2 exposure conditions. For Class N exposure conditions, the specification might be relaxed to a 0.50 maximum w/cm, but only subject to the local shotcrete practice demonstrating that such shotcrete had suitable shooting characteristics.

Dufour et al. (2006) provide a review of the *State-of-the-Art Specifications for Shotcrete Rehabilitation Projects* as developed by the Ministry of Transportation Quebec (MTQ). MTQ shotcrete rehabilitation projects are mainly directed at repair of bridges, elevated freeway structures and other highway-related infrastructure. Such structures are subjected to a very severe exposure environment with frequent cycles of freezing and thawing and copious application of deicing chemicals. As such the structures are considered to be subjected to a CSA A23.1-19 Class C-1 exposure category. With over 40 years of shotcrete repair experience, the MTQ has developed the repair shotcrete mix performance requirements detailed in Table 11.3, which follows, for Dry-Mix Shotcrete and Table 11.4, which follows, for Wet-Mix Shotcrete.

Table 11.3 MTQ dry-mix shotcrete performance requirements

Minimum 28-day compressive strength, MPa	Minimum weight of cement, kg/m³ Type GUB-SF (Type I with silica fume)	Type HE (type III)	Maximum water-cementitious material ratio[1]	Minimum proportion by weight of 310 mm aggregate, %	Air content (plastic and hardened states), %	Minimum weight of synthetic fibre, kg/m³
35	450	460	Based on consistency (~0.40)	10	3.5 to 7.0	0.9

[1] Water-cementitious material ratio is not verified, given the nature of dry-mix shotcrete.

Table 11.4 MTQ wet-mix shotcrete performance requirements

Minimum 28-day compressive strength, MPa	Minimum weight of cement, kg/m³	Maximum water-cementitious material ratio	Minimum proportion by weight of 10 mm aggregate, %	Air content,[1] %	Slump, mm	Minimum weight of synthetic fibre, kg/m³
35	410	0.40	25	10 to 15	100 ± 30	0.9

[1] Air content is measured after the addition of high-range water-reducing admixture, if required, before pumping.

In addition to the above types of specified performance requirements for infrastructure rehabilitation shotcretes, other performance parameters may be specified, depending on the specifics of the project. For example, with fibre-reinforced shotcretes, there may be requirements to meet certain toughness performance requirements, e.g. There may be a requirement to meet a Toughness performance Level III in tests conducted to ASTM C1609 (Morgan et al., 1995); see Section 6.9 in this book for a definition of Toughness Performance Levels. On some fibre-reinforced shotcrete tunnelling and mining projects there may be a requirement to meet a minimum Joules energy value in the ASTM C1550 round panel test.

The ASTM C642 Boiled Absorption (BA) and Volume of Permeable Voids (VPV) test is often also specified for shotcretes used in infrastructure rehabilitation. Maximum limits of 8% BA and 17% VPV are commonly specified for such shotcretes. This test is of value in that it can identify defective shotcrete caused by problems, such as poor application techniques (e.g. insufficient impacting velocity or shooting at too acute an angle), or excessive accelerator addition, where the use of accelerators is specified.

In aggressive freeze/thaw exposure environments, the project specification may require demonstration in preconstruction testing that the shotcrete is durable when subjected to 300 cycles of freezing and thawing in the ASTM C666 Procedure A test. Durability Factors in excess of 80 are generally considered to demonstrate freeze/thaw durable shotcrete in this test (Morgan, 1991). In addition, some specifications require the potential freeze/thaw durability of the shotcrete to be demonstrated in preconstruction air-voids parameters testing to ASTM C457. The MTQ specifications require hardened wet-mix shotcrete to have an average air-void spacing factor not exceeding 0.230mm with no individual result greater than 0.260 mm. For dry-mix shotcrete, MTQ specifications require the average air-void spacing factor to not exceed 0.300 mm with no individual result greater than 0.320 mm (Dufour et al., 2006). These recommendations are based on the results of extensive research into the freeze-thaw durability of shotcretes conducted at Université Laval in Quebec City.

In situations where the shotcrete is subjected to exposure to deicing chemicals, the specifications may require preconstruction salt scaling testing to be conducted on the shotcrete to ASTM C672. A limit of maximum 1 kg/m^2 scaling mass loss after 50 cycles in this test is considered an industry standard (Beaupré et al., 1994; Dufour et al., 2006). The test has, however, been criticized by some as being excessively aggressive and some authorities have come up with modified versions of this test which they consider better reflect likely field performance for shotcretes subjected to deicing chemicals.

11.6 SHOTCRETE MATERIALS, MIXTURE PROPORTIONS AND SUPPLY

The same basic materials used in conventional structural shotcretes are also generally used in shotcretes for infrastructure rehabilitation, but often with some modifications. For example, in addition to Portland cement, supplementary cementing materials (such as fly ash, silica fume, ground granulated blast furnace slag, or calcined metakaolin), suitably graded coarse and fine aggregates and air-entraining and water-reducing admixtures, repair shotcretes may also be formulated with one or more of the following types of materials:

a) Liquid shrinkage-reducing admixtures in wet-mix shotcrete (Morgan et al., 2001);
b) Type K expansive cements;
c) Various types of fibres (e.g. steel, polypropylene, carbon, polyvinyl alcohol or natural fibres); and
d) Special types of set accelerators (powdered addition during blending with dry-mix shotcretes and liquid addition at the nozzle with wet-mix shotcretes).

While conventional ready-mix batching, mixing and supply is often used in shotcrete rehabilitation projects, there is a large market for dry-blended bagged shotcrete supply. There are a number of companies in North America which have developed a suite of different dry-bagged shotcrete repair materials. They are typically supplied in either paper bags (30 kg) or bulk bin bags (up to 1000 kg). Some suppliers have developed special rapid setting, hardening and strength gain products based on alternative cements to Portland cement (e.g. modified high aluminate-based cements, or calcium sulfoaluminate cements) (Ballou, 2013). Such products are very useful for remedial works in intertidal regions in marine projects, permafrost or frozen ground applications, or where the repaired structure has to be returned to service very rapidly. Some companies have also developed shotcretes with high acid attack and sulphate resistance for use in projects such as rehabilitation of sewers or molten sulphur pits. Such products can be formulated for use in either the wet-mix or the dry-mix shotcrete processes. Wet-mix shotcretes can be batched using conventional transit concrete mixers, or dry-to-wet mobile batching equipment, such as that shown in Figure 11.2.

Dry-mix bagged shotcretes are typically discharged into predampening augers which discharge the shotcrete directly into the shotcrete gun, with remaining water addition at the nozzle (see Figure 10.17).

Table 11.5 provides an example of a wet-mix shotcrete mixture design used over a 10-year period for rehabilitation of about 2 km of shipping berth faces in an intertidal region in the Port of Saint John, New Brunswick (Gilbride et al., 1996).

Figure 11.2 Mobile batching equipment producing wet-mix shotcrete from dry bagged materials.

Table 11.5 Wet-mix shotcrete mixture design for shipping berth face
rehabilitation at the Port of Saint John, New Brunswick

Material	Mix proportions, kg/m³
Normal Portland cement (Type 10)	400
Silica fume	56
10 mm coarse aggregate (SSD)	460
Concrete sand (SSD)	110
Water	180
Water-reducing admixture	2 L
Superplasticizer	7 L
30 mm steel fibre	60
Air-entraining admixture	As required for
Air content (in place)	7 ± 1%
TOTALS:	2265
Slump	80 ± 20 mm
Minimum 28 compressive strength	40 MPa

Table 11.6, which follows, provides an example of a dry-mix shotcrete mixture design used by the MTQ for shotcrete repair of the Metropolitain Boulevard elevated freeway structure in Montreal, Quebec for 5 years from 1989 to 1994 (Bertrand and Vezina, 1995).

Table 11.6 Dry-mix shotcrete used for repair of Metropolitain
Boulevard, Montreal, Quebec

Material	Mix proportion
Cement type 10SF (8% silica fume), kg/m³	450
Coarse aggregate 10–2.5 mm, kg/m³	235
Fine aggregate, kg/m³	1510
Polypropylene, kg/m³	1.0
Air-entraining agent, L/m³	1 to 2

11.7 SHOTCRETE APPLICATION AND FINISHING

The general application and finishing best practises for wet-mix and dry-mix shotcrete application and finishing described in Chapter 9 also apply to shotcrete for infrastructure rehabilitation. In particular, it is important to:

a) Provide suitable access for the nozzlemen, helpers and finishers so that they can work safely with free unhindered access to the work;

b) Provide sufficient lighting and ventilation so that the nozzleman and crew have an unhindered view of the shooting area;

c) Use good shotcrete nozzling techniques as detailed in ACI 506R. In particular:

- Orient the nozzle at right angles to the receiving surface, except as required to fill corners and edges and encase inserts and large diameter reinforcing bars (the nozzleman may have to shoot at an angle from both sides of such elements to achieve proper encapsulation with shotcrete);
- Optimize the combination of air volume and distance of the shotcrete from the receiving surface to achieve maximum consolidation of the shotcrete and full encapsulation of reinforcing steel and any embedments;
- Have a blow-pipe operator work in tandem with the nozzleman to keep the area about to be shotcreted free of rebound and build-up of overspray;

d) When applying shotcrete in more than one layer, trim the initial layer with a cutting rod, or brush with a stiff bristle broom to prepare a surface suitable for application of the next layer of shotcrete;

e) Allow the initial shotcrete layer to stiffen sufficiently before application of the finishing layer of shotcrete (in order to avoid pulling sags and tears into the initial shotcrete layer during finishing operations);

f) Use shooting wires (or *pencil rods* in curved surfaces) to control the finished line and grade and tolerance; and

g) Finish shotcrete to specified line and grade and tolerance and apply specified type of finish.

11.8 CURING AND PROTECTION

On completion of finishing it is important to protect the shotcrete from rapidly drying out, as this can cause plastic shrinkage cracking and/or *crazing* (fine pattern cracking in the hardened shotcrete surface). This can be accomplished by using techniques such as erection of windbreaks and sunshades, fogging/misting, or spray application of evaporation retarders to the finished shotcrete surface.

As soon as the shotcrete has taken a hard set it should be cured. Curing is best achieved with moist curing using methods such as:

a) Wrap the shotcrete repairs in wet burlap covered with a plastic sheet, or use a presaturated plastic-coated non-woven synthetic or natural fabric;

b) Where conditions permit, install sprinklers or soaker hoses to keep the shotcrete continuously wet for the specified period; and

c) Moist curing should be maintained for at least 7 days.

When moist curing it is important to keep the shotcrete continuously wet and avoid procedures that allow the shotcrete to undergo cycles of wetting and drying during the curing process.

Where moist curing is not suitable because of logistical or other constraints, spray-on curing compounds can be used. They are less desirable than moist curing, as they do not provide the additional water that shotcrete needs for optimal hydration and minimizing the potential for autogenous and drying shrinkage-induced cracking (Aïtcin, 1999). They are, however, considerably better than providing no curing protection at all.

In addition to moist curing, or the use of spray-on curing compounds, the shotcrete should be protected against adverse thermal effects. In hot weather conditions, shotcrete application should be suspended if the ambient temperature rises above 35°C, unless suitable hot-weather protection measures are adopted. In cold weather conditions, shotcrete work should be suspended if the substrate temperature is below 5°C and/or the ambient temperature is forecast to fall below 5°C, unless suitable cold weather protection measures are undertaken. For example, in Edmonton and Calgary in Alberta, shotcrete construction of major structures has proceeded throughout the winter by construction of suitable heated enclosures with moist curing. Work has typically only been suspended when ambient temperatures fall below −20°C (it simply gets too difficult to maintain shotcrete supply under such conditions).

During shotcrete construction of the Whistler 2010 Olympics bobsleigh/luge track, all shotcrete application, finishing and wet curing was conducted inside a travelling tent in which the temperature and humidity was controlled. In the summer, the tent provided protection against the drying effects of wind and solar radiation and shutdowns in construction because of rain. In the winter, the tent provided protection against wind and snow and a heated enclosure. This enabled shotcrete construction to proceed throughout the year in harsh environmental conditions. Figure 9.36 shows shotcrete work inside the tent at the Whistler project.

11.9 EXAMPLES OF SHOTCRETE REPAIR AND REHABILITATION OF INFRASTRUCTURE

11.9.1 Bridges and highway infrastructure

Dry-mix shotcrete has been widely used in North America for bridge and highway infrastructure rehabilitation for over a century. Wet-mix shotcrete has been used for over 60 years for such applications. The first author has personally been involved in shotcrete repair of numerous bridges in Canada and the USA for over 40 years. He has examined the performance of over 60 shotcrete repaired bridges in Canada (Morgan and Neill, 1991). A few examples of shotcrete repair of bridges in North America follow.

11.9.1.1 Ministry of Transportation Quebec (MTQ) and City of Montreal

The MTQ has used dry-mix shotcrete since the 1980s in bridge infrastructure rehabilitation. The current MTQ shotcrete specification has evolved from a specification first introduced over 50 years ago (Dufour et al., 2006). The MTQ permits the use of either wet or dry-mix shotcrete on vertical surfaces, but only allows the use of dry-mix shotcrete on overhead surfaces. Starting in 1990 the City of Montreal spent over $80 million in shotcrete repair of over 5000 columns and the soffits of the 10 km long Metropolitain Boulevard elevated freeway structure crossing the city. This work was done using dry-mix air-entrained shotcrete (Bertrand and Vezina, 1995). Figure 11.3 shows shotcrete repair being carried out on the Metropolitain Boulevard.

11.9.1.2 Ministry of Transportation Ontario (MTO)

In the 1980s, the Ministry of Transportation of Ontario (MTO) used latex-modified shotcrete for repair of bridge components such as beams, columns, abutments and arches. The performance of such repairs was, however, often less than satisfactory because of difficulties in application and finishing of the latex modified shotcrete used and its susceptibility to plastic and restrained drying shrinkage cracking (Morgan and Neill, 1991; Hutter and Singh, 2012). Figure 11.4 shows an example of pattern cracking in a latex-modified shotcrete repair of a bridge abutment in Ottawa, Ontario.

In 1990, after extensive literature and laboratory research, the MTO decided to repair the open-spandrel concrete arch Magnetawan River Bridge using a prepackaged silica fume modified shotcrete instead of using latex

Figure 11.3 Shotcrete repair of Metropolitain Boulevard elevated freeway structure.

(Photo courtesy Jacques Bertrand.)

Figure 11.4 Pattern cracking in latex-modified shotcrete repaired part of bridge abutment in Ottawa subjected to direct sun exposure.

Figure 11.5 Magnetawan River Bridge repaired with shotcrete.

modified shotcrete. Based on the successful performance of this project the MTO has since repaired over 65 structures using such silica fume modified shotcrete (Hutter and Singh, 2012). The use of latex-modified shotcrete has been largely discontinued. Figure 11.5 shows the shotcrete repaired Magnetawan River Bridge.

Figure 11.6 Shotcrete repair of bridges piers in bridge over the North Saskatchewan River.

11.9.1.3 Alberta bridge repairs

Since the early 1980s, dry-mix steel fibre-reinforced shotcrete has been used for repair of many bridges in Alberta (Carter, 1985; Johnston and Carter, 1989). In 1990, the first author examined eight such bridges and found the repairs to all be in good to excellent condition (Morgan and Neill, 1991). Figure 11.6 shows dry-mix steel fibre-reinforced shotcrete repair of high bridge piers in the North Saskatchewan River in Drayton Valley, Alberta. The repairs were required due to extensive salt scaling and reinforcing steel corrosion-induced delamination and spalling of the original reinforced concrete in the piers, as a result of leaking expansion joints (i.e., moisture carrying deicing salts) in the bridge deck above.

11.9.1.4 Oregon City Arch Bridge

The Oregon City Arch Bridge spans the Willamette River near Portland, Oregon. The bridge is 274 m long, including the viaduct approaches. The main span of the bridge is a C.B. McCullough design through-deck steel box girder arch that is believed to be unique in North America. The bridge, which was completed in 1922, however, has the appearance of a concrete arch bridge. This is because the steel components of the bridge were encased with a mesh reinforced *gunite* (sand/cement dry-mix shotcrete), ranging in thickness from 50 to 150 mm. The prime purpose of this *gunite* application was to protect the steel members from the corrosive effects of emissions from a nearby pulp mill and other industries. Figure 11.7 shows the bridge during original construction in 1922. Figure 11.8 shows *gunite* application

Figure 11.7 Oregon City Bridge during construction in early 1920s.
(Photo courtesy Marcus von der Hofen.)

Figure 11.8 Application of *gunite* to top arch rib of Oregon City bridge.
(Photo courtesy Marcus von der Hofen.)

Figure 11.9 Wet-mix shotcrete placement inside steel box beam arch.
(Photo courtesy Marcus von der Hofen.)

to the top of the arch rib during initial construction. von der Hofen (2012) provides a description of this original work.

This *gunite* encasement of the steel members provided remarkably durable performance for nearly 90 years, but in 2010 a decision was made to remove all the existing *gunite* and replace it with a modern silica fume modified wet-mix shotcrete, as part of a major rehabilitation of the bridge (von der Hofen, 2013). After removal of the *gunite*, the steel was grit-blasted to a white metal finish. This was found to be necessary to satisfy the specified minimum 1.0 MPa bond strength for the replacement shotcrete. Figure 11.9 shows wet-mix shotcrete placement inside the arches. The remedial work was successfully completed in 2012 (von der Hofen, 2013).

11.9.2 Marine structures

Shotcrete has been widely used in North America for over 100 years for rehabilitation of marine structures. Marine structures that have been repaired with shotcrete include piers, wharfs, jetties, sea walls, light stations, dry docks, bridges, undersea tunnels, barges and floating concrete ships. The first author has been involved in shotcrete repair of all of these types of structures, and a few examples follow.

11.9.2.1 Canada Place, Vancouver Harbour, British Columbia

Between 1983 and 1984, over $2 million was spent in shotcrete repair of the Pier B-C in Vancouver Harbour, which supports the Canada Place Trade and Convention Centre, Cruise Ship Terminal and Pan Pacific Hotel. Dry-mix shotcrete was used to repair deteriorated and damaged precast piles and cast-in-place reinforced concrete sea walls, pile caps, beams, stringers and deck slab soffits in intertidal and salt spray exposure environments. The work was started using a conventional dry-mix shotcrete. There was, however, a need to enhance productivity when working in intertidal regions in order to have the structure ready for the EXPO-86 World Fair. Trials were conducted with a silica fume modified dry-mix shotcrete. It was found to markedly improve the adhesion, cohesion, thickness of build-up and resistance to sagging and sloughing without the need for use of an accelerator. Most importantly, the silica fume provided excellent wash-out resistance to the freshly placed shotcrete. This allowed for a substantially increased shotcreting *window* when working in intertidal regions and enabled the work to be completed on time. Figure 11.10 shows a view of the completed Canada Place project. This pioneering project marked the first use of silica fume in dry-mix shotcrete for remedial work in Canada and has since led to the routine use of silica fume in shotcrete remedial work in marine and other

Figure 11.10 Completed Canada Place project in Vancouver Harbour.
(Photo courtesy Dallas Morgan.)

infrastructure throughout North America and elsewhere in the world. When re-examined in 2015, after over 30 years of service, the shotcrete repairs were observed to be still in good condition.

11.9.2.2 Port of Saint John, New Brunswick

The Port of Saint John in New Brunswick is located in the Bay of Fundy and has one of the highest tidal ranges of any major port in the world. With a typical tidal range of 8.5 m, it presents a very aggressive exposure environment for concrete structures in the harbour. There are nearly 2 km of concrete shipping berth faces in the harbour, many of them constructed from the 1910s to the 1930s. Deterioration of the mass concrete berth faces has been caused by factors such as ship impact damage, exposure to strong currents laden with salt and abrasive sediments, alkali-aggregate reactivity and most significantly damage from between 200 to 300 cycles of freezing and thawing in the intertidal range each year. Some of the earliest shipping berth faces were abandoned because the deterioration was too severe to justify rehabilitation (one could climb through holes in some of the berth faces at low tide). Some 1600 lineal metres of the shipping berth faces were, however, deemed repairable and between 1986 and 1996 they were rehabilitated using an anchored and bonded air-entrained, steel fibre-reinforced wet-mix silica fume modified shotcrete (Gilbride et al., 1988). Figure 11.11 shows a typical deteriorated section of berth face prior to shotcrete repair.

Figure 11.11 Deteriorated section of shipping berth face prior to repair.

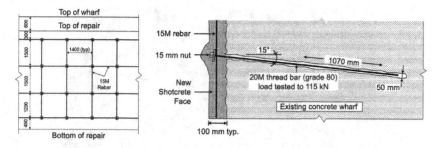

Figure 11.12 Schematic of anchor and shotcrete repair.

Figure 11.12 shows a schematic of the anchor and shotcrete system used in the repairs

The shotcrete work was typically carried out from either floating barges, or swing stages on the falling tide. The silica fume in the mix provided the freshly placed shotcrete with excellent wash-out resistance against the rising tide and wave action. Compressive strengths at 28 days typically ranged between 40 and 50 MPa and boiled absorption values were typically in the 5.1 to 7.6% range. As-batched air contents were designed to be in the 7 to 10% range and as-shot air contents were typically in the 4.5 to 7.1% range. Most spacing factor values were less than 0.260 mm (Gilbride et al., 1988). As such, the shotcrete was expected to be freeze-thaw durable. In 1995, after nearly 10 years in service, a survey of the condition of the shotcrete in the berth faces was conducted (Gilbride et al., 1996). Other than for some restrained drying shrinkage cracks and a few peeling type delaminations at some featheredged construction joints, the shotcrete was observed to be in good condition. There was no evidence of any freeze/thaw damage, in spite of the repaired berth faces having been subjected to over 2000 cycles of freezing and thawing. In 2015, after nearly 30 years in service, Gilbride reported that the shotcrete resurfacing of the shipping berth faces was still performing well in this harsh marine environment. Figure 11.13 shows a typical shotcrete resurfaced berth face after nearly 10 years in service.

11.9.2.3 Haut-Fond Prince Lighthouse, Gulf of St. Lawrence, Quebec

The Haut-Fond Prince lighthouse located in the Gulf of St. Lawrence, near Tadoussac, Quebec was constructed in 1964. The steel and reinforced concrete components forming the pier base structure suffered severe abrasion and erosion deterioration over the years from wave action and the high pressure of ice grinding on the intertidal parts of the structure in winter months. Some sections of the pier were eroded to depths of as much as 1.5 m. Repair was urgently needed to prevent undermining of the structure, and in 1996 a repair programme was carried out (Gendreau et al., 2009). Figure 11.14 shows a general view of the lighthouse after completion of the repair.

Figure 11.13 Repaired section of berth face after nearly 10 years in service.

The repair consisted of removal of damaged steel plates and deteriorated concrete and application of an air-entrained, dry-mix, steel fibre-reinforced, silica fume modified shotcrete. The work was particularly challenging, as shotcrete had to be applied in intertidal regions from an inflatable boat, under conditions of strong tidal action and waves impacting the freshly applied shotcrete. Dry-bagged shotcrete material and shotcreting equipment was stored on a barge anchored next to the work. Figure 11.15 shows shotcrete application in progress.

The dry-mix shotcrete mixture proportions used are given in Table 11.7. The steel fibre was added to increase resistance to restrained shrinkage cracking and improve impact resistance from ice flows. A liquid air-entraining

Figure 11.14 General view of Haut-Fond Prince Lighthouse after shotcrete repair. (Photo courtesy Antoine Gagnon.)

admixture was added to produce a freeze/thaw durable shotcrete with an air-void spacing factor lower than 0.300 mm. The shotcrete was stored in a hold in the barge heated to about 30°C and hot water was added during shooting such that the resultant shotcrete had a temperature of about 25°C. This, in conjunction with the use of a CSA Type HE High Early Strength Cement, together with addition of a set accelerator, enabled the shotcrete to set, harden and develop compressive strength such that it was not damaged by tidal currents and wave action. The specified minimum compressive strength of 20 MPa at 7 days under field cure conditions was readily met with results as high as 39 MPa being achieved. The applied shotcrete satisfied all the specified performance requirements. The structure was inspected after four years in service and the shotcrete repairs were observed to be providing excellent performance with no damage from freezing and thawing cycles, or ice scour.

Figure 11.15 Shotcrete application to Haut-Fond Prince lighthouse from an inflatable boat. (Photo courtesy Denis Beaupré.)

Table 11.7 Dry-mix shotcrete mixture proportions used at Haut-Fond Prince Lighthouse repair

Material	Percentage of dry materials mass, %
Type 30 cement	20.0
Silica fume	2.5
Sand (0 to 5 mm)	61.0
Coarse aggregate (2.5 to 10 mm)	14.8
Set accelerator	1.0
Steel fibres	1.7

11.9.2.4 Stanley Park Seawall, Vancouver, British Columbia

The Stanley Park Seawall is a 10 km long combined walkway and cycle path along the oceanfront in English Bay, Burrard Inlet and Coal Harbour in Vancouver, British Columbia. It is the most widely used public recreational facility in Vancouver, with over one million visitors a year. The seawall is primarily constructed of granite masonry blocks with mortared joints, with an asphalt pavement surface with anchored granite edge coping stones. Construction of the seawall started in the early 1920s as an erosion control measure and took 53 years to build. For 32 years, construction of the seawall was under the direction of James Cunningham, an immigrant Scottish stonemason, who devoted most of his life to the project.

The seawall is subjected to daily tidal action and waves. In addition, during winter storms it can be subjected to severe impact from floating logs, which are common in the ocean around Stanley Park. The majority of the seawall has demonstrated remarkable durability, considering its age and the marine exposure conditions. By 2000, however, there were numerous locations, comprising about 500 m in total length, where wave and tidal action had caused scour and erosion in the predominantly sandstone substrate, undermining the seawall. A decision was made to repair the seawall in these undermined areas using an air-entrained, wet-mix, macrosynthetic fibre-reinforced shotcrete with silica fume added for enhanced resistance to wash-out in these environmentally sensitive intertidal regions (Morgan et al., 2004). Figure 11.16 shows one such location near Siwash Rock, where a total thickness of about 2.5 m of shotcrete was applied in three passes to underpin the seawall in a severely scour-damaged zone.

Details of the shotcrete mixture design used and specified, and actual shotcrete performance are provided in Table 11.8.

The shotcrete was supplied in 800 kg bulk bin bags which were discharged into a 2 m^3 rotating drum mixer mounted on a flat-bed truck. All shotcrete equipment and materials were mounted on a shotcrete *train* which moved along the seawall performing the underpinning repairs where required on the seawall. The shotcrete work was performed at low tides and because of environmental protection measures, only the nozzleman and his helper were

Figure 11.16 Shotcrete underpinning of Stanley Park Seawall at Siwash Rock.

Table 11.8 Stanley Park Seawall shotcrete mix design and performance requirements

Material	Mass, kg/m³	
Cement, Type GU	400	
Silica fume	45	
Fly ash	30	
Coarse aggregate (10–2.5 mm)	450	
Fine aggregate	1210	
Water-reducing admixture	Standard dose	
superplasticizer	As required for 60 ± 20 mm slump	
Air-entraining admixture	As required for 7–10% air content at pump	
	As required for 4 ± 1% air content as-shot	
Total mass	2320	
Hardened shotcrete properties	*Specified*	*Typical values*
Compressive strength on cores	Min. 30 MPa at 7 Days	47 MPa
	Min. 40 MPa at 28 Days	54 MPa
ASTM C642 boiled absorption	Max. 8%	5.0%
ASTM C642 volume of permeable voids	Max. 17%	11%

allowed on the beach during shooting operations. On relatively calm days, the nozzleman was able to continue shooting until about half an hour before the incoming tide reached the work, with no washout or detrimental effects on the freshly installed shotcrete. On windy days, with more severe wave action, shotcrete application was terminated about an hour before the incoming tide reached the work. Environmental monitoring showed no detrimental effects on the quality of seawater (alkalinity, suspended solids and turbidity) after submersion of the work by the incoming tides.

In addition to repair of the masonry seawall, a 215 m long section of the even older Devonian Park portion of the Seawall, originally constructed in 1918, was repaired with shotcrete. Figure 11.17 shows shotcrete repair being carried out on a 3.7 m high section of this seawall. Repair was carried out on a deteriorating 200 mm thick reinforced concrete facing to a rockfill providing protection to the seawall. The same shotcrete mix and process utilized for repair of the masonry seawall was successfully used to repair the Devonian Park seawall.

11.9.3 Dams and hydraulic structures

Shotcrete has been used for over 100 years for repair and rehabilitation of deteriorated hydraulic structures, such as dams (upstream faces and downstream spillways, intake structures, draft tubes and low-level outlet

Figure 11.17 Shotcrete repair of deteriorated concrete facing to Devonian Park seawall.

structures). Heere et al. (1996) provide examples of shotcrete repairs to four British Columbia Hydro Dams, which ranged in age from 65 to 80 years old at the time of shotcrete repair. In addition, shotcrete has been used to rehabilitate a range of other hydraulic structures, including aqueducts, water retention tanks, swimming pools, sewage treatment structures and industrial water treatment facilities. The sections, which follow, provide some case history examples of repair and rehabilitation of different types of hydraulic structures in which the authors have been involved.

11.9.3.1 Jordan River Dam, Vancouver Island, British Columbia

The Jordan River Dam is a 40 m high Ambersen buttress type dam built in 1912–1913 in Southern Vancouver Island, British Columbia (Heere et al., 1996). It is comprised of inclined reinforced concrete slabs resting on downstream buttresses. Figure 11.18 shows the seismically retrofitted dam in 1990. The slabs are 1.4 m thick at the base of the dam, tapering to 0.4 m thick at the top. Over the years, the slabs and buttress elements progressively deteriorated as a result of water leaking through joints in the slabs above the buttresses, leaching and frost action. In addition, there was some abrasion and wear on the upstream face of the dam from logs and ice abrasion as the water level in the dam rose and fell. Also, the low-level outlet structures were eroded from high-velocity water flows.

Figure 11.18 Seismically retrofitted Jordan River Dam in 1990.

Over the years, a series of shotcrete repairs were carried out to maintain the dam in a serviceable condition, culminating in a major seismic retrofit of the dam in 1990. Many of the repairs were conducted using the shotcrete technology of the day. Brief examination of these repairs reflects the progress in shotcrete repair technology in Canada. During the period 1969–1971, the upstream face of the dam was repaired using a gunite-type dry-mix shotcrete reinforced with a 75 × 75 mm grid of 4 mm dia. welded wire mesh with shotcrete applied in a 75 to 100 mm thick layer. A 20 mm thick layer of unreinforced dry-mix shotcrete of similar composition was applied to the buttress elements on the downstream face. Compressive strength of the original concrete was highly variable (the original concrete was placed at a quite fluid consistency, using *puddling sticks* and displayed pronounced segregation within lifts). Strengths in cores from the slab concrete ranged from 19 to 33 MPa and averaged about 26 MPa in tests conducted by Heere in 1994. Strengths in cores from the buttress concrete ranged from 6 MPa to 39 MPa and averaged 18 MPa in 1994.

Deterioration of the dam continued, and in 1989 major repairs to leaks at joints in the slabs in the upstream face of the dam were conducted. These repairs were carried out using dry-mix, steel fibre, reinforced, silica fume modified shotcrete. In 1990 the old dry-mix shotcrete repairs to the downstream buttresses, which had largely debonded (as a result of the poor quality of concrete to which they were applied), were removed. The lower parts of the buttresses were massively seismically strengthened, with new reinforcing and cross-beams using cast-in-place concrete. The upper tiers of the buttresses were encapsulated in an air-entrained, wet-mix, silica fume modified shotcrete, a minimum 65 mm thick, reinforced with anchored hook dowels, rebar and mesh. Testing by Heere in 1994 (Heere et al., 1996) of the shotcrete applied to the buttresses in 1990 demonstrated that the shotcrete was of excellent quality. Both the dry-mix shotcrete repairs to the upstream face applied in 1989, and the wet-mix shotcrete repairs applied as part of the seismic retrofit of the downstream buttresses in 1990 continue to provide good performance.

11.9.3.2 Wachusett Aqueduct, Massachusetts

In 2001–2002, the historic 11 km long Wachusett Aqueduct in Eastern Massachusetts was rehabilitated with wet-mix shotcrete (Town, 2004). The original aqueduct was constructed between 1897 and 1903 and was the primary source of drinking water for the City of Boston. The original aqueduct was horseshoe-shaped and 3.35 m high. The sidewalls up to the *spring line* and invert were constructed of dressed brick ashlar masonry. The crown of the original aqueduct (from 9 o'clock to 3 o'clock) was constructed with unreinforced concrete. Figure 11.19 shows part of the aqueduct before shotcrete lining.

In the 1960s, new water supply systems were developed for Boston and the aqueduct ceased to be used. By 1999, however, water demand in the area required the Wachussett Aqueduct to be put back into service. The first author was involved in this restoration project, which consisted primarily of application of 75 mm thick of wet-mix shotcrete through anchored wire mesh reinforcement to line the aqueduct. Over 11,500 cubic meters of

Figure 11.19 Wachussett aqueduct before shotcrete lining.

Figure 11.20 Wachussett aqueduct after shotcrete lining.

wet-mix shotcrete were applied. The shotcrete lining was designed to strengthen the structure, control groundwater inflow into the aqueduct, and provide a smooth tunnel surface to maximize the volume of water flowing through the tunnel. The lining was finished to an exacting cast-concrete equivalent finish. Figure 11.20 shows a section of the completed shotcrete-lined aqueduct. The shotcrete lining was completed within 18 months and provided better water flow capacity than the original brick ashlar and cast concrete aqueduct, in spite of the reduction in cross-section area, because of the improved lining smoothness achieved with the shotcrete.

11.9.3.3 Ruskin Dam, British Columbia, Seismic Retrofit

The Ruskin Hydroelectric Dam is located on the Stave River, about 60 km east of Vancouver, BC. The dam was constructed in 1929 and 1930 and is a mass concrete gravity structure situated in a narrow valley and founded predominantly on bedrock. The dam is 130 m long at the road deck level and goes over an 85 m long, seven-bay radial-gated spillway straddled by two 45 m long non-overflow sections. The dam is 58 m high from its deepest foundation to the road deck on the dam crest. There is a stepped cast concrete structure on the left abutment of the dam (looking upstream). Figure 11.21 shows a general view of the dam and 105 MW generating station in 2008, when it was nearly 80 years old.

The Ruskin Dam was built long before the development of air entrainment to provide freeze/thaw durability to concrete. Consequently, the spillway face suffered some deterioration from frost action, as well as erosion/abrasion from water and water-borne debris. In 1954, some patch repairs

Figure 11.21 Ruskin dam and generating station.

were made to the spillway face using mesh-reinforced dry-mix shotcrete. But deterioration continued in adjacent non-repaired parts of the spillway, and in 1973 a major remediation programme was undertaken to completely resurface the entire spillway and adjacent stepped concrete structure. This was done using dry-mix shotcrete reinforced with a 5 mm diameter welded-wire mesh reinforcement. Shotcrete thicknesses on the spillway varied from about 75 mm to 200 mm on the spillway, and 75 to 150 mm on the stepped structure. This remedial work extended the service life of the dam by over 40 years.

In the mid-2000s, BC Hydro, the owner and operator of the dam and generating station determined that the spillway radial gates were seismically deficient by current seismic standards and decided to replace the existing seven radial gates with a new five-gated structure which meets current seismic requirements. In 2008, a study was commissioned to conduct a detailed survey of the condition of the spillway and adjacent stepped structure. A detailed condition survey was carried out on the spillway surface from a rolling swing-stage. A combination of visual examination, photographic documentation, non-destructive testing (NDT) using impact echo, coupled with sounding for delaminations using chain drag and hammer sounding was performed. In addition, cores were extracted at selected locations to verify findings from NDT, as well as to provide specimens for determination of compressive strength and Boiled Absorption (BA) and Volume of Permeable Voids (VPV) in both shotcrete and substrate concrete. Details of the results and findings of this study are provided in a paper by Zhang et al. (2011). The study determined that while the shotcrete repaired spillway face was in reasonably good overall condition, considering it had provided 35 years of service, there was distress in the form of cracking, delaminations at construction joints with feathered edges, and more deep-seated delaminations either at the shotcrete/concrete interface, or deeper in the substrate concrete in a number of locations.

BC Hydro decided that in order to extend the service life of the Ruskin Dam by at least another 50 years, that as part of the seismic retrofit programme they would resurface the spillway structure and adjacent stepped structure. For the stepped structure, this was done by removing the existing shotcrete resurfacing and weak substrate concrete, and resurfacing it with a bonded and anchored cast-in-place steel fibre-reinforced concrete. This remedial solution was selected because cast-in-place concrete is better suited to construction of the horizontal parts of the steps than shotcrete.

By contrast, for the sloping spillway surface, shotcrete was selected as the preferred construction process. A wet-mix, steel fibre-reinforced silica fume modified shotcrete was specified for use on the project. Existing dry-mix shotcrete was required to be removed to the extent necessary to allow for a minimum 150 mm thickness for the new bonded shotcrete overlay. Initially, the bulk of the shotcrete and concrete removal was accomplished with high-pressure water demolition, with chipping hammers being used as needed. In many places, the shotcrete thickness was greater than 150 mm because of a need to remove delaminated or deteriorated substrate concrete. To speed up the concrete and overlay shotcrete removal process, the contractor changed to a system of diamond wire cutting slabs out of the surface of the spillway, followed by high-pressure water blasting to achieve the specified surface roughness profile. The shotcrete was anchored with 15M L-Bar anchors at 1.2 m on centre vertically and horizontally, with 15M reinforcing steel spanning vertically and horizontally between the anchors. Figure 11.22 shows a prepared substrate, with anchors and reinforcing steel installed, ready for shotcreting. The specified performance requirements for the shotcrete were as detailed in Table 11.9.

Shotcrete installation commenced in 2015. Both preconstruction and construction test results readily satisfied Table 11.9 specified performance requirements. Figure 11.23 shows shotcrete application from a rolling swing stage. Figure 11.24 shows the shotcrete finishing work in progress. The shotcrete was specified to have a steel trowel finished surface with a surface tolerance not exceeding 6 mm under a 3 m straightedge placed anywhere on the spillway on straight sections. Shooting wires were installed to control line and grade and the shotcrete was trimmed to the shooting wires with cutting rods, prior to finishing with bull floats and steel trowels. Careful attention to rigorous moist curing was required to minimize the occurrence of restrained drying shrinkage cracking, particularly for shotcrete placed during hot summer conditions where temperatures often exceeded 30°C and strong drying wind conditions frequently occurred.

Figure 11.22 Spillway surface prepared for shotcreting with installed anchors and reinforcing steel.

Table 11.9 Specified shotcrete performance requirements

Test description	Test method	Age, days	Specified requirement
Maximum water/cementitious ratio	—	—	0.40
Air content (as-shot)	CSA A23.2-4C	—	4 ± 1%
Slump at discharge into pump, mm	CSA A23.2-5C	—	60 ± 20
Maximum compressive strength	CSA A23.2-14C	7 28	30 MPa 40 MPa
Maximum boiled Absorption	ASTM C642	7	8%
Maximum vol. of Permeable voids	ASTM C642	7	17%
Minimum flexural toughness	ASTM C1609	28	Level III[1]
Minimum bond pull-off strength	CSA A23.2-6B	28	1.0 MPa

[1] Based on 4.0 MPa at 28 days desig flexural strength

Figure 11.23 Shotcrete application on Ruskin Dam spillway surface from a rolling swing stage.

Figure 11.24 Finishing shotcrete spillway surface.

11.9.4 Miscellaneous shotcrete repairs/retrofit

In addition to the structures already described, the authors have been involved in many other types of projects where shotcrete has been used for repair/strengthening or seismic retrofit (Chan and Morgan, 2000). Examples include:

a) Jacketing and strengthening of cracked and leaking grain silos (Collins et al., 1997);
b) Repair of corrosion damaged bulk shipping facilities such as potash, coal and sulphur load-out dumper pits, loading towers and conveyors, and dome structures (Morgan, 2006);
c) Repair and strengthening of large diameter corrugated metal culverts;
d) Repair of wastewater and sewage conveyance pipes and treatment tanks;
e) Repair of oil sands processing tanks;
f) Repair of corrosion damaged beams, columns, and soffits of slabs in pulp and paper mills;
g) Seismic retrofit of heritage and other reinforced concrete and masonry structures (Heere et al., 1999; Morgan and Zhang, 2009);
h) Seismic retrofit of parking structures, schools and other buildings; and
i) Repair of World War I and II floating concrete ships (McAskill et al., 1994; McAskill and Heere, 2004).

Brief descriptions of a few of these projects follow.

11.9.4.1 Prince Rupert Grain Silos

The Prince Rupert Grain Terminal is located on the Northwest coast of British Columbia near the Alaskan panhandle and was built in 1985 as part of a major strategic development for the export of Canada's grain to Pacific nations. It handles about one-fifth of Canada's total wheat production but also handles barley, canola and other grains. The main grain storage facility at the terminal consists of 60 reinforced concrete silos arranged in three 20-silo clusters. Figure 11.25 shows a partial view of the silo complex.

The silos were designed and constructed in accordance with the then-prevailing ACI design code for silos (ACI 313R). When grain is unloaded from silos it is not uncommon for the grain to bridge and then discharge with impact as the bridge breaks. Over time, repeated impact loads can give rise to fatigue-induced cracking in the lower two-thirds of the grain silos. This occurred within four years of construction of the silos and was a concern to the owner, as the cracks provided a path for water entry to the stored grain, and also started to initiate corrosion of reinforcing steel. After an extensive structural review of the behaviour of the silos, a decision was made to strengthen the silos and remediate the cracking concerns by

Figure 11.25 Prince Rupert Grain Terminal grain silos.

(Photo courtesy American Shotcrete Association)

constructing a reinforced shotcrete jacket around the exterior of all the grain silo clusters. A paper by Collins et al. (1997) provides details of the remedial work undertaken. The first author was involved in an investigation of the cracking which occurred in the silos and provided the mixture design for the wet-mix silica fume modified shotcrete used for the remedial work. The shotcrete was supplied by ready-mix concrete trucks and was applied by hand nozzling from suspended swing stages, as shown in Figure 11.26.

11.9.4.2 Historic Masonry Building Seismic Retrofit, Vancouver, British Columbia

The Wing Sang Building is the oldest heritage masonry structure in Chinatown in Vancouver, British Columbia. The front (South) building was first built by a Chinese immigrant, Yip Sang, as a two-story brick structure in 1889, with a third floor being added in 1901. His import business thrived, as did his family, and in 1912 he built a back (North) six-storey brick masonry building to house his four wives and 23 children. Over the years the buildings deteriorated, being of simple brick masonry construction with interior timber framing and flooring, which were highly deficient by modern seismic standards. It would have been a simple solution to demolish and replace the buildings with a modern high-rise tower. However, in the late 2000s a successful Vancouver realtor, with a penchant for historic structures preservation purchased the property and seismically retrofitted it as his offices and an art gallery. Morgan and Zhang (2009) provide a detailed description of the seismic retrofit carried out on this building.

Figure 11.26 Reinforced shotcrete jacket construction at Prince Rupert Terminal grain silos.

(Photo courtesy American Shotcrete Association)

11.9.4.3 Rehabilitation of Historic High-Rise Building, Vancouver, British Columbia

The Vancouver Block Building was built in 1911 and was one of the first high-rise buildings constructed in downtown Vancouver. This 15-storey high-rise building was constructed with a steel frame, with stucco clad brick masonry walls on the North and South sides of the building and architectural glazed terracotta hollow brick cladding on the East and West sides of the building. Figure 11.27 shows a general view of the North and West faces of the building and clock tower, during rehabilitation.

In the late 1990s cracks were discovered in the exterior plaster clad brick masonry walls and some terracotta elements. An investigation found that decades of exposure to wind-driven rain had resulted in water penetrating through the walls to the structural steel framing. This had resulted in varying degrees of corrosion of the steel column and beam elements and the steel corrosion products were causing the observed plaster cracking. In places the corrosion was sufficiently severe to have caused complete loss of steel in I-beam flanges. A structural engineer was hired, and a detailed remedial design implemented.

Heere et al. (1999) provide details of the remedial work undertaken. Briefly, it involved segmental removal of plaster and brick masonry along

Figure 11.27 View of north and west faces of Vancouver block during rehabilitation.

all exterior wall beam and column lines on the North and South sides of the building. Corrosion product was removed from steel elements using a combination of needle scaling and grit blasting. Where needed, customized steel profiles were welded to the webs of the steel beams and columns. Rather than simply replacing the brick and plaster along beam and column lines, the structure was strengthened, and steel framing protected by installing reinforcing steel and then shotcrete. The work was done from either scaffolding, or swing stages. The South wall was shot first with a dry-bagged premix shotcrete applied using the dry-mix shotcrete process. While the dry-mix shotcrete process worked well in terms of the ability to use lighter equipment, and the ease for stop-and-go and clean-up operations, it did create some problems with control and removal of dust and rebound.

Repair on the North face involved working over a neighbouring property with high pedestrian traffic and the owner asked if the wet-mix shotcrete process could be used to repair the North face, since it produces significantly less dust and rebound than the dry-mix shotcrete process. The shotcrete pump was set up on the second floor and the challenge was to pump the shotcrete up to 13 stories high. This was successfully achieved using a powerful small-line shotcrete pump with a 75 mm diameter swing valve and 50 mm diameter shotcrete line and a specially designed silica fume modified shotcrete with 10 mm maximum size aggregate. The shotcrete was pumped vertically through a fixed steel slick line which was then connected at every floor to a 50 mm diameter rubber hose that conveyed the shotcrete horizontally to the nozzle where the shotcrete was being applied. Figure 11.28 shows a nozzleman applying shotcrete to a prepared column line from a

Figure 11.28 Nozzleman applying shotcrete to a prepared column line from a swing stage.

swing stage. After a sufficient period of moist curing, the shotcrete was allowed to dry out before the North and South walls received a new coat of elastomeric paint.

REFERENCES

AASHTO-AGC-ARTBA Joint Committee Task Force 37 Report. 1998. *Guide Specifications for Shotcrete Repair of Highway Bridges* American Association of State Highway and Transportation Officials. 101 p.

ACI 207.6-17. 2017. *Report on the Erosion of Concrete in Hydraulic Structures.* American Concrete Institute. 33 p.

ACI 210R-93(98). 1998. *Erosion of Concrete in Hydraulic Structures.* American Concrete Institute. 34 p.

ACI 313R. *Standard Practice for Design and Construction of Concrete Silos and Stacking Tubes for Storing Granular Materials.* American Concrete Institute.

ACI 506R-06. 2016. *Guide to Shotcrete.* American Concrete Institute 40 p.

ACI-ICRI. 2013. *Concrete Repair Manual.* 4th edition. American Concrete Institute.

ACI RAP-6. 2005. *Vertical and Overhead Spall Repair by Hand Application.* American Concrete Institute. 5 p.

Aïtcin, P. -C. 1999. Demystifying Autogenous Shrinkage. *Concrete International.* Vol. 21. No. 11. 54–56.

ASTM International C1550-10. 2010. *Standard Test Method for Flexural Toughness of Fiber Reinforced Concrete (Using Centrally Loaded Round Panel)*. 14 p.

ASTM International C1609-05. 2005. *Standard Test Method for Flexural Performance of Fiber Reinforced Concrete (Using Beam with Third-Point Loading)*. 8 p.

ASTM International C642-06. 2006. *Standard Test Method for Density*. Absorption and Voids in Hardened Concrete. 3 p.

ASTM C457. 2016b. *Standard Test Method for Microscopical Determination of Parameters of the Air-Void System in Hardened Concrete*. 7p. ASTM International. https://doi.org/10.1520/C0457_C0457M-16

ASTM International C666-03. 2003. *Standard Test Method for Resistance of Concrete to Rapid Freezing and Thawing*. 6 p.

ASTM C672. 2012. *Standard Test Method for Scaling Resistance of Concrete Surfaces Exposed to Deicing Chemicals*. 7p. ASTM International.

Ballou, M. 2013. Rapid-Setting Cement in Shotcrete. *Shotcrete Magazine* Spring, 2013. 46–47.

Beaupré, D., Talbot, C., Gendrau, M., Pigeon, M. and Morgan, D. R. 1994. Deicer Salt Scaling Resistance of Dry and Wet-Process Shotcrete. *ACI Materials Journal*. Vol. 91. No. 5. September–October. 487–494.

Bertrand, J. and Vezina, D. 1995. *The Development of Air Entrained Durable Shotcrete for Structural Repairs. Shotcrete for Underground Support VII*, Telfs, Austria, June 11–15, 1995, Amercian Society of Civil Engineers, 58–65.

Carter, P. 1985. Bridge Repair with Steel Fibre Shotcrete, ACI Fall Convention. *Seminar on Concrete Rehabilitation with Shotcrete, 1985*, Chicago, 16 p.

Chan, C. and Morgan, D. R. 2000. Infrastructure Repair and Rehab with Shotcrete. *CE News*, March 2000, 66–71.

Collins, M., Adebar, P., Seabrook, P. T., Kuchma, D. and Sacre, P. 1997. External Repair of Cracked Grain Silos. *Concrete International*. Vol. 19. No. 11. November. 22–28.

CSA. 2019e. *A23.1/A23.2 Concrete materials and methods of concrete construction/Test methods and standard practices for concrete*. 690p. Canadian Standards Association.

CSA-A864. 2005. *Guide to the evaluation and management of concrete structures affected by alkali-aggregate reaction*. 108p. Canadian Standards Association.

Dufour, J. -F., Reny, S. and Vezina, D. 2006. State-of-the-Art Specifications for Shotcrete Rehabilitation Projects. *Shotcrete Magazine* Fall 2006 4–11.

Emmons, P. H. 1993. *Concrete Repair and Maintenance Illustrated: Problem Analysis: Repair Strategy: Techniques*. R.S Means. 314 p.

Gendreau, M., Beaupré, D., Lacombe, P. and De Montigny, J. 2009. Use of Dry-Mix Shotcrete to Repair a Lighthouse Structure. *Shotcrete Magazine* Winter 2009, 32–37.

Gilbride, P., Morgan, D. R. and Bremner, T. W. 1988. Deterioration and Rehabilitation of Berth Faces in Tidal Zones at the Port of Saint John. *ACI SP-109, Concrete in Marine Environment*, 1988, 199–227.

Gilbride, P., Morgan, D. R. and Bremner, T. W. 1996. Performance of Shotcrete Repairs to Berth Faces at the Port of Saint John. *Odd Gjorv Symposium, CANMET/ACI International Conference on Performance of Concrete in Marine Environment, St. Andrews-by-the-Sea*, New Brunswick, August 4–9, 1996, 163–171.

Heere, R., Morgan, D. R., Banthia N. and Yogendran, Y. 1996. Evaluation of Shotcrete Repaired Dams in British Columbia. *Concrete International*. Vol. 18. No. 3. March. 24–29.

Heere, R., Morgan, D. R., McAskill, N. and Knowlton, T. 1999. Shotcrete Rehabilitation of a Vancouver, BC, Historic High-Rise Building. *Shotcrete Magazine*. Vol. 1, No. 4. November. 10–13.

ICRI 310.1R-2008. 2008. *Guideline for Surface Preparation for the Repair of Deteriorated Concrete Resulting from Reinforcing Steel Corrosion.* International Concrete Repair Institute. 12 p.

ICRI 310.2R-2013. 2013. *Selecting and Specifying Concrete Surface Preparation for Sealers, Coatings, Polymer Overlays and Concrete Repair.* International Concrete Repair Institute. 48 p.

ICRI 310.3R-2014. 2014. *Guideline for the Preparation of Concrete Surfaces for Repair Using Hydrodemolition Methods.* International Concrete Repair Institute. 28 p.

von der Hofen, M. 2012. The Oregon City Bridge (Part I). *Shotcrete Magazine* Fall 2012. 30–32.

von der Hofen, M. 2013. The Oregon City Bridge (Part II). *Shotcrete Magazine* Fall 2013. 22–24.

Hutter, J. and Singh M. 2012. The Use of Shotcrete as a Repair Process for Ontario Bridge Structures. *Shotcrete Magazine* Winter 2012. 22–27.

Johnston, C. D. and Carter, P. D. 1989. Fiber Reinforced Concrete and Shotcrete for Repair and Restoration of Highway Bridges in Alberta. *Transportation Research Board, 68th Annual Meeting*, January 22–26, 1989.

McAskill, N. A. and Heere, R. 2004. Shotcrete Repair of WWII Concrete Hulks. *Shotcrete Magazine*, Summer 2004, 10–14.

McAskill, N. A., Morgan, D. R., Hatch, D. and Osualdini, M. 1994. Evaluation and Restoration of World War I and II Concrete Ships. *ACI/CANMET Third International Conference on Durability of Concrete*, Nice, France, May 22–27, 1994, 14 p.

Morgan, D. R. 1991. Freeze Thaw Durabilty of Steel and Polypropylene Fibre-reinforced Shotcretes. *ACI SP-126, CANMET/ACI International Conference on Durability of Concrete*, 901–911.

Morgan, D. R. 1996. Compatibility of Concrete Repair Materials and Systems. *Construction and Building Materials*. Vol. 10. No. 1. 56–67.

Morgan, D. R. 1997. Shotcrete Repair of Infrastructure in North America. *Betoninstandsetzung 1997*, Innsbruck, Austria, January 30–31, 1997, 28 p.

Morgan, D. R. 2006. Advances in Shotcrete Technology for Infrastructure Rehabilitation, *Shotcrete Magazine* Winter 2006. 18–27.

Morgan, D. R., Chen, L. and Beaupré, D. 1995. Toughness of Fiber Reinforced Shotcrete. *Shotcrete for Underground Support XII*, Edited by Klappperich, H., Pottler, R. & Willocq, J., Telfs, Austria, Published by ASCE, 66–87.

Morgan, D. R., Ezzet, M. and Pfhol, C. 2004. Rehabilitation of the Seawall at Stanley Park Vancouver, BC, Canada with Synthetic Fibre-reinforced Shotcrete. *Shotcrete: More Engineering Developments, Proceedings of the 2nd International Conference on Engineering Developments in Shotcrete*, Edited by Bernard, E.S., Cairns, Australia, October 2004, Taylor and Francis, 201–208.

Morgan, D. R., Heere, R. Chan, C., Buffenbarger, J. K. and Tomito, R. 2001. Evaluation of Shrinkage-Reducing Admixtures in Wet and Dry-Mix Shotcretes. *Shotcrete: Engineering Developments, Proceedings of the International Conference on Engineering Developments in Shotcrete*, Edited by Bernard, E.S., Hobart, Tasmania, April 2001, 185–192.

Morgan, D. R. and Neill, J. 1991. Durability of Shotcrete Rehabilitation Treatments of Bridges. *Transportation Association of Canada Annual Conference*, Winnipeg, Manitoba, September 15–19, 1991, 36 p.

Morgan, D. R. and Zhang, J. 2009. Seismic Retrofit of Historic Wing Sang Building. *Shotcrete Magazine* Winter 2009. 8–12.

Taylor, G. 1995. Repair. *Sprayed Concrete, Properties, Design and Application*, Edited by Austin, S. & Robbins, P., Published by Whittles Publishing, Scotland, Chapter 14, 287–296.

Town, R. 2004. Restoring the Century Old Wachusett Aqueduct. *Shotcrete Magazine* Summer 2004. 16–18.

Transportation Association of Canada. 1992. *Recommended Practice for Shotcrete Repair of Highway Bridges*. Canadian Strategic Highway Research Program (C-SHRP). 84 p.

Zhang, L., Ezzet, M., Shanahan, N., Morgan, D. R. and Sukumar, P. K. 2011. Ruskin Dam Spillway Shotcrete Assessed. *Concrete International*. Vol. 33. No. 2. 37–43.

Chapter 12

Ground support and shoring

12.1 INTRODUCTION

Some of the earliest uses of shotcrete were for ground support and shoring. As noted in Figure 3.3, dry-mix shotcrete (*gunite*) was used for slope stabilization purposes by the US Army Corps of Engineers on the Panama Canal construction as early as 1911. Next to swimming pools and underground support in tunnels and mines, ground support and shoring represent the largest uses of shotcrete in North America and probably worldwide. There are many different types of ground support and shoring projects which have used shotcrete. These include:

a) Earth and rock slope stabilization;
b) Soil nailed wall construction;
c) Temporary stressed tie-back wall construction;
d) Permanent structural walls;
e) Underpinning buildings and structures;
f) Canal linings; and
g) Creek and river levee stabilization.

The sections, which follow, examine some of these various uses of shotcrete in ground support and shoring applications.

12.2 EARTH AND ROCK SLOPE STABILIZATION

Shotcrete has been used for over 100 years for earth and rock slope stabilization. As mentioned in Chapter 3, up until the mid-1950s, such work was nearly all carried out with the dry-mix shotcrete (*gunite*) process. The wet-mix shotcrete process was introduced in the mid-1950s and, mainly because of its greater rate of application (and hence increased productivity with reduced costs), increasingly became the preferred method for soil and rock slope stabilization, to the extent that the wet-mix shotcrete process now dominates for such applications in most countries around the world.

DOI: 10.1201/9780429169946-14

Prior to the 1970s, most shotcrete used for earth and rock slope stabilization was reinforced with either conventional reinforcing steel, or more commonly welded wire mesh fabric. Since the mid-1970s, when steel fibre-reinforced shotcrete (SFRS) was first used for rock slope stabilization at the Ririe Dam in Idaho (Kaden, 1974), SFRS has increasingly been used, in lieu of welded wire mesh, for such applications. Steel fibre reinforcement has been used in both wet-mix and dry-mix shotcretes. In the late-1980s, macrosynthetic fibres were developed for use in shotcrete and they rapidly found use in earth and rock slope stabilization projects (Morgan, 1995, 2000). Macrosynthetic fibres have, however, mainly been used in wet-mix shotcrete.

Examples of some types of earth and rock slope stabilization projects, in which the authors have been involved, include:

a) Stabilizing city-block-size deep excavations (up to 30 m deep) for below-ground parking structures beneath subsequently constructed high-rise buildings, using stressed tie-back anchors or passive soil-nail anchors with shotcrete facing;
b) Underpinning existing buildings and structures, in conjunction with the use of stressed tie-back anchors (Abbott, 2001, 2010);
c) Stabilizing highway and railway cuts with vertical or sloping walls. Such walls may have a natural rough *as-shot* finish, or a sculpted and often pigmented architectural shotcrete finish (FHWA, 1998; Harrison, 2015);
d) Adding additional traffic lanes under bridge overpasses by removal of sloped bridge abutments, and construction of vertical or near-vertical reinforced shotcrete walls;
e) Support of excavations in highway and railway *cut-and-cover* tunnelling projects (Abbott, 2010);
f) Stabilizing mountain slopes and bluffs (Chan et al., 2002);
g) Creek stabilization and protection from erosion from storm and debris flow events (Hungr and Skermer, 1998);
h) Protection of ocean-front bluffs and seawalls from erosion, scour and undercutting (Morgan et al., 2004);
i) Stabilizing deteriorating mechanically stabilized earth walls (Heere et al., 2001); and
j) Protection of gabion basket-lined river channels and levees from damage and erosion (e.g. Mapocho River running through Santiago, Chile).

The sections, which follow, show some examples of such shotcrete applications.

12.3 STABILIZING EXCAVATIONS

Shotcrete has long been used along the West coast of North America (Los Angeles, San Francisco, Seattle and Vancouver), and now increasingly elsewhere in North America for stabilizing deep excavations for below-ground parking structures. Many of these excavations are of city-block size dimensions. Depths of these excavations range from 3 m (for one floor of below-ground parking) to as much as 30 m (for 8 or more floors of below-ground parking). Stressed tie-back anchors with reinforced shotcrete facings are commonly used for stabilizing the perimeter walls where favourable ground conditions exist. For example, in downtown Vancouver, BC, the geological conditions prevailing are comprised predominantly of sedimentary deposits, including conglomerate, sandstone, siltstone and shales. Such ground conditions are generally well suited to excavation and stabilizing using this construction method. In fact, in the past several decades, most of the stabilization of deep excavations in the downtown Vancouver, BC core have been constructed using this method.

After investigation of the ground conditions prevailing on the site, the geotechnical engineer-of-record designs an excavation and shoring sequence. The following is a brief description of this construction method:

1. *Excavate berm 1m wide then slope at 1:1 as shown in Figure 12.1*
2. *Install anchors through berm. Anchors will have free-length sleeved to de-bond. A high early-strength silica fume modified grout is used to facilitate tensioning anchors the next day.*
3. *Day 2 – excavate alternating 2 anchor panels (depending on soil quality this may be increased or decreased) – then shotcrete panels.*

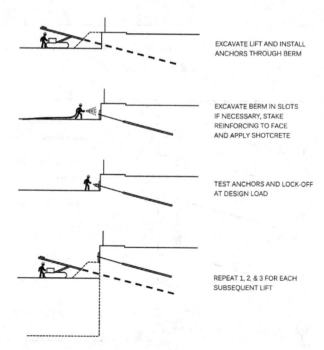

EXCAVATE LIFT AND INSTALL
ANCHORS THROUGH BERM

EXCAVATE BERM IN SLOTS
IF NECESSARY, STAKE
REINFORCING TO FACE
AND APPLY SHOTCRETE

TEST ANCHORS AND LOCK-OFF
AT DESIGN LOAD

REPEAT 1, 2, & 3 FOR EACH
SUBSEQUENT LIFT

Figure 12.1 Typical anchored shotcrete diaphragm installation procedures.

4. *Day 3 – proof test each anchor to 1.25 (sometimes 1.33) design load and lock off. Excavate adjacent panels which already have anchors installed, and repeat process*

Figures 12.1–12.4 show this construction process.

Figure 12.2 Sequential panel excavation and shotcrete shoring method. (Photo courtesy Abbott Consulting & Management.)

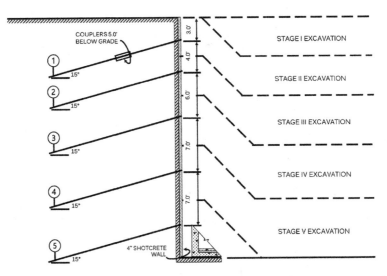

Figure 12.3 Typical shotcrete with stressed anchor tie-back cross-section.

Figure 12.4 Stabilized excavation for a below-ground parking structure in down-town Vancouver, BC.

(Photo courtesy Abbott Consulting & Management.)

On completion of stabilization of the excavation, construction of the parking structure can then proceed. This usually involves installation of a waterproofing membrane to the shotcreted excavation, followed by construction of the reinforced concrete perimeter walls, columns, beams, ramps and suspended parking slabs. Up until the late 1990s, most of the perimeter walls were constructed using conventional formed, cast-in-place reinforced concrete methods. Since the 2000s, however, many of the below-ground parking structure projects in Vancouver, BC and Calgary Alberta (as well as in other cities along the west coast of the USA) have used structural shotcrete methodology to construct the perimeter walls. The use of shotcrete, in lieu of formed cast-in-place concrete, eliminates the need for formwork and this has proven to be attractive to contractors and owners because of overall time and materials cost savings. The construction of such reinforced shotcrete walls is described in the preceding Section 10.1.

12.4 UNDERPINNING BUILDINGS AND STRUCTURES

Shotcrete has proven to be a valuable means for underpinning buildings and structures. The methodology used is really a variant on the method used for stabilizing excavations with stressed tie-back anchors with shotcrete facing, as described in the preceding Section 12.3. Abbott (Abbott, 2001) provides an interesting case-history example of one such project to underpin a deteriorated three-story brick masonry building on a rubble foundation in downtown Vancouver, BC, so that a deep excavation could be constructed in the lot adjacent to this brick masonry building. The perimeter brick masonry wall adjacent the proposed new excavation was so unstable that a decision was made to first reinforce and strengthen it, prior to undertaking the underpinning. A grid of reinforced shotcrete was installed over the entire brick wall, with ties through the floor joists at the four floor levels. Part of this construction is shown in Figure 12.5.

After strengthening and stabilizing the brick masonry wall with reinforced shotcrete, underpinning commenced. Underpinning used a 1 to 4 sequenced panel numbering system for segmental excavation. Figure 12.5 shows the underpinning completed to the full 14 m depth of the excavation. Colour changes at the edges of individual panels (because of the effects of overspray) provide a visual indicator of the sizes of individual panels shot.

Figure 12.5 Underpinning under a stabilized and strengthened brick masonry wall.

(Photo courtesy Abbott Consulting & Management.)

12.5 SOIL NAILING

Soil nailing is a construction technique used in certain types of ground to create stable sloped or vertical surfaces. It is usually used in conjunction with reinforced shotcrete to produce a stable temporary or permanent wall able to retain the ground behind it. While the method is referred to as *soil nailing*, it has been used in a wide variety of ground conditions, ranging from soils to weathered rock and even some types of unweathered rock. The method is an off-shoot of the New Austrian Tunneling Method (NATM) described in Chapter 13 of this book and involves the concept of passive reinforcement of the ground with closely spaced reinforcing steel bars, called nails. Holes are drilled horizontally or sub-horizontally into the ground and the nails, with spacers to centre them in the holes are fully grouted with Portland cement-based grouts. The nails are passive and develop their reinforcing action through nail-ground interactions as the ground deforms during and after construction (FHWA,1998). Figure 12.6 shows a schematic

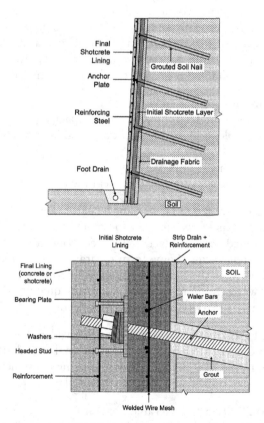

Figure 12.6 Schematic of a soil nailed shotcrete faced excavation stabilization (top) and an illustration of a typical installed and grouted soil nail anchor (bottom).

of a soil-nailed wall along with an illustration of a typical grouted soil nail anchor.

Soil nailing had its origins in Europe in the early 1970s. One of the first uses of soil nailing in North America was reportedly for stabilization of a 13.7 m deep foundation excavation in dense silty sands at the Good Samaratin Hospital in Portland, Oregon in 1976 (FHWA, 2015). A national guideline publication for soil nailing was developed in Japan in 1987. In 1996 (subsequently revised in 1998), the U.S Department of Transportation, Federal Highway Administration, issued a publication: *Manual for Design & Construction Monitoring of Soil Nail Walls* (FHWA, 1998). This 530-page publication provides a very comprehensive guide to all aspects of shotcrete soil-nail wall design and construction. It is complemented by the *Soil Nail Walls Reference Manual* published by the FHWA in 2015 (FHWA, 2015).

In the over 40 years that soil-nail wall construction has been used, it has proven to be a technically sound and cost-effective alternative to conventional retaining wall construction, which often requires a cut excavation and backfilling. It is, however, only suited to use in ground which is able to stand unsupported one to two metres high for a minimum of two days when cut vertically or near vertically and is suitable for installation of soil nails. It is well suited to use in stiff to hard fine-grained soils and dense sands and gravels with good cohesion and evenly weathered rock with no planes of weakness. It is not suitable for ground conditions, such as the following:

a) Clean sands and gravels lacking cohesion;
b) Soft clays with a high swelling or creep capacity;
c) Soils with cobbles and boulders that make soil nail anchor installation difficult;
d) Soils with a high groundwater table; and
e) Highly corrosive soils which could degrade the soil nails.

With respect to the shotcrete facings, in the early years of soil nailing they were largely viewed as *temporary* with permanent slope stabilization being provided by formed, cast-in-place reinforced concrete walls constructed against the shotcrete facing. Some form of drainage or waterproofing was often provided between the shotcrete facing and permanent concrete wall to control groundwater. In more recent years, as the quality and durability of shotcrete has improved, two things have happened:

a) The initial shotcrete lining is now being considered as permanent and is being incorporated into the permanent final wall design; and
b) Increasingly, the final permanent wall is being constructed with structural shotcrete rather than formed cast-in-place concrete.

In the 1980s to 2000s, a considerable number of permanent shotcrete soil-nail walls were constructed in deep parking structure foundation walls under high-rise buildings in the west coast of the USA (Los Angeles, San Francisco and Seattle areas). The permanent shotcrete walls were constructed from the top down to depths of up to 30 m below grade. Depending on ground conditions, the following construction method was typically used:

a) Soil was segmentally removed in 1 to 2 m high lifts, and soil nails installed and grouted;

b) This process was repeated until an entire lift was excavated and anchored;

c) Synthetic drainage fabric strips were installed vertically against the excavated earth face at spacings suitable for the prevailing site conditions. Horizontal drainage strips were also installed at the base of the shotcrete lift;

d) An initial layer of shotcrete was applied at soil nail anchor points and bearing plates installed connecting the soil nails to the shotcrete;

e) Reinforcing steel for the permanent structural wall was installed and wet-mix shotcrete was applied to the full thickness from the bottom up, using the ACI 506R-16 bench shooting technique;

f) Shooting wires were installed to control final line and grade and the wall (which sometimes also included pilasters) was cut and trimmed and finished to the specified architectural finish;

g) The bottom of the shotcrete lift was either shot against an inclined form board, or trimmed while still plastic to create an approximately 45-degree horizontal joint; and

h) Steps a) to g) above were then repeated as many times as necessary to get to the bottom of the excavation, with the vertical drainage strips extending down to the base of the wall where they connected to a footing drain, which in turn discharged water into a sump with pumps to remove water.

Entire city-block size foundation perimeter walls have been constructed using this method. It has proven to be economically attractive, as once constructed, the owner not only has a fully supported excavation but also has a permanent perimeter foundation wall. This method has worked well in drier climates with little groundwater. Performance has, however, not always been as favourable in wetter climates with more groundwater. On some projects, groundwater has penetrated through the permanent structural shotcrete walls, with the most vulnerable place for leakage being at the horizontal construction joints. This has resulted in ongoing maintenance problems for owners, and the method has tended to fall out of favour in some areas, particularly in locations with wetter climates and/or unfavourable groundwater conditions.

To mitigate the water penetration issues referred to above, since the 2000s there has been an increased tendency to go to a three-stage shotcrete construction process:

a) Permanent structural shotcrete is still used for top-down soil-nail wall construction;

    b) This is followed by installation of a complete waterproofing membrane around the entire shotcrete-lined excavation; and

    c) A permanent structural shotcrete wall is then constructed from the bottom up (as described in Chapter 10).

A variety of different systems have been used for waterproofing of below-grade structural shotcrete walls. Both membrane and integral shotcrete waterproofing systems have been used (Klein, 2007 and Darling and Cao, 2009). Darling and Cao provide a detailed description of a membrane system that has been successfully used on a number of deep foundation projects in North America. The membrane consists of a polymer-mesh-reinforced cavity sandwiched between a plastic film and a nonwoven semipermeable geotextile. The composite membrane serves as a carrier for post-shotcrete installation injection of a hydrophilic grout through injection ports installed in the membrane. When the grout is injected, it fills the cavity created by the mesh layer in the membrane and fills any voids in, or between the shotcrete layers. This provides a waterproofing system that is fully adhered to shotcrete layers and can seal any voids at shotcrete construction joints. Figure 12.7 shows one such structural shotcrete wall placed and finished over the membrane system described above.

Figure 12.7 Completed structural shotcrete wall placed over a grouted waterproofing membrane.

(Photo courtesy Johnson Western Gunite.)

12.6 CUT AND COVER TUNNELS

Shoring with stressed tie-back rock bolts and temporary shotcrete facing has proven to be an effective means of construction of excavations for cut and cover tunnelling. A good example of this is the shoring for the cut and cover tunnel segment of the Canada Line rapid transit project between downtown Vancouver and Richmond, BC and Vancouver International Airport. The design/build contractor selected for the project elected to use the cut and cover method for construction of the tunnel in this segment, in lieu of a bored tunnel. This was in part because construction of the tunnel section of the Canada Line project was on the *critical path* for completion of the project in time for the 2010 Winter Olympic Games in Vancouver and Whistler, BC. In addition, this method allowed work to be carried out at multiple headings.

Abbott (2010) provides a detailed description of this project. It represents one of the largest shotcrete shoring projects ever undertaken in North America and the statistics are impressive. Double-sided shoring was performed on a 6.2 km long trench excavated in a major road corridor with commercial and residential buildings on either side. Some 530,000 m^3 of ground was excavated, including 30,000 m^3 of rock. Approximately 15,000 m^3 of wet-mix shotcrete was used to provide over 100,000 m^2 of tie-back anchored shotcrete shoring and underpinning. Over 26,000 tensioned anchors were installed. Challenges encountered included relocating and/or diverting and supporting sanitary and storm sewers, water mains, fibre optic cables, and gas and electrical lines. Also, anchors were not allowed to encroach on neighbouring private properties, and this required some innovate solutions. The shotcrete shored walls had to be constructed to a ±25 mm tolerance to meet the requirements for use of the contractors' collapsible box formwork in the cast-in-place concrete tunnel construction.

There were three different tunnel configurations:

1. Side-by-side in wider tunnel alignment sections where space permitted (4.2 km);
2. Stacked tunnels in business sections where access space was smaller (1.2 km); and
3. Roll-over sections where there was a transition from side-by-side to stacked sections (0.8 km).

Figure 12.8 shows schematics of each of these types of sections, together with typical stressed anchor configurations.

Shotcrete wall thickness was a minimum of 100 mm, but in areas where services had to be supported and in underpinning of buildings at stations the shotcrete was as much as 150 to 200 mm thick. The shotcrete had a design compressive strength of 35 MPa at 28 days and was reinforced with one

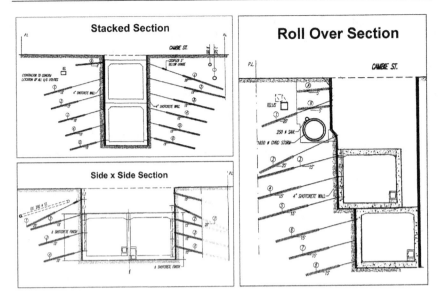

Figure 12.8 Canada Line cut and cover tunnel different tunnel sections. (Drawing courtesy Abbott Consulting & Management.)

layer of 102 mm × 102 mm-MW13.3/MW13.3 welded wire mesh. An additional layer of mesh was installed at anchor heads and additional reinforcing steel was provided where required in weaker ground conditions. A high early strength silica fume modified grout with a minimum compressive strength of 40 MPa at 24 hours was used so that the anchors could be tested for load the next day. All anchored shoring panels were shotcreted the same day. This was essential to keep up with the excavation and maintain productivity and schedule on the project. One part of the cut and cover tunnel was excavated through a fairly fragmented basalt, which left an irregular rock surface. This made contouring the mesh difficult in this zone and a macro-synthetic fibre reinforcement, at an addition rate of 4.6 kg/m^3, was used for shotcrete reinforcement in this zone, in lieu of wire mesh reinforcement. Silica fume modified shotcrete mixtures were used in wet areas and difficult to apply locations.

Once the shoring had reached the required grade, the cast-in-place concrete base slab was poured and finished. This was followed by fixing the reinforcing steel and setting the four sets of rolling 20 m long steel box forms for the final cast-in-place concrete tunnel sections. A strip of waterproofing membrane was adhered to the shotcrete in 1 m wide strips at all joints in the concrete wall sections, prior to concreting. The steel box forms were typically collapsed and recycled every three days. Figure 12.9 shows a view of an excavated and shored stacked tunnel section. Figure 12.10 shows

Figure 12.9 Shored cut and cover excavation in a stacked section.

(Photo courtesy Abbott Consulting & Management.)

steel box forms being set in a side-by-side shored tunnel section. Shoring was completed in July 2008 and the Canada Line opened to full operation in August 2009, which was 15 weeks ahead of schedule and well within time for the 2010 Winter Olympic Games.

12.7 STABILIZING MOUNTAIN SLOPES AND BLUFFS

Some of the earliest uses of shotcrete in the West of North America have been for stabilizing mountain slopes and bluffs to protect infrastructure, such as hydraulic structures (dams, spillways and canals) and highways and railways from damage from rock-falls and debris events. Shotcrete continues to be widely used for such purposes (Chan et al., 2002). Both wet and dry-mix shotcrete have been used and prior to the 1970s, most such work

Figure 12.10 Steel box forms being set in a shored side-by-side tunnel section. (Photo courtesy Abbott Consulting & Management.)

was carried out with wire mesh reinforcement with anchor bolts installed as appropriate.

Installation of wire mesh is, however, not without its challenges. After rock scaling and bolting, wire mesh is attached to the rock face by workers either rappelling from the top of the slope on secured ropes or working out of a crane basket or manlifts. In schistose type rocks, which can be scaled to provide fairly flat faces, it can be relatively easy to install sheets of wire mesh. More commonly, however, the scaled rock face can be very irregular with substantial asperities. This not only makes it difficult to install the wire mesh fabric, but also results in consumption of larger quantities of shotcrete to fill the *valleys* behind the mesh and provide the necessary cover to the steel mesh for corrosion protection. Figure 12.11 shows a schematic of shotcrete installed over mesh.

With the introduction of steel fibre-reinforced shotcrete in the 1970s, and subsequently macrosynthetic fibre-reinforced shotcrete in the late 1980s (Morgan, 2000), fibre-reinforced shotcrete increasingly became the preferred product/process for rock slope stabilization. The use of fibre-reinforced shotcrete not only eliminated the time-consuming and sometimes hazardous process of installing wire mesh on prepared rock faces but also resulted in lower consumption of shotcrete, as is graphically illustrated in Figure 12.11.

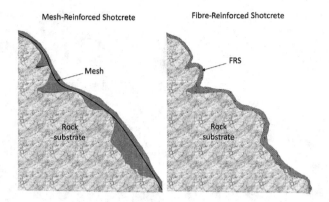

Figure 12.11 Schematic of rock slope stabilization with mesh-reinforced shot-crete compared to fibre-reinforced shotcrete.

Figure 12.12 Rock slope stabilization at the Ririe Dam on the Snake River in Idaho with steel fibre-reinforced dry-mix shotcrete in 1972.

Figure 12.12 shows a historic photo of the first use of steel fibre-reinforced shotcrete in North America for rock slope stabilization at the Ririe Dam on the Snake River in Idaho in 1972 (Kaden, 1974). Figure 12.13 shows the first use of steel fibre-reinforced shotcrete in Canada in 1979, where dry-mix steel fibre-reinforced shotcrete was used to stabilize a railway embankment in Burnaby, BC (Morgan, 2000).

Figure 12.13 Railway embankment stabilization with dry-mix steel fibre-reinforced shotcrete in Burnaby, BC, Canada in 1977.

In 2011 and 2012, BC Hydro carried out a major rock slope stabilization project on a 60 m high bluff above the concrete spillway to the massive 183 m high W.A.C. Bennett dam in Northern British Columbia. Construction of the dam started in 1961 and was completed in 1967, but over the 45 years it has been in service, BC Hydro has been faced with ongoing maintenance costs to maintain stability and control rockfalls from this high bluff. The rock slope stabilization work was conducted in 2011 and 2012 and included blasting to remove some 175,000 m³ of rock. This was followed by rock scaling and bolting, followed by application of steel fibre-reinforced silica fume modified shotcrete applied by the dry-mix shotcrete process. The final step was systematic pattern bolting through the installed shotcrete layer. Shotcrete was applied from wheeled manbaskets suspended from cranes. Figure 12.14 shows the shotcrete work in progress. Work was made challenging by the considerable heights and high winds that frequently blew down the canyon, but the contractor developed a method to stabilize the basket against the rock face from wind forces and counteract the thrust from the shotcrete nozzle. Shotcrete was applied to sloping, near-vertical and even overhead surfaces on the underside of projecting ledges.

Figure 12.14 Shotcrete application on rock bluff at W.A.C. Bennett Dam in Northern British Columbia.

(Photo courtesy Lihe (John) Zhang, LZhang Consulting & Testing Ltd.)

12.8 STABILIZING CREEKS

Shotcrete has been widely used in the mountainous regions of North America, not only to stabilize rock slopes, but also to stabilize creeks against erosion and scour from storm and debris events. A good example of this is the work that has been done along the *Sea to Sky* corridor along Howe Sound, between Horseshoe Bay and Squamish in British Columbia. The Coastal Mountains along Howe Sound drop steeply from nearly 1800 m elevation right into the ocean. With frequent landslides, rock falls, avalanches and debris flows, this has created a hazardous and challenging environment for the road and rail corridors, and various small villages scattered along Howe Sound. A good example of this is a major debris event that occurred in 1983 in Alberta Creek, which passes through the Village of Lions Bay. Heavy rains on snow-covered mountain slopes above the village produced very large stream flows, which created instability of the stream banks, causing loose overburden, snow, ice and trees to slump into the flowing water. The resulting debris flow moved in a series of surges down Alberta Creek (average slope of about 16 degrees), with flow velocities of 2 to 9 m/sec and transported some 20,000 m³ of debris (Hungr and Skermer, 1998).

The debris flow fanned out into the ocean, but not before seriously damaging or destroying 5 bridges and 5 homes and killing several people.

In response to this catastrophe, the BC Ministry of Highways embarked upon an extensive program to control debris events along the Howe Sound corridor. In the Lions Bay area, two major defensive strategies were developed: debris dams to catch the debris flow; and chutes (canals) to send the debris event in a controlled manner into the ocean. In the case of Alberta Creek, the topography was not suited to construction of a debris dam and so an 800 m long-slipformed high-strength (60 MPa at 28 days design strength mix designed by the first author) reinforced concrete chute was constructed.

In the case of three creeks near Lions Bay (Harvey, Charles and Mosquito creeks), catchment areas were excavated in the mountain side and debris dams were constructed. The debris dams were designed to catch calculated debris flows (boulders, rocks trees, etc.), but allow water, snow and ice slush, and sands and gravels to pass. After the debris event has ceased, backhoes and trucks are used to remove the debris from the dam, so that it is ready for the next debris event. Steel fibre-reinforced wet-mix shotcrete was used to stabilize the steep slopes of the excavated catchment areas above the debris dams in all three of these creeks. Stabilization work was also conducted in the creek beds below Charles Creek and Harvey Creek.

Conventional means of trying to stabilize and reinforce creek beds and protect bridge abutments for bridges passing over creeks from erosion and scour in British Columbia typically consisted of placing graded boulders and quarried rock in the base and sides of the creeks, and then *slush-grouting* with Portland cement-based grouts between the boulders. This approach has, however, met with variable success. While it has worked reasonably well in creeks with less steep slopes, it has not always fared well on steep mountain slopes (i.e., between 15- and 20-degree slopes, or greater). During extreme storm events, high hydraulic gradients from water getting under the slush-grouted boulder/rock lining have destroyed the lining, creating a debris event with severe erosion and scour of the stream bed and bridge abutments (Such events occurred twice in a creek on the new Coquihalla highway near Hope, BC in the late 1980s).

In the case of Harvey Creek, which has an average slope of about 21 degrees at the outlet below the debris dam, the design engineers came up with an innovative solution to protect against such an occurrence (Hungr et al., 1987). After creating a channelized shape for the creek bed, using heavy earth moving equipment, the contractors constructed what amounted to a structural inverted waffle-slab with boulders, varying in dimensions from 0.75 m to 1.5 m in nominal diameter, embedded into the waffles. This structure served to provide high resistance against uplift forces, as well as providing an aesthetically pleasing boulder-strewn creek appearance with excellent energy dissipation for water flowing down the creek at high stream flows.

The structure was constructed by first installing water pressure relief plastic pipes in the base and sides of the creek and then installing about a 300 mm thick layer of SFRS (designed by the first author) lining, applied by the wet-mix shotcrete process. Lifting bolts were pre-inserted in the individual boulders, and they were *plumbed* into the freshly applied shotcrete using backhoes. The boulders were carefully placed such that they *squished* into the shotcrete to provide a minimum 100 mm spacing between individual boulders, thus creating the structural waffle-slab effect. Shotcrete was applied by hand nozzling to the *spring line* of the boulders and a pencil vibrator was inserted to ensure full consolidation of the shotcrete around all boulders. The appearance of the end product is illustrated in Figure 12.15. Since construction, the debris dam has caught several debris events and the creek bed structure has provided over 35 years of excellent performance

Figure 12.15 Placement of boulders in freshly applied wet-mix steel fibre-reinforced shotcrete in Harvey Creek, Lions Bay Village, BC.

(Photo courtesy Dallas Morgan.)

Figure 12.16 Steel fibre-reinforced shotcrete lining at Two Mile Creek, Coquihalla Highway, Hope, BC.

with no significant erosion, scour or damage to the creek bed, or bridge abutments in the several bridges between the debris dam and the ocean. This represents an innovative and very successful use of SFRS.

In the case of Charles Creek near Lions Bay and Two Mile Creek on the Coquihalla Highway near Hope, BC, a more conventional canal type lining was constructed to protect the creek bed and bridge abutments from erosion and scour. These linings were constructed using high strength (60 MPa at 28 days) steel fibre reinforced silica fume modified shotcrete (SFRS). Figure 12.16 shows a picture of the 300 mm thick shotcrete lining on Two Mile Creek shortly after construction in the mid 1980s. The channel is subjected to continuous abrasion and wear from gravel and rocks carried by the creek and has passed several debris events since its construction. The condition of the shotcrete lining was examined after 30 years in service. Performance of the lining was not as good as that observed in the *boulder strewn* Harvey Creek lining, as there was some loss of section in the floor of the channel from abrasion and erosion. Remediation with installation of a new SFRS bonded overlay should, however, be able to provide the channel with another 30 years of service before further remedial interventions are required.

REFERENCES

Abbott, R. W. 2001. Shotcrete Solution to Tricky Underpinning Problem. *Shotcrete Magazine, American Shotcrete Association* Summer, 2001. 12–14.

Abbott, R. W. 2010. Canada Line Cut and Cover Tunnel Shotcrete Shoring. *Shotcrete Magazine, American Shotcrete Association* Winter, 2010. 20–24.

ACI 506R-16. 2016d. *Guide to Shotcrete*. American Concrete Institute. 52p.

Chan, C., Heere, R. and Morgan, D. R. 2002. Shotcrete for Ground Support: Current Practices in Western Canada. *Shotcrete Magazine, American Shotcrete Association, Part I* Winter, 2002. 14–19. Part II Spring 2002. 12–15.

Darling, J. and Cao, X. 2009. Waterproofing Below-Grade Shotcrete Walls.. *Shotcrete Magazine, American Shotcrete Association* Winter, 2009. 38–40.

FHWA (1998), US. Department of Transportation, Federal Highway Administration, Publication No. FHWA-SA-96-069R, (Revised October, 1998), Manual for Design and Construction Monitoring of Soil Nail Walls, 530 p.

FHWA (2015), US. Department of Transportation, Federal Highway Administration, Publication No. FHWA-NH1-14-007, FHWA GEC 007, Soil Nail Walls - Reference Manual, 425 p.

Harrison, W. 2015. Sustainable Transportation Retaining Walls. *Shotcrete Magazine, American Shotcrete Association* Spring, 2015. 32–33.

Heere, R., Morgan, D. R. and Jungaro, S. 2001. Shotcrete Retrofit of a Mechanically Stabilized Earth Wall. *Shotcrete Magazine, American Shotcrete Association* Summer 2001. 8–10.

Hungr, O., Morgan, G. C., VanDine, D. F. and Lister, D. R. 1987. Debris Flow Defences in British Columbia. *Debris Flows/Avalanches: Process, Recognition, and Mitigation*, Edited by Costa, J. E. & Wiezorek, G. F., Published by Geological Society of America, Reviews in Engineering Geology, Vol. 7, 201–222.

Hungr, O. and Skermer, N. 1998. Debris Torrents and Rockslides, Howe Sound to Whistler Corridor. *Technical Tour Guidebook, Trip 6*, Edited by Clague, J., Vancouver, Publisher by Technical Tour Guide Books, 8th IAEG Congress, September, 1998, 21–25.

Kaden, R. 1974. Slope Stabilized with Steel Fibrous Shotcrete. *Western Construction* April, 1974. 30–33.

Klein, K. 2007. Proactive Waterproofing. *Concrete Construction* March, 2007. Vol. 52 No. 3. 36.

Morgan, D. R. 1995. Sprayed Concrete: Properties, Design and Application. *Chapter 11 Special Sprayed Concretes*, Edited by Austin, S. & Robins, P., Scotland, Published by Whittles Publishing, 229–265.

Morgan, D.R. 2000. Evolution of Fibre Reinforced Shotcrete. *Shotcrete Magazine, American Shotcrete Association* May, 2000. 8–11.

Morgan, D.R., Ezzet, M. and Pfhol, C. 2004. Rehabilitation of the Seawall at Stanley Park, Vancouver BC, Canada with Synthetic Fibre Reinforced Shotcrete. Shotcrete: More Engineering Developments, *Proceedings of the 2nd International Conference on Engineering Developments in Shotcrete*, Edited by Bernard, E.S., Cairns, Australia, October 4, 2004, published by Taylor and Francis, 201–208.

Chapter 13

Underground support in tunnels

13.1 REFERENCE MATERIAL

In all of shotcrete technology, there are probably more reference publications on shotcrete for underground support in tunnels and mines than on any other topic. This is not surprising, given that worldwide there is probably more shotcrete used in underground support than in any other shotcrete application. In North America, swimming pool construction is touted as the largest consumer of shotcrete, but this would be followed by shotcrete for underground support. There have been several different conference series dealing with shotcrete for underground support. The following is a list of proceedings from some of these conference series:

13.1.1 Engineering Foundation (US) and Engineering Conferences International *Shotcrete Conferences*

1. Use of Shotcrete for Underground Structural Support, South Berwick, Maryland, USA, 1973, Published by ASCE, Editor J.R. Graham, 1974, 467 p. (Also ACI SP-45).
2. Shotcrete for Ground Support II, Easton, Maryland, USA, 1976, Published by American Concrete Institute, ACI SP 54, Editor J.A. Veltrop, 766 p.
3. Shotcrete for Underground Support III, St. Anton, Austria, 1978, Editor L.F. Platnik,
4. Shotcrete for Underground Support IV, Paipa, Colombia, 1985, Published by Engineering Foundation, Editors E. King and A. Murlando, 173 p.
5. Shotcrete for Underground Support V, Uppsala, Sweden, 1990, Published by ASCE, Editors J. Sharp and T. Franzen, 559 p.
6. Shotcrete for Underground Support VI, Niagara-on-the-Lake, Ontario, Canada, 1993, Published by ASCE, Editors D. Wood and D.R. Morgan, 198 p.

DOI: 10.1201/9780429169946-15

7. Shotcrete for Underground Support VII, Telfs, Austria, 1995, Published by ASCE, Editors H. Klapperich, R. Pottler and J. Wilcoq, 313 p.
8. Shotcrete for Underground Support VIII, Campos do Jordao, Brazil, 1999, Published by ASCE, Editors T. Celistino and H. Parker, 349 p.
9. Shotcrete for Underground Support IX, Kyoto, Japan, 2002, Published by Japan Tunneling Association, Editors K. Ono and D.R. Morgan, 337 p.
10. Shotcrete for Underground Support X, Whistler, British Columbia, Canada, 2006, Published by ASCE, Editors D.R. Morgan and H. Parker, 382 p.
11. Shotcrete for Underground Support XI, Davos, Switzerland, 2009, Published by Engineering Conferences International, Editors F. Amber and K. Garshol, 239 p.
12. Shotcrete for Underground Support XII, Singapore, 2015, published by Engineering Conferences International, Editors L. Ming, O. Sigl and G. Li,
13. Shotcrete for Underground Support XIII, Kloster Irsee, Germany, 2017, Published by Engineering Conferences International, Editors D. Mahner, M. Beisler and F. Heimbecher.
14. Shotcrete for Underground Support XIV, Pattaya, Thailand, 2019, Published by Engineering Conferences International, Editors M. Beisler, P. Ngamsantikul and H. Klapperich.

13.1.2 Norwegian Concrete Association Shotcrete Symposia

Sprayed Concrete: Modern Use of Wet Mix Sprayed Concrete for Underground Support

1. First International Symposium on Sprayed Concrete, Fagerness, Norway, 1993, 464 p.
2. Second International Symposium on Sprayed Concrete, Gol, Norway, 1996, 433 p.
3. Third International Symposium on Sprayed Concrete, Gol, Norway, 1999, 525 p.
4. Fourth International Symposium on Sprayed Concrete, Davos, Switzerland, 2002, 365 p.
5. Fifth International Symposium on Sprayed Concrete, Lillehammer, Norway, 2008, 346 p.
6. Sixth International Symposium on Sprayed Concrete, Tromsø, Norway, 2011.
7. Seventh International Symposium on Sprayed Concrete, Sandefjord, Norway, 2014, 458 p.
8. Eight International Symposium on Sprayed Concrete, Trondheim, Norway, 2018, 353 p.

13.1.3 Australian Shotcrete Conferences

1. Shotcrete: Techniques, Procedures and Mining Applications, Symposium, Kalgoorlie, Western Australia, 1996, Published by Rock Technology, Edited by C. Windsor.
2. Shotcrete: Engineering Developments, Proceedings First International Conference on Engineering Developments in Shotcrete, Hobart, Tasmania, Australia, 2001, Published by A.A. Balkema, Editor S. Bernard, 291 p.
3. Shotcrete: More Engineering Developments, Proceedings Second International Conference on Engineering Developments in Shotcrete, Cairns, Australia, 2004, Published by CRC Press, Editor S. Bernard, 291 p.
4. Shotcrete: Elements of a System, Third International Conference on Engineering Developments in Shotcrete, Queenstown, New Zealand, 2010, Published by CRC Press, Editor S. Bernard, 299 p.

The above series of Conference Proceedings provide a comprehensive overview of the advances in shotcrete for underground support from 1973 to 2019. The Engineering Foundation and Engineering Conferences International sponsored conferences are particularly useful, in that they have been held in North and South America, Europe and Asia. This has facilitated international exchange on state-of-the-art developments on shotcrete for underground support in different regions of the world. The Norwegian Concrete Association sponsored conferences were also international in scope, but mainly highlighted shotcrete for underground support developments in Europe in general and the Scandinavian countries in particular. The Australasian Conferences, while also international in scope, primarily emphasized shotcrete for underground support in tunnels and mines in Australia and New Zealand. The first author had the privilege to attend 14 of the above conferences over nearly three decades (1990–2019) and act as Co-Chair and Editor for three of the Engineering Foundation conferences.

In addition to the above conference series, there have been a number of shotcrete colloquia and conferences in Germany, Austria and Switzerland, with proceedings published in German. These are not referenced in this book. In Africa, The Southern African Institute of Mining and Metallurgy published the proceedings of: *Shotcrete for Africa*, Misty Hills, Johannesburg, 2009, Editor A. Boniface, 418 p. This shotcrete proceedings, while international in scope, dealt mainly with shotcrete developments in mines and tunnels in Southern Africa.

13.1.4 International Tunneling Association

In addition to the above conference series publications, the International Tunneling Association (ITA) Working Group 12: *Sprayed Concrete Use*, has been a very active committee. The committee is comprised of invited individual members from member countries and has published a number of documents on various aspects of shotcrete for underground support in tunnels and other underground openings. Some of the published documents are listed below.

1. Shotcrete in Tunneling Status Report 1991, T. Franzen, Published by Swedish Rock Engineering Research Foundation, 1991.
2. Shotcrete for Rock Support: A State-of-the-Art Report with Focus on Steel Fibre Reinforcement, T. Franzen, Tunneling and Underground Space Technology, Vol.7, No.4, October, 1992, 383–391.
3. Shotcrete for Rock Support: A Summary of the State-of-the-Art in 15 Countries, T Franzen, Tunneling and Underground Space Technology, Vol.8, No.4 October, 1993, 441–470.
4. Health and Safety in Shotcreting, K. Ono, Tunneling and Underground Space Technology, Vol. 11, No. 4, 1996, 391–409.
5. Sprayed Concrete for Final Linings ITA Working Group Report, T. Franzen, K. Garshol and T. Tomisawa, Tunneling and Underground Space Technology, Vol. 16, No. 4, 2001, 295–309.
6. Lining of Tunnels Under Groundwater Pressure, T. Franzen and T.B. Celistino, ITA Downunder- 2002, Congress Proceedings, Vol.1, 481–487.
7. Shotcrete and Waterproofing of Operational Tunnels, T. Celistino, Proceedings ITA Workshop on Waterproofing, Sao Paulo, Brazil, 2005, 5 p.
8. Shotcrete for Rock Support: A Summary Report on State-of-the-Art, K. Garshol, ITA Report No. 005, May 2010, 14 p.
9. Permanent Sprayed Concrete Lining, ITA Working Group 12 and ITAtech, ITA report No.24, October 2020, 55 p.

These ITA Working Group 12: Sprayed Concrete reports provide a comprehensive overview of advances in shotcrete for underground support over the period 1990 to 2020. In addition, useful information regarding spray applied waterproofing membranes for use in waterproofing tunnels and other underground openings is provided in:

ITAtech Design Guidance for Spray Applied Waterproofing Membranes, ITA Activity Group No.2, April 2013, 62 p.

13.1.5 Other reference sources

Useful information is also provided in a number of other publications including:

1. ACI 506R-16 Guide to Shotcrete, 2016, 40 p.
2. ACI 506.5R-09, Guide for Specifying Underground Shotcrete, American Concrete Institute, 2009, 52p.

3. Guideline Sprayed Concrete, Austrian Society for Construction Technology, 2013.
4. European Standard EN 14487, Sprayed Concrete, Parts 1 and 2.
5. European Standard EN 14488, Testing Sprayed Concrete, Parts 1 to 5.
6. The book *Sprayed Concrete Linings* by Alun Thomas, published by Taylor and Francis, 2008, 237 p.
7. The book, *Sprayed Concrete: Properties, Design and Application*, by S. Austin and P. Robbins, published by Whittles Publishing, 1995, 382 p.
8. Institution of Civil Engineering (UK), Sprayed Concrete Linings (NATM) for Tunnels in Soft Ground, Design and Practice Guide, 1996, 84 p.
9. RTC. (2019). Guideline on the Applicability of Fibre-Reinforced Shotcrete for Ground Support in Mines. Rock Tech Centre – MIGS III – WP 24, 53 pages.

In addition to the above publications, the American Shotcrete Association (ASA) publishes *Shotcrete Magazine*. Four editions have been published per year (Spring, Summer, Fall and Winter) since 1999. Several of these issues have had a theme of Shotcrete in Tunneling, or Mining, or Underground Support. In addition, the ASA Underground Committee has published two position statements regarding shotcrete use underground. These are:

1. Position statement #1: Spraying Shotcrete Overhead in Underground Applications, 2019, 5 p.
2. Position statement #2: Spraying Shotcrete on Synthetic Sheet Waterproofing Membranes, 2019, 3 p.

A search of the archives (www.shotcrete.org) shows that by the end of 2020, over 100 articles have been published in Shotcrete Magazine relating to various aspects of tunnelling, mining or underground support. These articles provide a good overview of the development of shotcrete in the underground environment internationally, but in North America in particular.

13.2 INTRODUCTION

The main reasons for using shotcrete for lining underground openings are:

1. To prevent or minimize rock displacement in loosening ground by:
   a. Stiffening and strengthening the rock mass by filling open joints and fractures;
   b. Transferring the rock load to adjacent stable rock through adhesion and/or shear; and
   c. Acting as a membrane in bending or tension when shotcrete bond is low and the shotcrete layer is continuous.

2. In oxidizing and slaking ground to seal the rock and prevent ravelling and sloughing which occur because of exposure of the rock to moist air and/or groundwater; and

3. To control water and ice formation by redirecting, draining or stopping water flow.

The first reported use of shotcrete for underground support in North America was the use of *gunite* in the Brucetown Experimental Mine in 1914 by George Rice, Chief Engineer with the Pittsburgh Bureau of Mines. It was used primarily to protect and maintain excavated rock surfaces from deterioration from exposure to water and air (Kobler, 1966). Thereafter, for the next three decades, *gunite* continued to be used in underground applications in many tunnels and mines across North America, although mainly in semi-structural applications. Virtually all of this shotcrete was *gunite* applied by hand nozzling. See Figure 13.1, which follows, of an example of an early shotcrete application in a tunnel.

Major breakthroughs in the use of shotcrete for underground support arose after the Second World War, initially in Europe in the mid 1950s, and subsequently in South America and Asia (Barton et al., 1995; ITA-Austria, 2012). Important features in these breakthroughs included the development of machines which allowed coarse aggregates to be incorporated in dry-mix shotcretes, the development of the wet-mix shotcrete application process and the development of remotely controlled manipulator arm shotcrete placement (now sometimes referred to erroneously as *robotic* shotcrete placement).

Also critical to the use of shotcrete in underground support was the development of design methodologies that allowed engineers to replace conventional steel sets and timber lagging type designs, or cast-in-place reinforced

Figure 13.1 Early shotcrete application in a tunnel.

concrete lining designs, with rock bolt and shotcrete designs. Pre-eminent amongst these design methodologies was the so-called *New Austrian Tunnelling Method (NATM)* which was developed by Rabcewicz and his colleagues in Austria in the late 1950s and early 1960s (Rabcewicz, 1964/1965). This was followed by the development of the so-*called Norwegian Method of Tunneling (NMT)* in the 1970s (Barton et al., 1995).

In North America, dry-mix shotcrete in conjunction with rock bolts and mesh reinforcement and other types of reinforcement (e.g. lattice girders and/or steel sets) was used in construction of eleven Washington DC subway stations during the 1970s and 1980s (Plotkin, 1981). In Canada, permanent dry-mix coarse aggregate shotcrete linings with mesh reinforcement and rock bolts were used in construction of the Canadian National Railways Tunnel (Thornton Tunnel) near the Burrard inlet in Vancouver, British Columbia in 1968 (Mason, 1968). Also, mesh reinforced dry-mix coarse aggregate shotcrete, in conjunction with steel sets was used in construction of reinforced linings in a subway tunnel in Toronto in 1961 (Kobler, 1966). The first major use of the NATM process in Canada [although the designers referred to it as the Sequential Excavation Method (SEM)], was construction of the underground Grandin Metro Station in soft ground in downtown Edmonton, Alberta in 1989 (Brandt and Phelps, 1989).

13.3 NEW AUSTRIAN TUNNELING METHOD (NATM)

The NATM method was primarily developed for tunnelling in weak or squeezing ground. Rabcewicz stated the goals of NATM as:

a) *To provide safe and economic support in tunnels excavated in materials incapable of supporting themselves, e.g. crushed rock, debris, and even soil. Support is achieved by mobilizing whatever humble strength the rock or earth possesses; and*
b) *To use surface stabilization by a thin auxiliary shotcrete lining, suitably reinforced by rock bolting and closed as soon as possible by an invert.*

Many hundreds of papers have been published in the technical literature on various aspects of the development and use of NATM for construction of tunnels and other underground openings on projects around the world. Many hundreds of different tunnels and other underground openings have been constructed using the NATM method most successfully (ITA-Austria, 2012), but with some noted failures (Institute of Civil Engineering (UK), 1996). The Austrian Chapter of the International Tunneling Association publication *50 Years of NATM* (ITA-Austria, 2012) provides many examples worldwide of completed NATM projects. It provides a comprehensive overview of the historical development and advances in the use of the NATM process over a 50-year period. Over 200 references pertinent to NATM are cited in this publication. (Note: In the United Kingdom the term

Sprayed Concrete Lining (SCL) is often used to describe the NATM process. In North America the term *Sequential Excavation Method* (SEM) is often used to describe the NATM process.)

It is not proposed in this book to elaborate in detail on the principles of NATM design and construction. This would be a book topic unto itself. Barton (Barton et al., 1995) provides a useful summary of the principles of NATM design, together with some examples of different NATM projects. Conceptually the NATM process involves stabilizing the ground around an underground excavation in the most safe and economic manner possible by utilizing the bearing capacity of the ground with the help of shotcrete and other support elements, together with continuous measurement of ground and lining deformations and stresses during the construction process.

Figure 13.2 provides an example of a typical cross-section in a NATM design. The design consists of rock bolts, an initial mesh reinforced shotcrete lining, a drainage fabric covered by a welded waterproof membrane and a formed, cast-in-place reinforced concrete final lining. Many hundreds of tunnels and other underground openings and thousands of kilometres of tunnels have been constructed all over the world in the past 50 years using such NATM design concepts (ITA-Austria, 2012).

With respect to shotcrete, an important aspect to note in such designs is that in the 1960s to 1990s the initial shotcrete lining was considered by

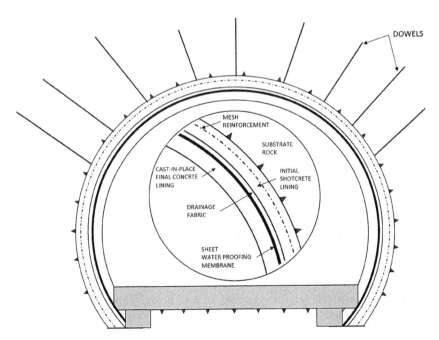

Figure 13.2 Cross-section of a typical NATM tunnel with initial shotcrete lining and cast-in-place final concrete lining.

many designers to be *temporary shotcrete*, i.e. the initial shotcrete lining was not considered to be *structural* and the thick, reinforced concrete inner lining was required to provide the permanent structural support for the tunnel. As such, less emphasis was placed on the quality of the initial shotcrete lining and there was an unfortunate trend that developed. Lower quality, permeable, less durable shotcretes, with core compressive strengths often as low as 20 to 25 MPa at 28 days (and sometimes even lower in tunnels in Japan), were permitted to be used in the initial lining. Shotcrete quality was driven by construction considerations, in particular a demand for shotcretes that would have very rapid stiffening and setting characteristics, an ability to be applied in great thicknesses (up to as much as 500 mm in a single pass) and have very rapid early strength development (2 to 12 hours). This was typically achieved by using high addition rates of either high alkali-based accelerators (typically sodium and potassium aluminates), or sodium silicates added at the shotcrete nozzle. Alkali-based accelerators were often added at dosages of 8 to 12% by mass of cement and in some tunnels, sodium silicates were added at dosages as high as 20% by mass of cement. Such high accelerator addition rates substantially downgraded the later age (28 days and more) compressive strength of the shotcrete, increased permeability and reduced durability.

While such *temporary shotcrete* was generally able to provide the necessary characteristics for ground support and advancing the tunnel, in a number of projects in Europe and elsewhere it had unfortunate unintended consequences for the long-term tunnel performance. Groundwater leaching through the permeable initial shotcrete lining dissolved calcium hydroxide and alkalis in the cementitious component of the shotcrete, creating a highly alkaline leachate (pH 11 to 13). Such highly alkaline solutions migrated through to the drainage fabric and then down into the drainage pipes in the invert, where they would often precipitate, causing occlusion and blockages in the drainage pipes. Considerable costs have been incurred to send high-pressure water jets down the drainage pipes to remove occluded materials, and this procedure is required to be repeated from time to time.

There were also major negative environmental consequences. The highly alkaline waters leaching from the tunnels were being discharged into regional drainage habitats, killing fish and other aquatic species. Owners of tunnels were made to install expensive treatment facilities at the drainage outlets from the tunnels to buffer and neutralize the alkaline waters before discharge into the regional drainage systems. These treatment facilities need to be operated in perpetuity. Some jurisdictions banned the use of shotcrete-lined tunnels in their districts because of this issue.

In Scandinavia (Barton et al., 1995) and North America (Chan et al., 2002), with the advent of the use of steel fibre in shotcrete in the late 1970s and silica fume in the 1980s, permanent shotcrete linings with high quality (specified compressive strengths in shotcrete cores of 35 to 40 MPa at 28 days), low permeability, low leachability and good durability were being

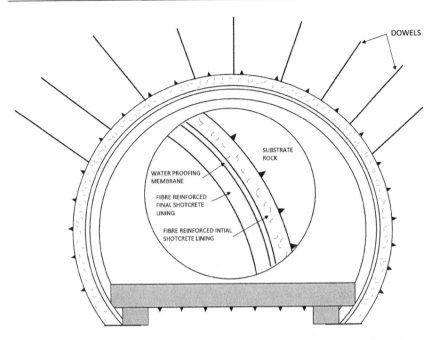

Figure 13.3 Cross-section of a NATM tunnel with initial and final fibre-reinforced shotcrete lining.

used for underground support in tunnels and mines. These projects demonstrated that it was possible to provide high quality, permanent, durable shotcrete linings, with shotcretes well suited to the construction process, using either the wet or dry-mix shotcrete processes. These findings gave rise to an interest in the concept of a *single shell* shotcrete lining (i.e., a lining comprised of a high-quality initial shotcrete lining (with or without a waterproofing membrane), and a final (inner) reinforced permanent shotcrete lining, in lieu of a cast-in-place final concrete lining. Such tunnel lining designs are referred to in parts of Europe as *monocoque* linings (Gebauer et al., 1991) and are considered to be an extension of the NATM (see Figure 13.3).

Also see the ITA Working Group #12 and ITAtech, ITA report No.24 (October 2020) on *Permanent Sprayed Concrete Linings* for comprehensive information on this topic.

13.4 NORWEGIAN METHOD OF TUNNELING (NMT)

Much of the tunnelling work done in the Scandinavian countries has been in harder, jointed rock, which has been excavated using drill and blast methods. This excavation process often resulted in *overbreak*, with irregular rock surface profiles. Such excavation profiles are not well-suited for use of the NATM process (Barton et al., 1995). Prior to the 1970s, such drill and blast excavated tunnels, where required, were supported by rock bolts and mesh covered with a plain shotcrete. These single shotcrete lining systems, while they worked reasonably well, were not optimal from either a cost or technical performance perspective. This is because of the large volumes of shotcrete required to fill the voids behind the mesh, as well as the difficulties sometimes encountered in getting good bond of the shotcrete to the rock behind the mesh and fully encapsulating the mesh. With the advent of steel fibre-reinforced shotcrete (SFRS) in the 1970s, these concerns could be ameliorated, as illustrated in Figure 12.11.

By introduction of SFRS, this was a seminal moment in the development of the *Norwegian Method of Tunneling (NMT)* as we know it today. The NMT is based on a quantitative (numerical) rock mass classification system (the so-called *Q-System*), developed by Barton and his colleagues (Barton et al., 1974). An updated version of the NMT and *Q-System* published by Grimstad and Barton in 1993 (Grimstad and Barton, 1993) is shown in Figure 13.4.

Briefly, this design method makes recommendations for various reinforcement categories depending on rock mass classifications (rock classes varying

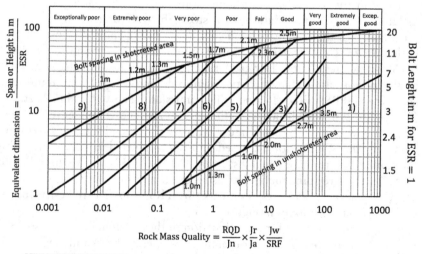

$$\text{Rock Mass Quality} = \frac{RQD}{Jn} \times \frac{Jr}{Ja} \times \frac{Jw}{SRF}$$

REINFORCEMENT CATEGORIES
1) Unsupported
2) Spot bolting, sb
3) Systematic bolting, B
4) Systematic bolting (and unreinforced shotcrete, 4-10cm, B(+S))
5) Fiber reinforced shotcrete and bolting, 5-9cm, Sfr+B

6) Fiber reinforced shotcrete and bolting, 9-12cm, Sfr+B
7) Fiber reinforced shotcrete and bolting, 12-15cm, Sfr+B
8) Fiber reinforced shotcrete > 15cm, reinforced ribs of shotcrete and bolting, Sfr, RRS+B
9) Cast concrete lining, CCA

Figure 13.4 Rock Mass classification-permanent support recommendations based on Q and NMT (Grimstad and Barton, 1993).

(Graph courtesy Geolog Eystein Grimstad and Dr Nick Barton.)

Table 13.1 Excavation Support Ratio (ESR) for a variety of underground excavations

Type of excavation		ESR
A	Temporary mine openings, etc.	ca.3–5?
B	Permanent mine openings, water tunnels for hydropower (excluding high-pressure penstocks), pilot tunnels, drifts and headings	1.6
C	Storage Caverns, water treatment plants, minor road and railway tunnels, surge chambers, access tunnels, etc.	1.3
D	Power stations, major road and railway tunnels, civil defence chambers, portals, intersections	1.0
E	Underground nuclear power stations, railway stations, sports and public facilities, factories	ca. 0.8?

from *exceptionally good* to *exceptionally poor*), and the underground opening span or height divided by the excavation support ratio (ESR). The ESR varies, depending on the type of structure being constructed, as shown in Table 13.1 (Barton et al., 1995).

Included in Figure 13.4 are recommendations for anchor bolt lengths and spacings in the varying ground conditions and opening dimensions. Also included are recommendations for steel fibre-reinforced (Sfr) shotcrete thicknesses for the varying ground conditions and opening dimensions, and in the case of *reinforcement category 8*, a requirement for reinforcing ribs in the Sfr shotcrete. What is, however, missing in Figure 13.4 is a quantification of the performance characteristics required for the steel fibre-reinforced shotcrete (SFRS). Recognizing this omission, Papworth in Australia (Papworth, 2002) published a modified version as shown in Figure 13.5. He added a row at the top of the figure with recommended toughness requirements for the SFRS in Joules, based on tests conducted in accordance with the Round Determinate Panel test (now ASTM C1550), as shown in Figure 13.5. There were some merits in this recommendation, but more appropriately, the varying energy requirements for SFRS in Joules are best included in the different *envelopes* in Figure 13.6.

Recognizing the need for quantification of the different energy-absorbing requirements for SFRS for the different *envelopes* in the Q and NMT chart, Grimstad published the revised version shown in Figure 13.6 in 2002 (Grimstad et al., 2002). Barton and Grimstad (Barton and Grimstad, 2014) commented as follows with respect to Figure 13.6: *Note energy absorption classes E=1000 Joules (for highest tolerance of deformation), 700 Joules and 500 Joules in remainder (when there is lower expected deformation).*

It should be noted that the energy absorption recommendations in Figure 13.6 are based on tests conducted using the EFNARC edge supported square panel test (EN 14488-5, 2006) shown in Figure 13.7. While this test method

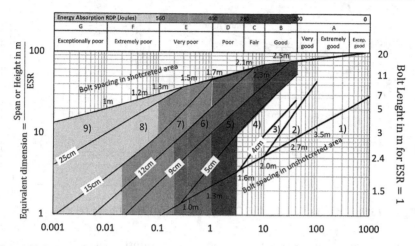

Figure 13.5 Papworth's modification to the Grimstad and Barton Q and NMT chart.

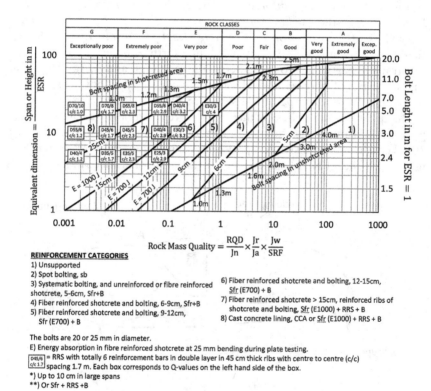

$$\text{Rock Mass Quality} = \frac{RQD}{Jn} \times \frac{Jr}{Ja} \times \frac{Jw}{SRF}$$

REINFORCEMENT CATEGORIES

1) Unsupported
2) Spot bolting, sb
3) Systematic bolting, and unreinforced or fibre reinforced shotcrete, 5-6cm, Sfr+B
4) Fiber reinforced shotcrete and bolting, 6-9cm, Sfr+B
5) Fiber reinforced shotcrete and bolting, 9-12cm, Sfr (E700) + B

6) Fiber reinforced shotcrete and bolting, 12-15cm, Sfr (E700) + B
7) Fiber reinforced shotcrete > 15cm, reinforced ribs of shotcrete and bolting, Sfr (E1000) + RRS + B
8) Cast concrete lining, CCA or Sfr (E1000) + RRS + B

The bolts are 20 or 25 mm in diameter.
E) Energy absorption in fibre reinforced shotcrete at 25 mm bending during plate testing.
[D45/6 c/c 1.7] = RRS with totally 6 reinforcement bars in double layer in 45 cm thick ribs with centre to centre (c/c) spacing 1.7 m. Each box corresponds to Q-values on the left hand side of the box.
*) Up to 10 cm in large spans
**) Or Sfr + RRS +B

Figure 13.6 Rock mass classification-permanent support recommendations based on Q and NMT, with energy absorption requirements for SFRS (Joules).

(Graph courtesy Geolog Eystein Grimstad and Dr Nick Barton.)

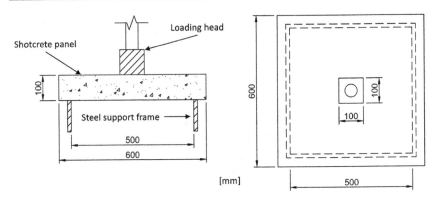

Figure 13.7 Schematic of EFNARC edge supported toughness test plate.

is used in much of Europe and in some other countries, it is seldom used in North America. The *ASTM C1609 Standard Test Method for Flexural Performance of Fibre-Reinforced Concrete (Using Beam With Third-Point Loading)*, and the *ASTM C1550 Standard Test Method for Flexural Toughness of Fibre-reinforced Concrete (Using Centrally Loaded Round Panel)* are the methods widely used in North America and elsewhere (Australia in particular) to characterize the toughness and energy-absorbing characteristics of fibre-reinforced shotcretes. Figure 13.8 shows a schematic of a round determinate panel test set-up to ASTM C1550.

The question thus arises: Is there any correlation between the EFNARC plate test and any of these other test methods. Bernard in Australia (Bernard, 2002) conducted extensive comparison testing of fibre-reinforced shotcretes using both the EFNARC square panel test and round determinate panels

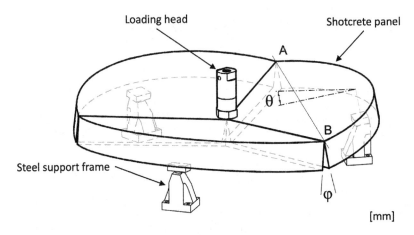

Figure 13.8 Schematic of ASTM C1550 round panel test.

(Schematic courtesy E. Stefan Bernard.)

and reports the following correlation: Energy in Joules in EFNARC Plate Test at 25 mm deflection = 2.5 × Energy in Joules in ASTM C1550 Round Panel Test at 40 mm deflection. DeRivaz (2014), however, warns that there might not be such a direct correlation between the edge-supported EFNARC square panel test and ASTM C1550 round determinate panel test. The loading conditions and test setup between the two test methods are fundamentally different. The EN14488-5 test procedure uses a rather stout square plate (600 × 600 × 100 mm) which is tested in a statically indeterminate setup which allows for load redistribution (i.e., total number of cracks unknown) and creates both flexural and punching shear stresses. The ASTM C1550 test procedure uses a more slender round panel (ϕ800 × 75 mm) which is statically determinate and does not allow for load redistribution between different cracks and where flexural stresses are predominant. It is not a substitute for an indeterminate test setup that allows for mobilizing the FRS in hyperstatic conditions and generating a multicracking response such as the EFNARC square panel allows (RTC, 2019). Different and varying correlation factors between these two test methods have been found for more modern fibre-reinforced shotcrete mixtures and their response to the testing conditions (Gagnon and Jolin, 2008).

It is interesting to note that the Australian Shotcrete Society (AuSS, 2010) came up with the recommendations in Table 13.2 for shotcrete toughness based on Joules energy in the ASTM C1550 Round Panel Test.

The Q-System for rock mass classification has now been used for over 40 years for assisting in selection of reinforcement systems for rock tunnels and caverns. During the past 30 years, the use of mesh reinforcement has been largely eliminated in Scandinavia and most NMT tunnels; design has been based on the use of steel fibre-reinforced shotcrete (SFRS). Many hundreds of underground structures and thousands of km of tunnels have been successfully constructed using the single shell SFRS NMT method in Scandinavia and elsewhere in the world (Barton and Grimstad, 2014). Much of the tunnelling work carried out in hard rock tunnels and mines in North America since the early 1980s has also used fibre-reinforced shotcrete in single shell lining systems analogous to the NMT designs. The sections, which follow, provide some case history examples of applications of such systems in tunnels and mines in North America in which the first author was involved.

Table 13.2 Typical toughness values specified in Australian mining projects

Specified type of support	ASTM C1550 toughness at 40 mm deflection
Non-structural or low deformation	280 J
Moderate ground support	360 J
High-level ground support	450 J

13.5 ROCKY MOUNTAIN RAILWAY TUNNELS

In 1980, the government of British Columbia in Canada initiated a CAN$3.5 billion North East Coal Development Project. Included in this massive resource development project was construction of a 130 km long railway line through the Rocky Mountains. This railway line had four tunnels: two long tunnels, the Table tunnel (9 km) and Wolverine tunnel (6 km), and two short tunnels, the km 80 tunnel (270 m) and km 86 tunnel (370 m). All tunnels were driven using the drill and blast method (Morgan and McAskill, 1984).

The standard tunnel section was a horseshoe-shaped (with straight legs) profile: 5.480 m wide and 5.725 m high to the spring line, with a 2.740 m radius semicircular arch. A decision was made to electrify the line. This eliminated the need for a permanent ventilation system to handle diesel exhaust fumes and made the use of a single shell shotcrete lining viable, as opposed to a smooth cast-in-place final concrete lining.

In the two longer tunnels, shotcrete was only used where dictated by geological conditions. In the short tunnels, because of the very blocky, fractured and jointed nature of the blasted rock, the entire lengths of the tunnels were lined with shotcrete. The Wolverine tunnel and parts of the Table tunnel, which were started first, were lined with the then traditional mesh-reinforced shotcrete and rock-bolt system.

While this system worked, it was not optimal, either technically or economically. Installation of mesh was time consuming and resulted in the need for higher volumes of shotcrete per square meter to fill behind and encapsulate the mesh than steel fibre-reinforced shotcrete (SFRS) (see Figure 12.11). A decision was made to line the km 80 and km 86 tunnels and considerable lengths of the Table tunnel with SFRS. The sections, which follow, deal mainly with the SFRS lining of the km 80 and km 86 tunnels.

The contractors elected to use the dry-mix shotcrete process, with shotcrete supply in large (1558 kg) synthetic cloth bulk-bin bags. The shotcrete mixture design used is shown in Table 13.3.

The combined coarse aggregate (10 mm nominal maximum size) and fine aggregate (5 mm nominal maximum size) was designed to meet the ACI 506 grading No.2 requirements. The specified minimum compressive

Table 13.3 As-batched dry-mix shotcrete mixture proportions for 1.0 m³ shotcrete through the nozzle

Mix ingredients	Mass (kg)
Type I Normal Portland cement	460
10 mm coarse aggregate	520
5 mm fine aggregate	1220
Powdered aluminate-based accelerator	18
Hooked-end steel fibre	59

Table 13.4 Compressive strength test results from 75mm diameter cores from SFRS test panels

Date	Compressive strength, MPa					
	7 days			28 days		
Year-month-day	(a)	(b)	Average	(a)	(b)	Average
82-12-07	26.2	26.2	26.2	37.3	36.5	36.9
82-12-07	43.3	43.1	43.2	52.1	50.2	51.2
82-12-07	44.2	41.6	42.9	46.2	44.0	45.1
83-02-03	30.9	32.8	31.9	45.5	42.8	44.1
83-02-14	44.9	31.4	38.2	42.2	35.0	38.6
83-02-15	34.3	38.1	36.2	44.7	43.8	44.3
83-02-17	31.1	34.2	32.6	43.2	42.2	42.7
83-02-22	31.4	37.1	34.3	45.7	36.4	41.1
83-02-23	42.2	47.2	44.7	45.0	45.0	45.0
83-02-26	36.7	38.7	37.7	47.6	46.6	47.1
83-02-26	41.2	40.0	40.6	43.8	41.9	42.9
83-03-01	39.9	37.7	38.8	45.4	44.9	45.2
83-03-04	29.5	31.5	30.5	39.3	37.4	38.4
83-03-07	31.4	35.2	33.3	44.7	42.8	43.7
83-03-07	29.6	30.5	30.1	47.6	35.9	41.8
83-03-11	39.0	42.8	40.9	42.8	40.5	41.6
Average			36.4			43.1

strength requirement for cores extracted from shotcrete test panels (or the *in-situ* shotcrete lining, if necessary) was: 20 MPa at 7 days and 35 MPa at 28 days. Actual shotcrete compressive strength test results from the km 80 and km 86 tunnels over a three-month period are shown in Table 13.4.

It can be seen that the quality of the shotcrete applied was excellent. Compressive strength test results readily met the minimum specified performance requirements, averaging 36.4 MPa at 7 days and 43.1 MPa at 28 days, without any low test results.

Preconstruction testing was conducted to evaluate the toughness characteristics of the above shotcrete mixture design. Beams were cut from shotcrete test panels and tested to ASTM C1018 (the precursor to the current ASTM C1609 test method). A minimum *Toughness Performance Level* III (Morgan, Chen and Beaupré, 1995) was specified and it was found that this was readily achieved at a fibre addition rate of 0.75% volume (59 kg/m^3). Beam testing was not conducted as part of the regular Quality Control (QC) testing on the project. Rather, the steel fibre addition rates in the shotcrete batch records were scrutinized.

The construction schedule dictated that the km 80 and km 86 tunnels be constructed during the winter of 1982–1983. With outside temperatures as

Figure 13.9 Shotcrete placement near hoarded tunnel portal from a man-lift.

low as −30°C and temperatures inside the tunnel down to −10°C, cold weather shotcreting practices had to be implemented. After completion of excavation, the ends of the tunnels were hoarded in with large insulated timber and plywood panels, as shown in Figure 13.9. Large barn doors were built into the hoarded panels to facilitate movement of equipment and materials into the tunnels. Two large diesel forced air furnaces were installed outside the tunnel at one end. A ventilation fan was installed at the other end, creating a forced flow of warm air through the tunnel. A period of heating of about 7 to 10 days was required to heat the air in the tunnel to about 10°C and the rock to a temperature of 5 to 8°C. Shotcreting was only permitted when the air, rock and shotcrete temperatures were all above 5°C. (Note: if this is not done, experience on other underground projects in Canada has shown that the shotcrete can be very slow to set, harden and gain early and later age compressive strength.)

Water control prior to shotcrete installation was accomplished by drilling 20 mm diameter drainage holes into wet areas and inserting snug-fit plastic drainpipes into the holes. In seeping seams, oakum caulking rope was pressed into cracks to divert water to the installed drain pipes. Shotcrete was then applied. After the shotcrete had developed sufficient strength, the drain holes were grouted and plugged to protect against water and ice formation in the electrified tunnels.

The prebagged shotcrete was discharged into a predampener to achieve a moisture content of about 3 to 4 % prior to discharge into the hopper of a Meyco GM 60 rotating barrel feed dry-mix gun. The remainder of the mixing water was added at a water ring, which was located about 3 m back from the end of the nozzle. It was found that this set-up provided a more uniform wetting out of the shotcrete, with reduced rebound and tendency for the creation of dry pockets and *sand lenses*.

Shotcrete was placed in at least two passes to a minimum thickness of 50 mm in the *back* of the tunnel above the *spring line*. In places where rock conditions dictated, SFRS was applied at thicknesses up to 100 mm. In the walls below the *spring line*, a minimum thickness of 25 mm of SFRS was applied. Rock bolts were installed as needed and as determined by the geological engineer of record.

A rigorous Quality Assurance (QA) monitoring and Quality Control (QC) testing programme was implemented on the project and was able to verify that, with a few exceptions, the Owner was provided with a high quality, durable shotcrete lining. Indeed, after some now over three decades in service, the SFRS is still providing durable performance. One exception was in an area of a week's shotcrete production in one of the longer tunnels, where QC testing on test panels showed lower than specified compressive strengths at 7 and 28 days. Also, tests to ASTM C642 produced values of *Boiled Absorption* above the maximum allowable value of 8%, and *Volume of Permeable Voids* above the maximum allowable value of 17%. Cores extracted from the *in-situ* tunnel lining in the area of interest confirmed the panel test results. Investigation found that the non-conforming test results were attributable to an accidental overdosage of the shotcrete set accelerator in shotcrete that was batched using a mobile batching unit. The shotcrete in this zone was on the *critical path* for installation of the overhead electrification and was consequently not able to be removed and replaced. The shotcrete lining in this zone experienced deterioration in service from the combined effects of leaching and frost action. Remedial works have subsequently had to be implemented in this zone to remove and replace the defective shotcrete.

In summary, the SFRS lining of the km 80 and km 86 tunnels (and parts of the Table tunnel) was the first major tunnelling contract completed in Canada using SFRS. It demonstrated that SFRS provides a viable alternative to mesh reinforced shotcrete for lining of underground openings, from a technical, economic and practical application perspective. Subsequent to this project, many hundreds of underground openings have been lined with SFRS in North America and elsewhere in the world (Morgan, 1991; Vandewalle, 1996).

13.6 STAVE FALLS HYDROPOWER PRESSURE TUNNELS

The Stave Falls dam and powerhouse is located 65 km East of Vancouver, British Columbia, Canada. Construction of the original dam and powerhouse was started in 1909. Installation of the five generators in the powerhouse was completed between 1911 and 1925. With a capacity of 52.5 MW once all five horizontal double-Francis turbine-generators were installed, it was the largest source of hydroelectric power in British Columbia at that time. By the 1990s, the powerplant was 80 years old and service was becoming unreliable. The owners, BC Hydro, decided to decommission the existing Powerhouse (it is now a visitors' centre and National Historic Site of Canada) and replace it with a new powerhouse with 90 MW of installed power generated by two 45 MW Kaplan turbines and generators. Work on the Powerplant Replacement Project began in 1993 and was completed in 1999.

As part of the Powerplant Replacement Project, two water pressure tunnels were constructed (Ripley et al., 1998). One tunnel was 183 m long and the other 200 m long. Both tunnels have a straight-leg horseshoe cross-section, with a nominal height and width of 6.7 m, as shown in Figure 13.10. The maximum grade in the tunnels is 18.8% and the elevation gain from the powerhouse to the intakes is 27.2 m. The maximum static head in the tunnels is 46 m at tunnel centreline and the maximum design flow is 140 m³/sec per tunnel.

The tunnels were excavated full-face by drill and blast starting from the powerhouse excavation (see Figure 13.11). Rock bolts were installed within 25 m of the excavation face, as directed by the geotechnical engineer and consisted of 2.4 m and 3.6 m long, 25 mm diameter resin-grouted rock bolts. In addition, shorter 0.75 m long shotcrete anchor bolts, complete with *bow-tie* anchor plates were installed intermediate between rock bolts to achieve a net spacing of approximately 1.5 m between anchor points. Shotcrete anchor plate details are shown in Figure 9.13. This shotcrete

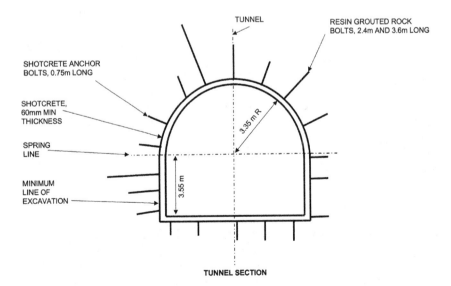

Figure 13.10 Typical tunnel geometry details.

Figure 13.11 Tunnel portals at powerhouse excavation.

anchor plate detail had been previously successfully used on other BC Hydro and BC Ministry of Transportation tunnelling and rock slope stabilization projects to tie steel fibre-reinforced shotcrete (SFRS) to the anchor bolts.

During the design phase of the project, two alternative lining systems were considered for the tunnels:

a) Unlined tunnel with local rock bolts and shotcrete installed as required to provide long term rock support; and
b) Shotcrete lined tunnels with full perimeter support of the walls, crown and invert with SFRS.

Option (b) above was found to need fewer rock bolts than option (a) to provide the required rock support, and also offered the following advantages:

1. Reduced hydraulic roughness (estimated Mannings roughness coefficients of 0.032 for the unlined tunnels option and 0.024 for a minimum 60 mm SFRS thickness). Substantial reductions in head loss were calculated for the full perimeter lining with the SFRS option and supported the use of tunnels with a lesser width [6.7 m for option (a) vs 7.2 m for option (b)];
2. Rocktraps eliminated;
3. Shorter transitions at intakes and at the steel linings at the powerhouse intake;
4. Decreased grouting at transitions;

5. Drain-holes eliminated;
6. Decreased operating leakage; and
7. Decreased tunnel maintenance.

The net effect was an estimated construction cost savings of CAN$ 400,000 by using option (b). More details regarding other design considerations for the tunnels, including rock mass quality, internal water pressures and the issue of *hydraulic jacking* and the effects of external water pressures when the tunnels are dewatered are dealt with in the publication by Ripley et al. (1998).

The following were identified as key requirements for the shotcrete lining to meet the project design requirements:

1. Adequate thickness to achieve the required smoothing effect;
2. Good quality bond of the shotcrete to the rock to minimize spalling;
3. Good quality strength, density and compaction to maximize durability;
4. Steel fibre reinforcement to minimize shrinkage and stress cracks;
5. Full perimeter application to minimize leakage out of the operating tunnels; and
6. Anchoring of the shotcrete to the rock bolts and shotcrete anchor bolts to promote composite action of the rock/rock bolt/shotcrete structure.

Performance-based specifications were prepared for the SFRS for the project. This allowed the contractor to select the most economical combination of materials, equipment and methods to meet the specified performance requirements for the SFRS tunnel lining. The contractor elected to carry out the shotcrete lining work using hand-applied wet-mix shotcrete. Table 13.5 summarizes the specified performance requirements for the project.

Table 13.5 Stave falls tunnels SFRS performance specification

Property	Age, days	Specified limits
Maximum water: cement ratio	—	0.45
Air content – as-shot, %[1] CSA A23.2-4C	—	4 ± 1 %
Slump, mm CSA A23.2-5C	—	80 ± 30
Minimum compressive strength, MPa CSA A23.2-14C	7	30
	28	40
Maximum boiled absorption %	7	8
Max. volume of permeable voids % ASTM C642	7	17
Minimum flexural strength, MPa	7	4.0
Min. flexural toughness ASTM C1018 & Morgan, 1995	7	Toughness performance level III
Minimum steel fibre content	—	6 0 kg/m³
Minimum silica fume content	—	50 kg/m³

[1] Air content determined on shotcrete shot into CSA-A23.2-14C air pressure meter

Table 13.6 Wet-mix SFRS mix design

Material	Mass, kg	Bulk density, kg/m³	Volume, m³
Portland cement, type 10	385	3150	0.1222
Silica fume	50	2100	0.0238
Steel fibres	59	7860	0.0075
Coarse aggregate, 14–5mm	520	2759	0.1885
Fine aggregate, SSD	1200	2662	0.4508
Water	180	1000	0.1800
Water-reducing admixture	1.76 L	1000	0.0018
Superplasticizer	3.5 L	1000	0.0035
Air-content as-shot	4.0 %		0.0408
TOTAL	2399		1.0188

Slump (after superplasticizer addition) −70 ± 20 mm.
Water:(cement+silica fume) ratio = 0.41.
Calculated plastic density = 2355 kg/m³.
Accelerator added at nozzle as required.

Preconstruction trials were carried out to qualify the contractor's proposed shotcrete mix. Details of the final mixture design approved for the project, as a result of demonstrated performance in the preconstruction trials, are provided in Table 13.6.

Silica fume was added to the mix at an addition rate of 13% by mass of cement in order to enhance adhesion/cohesion, thickness of build-up and minimize sloughing (fall-out) of freshly applied shotcrete. Liquid accelerator was added at the shotcrete nozzle for the same purposes. The use of silica fume reduced the amount of accelerator required to be added at the nozzle to provide the shotcrete with suitable application characteristics. The contractor tried different brands of accelerators, some of which worked better than others, ultimately settling on a modified sodium silicate-based product (Alkali free aluminium sulphate compound-based accelerators were not yet available in Canada at the time this work was conducted).

The steel fibre used was a collated, hooked-end, high tensile strength product which had demonstrated good toughness performance characteristics on previous SFRS projects in Canada and in the preconstruction trials. Initially, it was added at an addition rate of 59 kg/m³ (0.75% vol). At this addition rate, the SFRS consistently produced *Toughness Performance Levels (TPL)* which exceeded the specified minimum flexural strength of 4.0 MPa at 7 days and minimum TPL III level at 7 days. Based on these findings, the contractor was permitted to reduce the steel fibre addition rate to 55 kg/m³ (0.70% vol). At this addition rate, the SFRS consistently satisfied the specified flexural strength (min 4.0 MPa at 7 days) and TPL III at 7 days as required in routine QC testing, and as demonstrated in Table 13.7.

Table 13.7 Toughness of SFRS (steel fibre addition of 55 kg/m³) at 7 days

Panel No.	First crack flexural strength MPa	Ultimate flexural strength MPa	ASTM C1018 toughness parameters		Japanese toughness factor kN.mm	Japanese toughness factor MPa	Toughness perf. level
			R 10, 30	R 30, 60			
10	4.50	4.50	79.3	66.4	23.23	3.05	IV
11	4.84	4.84	67.0	59.9	28.65	3.00	IV
12	3.86	3.86	82.8	73.4	22.44	3.04	IV
13	5.13	5.15	77	63.1	23.88	3.38	IV
14	5.07	5.07	75.5	67.8	21.27	3.39	IV
15	4.29	4.29	75.2	65.6	19.62	2.94	III–IV
16	4.56	4.56	76.2	65.0	21.42	3.00	IV
17	4.60	4.60	78.5	71.8	23.41	3.25	IV
18	6.22	6.22	75.5	59.6	26.55	3.87	IV
19	5.80	5.80	70.7	57.9	23.58	3.37	IV
20	4.67	5.07	104	89.6	28.26	3.91	IV–V
21	4.36	4.65	103	87.2	27.46	3.71	IV
22	4.69	4.69	72.7	63.4	20.96	2.98	IV
23	4.04	4.04	62.7	58.3	16.32	2.28	III–IV
24	4.83	4.94	97.3	86.3	28.60	4.04	IV–V
25	4.85	4.85	77.2	66.3	22.04	3.18	IV
26	4.96	5.04	87.7	83.7	27.21	3.85	IV–V
27	4.40	4.77	100.7	89.2	27.31	3.85	IV
28	3.86	3.98	87.0	75.7	20.82	2.90	IV
29	5.27	5.27	89.5	70.2	27.10	3.78	IV
30	4.18	4.18	84.5	76.3	22.36	3.08	IV
31	4.44	4.44	78.0	70.3	23.72	3.29	IV
32	4.59	4.59	64.3	53.8	20.64	2.88	III
33	4.91	4.91	82.3	72.8	23.48	3.43	IV
34	5.69	5.69	71.7	59.7	23.48	3.27	IV
35	3.85	3.85	82.5	76.8	20.86	2.74	IV
36	5.02	5.04	88.7	78.2	27.36	3.68	IV
Mean	4.72	4.77	81.2	70.7	23.41	3.30	IV
Stand. Dev.	0.58	0.57	11.0	10.2	3.18	0.43	
Spec.	Min. 4	Min. 4					Min. III

With respect to other shotcrete properties, cores extracted from QC test panels with SFRS with 55 kg/m³ steel fibre (with a few exceptions), satisfied the specified minimum compressive strength of 30 MPa at 7 days (average 36.1 MPa) and 40 MPa at 28 days (average 53.1 MPa). Similarly, the SFRS (with two exceptions) satisfied the ASTM C642 specified allowable maximum values *for Boiled Absorption* (Max 8%) and *Volume of Permeable Voids* (Max 17%). The two cores which failed to meet the ASTM C642 values also had the lowest compressive strengths. The few low test results were attributed to accelerator overdosage.

Prior to shotcrete application, all rock surfaces were washed with pressure hoses to remove any materials potentially deleterious to shotcrete/rock bond (e.g. loose rock, dust from blasting, diesel fumes from excavation equipment, etc.). The rock surface was then allowed to dry-back to a *Saturated Surface Dry (SSD)* condition prior to any shotcrete application. (Note: It is very important that shotcrete not be applied to rock surfaces with liquid water present, as this can be very detrimental to the quality of shotcrete bond to the rock.) Areas of water flow into the tunnels were handled by installation of drainpipes. The contractor elected to use the following sequence of shotcrete installation:

1. First, the contractor installed a graded bed of tunnel muck on the invert, to provide a smooth working surface for the manlift and protect the invert from accumulation of shotcrete rebound;
2. Shotcrete was then applied to the walls, starting at about 0.5 m above the invert, progressing up to the crown;
3. The crown was typically shot in two lifts, with the first lift being allowed to reach initial set prior to application of the second lift. The shotcrete anchor bolt *bow-tie* plates were typically set to be covered in the second lift of shotcrete;
4. After completion of shotcrete placement for the walls and arch, the rebound and tunnel muck in the invert was removed and the invert was cleaned by a combination of water pressure washing and the use of an air blow-pipe; and
5. Shotcrete anchor bolts and *bow-tie* plates were then installed in the invert and SFRS applied to the SSD rock in the invert and lower 0.5 m of the walls.

Shotcrete was supplied to the project in ready-mix concrete trucks from a nearby batch plant. The trucks were able to back up into the tunnel to discharge shotcrete into a swing-tube shotcrete piston pump. Liquid accelerator was added at the nozzle by an accelerator dosing pump. Access to the upper walls and arch of the tunnels was provided by a rough terrain manlift with a work platform. Shotcrete sloughing occurred in some wet (seeping) locations, or where the contractor applied the shotcrete too thick in a single pass. Sloughed areas were removed prior to initial set, trimmed and replaced.

In addition to lining the full perimeter of the tunnels with SFRS, the transition zone from the 6.7 m wide × 6.7 m high horseshoe-shaped tunnels to the circular 6.1 m diameter steel pipes entering the powerhouse was accomplished using structurally reinforced SFRS. This required the use of shotcrete up to 1.5 m thick. The shotcrete was applied in layers up to 200 mm thick in the arch and 500 mm thick in the invert. Each layer was allowed to achieve initial set prior to application of the next layer of shotcrete. This resulted in substantial time and cost savings relative to a formed, cast-in-place concrete construction of this transition zone.

The hardened shotcrete was sounded prior to substantial completion of the tunnel and a number of test holes were cored to check shotcrete/rock bond. No debonded areas were identified in the completed shotcrete lining prior to commissioning of the tunnels. After about four years in service, the tunnels were dewatered as part of a powerhouse maintenance program. The SFRS lining was observed to be in good condition, with no evidence of SFRS delaminations. Also, no evidence of water leakage from hydraulic jacking was reported during operation of the water pressure tunnels.

In summary, this case history example demonstrates that SFRS can be a very effective water pressure tunnel lining system from technical, cost and construction perspectives. Since this project, many other water pressure tunnels have been lined with SFRS in British Columbia and elsewhere in the world (In 2000 Morgan compiled a list of 20 such tunnels in North and South America, South Africa, India and Europe; and there have been many more since then). A good recent example of this is the retrofit of a hydroelectric draft tube ceiling in a US Army Corps of Engineers project in Washington State in 2019 (Radomski et al., 2019).

REFERENCES

ACI 506R-16. 2016e. *Guide to Shotcrete*. American Concrete Institute. 52p.

ASTM C642. 2013e. *Standard Test Method for Density, Absorption and Voids in Hardened Concrete*. 3p. ASTM International. https://doi.org/10.1520/C0642-13

ASTM C1550. 2020b. *Standard Test Method for Flexural Toughness of Fiber-Reinforced Concrete (Using Centrally Loaded Round Panel)*. 14p. https://doi.org/10.1520/C1550-20

ASTM C1609. 2019b. *Standard Test Method for Flexural Performance of Fiber Reinforced Concrete (Using Beam with Third Point Loading)*. 9p. https://doi.org/10.1520/C1609_C1609M-19A

AuSS. 2010. *Shotcreting in Australia: Recommended Practice*. Concrete Institute of Australia & Australian Shotcrete Society. CIA Z5-2010. 84 p.

Barton, N. and Grimstad, E. 2014. Q-System Application in NMT and NATM and the Consequences of Overbreak. *Seventh International Symposium on Sprayed Concrete*, Sandjeford, Norway, 33–49.

Barton, N., Grimstad, E and Palmstrom, A. 1995. Design of Tunnel Support. *Sprayed Concrete: Properties, Design and Application*, Edited by Austin, S. & Robins, P., Published by Whittles Publishing Services, 150–170.

Barton, N., Lien, R. and Lunde, J. 1974. Engineering Classification of Rock Masses for the Design of Tunnel Support. *Rock Mechanics*. Vol. 6. No. 4. 189–236.

Bernard, E. S. 2002. Correlations in the Behaviour of Fibre-reinforced Shotcrete Beams and Panels. *Materials and Structures, RILEM.* Vol. 35. April. 156–164.

Brandt, J. R. and Phelps, D. J. 1989. Design and Construction of Tunnels for the Edmonton LRT. *7th Canadian Tunneling Conference.*

Chan, C., Heere, R. and Morgan, D. R. 2002. Shotcrete for Ground Support: Current Practices in Western Canada. *Shotcrete Magazine, Part I.* Vol. 4. No. 1. Winter. 14–19 and *Part II.* Vol. 4. No. 2. Spring 2002. 12–15.

CSA. 2019f. *A23.1/A23.2 Concrete materials and methods of concrete construction/Test methods and standard practices for concrete.* 690p. Canadian Standards Association.

DeRivaz, B. 2014. Test Method of Sprayed Concrete-Energy Absorption of EN14488-5 and Residual Strength of EFNARC. *Seventh International Symposium on Sprayed Concrete,* Sandjeford, Norway, 124–135.

European Standard EN 14488-5. 2006. *Testing sprayed concrete: Determination of energy absorption capacity of fibre reinforced slab specimens.*

Gagnon, A. and Jolin, M. 2008. A New Approach for Fibre-Reinforced Shotcrete under Dynamic Loading. *8th International Symposium on Sprayed Concrete, 2018,* Trondheim, Norway.

Gebauer, B., Lukas, W. and Kusterle, W. 1991. Monocoque Shotcrete Lining. *World Tunneling* October. 357–360.

Grimstad, E. and Barton, N. 1993. Updating the Q-System for NMT. *First International Conference on Sprayed Concrete,* Fagerness, Norway, 44–66.

Grimstad E., Kankes, K., Bhasin, R. K., Wold Magnussen, A. and Kaynia, A. 2002. Rock Mass Quality Q Used in designing Reinforced Ribs of Sprayed Concrete and Energy Absorption. *Proceedings Indian Rock Conference, INDROCK-ISRMTT,* New Delhi, November 28–29, 2002, 101–118.

Institution of Civil Engineers (UK). 1996. *Sprayed Concrete Linings (NATM) in Soft Ground: Design and Practice Guide.* Thomas Telford Publishing. 199. 84. EN 14488-5 (2006).

ITA-Austria. 2012. *50 Years of NATM: Experience Reports.* ITA-Austria. 236 p.

ITA. 2020. *Permanent Sprayed Concrete Lining.* ITA Working Group 12 and ITAtech, ITA report No.24. October 2020. 55p.

Kobler, H. G. 1966. Dry-Mix Coarse Aggregate Shotcrete. *Shotcreting* ACI SP-14, 33–58.

Mason, R. E. 1968. *Instrumentation of the Canadian National Railways Tunnel, Vancouver,* B.C., Master of Applied Science Thesis, University of British Columbia, 99 p.

Morgan, D. R. 1991. Steel Fiber Reinforced Shotcrete for Support of Underground Openings in Canada. *Concrete International.* Vol. 13. No. 11. 56–64

Morgan, D. R., Chen, L. and Beaupré, D. 1995. Toughness of Fiber Reinforced Shotcrete. *Shotcrete for Underground Support XII,* Edited by Klappperich, H., Pottler, R. & Willocq, J., Telfs, Austria, Published by ASCE, 66–87.

Morgan, D. R. and McAskill, N. 1984. Rocky Mountain Tunnels Lined with Steel Fibre-reinforced Shotcrete. *Concrete International,* Vol. 6. No. 12. December. 33–38.

Papworth, F. 2002. Design Guidelines for Use of Fiber Reinforced Shotcrete in Ground Support. *Shotcrete Magazine* Spring 2002. 16–21.

Plotkin, E. S. 1981. Tunnel Shotcrete Lining. *Concrete International.* Vol. 3. No. 1. 94–97.

Rabcewicz, L. V. 1964/1965. The New Austrian Tunneling Method. *Water Power, Part 1* November 1964. 511–515. Part 2, January 1965. 19–24.

Radomski, S. M., Morgan, D. R., Zhang, L. and Graham, D. 2019. Structural Modifications to Hydroelectric Turbine Draft Tube Ceiling. *Shotcrete Magazine, American Shotcrete Association* Summer, 2019 22–34.

Ripley, B. D., Rapp, P. A. and Morgan, D. R. 1998. Shotcrete Design. *Construction and Quality Assurance for the Stave Falls Tunnels, Canadian Tunneling* 141–156.

RTC. 2019. *Guideline on the Applicability of Fibre-Reinforced Shotcrete for Ground Support in Mines.* Rock Tech Centre – MIGS III – WP 24, 53 pages.

Vandewalle, M. 1996. *Tunneling the World.* Bekaert S.A, 247 p.

Chapter 14

Shotcrete in mining

14.1 INTRODUCTION

Shotcrete has been used for ground support in mines for over 100 years. As mentioned in Chapter 13, the first reported use of shotcrete in a mine was at the Brucetown Experimental Mine in Pennsylvania in 1914. There, the original sand-cement *gunite* (dry-mix shotcrete) system developed by Carl Akeley was used to protect exposed rock surfaces from exposure to air and water. This same system, albeit with advances in shotcrete mixture designs and application equipment continued to be used in underground mines in North America and elsewhere in the world through to the 1950s. During this period, it was, however, not the primary means of ground support and control in underground mines. Traditional ground support and control methods, such as timber and/or steel sets and timber lagging and rock bolts and screen (heavy-duty wire mesh) were the predominant methods used. *Gunite* was used as an auxiliary component of the support system in selected applications. It was found to be particularly helpful in protecting particular rock types, such as cretaceous shales and serpentinite schists from deteriorating from oxidizing and slaking. This helped stabilize the ground. The first author used dry-mix steel fibre-reinforced shotcrete for this purpose in a mine shaft on Vancouver Island and an exploratory adit and chamber for a hydroelectric project in central British Columbia in the 1980s, with good results.

The development in the 1950s of rotary barrel dry-mix shotcrete guns that were able to apply shotcrete, which incorporated coarse aggregate in the shotcrete mixture design and allowed for greater rates of shotcrete production (than what was possible with the original double pressure chamber guns), saw increasing use of shotcrete in mining applications, both above and underground (Yoggy, 2011). During the 1950s to the 1980s, most shotcrete applied in underground mines was dry-mix shotcrete applied by hand-held nozzles. By the early 1980s, however, specialized shotcrete spraying manipulators started to be used in mines in both above ground and in underground applications (Rispin et al., 2005). This resulted in substantial increases in shotcrete productivity and shotcrete, in conjunction with rock

DOI: 10.1201/9780429169946-16

bolts and different types of reinforcing (welded wire mesh, steel fibre, reinforcing steel bars, steel lattice girders), started to become accepted as the primary means of ground support in many mines in North America, and elsewhere.

This acceptance was not without its challenges, as initially many miners were sceptical about the ability of a relatively thin layer of reinforced shotcrete (typically 50 to 100 mm thick) to support the ground in challenging mining environments with high ground stresses and deformations and seismic (rock-burst) conditions. They were used to observing problem areas in the mines by the *loose* (fallen chunks of rock) found hanging in the overhead screen and many looked at shotcrete as *hiding potential problem areas*. It took many training sessions and seminars and case history examples to demonstrate how shotcrete worked to provide ground control and actually helped in identifying problem areas by identifying visible cracks in the shotcrete when there was significant ground movement (Larsen et al., 2009). Ground support strengthening could then be installed in areas where the shotcrete displayed significant cracking. Thompson et al. (2009) provide a useful overview of how cracks develop in shotcrete in rock under high stress and dynamic conditions and what constitutes significant cracking that would give rise to the need for remedial works.

The next major advance in shotcrete for use in mining was the development of the wet-mix shotcrete system. As mentioned in Chapter 3, while wet-mix shotcrete was first pumped and shot in the 1950s, it was not really until development of the swing-tube concrete pump in the 1970s that wet-mix shotcrete started to be used more widely in the construction industry (Yoggy, 2002) and the 1980s when it started to find use in tunnelling and mining projects in North America (Morgan, 1991). There were several advantages to the wet-mix shotcrete system, compared to the dry-mix shotcrete system. Prime amongst these was increased productivity. Wet-mix shotcrete could be applied at about four times the rate (cubic metres per hour) of that achievable with dry-mix shotcrete. At first, wet-mix shotcrete was hand applied by nozzlemen located in boom-mounted manlifts. Production rates of 7 to 9 m³/hour are cited as being typical for such hand-applied wet-mix shotcrete when using 50 mm diameter shotcrete delivery hoses (Rispin et al., 2005).

Productivity further increased once the spray nozzle was located on remote control manipulator arms (commonly referred to in the shotcrete industry as shotcrete *robots*). The *robot* arms could support up to 75 mm diameter shotcrete delivery hoses, which provided production rates as high as 25 m³/hour. This was huge for the mining industry as it permitted in-cycle ground support to be provided by the shotcrete process. By the 1990s, wet-mix robotically applied shotcrete was enjoying widespread use in many of the worlds large mechanized underground mines. Larsen et al. (2009) reported that in the 2000s the Vale Inco Frood and Stobie underground mines in Subury, Ontario used between 6000 and 8000 m³ per year of robotically applied wet-mix fibre-reinforced shotcrete. In countries such as Australia, since 2000, about half a million cubic metres of wet-mix fibre-reinforced shotcrete (initially steel fibre reinforced but now almost all macro-synthetic fibre reinforced) are applied annually in the metalliferous mines (Bernard et al., 2014).

14.2 CASE HISTORY EXAMPLES OF SHOTCRETE USE IN MINES

14.2.1 Vale Inco Mines in Canada

Larsen et al. (2009) provided a comprehensive review of the history of shotcrete use at the Vale Inco mines near Sudbury, Ontario, Canada. This review is useful in that it well demonstrates the evolution of shotcrete in mining in Canada. The following is a summary of key information from the Larsen et al. review.

The Vale Inco Sudbury operations have been in operation for over 100 years. They include five operating underground mines and collectively they represent the largest fully integrated base metals mining complex in the world, producing nickel, copper, cobalt and precious metals. Vale Inco first started to use a sprayed dry-mix mortar (*gunite*) in the 1970s as a water sealant for underground garages, shaft stations and lunchrooms. It was sprayed over existing rockbolts and screen and often painted white to improve lighting for the miners. Some attempts were made to use the *gunite* in operating headings, but it was deemed to be unsuitable as it tended to split, crack and spall in the intense dynamic conditions encountered in the mining operations. Larsen et al. (2009) report that this was likely because it was applied too thin and too late in the mining cycle, after the ground had already relaxed. Also, quality was an issue with reported inconsistent and often low flexural and compressive strengths.

Vale Inco did, however, not give up on shotcrete as a ground support tool and in the early 1980s shotcrete was used at the Creighton mine near Sudbury to supplement bolt and screen in high-stress conditions in a raise (Figure 14.1).

This application demonstrated the value of shotcrete for ground support when properly designed and applied. By the late 1980s, improved shotcrete mixtures and supply and application equipment were being introduced in the mines. Enhanced dry-mix shotcrete mixture designs incorporating 10 mm coarse aggregates with improved composite aggregate gradations blends were being used. The first author consulted to Vale Inco on the introduction of silica fume and steel fibre reinforcement into shotcrete for use in the Frood and Stobie mines. This resulted in a sea-change in the attitude towards the use of shotcrete as a primary ground support tool. By the late 1980s, these improved shotcretes were being used for ground support in

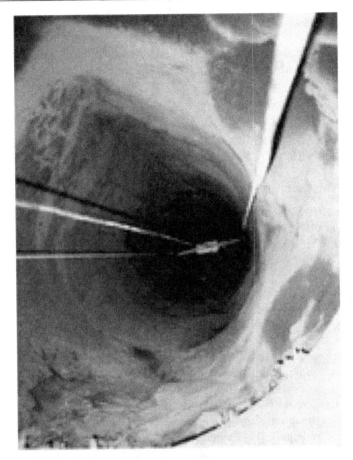

Figure 14.1 Shotcrete lining of raise in Creighton Mine.

(Photo courtesy Joseph Hutter.)

major excavations such as hoist rooms, garages and crusher stations. Shotcrete was applied over existing base support provided by items such as cable and grouted reinforcing bar bolts and screen and was found to improve the stability of the entire support system.

In the 1970s and early 1980s, most shotcrete was supplied bone dry in 30 kg paper bags, which were broken into hoppers. Nearly all shotcrete was applied by hand nozzling using dry-mix guns. These processes created unacceptable amounts of dust and rebound and were slow and laborious. By the late 1980s, key changes were made in equipment and supply methods. The small paper bags were replaced with large 1000 kg bulk-bin bags.

More rugged dry-mix shotcrete guns with higher rates of productivity and hopper hoods that reduced dust levels and protected workers arms were introduced. The shotcrete nozzle was taken out of the hands of the nozzleman and

Figure 14.2 Remote control shotcrete application with manipulator arm.
(Photo courtesy Joseph Hutter.)

placed at the end of a manipulator arm. The nozzleman now became the remote boom operator. This increased the comfort level of the nozzleman, created a safer working environment and greatly increased productivity (Figure 14.2).

Vale Inco found three key roles where shotcrete could be used to supplement bolt and screen:

a) For protection of the existing support from corrosion or from fly-rock damage from blasting in applications, such as secondary blasting chambers and top sills for vertical retreat mining;

b) For enhanced support in seismically active zones, such as rib pillars, crusher stations, headings at depth and crown pillar regions; and

c) For reconditioning or mining in difficult ground conditions, such as when mining through backfill, crushed zones, severely relaxed ground, large intersections, draw points and large permanent openings. In all these applications, the ground is usually completely mined and supported with the primary ground support, followed by application of the shotcrete in thicknesses typically ranging from 50 to 100 mm.

In the late 1980s, the Vale Inco Frood Mine used dry-mix shotcrete to support and recondition heavily deteriorated ground in gangways. Shotcrete was used to rehabilitate corroded bolt and screen and rotted timbers.

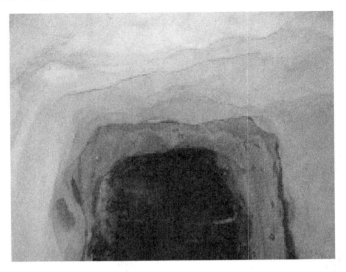

Figure 14.3 Shotcrete lined mesh-reinforced development heading in Frood Mine.
(Photo courtesy Joseph Hutter.)

The dry-mix shotcrete was initially supplied in bulk-bin bags, and later through a bulk carrier with a dry-mix gun mounted on the back. By 1990, shotcrete use grew beyond reconditioning and was also being used to construct dump walls, ventilation barricades, backfill barricades and ore-pass mantles. In the 1990s, the Frood mine also tested mesh-reinforced shotcrete as primary ground support in some production headings (Figure 14.3).

The shotcrete was required to provide stability in the crushed ground conditions and control large deformations. The following two-pass support procedure was implemented for each 3.6 m development round:

a) Apply plain shotcrete 50 to 100 mm thick to the back (overhead) and walls;
b) Allow the shotcrete to set, harden and gain strength for 8 hours;
c) Attach a screen (mesh) to the shotcrete with bolts; and
d) Apply a second layer of plain shotcrete 50 to 100 mm thick over the mesh.

Shotcrete was first used in the Vale Inco Stobie Mine in sublevel cave mining areas to provide corrosion protection to bolt and screen in the drill drifts, and to provide additional support to brows during production mining. By 1993, problems associated with drilling in the sublevel cave production headings led mining engineers to consider using shotcrete as a replacement for bolt and screen. They referred to this method as *boltless shotcrete*. This enabled Vale Inco to test the limits of a ground support system in which bolts were eliminated and the mesh-reinforced shotcrete played the primary support role.

The tests were conducted in three phases between 1993 and 1995. In Phase 1 testing in 1993 and 1994, a two-pass boltless mesh-reinforced shotcrete system was tested in a number of drill drifts in which remnant pillar mining was taking place. This trial demonstrated that the mesh-reinforced shotcrete performed well under production and blasting conditions and provided an important support role even when tensile cracking and rock fracturing occurred in the rock behind the shotcrete. It was, however, apparent that some reinforcement of the shotcrete was required to provide effective support in areas of moderate to high deformations and dynamic loading.

In 1994, Phase 2 testing was conducted in which mesh was replaced with steel fibre reinforcement. The steel fibre-reinforced shotcrete (SFRS) was applied to drifts which became the production headings for the sublevel cave mining. These trials demonstrated that with SFRS the necessity to rehabilitate the brows was significantly reduced relative to that required for conventional screen and bolt supported headings. It was also determined that 75 mm-thick SFRS was required to provide effective support during production mining. In Phase 3 operations in 1995, an SFRS system was used during the development phase and throughout the entire production phase. SFRS was used as part of the development mining cycle, as follows:

a) Drill, load, blast and muck the heading;
b) Scale the exposed rock using an air/water spray;
c) Apply 100 mm of SFRS to the back and walls using a steel fibre addition rate of 60 kg/m^3; and
d) Allow the shotcrete to cure for 12 hours before manpower re-entry under the SFRS.

The above trials demonstrated that the Phase 3 support method worked well for back support, and *this boltless shotcrete* support method has since been expanded to all sublevel cave development headings with good to very good ground conditions and low to moderate stress levels. It was also determined that all drift intersections be supplemented with 1.2 m long grouted reinforcing bar bolts on a 1.2 m square pattern. Further improvements in shotcrete materials and mixture designs enabled the 12 hour re-entry time to be reduced to 8 hours and the steel fibre addition rate to be reduced from 60 to 50 kg/m^3.

14.2.2 Northparkes E26 Mine, Australia

Northparkes E26 Mine near Parkes in New South Wales, Australia, is Australia's first block cave mine. This project is significant with respect to shotcrete in that between 1993 and 1997, some 16,700 m^3 of wet-mix SFRS were used in taking the mine from decline development to full production. Duffield (1999) provides a comprehensive overview of the use of shotcrete on this project. The following summarizes key information from the Duffield review. Key features in the block caving mining method used at the Northparkes mine include high production rates from multiple drawpoints in a hard blocky ore fractured along gypsum veins. The drawpoints are subjected to high abrasion from flow of the ore, as well as impact from secondary blasting and from the production load-haul-dump units (LHDs).

The blocky rock mass characteristics that made block caving an attractive mining method also necessitated a requirement for extensive ground support to prevent loosening of blocks from subsequent development blasting and extend the longevity of the underground excavations. It was determined early in the mine design that an integrated rock mass support system that would both support the rock after excavation and reinforce the rock mass to withstand the mining-induced stresses from the block caving sequence was required. SFRS in conjunction with the use of rockbolt and expanded metal strap (and steel sets in specific locations) was selected for this purpose. This support system was required to provide an abrasion-resistant lining for the 130 drawpoints, with low maintenance and hence, reduced operating costs and ensure a safe working environment (see Figure 14.4).

The shotcrete specification required minimum compressive strengths of 20 MPa in 3 days, 30 MPa at 7 days and 40 MPa at 28 days. In addition, a minimum flexural strength of 4 MPa at 7 days and 5 MPa at 28 days was specified. The steel fibre content was set at not less than 60 kg/m³. SFRS was applied as part of the extraction drive mining cycle after rockbolts, cable bolts and expanded metal straps had been installed. As the turn-outs for the

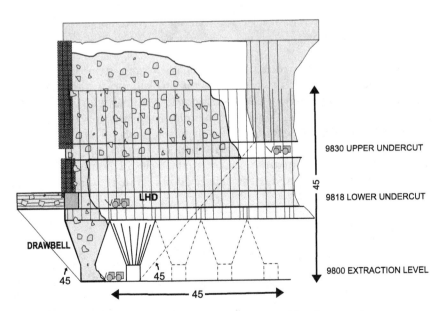

Figure 14.4 Section through drawbell in undercut sublevel extraction.

(Photo courtesy Stephen Duffield, Newcrest Mining Ltd.)

draw points were extracted, the SFRS was applied after every cut in order to maintain the integrity of the bullnose area.

The drawpoint lining system used at the Henderson Mine block caving operation in Colorado, USA was adapted for the Northparkes mine. It consisted basically of:

a) Rockbolts 2.4 m long fully resin grouted on a 1.0 m × 1.0 m spacing;
b) Expanded metal straps installed longitudinally into the drawpoint from the extraction drive and also pinned vertically in the brow area;
c) Cable bolts 6.0 m long fully cement grouted installed in the brow area;
d) Two steel sets; and
e) The steel sets were encased in SFRS to provide a tough, smooth lining system.

The final dimensions of the drawpoint were 3.8 m wide by 3.2 m high.

Duffield provides a detailed description of the method of constructing the drawpoints. He notes that it took up to 600 mm thickness of SFRS to completely encase the steel sets. They tried an alternative of forming and pumping a cheaper concrete to encase the steel sets, but this took four days to complete a drawpoint lining, compared to one day when using SFRS. One problem that was noted when using SFRS was abrasion wear and damage caused to the trailing electrical cable of the LHDs when they turned corners. This problem was resolved by application of a sprayed plain shotcrete without fibres over the SFRS at corners and hand trowelling it to a smooth finish (on subsequent block caves at Northparkes, macro-synthetic fibres were used to overcome this issue).

All SFRS was batched in a ready-mix concrete plant on the surface and transported down the decline in 4WD agitator trucks to the shotcrete rig underground. The round trip from the batch plant to the extraction level 480 m below the surface and back was about 11 km. Shotcrete was applied from three remote control manipulator arms (robots) sized for the work (see Figure 14.5).

In addition to the use of SFRS in the decline, extraction drifts and drawpoints, it was applied to rock surfaces in all the long-term mechanical and electrical installations to provide a safe, low maintenance working environment. Typically, 100 mm thickness of 40 MPa at 28 days SFRS was applied in installations, such as crusher chambers, main pump stations, underground workshop and control room, screen room, main conveyor decline, transfer conveyor drives, loading station, ore bins area and electrical substations. Duffield reports that the SFRS in all of the above installations has performed well, with no maintenance requirements.

Duffield concluded that during the four-year construction period of the mine, the SFRS proved itself as a versatile material that was quick to apply. He noted that by shotcreting the extraction level, excavations for mechanical and electrical installations and other openings subjected to mining stresses,

Figure 14.5 Remote control manipulator arm used to apply SFRS.
(Photo courtesy Stephen Duffield, Newcrest Mining Ltd.)

that a low maintenance environment with minimized operating costs has been achieved. More specifically, he reported that at that time (August 1999), the Northparkes E26 Mine was producing at the lowest cost per tonne of all Australian underground mines.

14.2.3 Cadia East Mine, Australia

In 2004, it was reported (Duffield, 2004) that the Cadia East Mine in New South Wales, Australia when fully developed would be the largest underground mine in Australia and one of the largest gold mines in the world. The mine uses a low-cost, bulk underground mining method known as panel caving to extract the ore. Panel caving is a natural caving method that uses ground stresses, rock structures and gravity to break the rock and propagate mining vertically. Cadia East has two panel caves with extraction levels at 1200 m and 1400 m beneath the surface.

Fibre-reinforced shotcrete has been an essential component to the safe and economical development of this mine. The main shotcreting application in the mine commenced in June 2010, and by the end of November 2013, some 59 km of shotcrete lined tunnels had been constructed using 115,000 m³ of fibre-reinforced shotcrete. This project is of interest in that it reflects changes that have occurred in shotcrete in mining in Australia in the 17 years after shotcrete work commenced at the Northparkes E26 Mine. It differs with respect to fibre-reinforced shotcrete technology from the Northparkes E26 Mine in that it used macrosynthetic fibre reinforcement, rather than steel fibre. This is reflective of the general trend for fibre-reinforced shotcrete in mines in Australia, as reported by Bernard et al. (2014).

Duffield (2014) provides a comprehensive overview of the use of macrosynthetic fibre-reinforced shotcrete (SnFRS) on this project. The following is a brief summary of the key information presented by Duffield in his overview of the project. During mine development, SnFRS was applied in all of the following major excavations:

a) Main decline: 9.1 km long at a gradient of 1 in 7;
b) Conveyor decline: 7.6 km long at a gradient of 1 in 5.3;
c) Crusher chambers: three major excavations, each with approximate dimensions of 40 m long by 12 m wide by 26 m high;
d) Undercut level: 3 km of tunnels; and
e) Extraction level: over 8 km of extraction drives, drawpoints and access drives.

All development was excavated using drill and blast with a fleet of four jumbo drill rigs backed up by 10 rock bolting jumbos. The SnFRS was applied in-cycle before rock bolting. A typical cycle consisted of the following activities: drill; charge and fire; clearance and re-entry; muck out; scale/hydroscale; spray shotcrete; rock bolt; survey mark-up for next round. The minimum standard of ground support consisted of 50 mm thickness of SnFRS with pattern bolting with 2.4 m long resin grouted reinforcement rock bolts. Depending on ground conditions, additional support was installed, such as steel mesh; cable bolts; a second layer of SnFRS; and where required, steel sets. Table 14.1 shows a typical SnFRS mixture design used on the project.

The mixture had a specified minimum compressive strength of 40 MPa at 28 days and a minimum toughness of 500 Joules in the ASTM C1550 round determinate panel test. Toughness performance requirements were achieved by using 9 kg/m³ of a high-performance macro synthetic fibre, with a good track record of performance in SnFRS in Australian mines, and elsewhere. The following admixtures were used in the shotcrete mixture:

a) Both low-range and high range water reducing admixtures to control water demand and hence the water cementing materials ratio (and consequent strength) of the mix;

Table 14.1 Typical SnFRS mix design

Ingredient	Quantity, kg/m³
River sand	1065
10/7 mm basalt aggregate	570
SL cement	400
Fly ash	55
High-range water-reducing admixture	2000 mL/m³
Liquid silica	7000 mL/m³
Low-range water reducer	1200 mL/m³

b) A liquid silica to enhance adhesion and cohesion of the mix and enhance thickness of build-up and reduce fall-out during shooting;

c) A hydration stabilizer to control the working life of the mix (maintain slump, pumpability and shootability for the required time); and

d) Set accelerator added at the nozzle to provide immediate stiffening of the applied shotcrete and rapid setting, hardening and early strength development of the shotcrete.

The shotcrete was batched in a ready-mix plant at the surface, which operated 24 hours a day all year. All shotcrete was transported to the operational headings at depths of up to 1400 m beneath the surface via the main decline by a fleet of 11 underground agitator trucks. The approximately 10 km long trip (one way) took about 2 hours; hence, the importance of using a hydration stabilizing admixture. It was added at the batch plant at a dosage rate of 2 litre/m^3. The agitator trucks carried an additional supply of hydration stabilizer in case of delays underground requiring retempering of the mix to further extend the working life. The shotcrete was applied using 5 to 6 spray robots at any one time. Some 25 to 30 headings were sprayed in a typical week and SnFRS production averaged about 2900 m^3 per month. Duffield (Duffield, 2014) concluded that at Cadia East, the use of SnFRs was essential for development of this world-class mining project. Without the application of a consistent, high-quality, high-capacity SnFRS on time and in the right locations, the project would have stopped.

14.3 SHOTCRETING IN COLD CONDITIONS IN MINES

The ACI 506.2 *Specification for Shotcrete* requires that shotcrete not be applied against frozen ground and to *stop shooting when ambient temperature is 40°F (4°C) and falling, unless adequate measures are taken to protect the shotcrete.* While this is good advice for general shotcrete production, the reality for a number of mines in Northern Canada and other northern countries is that shotcrete is sometimes required to be applied in permafrost ground conditions and often at ambient temperatures much below 4°C. Special shotcrete mixtures and procedures have been developed to enable shotcrete application in such conditions.

With respect to shotcrete mixture designs, different approaches have been adopted to enable shotcrete to be applied to frozen ground in either shaft sinking operations, where the ground is intentionally frozen prior to excavation and shotcrete installation, or in mining in permafrost ground conditions. Such approaches include:

a) In dry-mix shotcrete applications, introduction of a brine solution (calcium chloride based), in lieu of potable water at the shotcrete nozzle (Dufour, 2000);

b) In dry-bagged premix shotcrete, the use of special dry-powdered accelerators preblended in with the dry materials during batching (Atkinson and Martin, 2007);

c) The use of high aluminate cements, in either dry- or wet-mix shotcretes; and

d) The use of special rapid setting and hardening calcium sulfoaluminate cements (Ballou, 2013).

All the above approaches have the same common objectives: to provide an installed shotcrete that will adhere to the ground, without sloughing and rapidly set and develop heat of hydration such that it hardens and gains sufficient strength before the frozen ground conditions stop the hydration reactions, and further strength development. Such work can be further complicated by the shotcrete having to be applied in cold ambient conditions, with air temperatures sometimes as low as –25°C. The following sections provide some brief case history examples of where shotcrete has been applied in mines in cold conditions.

a) Kattiniq Mine, Quebec, Canada

Dufour provides an interesting example of dry-bagged premixed shotcrete supply and application in this mine a few hundred kilometres south of the Arctic Circle. Rock and ambient air temperatures typically ranged between –10°C and +3°C but reached as low as –25°C near some ventilation raises. Extensive laboratory trials to simulate field conditions were carried out before finalizing the mixture provided to the project. The addition of brine solution at the nozzle generated a very rapid heat of hydration reaction, as shown in Figure 14.6.

Mix A was designed for use in shotcrete applied to permafrost ground. Mix B was developed for underground construction of features, such as fences, barricades and sumps. Mix A was batched with a dry material's temperature of –10°C. After an initial temperature drop of about 2°C during the first minute after application, the shotcrete temperature at the rock surface in a 50 mm thick shotcrete application rose by about 8°C in a 20 minute period. This was sufficient for the shotcrete to develop rapid setting, hardening and compressive strength development, appropriate for the mine ground support requirements.

The shotcrete was batched into bulk bin bags near Montreal, Quebec, loaded onto barges and shipped up North (see Figure 14.7).

Warehouse facilities were not available on the surface at the time of development of the mine and so the dry bagged materials were stored outside where the dry materials reached temperatures as low as –15°C prior to application. Thermisters installed in the shotcrete, at the shotcrete/rock interface and at depths of 200 mm and 1.7 m deep into the rock demonstrated that the temperature in the rock rose by only 1°C at the 200 mm deep thermistor and was not influenced at depths below that. This demonstrated

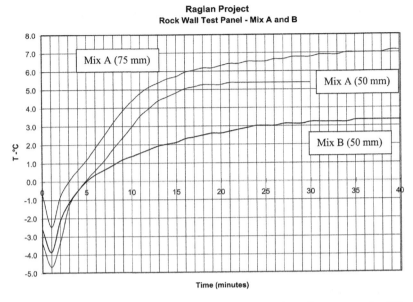

Figure 14.6 Temperature evolution of shotcrete rock wall test panels. (Mix A 50 mm and 75 mm thick and Mix B 50 mm thick); (graph courtesy Jean-François Dufour.)

Figure 14.7 Loading bulk bin bags of shotcrete onto barge for shipping.
(Photo courtesy Jean-François Dufour.)

that the shotcrete installation would have little thermal influence on permafrost ground conditions. Shotcrete application was successfully integrated into the mining cycle.

b) EKATI Diamond Mine, Northwest Territories, Canada

The first author was involved in the development of special dry-bagged premixed shotcrete for use in this mining project, located some 300 km Northeast of Yellowknife, in the Northwest Territories. Atkinson and Martin (Atkinson and Martin, 2007) provide a summary of the use of shotcrete in this challenging mining project. As part of the transition from an open cut pit to a combination of open-cut pit and underground mine, shotcrete was selected as the preferred method to stabilize the kimberlite ore drives. The main challenges facing the mine were the remote location and the low temperatures in which the shotcrete would be applied.

The mine site is serviced by air transportation 12 months of the year and an ice road built over frozen lakes and tundra from late January to mid March. All heavy construction materials for the entire year have to be moved to the mine site over the ice road during this short time period. During the first year of shotcrete application all the shotcrete supplied for the project was batched at the suppliers batch plant in Morinville, Alberta and shipped in bulk bin bags over the ice road to the mine site. Figure 14.8 shows trucks moving shotcrete materials to the mine site over the ice road.

All the dry shotcrete materials, including cement, silica fume, coarse and fine aggregates, steel fibres and powder accelerator were preblended and discharged into the bulk bin bags.

In subsequent years, however, the volume of shotcrete required was greater than could economically be met by this supply method. Consequently, the shotcrete supplier developed a shotcrete batch plant which was prefabricated and shipped to the mine site over the ice road during the winter of 2002. Local coarse and fine aggregates were processed and supplied to the

Figure 14.8 Trucks moving shotcrete materials over ice road to mine site. (Photo courtesy Richard Atkinson.)

Figure 14.9 Shotcrete manufacturing plant set up at mine site.
(Photo courtesy Richard Atkinson.)

batch plant and only the steel fibres and a *concentrate* of cement, fly ash and
accelerator was preblended and shipped in bulk bin bags over the ice road to
the mine site. The *concentrate*, steel fibres and local aggregates were blended
in the site batch plant to produce the dry-mix shotcrete required for the
project on a year-round basis. Figure 14.9 shows a picture of the batch plant.

A two-phase series of shotcrete trials was conducted to develop the special cold weather shotcrete required for this project. The shotcrete was
required to achieve initial set in approximately 10 minutes and a minimum
compressive strength of 8 MPa in 8 hours to meet mining objectives. In
Phase 1 shotcrete trials, the dry-mix materials were preconditioned to a
temperature of 12°C. The mix water added at the nozzle had a temperature
of 1°C. The mixed materials were stored in a freezer at –17°C until the time
of testing. Four different shotcrete mixture designs were tested in laboratory
trials and the mixture which best approached field performance requirements had a set time of less than 10 minutes and developed compressive
strength of 7 MPa in 8 hours and 12 MPa in 24 hours.

In Phase 2 trials, which were conducted at the shotcrete suppliers batch
plant in Morinville, Alberta in January 2002, full-scale shotcrete production
was carried out under the following conditions:

- Ambient air temperature –6°C to –8°C;
- Water temperature 12°C to 14°C; and
- Shot specimens stored in a freezer at –12°C until the time of testing.

Two mixtures were shot and tested and the mix which best met the mine performance requirements had compressive strengths of 9 MPa in 8 hours, 16 MPa in 12 hours, 36 MPa in 3 days and 38 MPa in 7 days. This mix has now been successfully used for ground support in the Ekati Diamond Mine for over a decade.

14.4 SHAFT LINING WITH SHOTCRETE

Shotcrete has long been used for shaft lining, in lieu of cast-in-place concrete lining. It is attractive for use in shaft sinking operations in that it eliminates the need for installation of formwork. Formwork installation is a time-consuming and costly component of traditional cast-in-place concrete linings in shafts. Prior to the 1980s, nearly all shotcrete shaft lining would have been performed using hand-applied dry-mix shotcrete. Working in shafts is a high-risk activity. It is typically accomplished through man access to the shaft via a hoist and stage. It adds significantly to the cost for the shaft development due to the specialized equipment and personnel that are required.

Recognizing the limitations of hand-applied shotcrete in shaft sinking operations, a number of agencies and contractors spent considerable effort in developing automated remote-controlled so-called *robotic* shotcrete lining systems which eliminated the need for man entry into the shafts. These automated *robotic* shotcrete lining systems are best suited to circular shafts, such as raise-bored shafts. One of the first published references on this topic was on work conducted by the US Bureau of Mines in 1977 (Monaghan et al., 1977). The goal of their development was to have a dry-mix shotcrete system which could operate in raise-bored shafts 2.7 m to 3.7 m in diameter, up to 300 m deep and place linings ranging in thickness from 50 mm to 150 mm thick. Having demonstrated the feasibility of the concept, a number of contractors in North America, Australia, South Africa and elsewhere took up the challenge to develop increasingly sophisticated remote control shotcrete *robot* shaft lining systems, which met or exceeded the initial US Bureau of Mines goals.

By the 1990s, dry-mix steel fibre-reinforced shotcretes were being routinely used in North America for lining raise-bored shafts up to 300 m deep (Morgan, 1991). Some contractors also developed remote-controlled *robotic* wet-mix shotcrete lining systems capable of application to such depths. Special rigging systems are required to hold the weight of the hose filled with wet-mix shotcrete in such applications and devices are required which control the rate of feed of shotcrete to the nozzle. Morgan et al. (2010) describe a rigging system used in a centrifugally sprayed concrete lining of a 3.5 m diameter 290 m deep raise-bored shaft that has also been used in wet-mix fibre-reinforced shotcrete lining of shafts. Both steel and macrosynthetic fibres have been used in such wet-mix shotcrete systems. Figure 14.10 shows an example of *robotic* application of wet-mix SFRS in a raise-bored shaft in North America.

Figure 14.10 Robotic application of wet-mix shotcrete in raise-bored shaft.
(Photo courtesy Kristian Loevlie.)

14.4.1 Remote-control shotcrete shaft lining in Australia

A review of the literature indicates that remote control *robotic* shotcrete lining is now being applied in shafts up to 8 m in diameter and up to 350 m deep. While the use of such remote-control systems has eliminated the need for man entry into the shaft, there are still hazards associated with manpower working around open shafts, either at the surface or sub-level in a mine. Contractors have gone to great lengths to minimize the hazards associated with such operations. Ford et al. (2010) provide a comprehensive overview of one method developed to minimize the hazards of remote-control shotcrete lining. They developed a special remote-control rig to control the lowering and raising of the shotcrete robot, hoses, winch cable and air lines into the shaft in a safe manner. Figure 14.11 shows a schematic of the set-up. The rig consists of a platform on which is mounted a winch and cable reel, a hose reel and a boom. The boom can be extended to centre the shotcrete robot in the shaft. A crane is mounted on the end of the boom to lift and lower the shotcrete robot into the shaft.

The following is a brief description of some of the other equipment and operational features in the remote-control *robotic* system utilized by Ford et al. (2010). The robot is fitted with three legs which keep the shotcrete nozzle centred in the shaft. The legs can be expanded to fit shafts of different diameters. The robot is also fitted with four infrared cameras mounted at 90 degrees to each other so that the shotcreting operations can be viewed at all times by the robot operator. Several LED lights are installed on the top of the robot to provide a clear picture to the operator. The footage from the cameras is recorded and is reviewed as part of the QC/QA operations.

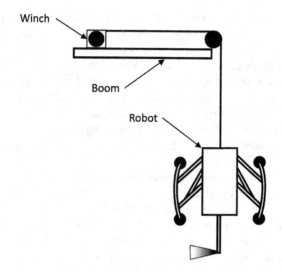

Figure 14.11 Schematic of remote-control shotcrete shaft lining rig.

(Sketch adapted from Ford et al., 2010.)

The robot was also equipped with a thickness scanning system which used an ultrasonic distance measuring device. The thickness of the shotcrete lining at any point could be measured by scanning the entire shaft, both before and after shotcrete spraying. More shotcrete could be applied in any areas indicating less than specified thickness.

Ford et al. (2010) reported that four shafts, with diameters ranging from 3.1 to 5.4 m and depths up to 185 m had been lined with dry-mix steel fibre-reinforced shotcrete. With respect to productivity, they indicated that on average a rate of 13 m³ of shotcrete could be applied in a 12 hour shift. This translated into a depth of about 17 m in a shift for a 5 m diameter shaft with shotcrete applied to a 50 mm thickness and with an allowance of 20% for rebound. They indicated that the robot system they utilized should be able to operate in shafts with depths up to about 350 m.

14.4.2 Hand-applied shaft lining of South Deep Mine Shaft Randfontein South Africa

Another good example of the use of hand nozzling to line a world-class shaft was the shotcrete lining of the South Deep Mine shaft near Randfontein in South Africa. Erasmus et al. (2001) provide a detailed description of this project. The South Deep mine is part of the largest single gold deposit known in the world. The complex ore body dips North/South at about 18 degrees between 2500 m and 3500 m beneath the surface. The thickness of the ore body varies from 1 m to 90 m and the mine has a planned life of 60 years at a rate of extraction of 220,000 reef tons per year. Ore was pre-extracted in the reel plane and the voids backfilled prior to sinking the shaft. Stresses in the shaft sidewall during shaft sinking and mining operations were calculated to result in strains of up to +/– 0.2 mm/m at depths of 2345 m to 2790 m where the shaft traversed the ore body. It was calculated that if a monolithic concrete lining was installed in this zone that it would be subjected to radial tensile stresses in excess of 8 MPa. The concrete lining could only be expected to withstand tensile stresses of up to 3 MPa before the onset of cracking. Based on this reasoning, it was decided to install a steel fibre-reinforced shotcrete lining to areas of the shaft where strains in excess of 0.2 mm/m were predicted.

A wet-mix stainless steel fibre-reinforced shotcrete was selected for this work because of its significantly higher ductility than monolithic concrete and calculated ability to withstand the predicted strains. Performance parameters included a minimum 60 MPa compressive strength at 28 days and an EFNARC minimum energy absorption of 1000 Joules at 28 days. In addition, because of concerns about sporadic incidences of strain bursting of shaft sidewalls at early ages, a minimum compressive strength of 5 MPa at 48 hours and 400 Joules energy absorption at 4 to 8 hours after shotcrete placement was specified. The mixture design developed contained Portland cement, superfine fly ash, silica fume, quartzitic aggregates, stainless steel fibres and synthetic microfibers. Chemical admixtures used included a hydration controlling admixture, internal curing agent, and an alkali-free accelerator added at the nozzle by an accelerator dosing pump. The stainless-steel fibre was selected because of the long-term durability requirements for the shaft lining in this very wet shaft.

Because of logistical constraints, it was decided to produce the shotcrete on the surface and lower the wet-mix shotcrete in a *kibble* with a waterproof canopy into the shaft, where it was discharged into the shotcrete pump. This method was used instead of a steel slick line to provide wet-mix shotcrete from the surface, because of the great depths of the works and the excessive amount of flushing and cleaning that would be required for the relatively small volumes of shotcrete that would be required per shift.

Shotcrete was hand-applied from a platform erected at the bottom of the shaft. The mine was very satisfied with the shaft development and reported that it was the deepest shaft ever to be sunk without a single fatal accident. They attributed this in large measure to the ability of the SFRS to prevent ground falls, as not a single incident of ground fall was reported since installation of the SFRS.

14.5 SUMMARY

In summary, the use of shotcrete in mining applications has come a long way since *gunite* was first used in the Brucetown Experimental Mine in Pennsylvania over a hundred years ago. While dry-mix hand-applied shotcrete still has its place and is used in many mining projects around the world, it is the use of high volume, robotically applied wet-mix fibre-reinforced shotcrete that has revolutionized ground support and other applications in mining. Not only has such shotcrete application made it technically and economically possible to develop large, mechanized mines that would otherwise not be able to be developed using older, more traditional ground support methods, but it has dramatically improved the health and safety aspects of modern mine development and reduced injuries and fatalities from ground fall and seismic events (rock bursts) (Bernard, 2013). As a consequence, in countries such as Australia over 500,000 cubic metres of robotically applied wet-mix fibre-reinforced shotcrete is used annually in underground mines (Bernard et al., 2014).

Shotcrete automation is continuing to evolve and miners such as Larsen et al. (2009) and Rispin et al. (2005) envisage the day when shotcrete application will be automated to the point where automated bulk shotcrete carriers controlled from the surface will deliver shotcrete to headings many kilometres away and the automated shotcrete sprayers will be remotely controlled by shotcrete nozzleman from the surface. This augurs well for the future of shotcrete in large, mechanized mining operations.

REFERENCES

ACI 506.2-13(18). 2018. *Specification for Shotcrete*. American Concrete Institute. 12p.

ASTM C1550. 2020c. *Standard Test Method for Flexural Toughness of Fiber-Reinforced Concrete (Using Centrally Loaded Round Panel)*. 14p. https://doi.org/10.1520/C1550-20

Atkinson, R. and Martin, M. W. 2007. Cold Weather Shotcrete in Canadas North Country. *Shotcrete Magazine. American Shotcrete Association* Fall 2007. 18–20.

Ballou, M. 2013. Rapid-Setting Cement in Shotcrete. *Shotcrete Magazine. American Shotcrete Association* Spring 2013. 46–47.

Bernard, S. 2013. Safe Support with Fibre Reinforced Shotcrete. *Tunneling Journal* August 2013. 44–47.

Bernard, S., Clements, M. J. K. and Duffield, S. 2014. Development of Macro-Synthetic Shotcrete in Australia. *Seventh International Symposium on Sprayed Concrete. Modern Use of Wet-Mix Sprayed Concrete for Underground Support*, Sandefjord, Norway, June 16–19, 67–75.

Duffield, S. 1999. Shotcrete Applications at Northparkes E26 Mine. *Shotcrete Magazine. American Shotcrete Association* August 1999. 18–24.

Duffield, S. 2014. Cadia East Project. *Shotcrete Magazine. American Shotcrete Association* Winter 2014. 16–21.

Dufour, J–F. 2000. Performance of Dry-mix Shotcrete in Permafrost Environment. *Shotcrete Magazine. American Shotcrete Association* August 2000. 28–32.

Erasmus, W. P., Swanepoel, C. D., Munro, D., Hague, I., Northcroft, I., Parrish, A. and Bassett, A. 2001. Shotcrete Lining of South Deep Shafts. *The Journal of the South Africa Institute of Mining and Metallurgy* July 2001. 169–176.

Ford, K., Spence, L., McGarva, D. and Calderwood, M. 2010. *Robotic Shotcrete Shaft Lining – A New Approach*, Edited by Bernard, S., Taylor and Francis Group, Shotcrete Elements of a System, 105–110.

Larsen, J., Thibodeau, D. and Hutter, J. 2009. A History of Shotcrete Use at Vale Inco. *Shotcrete Magazine. American Shotcrete Association* Spring 2009. 14–21.

Monaghan, D. A., Hoadley, D. J. and Anderson, G. L. 1977. Remote Shotcrete Lining of Raised Shafts. *ACI Symposium Paper*. Vol. 54. 225–240.

Morgan, D. R. 1991. Steel Fibre Reinforced Shotcrete for Support of Underground Openings in Canada. *ACI Concrete International*. Vol. 13. No. 11. November. 54–64.

Morgan, D. R., Loevlie, K. and Kwong, N. 2010. Centrifugal Sprayed Concrete for Lining Horizontal Pipes and Culverts and Vertical Shafts. *Shotcrete. Elements of a System*, Edited by Bernard, S., Taylor and Francis Group, 225–232.

Rispin, M., Gause, C. and Kurth, T. 2005. Robotic Shotcrete Applications for Mining and Tunneling. *Shotcrete Magazine. American Shotcrete Association* Summer 2005. 4–9.

Thompson, J. J., Joughin W. J. and Dube, J. 2009. Underground Monitoring to Determine the Interaction of Shotcrete and Rock Under High Stress and Dynamic Conditions. *Shotcrete for Africa Conference*, March 2–3, 2009, 46 p.

Yoggy, G. D. 2002. The History of Shotcrete: Part III. *Shotcrete Magazine. American Shotcrete Association* Winter 2002. 20–23.

Yoggy, G. D. 2011. Underground Shotcreting. *Shotcrete Magazine. American Shotcrete Association* Winter 2011. 8–11.

Chapter 15

Swimming pools and spas

15.1 INTRODUCTION

Since the earliest days of shotcrete, it has been used for construction of swimming pools and spas and other water retaining structures. There are good reasons for this. The versatility of shotcrete placement allows for the construction of monolithic pool shells of virtually any size and shape and reduces, or in the case of in-ground pools, largely eliminates the need for formwork, with resultant increased speed of construction and reduced costs relative to a conventional formed, cast-in-place concrete alternative. It also largely eliminates the need for construction joints in the pool shell.

Prior to the 1950s, all shotcrete pools were constructed using the *gunite* (dry-mix shotcrete) process. One of the first reported uses of *gunite* for swimming pool construction was for construction of a swimming pool at the Lehigh Country Club in Pennsylvania in 1936. The shotcrete was applied to an excavated rock substrate, which acted as a *form* for the shotcrete application (Samuels and Drakeley, 2016). Since then, many hundreds of thousands of swimming pools (and spas) have been constructed in North America using the shotcrete process. Swimming pool construction is reported to be the largest use of shotcrete in North America, with some 9 million m³ of shotcrete reported to have been used for swimming pool construction in 2008 (Drakeley, 2008). While dry-mix shotcrete still continues to be used, by the 1980s, wet-mix shotcrete was increasingly being used and by 2000 the majority of swimming pools were being constructed using the wet-mix shotcrete process.

There are several good reasons for this change from dry-mix to wet-mix shotcrete. Not only is the wet-mix shotcrete production rate (cubic meters/hour) much greater than for the dry-mix shotcrete process (by a factor of about 3 to 4), but there have also been problems with installed shotcrete quality and hence watertightness with *gunite* pools. (Yoggy, 2001; Lacher, 2007; Samuels and Drakeley, 2016). High-quality watertight pools have and continue to be constructed using the dry-mix shotcrete process (Oakes, 2016); unfortunately there have been many examples where this has not been the case.

DOI: 10.1201/9780429169946-17

There are a number of factors which have contributed to leaking swimming pool shells constructed with both the wet-mix and dry-mix shotcrete processes (Lacher, 2007; ASA Pool and Recreational Shotcrete Committee, 2015; Zynda, 2016). These include:

a) Work carried out by poorly trained and/or inexperienced shotcrete nozzlemen and crew, such that shotcrete is not applied at correct shooting orientation to the receiving surface, or with sufficient impacting velocity to properly consolidate the shotcrete and wrap around reinforcing steel and embedded items such as pipes and conduits;

b) Use of low strength shotcrete mixture designs with low cement contents (in an attempt to reduce shotcrete materials costs), which produce excessive rebound and lack sufficient paste to provide good adhesion and cohesion and wrap around reinforcing steel. Also, such mixes can have a higher than desirable water/cementing materials ratio, with consequent excess permeability, allowing for general water permeation through the pool shell;

c) Shooting mixes too dry, with consequent poor wrap around reinforcing steel and embedments and excessive rebound. Shotcrete should be applied at the *wettest stable consistency*, i.e. the consistency (slump) at which it will not sag or slough, for optimal encasement of reinforcing steel and embedments and to minimize rebound (Beaupré and Jolin, 2001);

d) Improper planning of the work with respect to shooting sequence. In large commercial swimming pools, the contractor will often first pour the floor slab, using conventional cast-in-place concrete placing and finishing techniques before shooting the walls. However, in many smaller and residential swimming pools, the entire pool will be constructed with shotcrete. In such circumstances, the *cove* between the walls and floor of the pool should be shot first, before shooting the walls, so that rebound and trimmings from finishing of the walls do not get trapped in this critical zone. If this is not done, leakage can occur at the wall/floor junction;

e) Rebound and trimmings from the shotcrete application and finishing processes should not be incorporated in the fresh shotcrete work. Rebound lacks sufficient paste and trimmings are not consolidated by the shooting process (Lacher, 2007; Zynda, 2016); and

f) Plastic and/or drying shrinkage cracking, caused by a failure to properly protect and cure the shotcrete during shotcrete placement, finishing, setting and hardening. Before setting, protection is best provided by fogging/misting. After setting and hardening, curing is best provided by wet curing; in pools this is best accomplished by using soaker hoses or covering the shotcreted surfaces with wet curing fabrics, followed by filling the pool with water as soon as the shotcrete has developed sufficient compressive strength to resist the water-induced loads. This also serves as a watertightness test for the newly constructed pool.

15.2 MIXTURE DESIGNS FOR POOLS

In North America, it has been common for a compressive strength of a minimum of 20 MPa (3000 psi) at 28 days to be specified for concrete and shotcrete for swimming pool and spa construction (Lacher, 2007). While such concrete or shotcrete may have adequate strength to resist structural loads, it is not considered adequate from a durability and serviceability perspective. In addition, if one were to actually try and make shotcrete with such a low strength, it would:

a) Lack sufficient paste content for good shootability (adhesion and cohesion with resistance to sagging and sloughing), and wrap around reinforcing steel and embedments;
b) Have high rebound; and
c) Have a water/cementing materials ratio in excess of 0.65, with consequent excessively high permeability.

So, the question arises: What is a suitable minimum compressive strength for swimming pools? Good guidance in this regard is provided in the ACI Committee 350 document *ACI 350 Code Requirements for Environmental Engineering Structures, Table 4.2*, which is reproduced in Table 15.1, which follows.

Table 15.1 ACI 350 code requirements for special exposure conditions

Exposure condition	Maximum water-cementitious materials ratio, by weight[1]	Minimum compressive strength, MPa
Concrete intended to have low permeability when exposed to water, wastewater, and corrosive gasses	0.45	28
Concrete exposed to freezing and thawing in a saturated condition or to deicing chemicals	0.42	31
Concrete exposed to corrosive chemicals other than deicing chemicals	0.42	31
For corrosion protection of reinforcement in concrete exposed to chlorides in tanks containing brackish water and concrete exposed to deicing chemicals, seawater, or spray from seawater	0.40	34

[1] A lower water-cementitious material ratio of higher strength may be required for durability of concrete exposed to sulphates

The ACI 350 code requires that in fresh-water pools, the concrete or shot-crete should have a minimum compressive strength of 27.5 MPa (4000 psi) and a maximum water/cementing materials ratio of 0.45. For saltwater pools, or where chloride-based deicing chemicals may be used in pool sur-rounds, the minimum compressive strength should be 34.5 MPa (5000 psi) and the maximum water/cementing materials ratio should be 0.40. The structural design engineer can, of course, specify higher compressive strengths, if required for structural purposes. The American Shotcrete Association *ASA Pool and Recreational Shotcrete Committee Position Statement #4* supports these requirements and notes that in reality a prop-erly designed, applied and cured shotcrete will routinely exceed 34.5 MPa (5000 psi) compressive strength at 28 days and that such a minimum com-pressive strength is desirable for enhanced durability.

15.3 WATERTIGHTNESS

A properly designed and constructed shotcrete swimming pool should be watertight. The American Shotcrete Association ASA Pool and Recreational Shotcrete Committee has issued: *Position Statement #4: Watertight Shotcrete for Swimming Pools* on this subject. They stress that watertightness is a crucial durability and serviceability requirement for any water retaining structure. They consider that shotcrete placement that allows water to pass through the pool shell is a sign of flawed material or placement techniques. This *Position Statement* #4 was issued in part to counteract the view being promoted by some shotcrete contractors that shotcrete swimming pools needed liners, coatings or tiling to make them watertight. (They espoused this opinion largely because of water leakage problems arising from one or more of the factors listed in Section 15.1 (a) to (f) above). There are many thousands of well-designed and constructed swimming pools, constructed by both the dry-mix and wet-mix shotcrete processes, that have demon-strated satisfactory watertightness in water leakage tests prior to installation of any linings, coatings or tiles. The installation of linings, coatings or tiles should be mainly an architectural aesthetic/functionality consideration.

15.4 COLD JOINTS

The American Concrete Institute (ACI) Concrete Terminology document defines a *Cold Joint* as: *a joint or discontinuity resulting from a delay in placement of sufficient duration to preclude intermingling and bonding of the material, or where mortar or plaster rejoin or meet.* In cast-in-place concrete construction, internal vibration is the most common method for providing adequate consolidation of the placed concrete. A cold joint is formed when an initial lift of concrete becomes too stiff for penetration by the vibrator used to consolidate a subsequent lift. This thus prevents the *intermingling of material* referred to in the above ACI definition. However, ACI 309R *Guide for Consolidation of Concrete* does indicate that if bond is obtained between cast sections, that a cold joint is avoided.

Most shotcreted swimming pools are constructed as monolithic shells, without any joints (Joints in pools are notoriously difficult to make watertight in the long term in conventional cast-in-place concrete construction). With small residential swimming pools, completion of the shotcrete application can usually be conducted within a day and the issue of joints does not arise. In larger commercial or competition-size pools, it may, however, take several days to complete the shotcrete installation and two types of joint may be encountered:

a) *Construction Joints*: i.e. intentionally produced joints, either vertical, sloped or horizontal, at the end of a day's construction; and
b) *Layer Joints*: i.e. joints which are present when the shotcrete is constructed in layers. A good example of this is when the initial lift of shotcrete is applied to first just encapsulate the outer layer of rebar (usually using bench shooting), and then a final top-down cover coat of shotcrete is applied and finished. The final layer may be applied either the same day, after the initial lift has stiffened sufficiently to withstand disturbance from installation and finishing of the final lift, or it may be applied days later, depending on the shotcrete contractor's construction schedule.

The question has sometimes been asked as to whether shotcrete *construction joints* or *layer joints* produce *cold joints* in swimming pool construction. The American Shotcrete Association ASA Pool and Recreational Shotcrete Committee has issued a *Position Statement #5: Monolithic Shotcrete for Swimming Pools (No Cold Joints)* on this topic and the answer is an emphatic NO. The reason for this is that while there is clearly no *intermingling* of shotcrete (as occurs in vibrated cast-in-place concrete process), when the substrate shotcrete has been properly prepared, and the shotcrete is properly applied, there is excellent bond between the layers of shotcrete at *construction joints* or in *layer joints*. This is because the high impacting velocity of the shotcreting process drives the cementing material paste into the critical bond interface with a high degree of consolidation. There are several laboratory studies (Beaupré, 1999; Trottier et al., 2002) and field reports (Hanskat, 2014; Zynda, 2016) to demonstrate that when proper shotcreting practices are implemented, it is almost impossible to identify where one layer stops and the other starts, and the shotcrete behaves monolithically.

Construction joints are best constructed by creating an approximately 45-degree joint by shooting and cutting and trimming the freshly applied shotcrete as required. Long tapered *featheredged* joints should be avoided, as they are susceptible to peeling type delaminations from drying shrinkage and thermal stresses (Morgan and Neill, 1991). Some structural engineers have questioned whether such 45-degree construction joints would leave a plane of weakness in the shotcrete. A comprehensive study (Trottier et al., 2002) investigated this issue. A series of large 1600 mm × 1600 mm × 75 mm panels were constructed with and without 45-degree construction joints in the middle of the panels, using the wet-mix shotcrete process. Plain shotcrete panels (without reinforcement) were produced, as well as panels reinforced with 102 mm × 102 mm × 4.1 mm/4.1 mm gauge welded wire mesh, panels reinforced with 40 kg/m³ of a hooked-end steel fibre and panels reinforced with 6.9 kg/m³ of a monofilament synthetic fibre. The panels were load tested to large deformations of up to 150 mm in the so-called *South African Waterbed Test* developed by Kirsten (Kirsten, 1992). A photo of the test is shown in Figure 15.1.

Trottier et al. demonstrated in this study that the presence of the construction joint had no negative effect on the flexural performance of the plain and steel and synthetic fibre-reinforced shotcrete panels. In the mesh-reinforced panels, there was some reduction in the load-carrying capacity in the panel with the joint, but this was attributed to some voiding at a double layer of mesh at the joint location. Based on the observed behaviour of the plain and fibre-reinforced shotcrete panels, Trottier et al. concluded that satisfactory performance would be achieved in mesh reinforced panels if overlapping of mesh at the construction joint was avoided.

Figure 15.1 Photo of *South African Water Bed Test.*

With respect to *layer joints* between a base shotcrete substrate and a second lift of shotcrete, there is plenty of evidence from both laboratory tests (Talbot et al., 1995) and field applications (Zynda, 2016) to demonstrate that when the shotcrete substrate has been properly prepared (is clean and free of overspray or other contaminants and is in an SSD condition) and the second lift of shotcrete is properly applied, that excellent bond strength is achieved between the shotcrete layers (see Section 6.9). In fact, in direct tensile bond testing of extracted cores, it is often difficult to even find the location of the bond plane.

15.5 EXAMPLES OF SHOTCRETE SWIMMING POOLS

As previously mentioned, there are many hundreds of thousands of shotcrete swimming pools in North America. There are entire publications, such as Water Shapes Magazine, devoted to the design and construction of swimming pools and spas and other water features, built by either cast-in-place concrete or shotcrete. Shotcreted pools can range from simple free-form, in-the-ground back-yard residential swimming pools, which can be shot in a day or less, to much more complex vanishing edge type pools and spas constructed on challenging sloping sites, to large scale commercial or competition swimming pools, with very exact dimensional tolerances. The American Shotcrete Association (ASA) holds an annual Outstanding Shotcrete Project Award in a variety of shotcrete categories, including *Outstanding Pool and Spa Project*. These award-winning projects provide outstanding examples of what can be achieved in the shotcrete swimming pool industry. Examples of a few award-winning projects follow.

15.5.1 Vanishing edge residential pool, Woodbury, Connecticut, USA

This ASA 2006 Outstanding Pool and Spa Project was built using the wet-mix shotcrete process (Drakeley, 2007). This vanishing edge pool was built in difficult terrain on the edge of a steep hill, posing challenges for the designer and builder. The pool and spa incorporated three levels of water in transit; a vanishing edge spa that spilled into the main pool, which in turn spilled over a vanishing edge into the lower surge pool, from which the water was recirculated into the spa.

The tiered design lent itself naturally to the contoured site, with the pools all founded on natural ledge rock hammered out to provide the required profiles and solid bedding for the shotcrete shells. Reinforcing rods were drilled into the ledge rock to act as bracing points for the footings and provide stability for the new shotcrete structure. After completion of excavation of the ledge rock, drainage stone and an underdrain dewatering system were installed to allow for continuous flow of groundwater. Single-sided forms were erected

Figure 15.2 Formwork and reinforcing for upper tier spa pool.

(Photo courtesy William T. Drakeley, Jr, Drakeley Pools.)

and plumbing and other embedments were installed. A double mat of 12.5 mm diameter bars spread a nominal 152 mm on centre vertically and horizontally were installed in the walls and floors, as shown in Figure 15.2.

The main pool dimensions (not including the spa and lower surge pool) were 10.6 × 6.1 m wide and 1.8 m deep. The floor thickness was 254 mm, and all vertical placements were approximately 457 mm thick. Critical to the success of this waterscape was precise control of the elevations and tolerance of the vanishing edge wall features, which had to be built to a finished shotcrete tolerance of 3 mm. This was achieved by precisely prebending the vanishing edge reinforcing steel to the required sloping shape, followed by installing it to the required elevation and tolerance. Guide wires were installed to control the finished shotcrete line and grade and tolerance.

Figure 15.3 Completed and filled upper spa pool spilling over vanishing edge.
(Photo courtesy William T. Drakeley, Jr, Drakeley Pools.)

A total of about 61 m³ of wet-mix shotcrete was supplied to the project by ready-mix trucks. All shotcrete was discharged within 90 minutes of the time of batching, as required by the ACI 506R Guide to Shotcrete. The shotcrete had a minimum design compressive strength of 28 MPa at 28 days and the tested compressive strength routinely exceeded these requirements. The shotcrete had 10 mm maximum size aggregate and a cement content of 475 kg/m³ and a specified air content of 10% at the pump to provide the shotcrete with freeze/thaw durability. Shotcrete application was by ACI Certified shotcrete nozzlemen and the shotcrete application process took two days to complete. After the placed shotcrete had been finished and set, soaker hoses were activated to keep the structure moist for 28 days.

After completion of curing, the final pool construction activities commenced, including: installation of copings, tiles and edge wall details. Activities prior to final filling of the waterscape included coating the shotcrete interiors with a plaster mix to give a deep-blue water look. Figure 15.3 shows a view of the completed upper spa pool with the water spilling over the vanishing edge to the lower main pool. The homeowner was delighted with the beautiful open line-of-sight effect.

15.5.2 Mountain pool, North Carolina, USA

This ASA 2015 Outstanding Pool and Recreational Project was built using the dry-mix shotcrete process (Oakes, 2016). The pool was built on the edge of a mountain slope and had a perimeter overflow spa, two sets of steps and an underwater lounging area; all built monolithically with dry-mix shotcrete. The pool had three vanishing edge sides, which were fully exposed to the elements and partially exposed to the viewer. The pool walls were 660 mm thick and 1.5 m high. The walls were reinforced with a double mat of 12.5 mm diameter rebar. There was a great deal of plumbing to shoot around, including a 150 mm diameter trunk line, with vertical risers every 1.5 m for the overflow water. The spa plumbing was very intricate and required attention to detail in shooting around the rebar, pipes and other embedments. There was over 27 m of vanishing edge and it was required to be constructed to a very exacting tolerance of 0.8 mm, to minimize the amount of water flowing over the edge and provide a uniform aesthetic effect.

Given the complexity of the pool, the contractor decided to shoot the floor first (including the cove with the walls). This provided a stable platform on which to work when shooting the walls and other features on days two and three. A blow pipe was used to help remove overspray and rebound from areas about to be shot and help in clean-up between shoots. Figure 15.4 shows shooting of the floor in progress. Where more than one layer of shotcrete was applied, care was taken to remove any laitance, dust or other contaminants and bring the existing shotcrete substrate to a clean SSD condition prior to application of the next lift of shotcrete. Figure 15.5 shows

Figure 15.4 Shooting the pool floor using the dry-mix shotcrete process.
(Photo courtesy Ryan Oakes, Revolution Gunite.)

Figure 15.5 Finished pool shell shortly after being shot.
(Photo courtesy Ryan Oakes, Revolution Gunite.)

part of the completed pool shell shortly after being shot and before application of surface finishes.

Of concern to the builder was the issue of the potential for the development of efflorescence on the exposed vanishing edge walls. This has been a common problem in both cast-in-place concrete and shotcrete pools. Not only is it unsightly, but it can also cause problems with exterior cladding materials, such as pool stuccos and tiles. Efflorescence is caused when water is able to penetrate the concrete or shotcrete pools at defects such as cracks (drying shrinkage or thermally induced, or caused by differential settlements), or through voids of incomplete consolidation such as *honeycomb* or cold joints in cast-in-place concrete, or *shadows* (porous zones or voids) behind rebar or piping, or other embedments in shotcreted pools. Water migrating through the concrete or shotcrete can dissolve soluble components of the hydrated cement paste, such as calcium hydroxide. On evaporating at a drying surface, the classically white efflorescent deposits can build up. On exposure to carbon dioxide in the atmosphere the calcium hydroxide is converted to calcium carbonate (Neville, 1996). The best ways to minimize, or eliminate the formation of efflorescence are to:

a) Implement designs and construction practices which reduce the potential for the formation of cracks; if cracks do occur, remediate them by methods such as epoxy injection or other suitable means;

b) Build water-tight pools, free from seepage through voids or porous areas in the concrete or shotcrete pool shell; and

c) Use concrete or shotcrete mixture designs with a low potential for production of calcium hydroxide in the hydrated cement paste, e.g. use pozzolanic materials such as fly ash, slag, silica fume, or calcined metakaolin to react with the calcium hydroxide and produce insoluble hydration products.

With respect to this shotcreted mountain pool shell, the designer and contractor were effective in controlling drying shrinkage cracking by implementing a rigorous wet-curing program. The newly applied shotcrete was wet cured using soaker hoses, which were left to flood the structure. The pool was cured in a flooded state for a month before application of final finishes. Also, by using a highly experienced ACI certified shotcrete nozzleman, who had shot over 1000 pools in the past 20 years, and rigorously following ACI 506 best shotcreting practices, the contractor produced a watertight pool with no leakage during ponding tests.

With respect to the shotcrete mixture design, the shotcrete contractor elected to incorporate silica fume in the dry-mix shotcrete. The silica fume was added to the volumetric batch trucks on site. Silica fume was used as it is an excellent pozzolan, i.e. it reacts with calcium hydroxide released during hydration of the Portland cement paste to produce calcium silicate hydrate, the main insoluble binder component of hydrated Portland cement. In short, silica fume addition is very effective in minimizing the amount of calcium hydroxide available to cause efflorescence. In addition, silica fume is very effective in increasing compressive strength and reducing the overall permeability of the shotcrete (Zhang et al., 2016). The design compressive strength for the shotcrete for this pool was 35 MPa at 28 days, but actual compressive strengths were as high as 58 MPa at 28 days. After a month of curing, there were no signs of moisture or efflorescence on exterior shotcrete surfaces. In effect, a watertight, efflorescence-free monolithic dry-mix shotcrete pool shell with low permeability and high compressive strength had been created.

The exterior exposed shotcreted pool surfaces were covered with a stucco product which matched the colour of the stone on the adjacent home. The interior of the pool and vanishing knife edges were finished with a 20-mm glass mosaic tile. Figure 15.6 shows a view of the completed pool adjacent to the house on a foggy day. The vanishing edge creates an ethereal quality.

15.5.3 Competition pool, Connecticut, USA

There has been a belief amongst certain design professionals that large commercial and competition-size swimming pools should be built using conventional formed and poured cast-in-place concrete construction

Figure 15.6 View of the completed pool on a foggy day.
(Photo courtesy Ryan Oakes, Revolution Gunite.)

methods rather than the shotcrete construction process. This view has
been based, in-part, on less than satisfactory experiences that some have
encountered with shotcrete, for reasons such as those detailed in Section
15.1. The reality is that a well-designed and constructed shotcrete pool
built as a monolithic shell should be as good as, or even better than a
formed, cast-in-place concrete pool. As previously mentioned, the *achilles heel* of large cast-in-place concrete pools is the need for construction
joints, both within the walls and floors and at the wall/floor junction. Such
joints incorporate waterstops and joint sealant materials. While in concept, waterstops should provide watertightness at joint locations, they are
vulnerable to leakage if less than perfectly constructed. Also, joint sealant
materials tend to break down with time and become a maintenance issue.
The first author has investigated a number of large cast-in-place concrete
water retaining structures, including swimming pools, where leakage has
occurred at joints for such reasons. The case history example described in
the section, which follows, provides an excellent example of the use of the
wet-mix shotcrete process to construct a large-competition-size swimming
pool as a monolithic shell, without joints with waterstops or joint sealant
materials, which provided a rapidly constructed, high-quality, watertight
structure (Drakeley, 2014).

The competition pool was constructed at a high school in Connecticut,
USA. This state-of-the-art 25 yard (22.86 m) long, eight-lane pool tapered in

depth from 2 to 4 m. It was designed for speed with gutters with an *automatic surge recovery* system, such that during swimming competitions waves would not rebound into the swimming lanes to slow down swimmers. The pool was initially designed for construction using the form and pour cast-in-place concrete system but did allow a shotcrete alternative in the bid. The shotcrete contractor submitted a bid and was able to demonstrate to the designer that he could provide a cost-competitive, joint-free, monolithic shotcrete shell alternative, which he guaranteed to be watertight before installation of the final tile lining (Drakeley, 2014).

There was a high water table at the site and so construction started with extensive excavation, followed by installation of a drainage/dewatering system. Next was placement of a gravel base on which the single-sided construction forms, reinforcing steel and pool plumbing were installed. The walls and floors were designed to be 305 mm thick, with offset (for shootability) double mats of No. 5 and No. 4 (15.9 mm and 12.5 mm diameter) reinforcing steel bars set at 305 mm on centre. Polymer chairs and wheel spacers were used to provide correct separation of the bars and full shotcrete cover to the wall and floor reinforcing steel. Shooting wires were used to define the line and grade for the bond beams, the shotcrete elevations for the floor's slope and the walls radiuses. Shotcrete application commenced in a planned systematic fashion for this multi-day shoot, starting with shooting of the wall-floor cove, as shown in Figure 15.7.

The shotcrete had a design minimum compressive strength of 28 MPa at 28 days, but actual 7-day compressive strengths reached 43 MPa. It took seven days to shoot and finish all the shotcrete. End-of-day construction

Figure 15.7 Start of shotcreting at wall/floor cove.

(Photo courtesy William T. Drakeley, Jr, Drakeley Pools.)

joints were shot to a 45-degree angle with an as-shot or broom finish. Rebound and cuttings and trimmings were collected and removed from the pool. They were not allowed to be incorporated into the work. Before start-up of shooting the next day, all joints were cleaned of any overspray or miscellaneous dirt and brought to an SSD condition. A total of some 268 m³ of shotcrete was applied. The floor was shot in sections, which were levelled with a power screed and then given a light broom screed for optimal bond of the subsequent ceramic tile bedding material. Final line and grade and tolerance were critical for aesthetic and functional reasons and were carefully controlled. After each day's shoot, soaker hoses were used to keep the shotcrete wet. After completion of construction of the shotcrete pool shell, wet curing was continued for 28 days. A week thereafter, the shotcrete pool shell was filled with water and no leakage was found. Figure 15.8 shows final installation of the 25 mm square tiles in the pool floor.

Figure 15.9 shows the completed swimming pool, filled and ready for competition. The design team was delighted with the final product, which satisfied all their performance requirements, and has since gone on to permit the use of shotcrete on their commercial projects throughout New England.

Figure 15.8 Final installation of ceramic tile in pool floor.

(Photo courtesy William T. Drakeley, Jr, Drakeley Pools.)

Figure 15.9 Completed competition pool, Connecticut.

(Photo courtesy William T. Drakeley, Jr, Drakeley Pools.)

REFERENCES

ACI CODE 350. 2006. *Code Requirements for environmental Engineering Concrete Structures.* American Concrete Institute. 488 p.

ACI CT-18. 2018d. *Concrete Terminology.* American Concrete Institute. 80.

ACI 309R-05. 2005. Guide for Consolidation of Concrete. American Concrete Institute. 36p.

ACI 506R-16. 2016f. *Guide to Shotcrete.* American Concrete Institute. 52p.

ASA Pool and Recreational Shotcrete Committee. 2015. Position Statement #4, Watertight Shotcrete for Swimming Pools. *Shotcrete Magazine. American Shotcrete Association* Winter 2015. 69–70.

ASA Pool and Recreational Shotcrete Committee. 2016. Position Statement #5, Monolithic Shotcrete for Swimming Pools (No Cold Joints). *Shotcrete Magazine. American Shotcrete Association* Fall 2016. 43–45.

Beaupré, D. 1999. Bond Strength of Shotcrete Repair. *Shotcrete Magazine. American Shotcrete Association* May 1999. 12–15.

Beaupré, D. and Jolin, M. 2001. Effect of Shotcrete Consistency and Nozzleman Experience on Reinforcement Encasement Quality. *Shotcrete Magazine. American Shotcrete Association* Fall 2001. 20–23.

Drakeley, W. 2007. Contemporary Edge. *Shotcrete Magazine. American Shotcrete Association* Spring 2007. 22–25.

Drakeley, W. 2008. Need for Nozzleman Certification in the Swimming Pool Industry. *Shotcrete Magazine. American Shotcrete Association* Winter 2008. 14–16.

Drakeley, W. 2014. Top of the Class. *Shotcrete Magazine. American Shotcrete Association* Summer 2014. 10–15.

Hanskat, C. S. 2014. *Shotcrete* Placed in Multiple Layers does NOT Create Cold Joints. *Shotcrete Magazine. American Shotcrete Association* Spring 2014. 40–41.

Kirsten, H. A. D. 1992. Comparative Efficiency and Ultimate Strength of Mesh- and Fibre-Reinforced Shotcrete as Determined from Full-scale Bending Tests. *Journal of the South African Institute of Mining and Metallurgy.* Vol. 92. No. 11/12. November/December. 303–323.

Lacher, R. 2007. Bad Benchmarks, Workmanship Issues in Swimming Pool Dry-Mix Construction. *Shotcrete Magazine. American Shotcrete Association* Spring 2007. 6–11.

Morgan, D. R. and Neill, J. 1991. Durability of Shotcrete Rehabilitation Treatments of Bridges in Canada. *Transportation Association of Canada Annual Conference,* Winnipeg. Manitoba, September 15–19, 37. Republished by the American Shotcrete Association in: D.R. Morgan. Shotcrete. *A Compilation of Papers.* 2008. 269–306.

Neville, A. 1996. *Properties of Concrete.* John Wiley & Sons Inc. Fourth ed. 513–514.

Oakes, R. 2016. Reflecting on a Shotcrete Pool. *Shotcrete Magazine. American Shotcrete Association* Winter 2016. 24–29.

Samuels, L. and Drakeley, W. 2016. Shotcrete Reborn. *Shotcrete Magazine. American Shotcrete Association* Spring 2016. 42–45.

Talbot, C., Pigeon, M., Beaupré, D. and Morgan, D. R. 1995. Influence of Surface Preparation on Long-Term Bonding of Shotcrete. *ACI Materials Journal.* Vol. 91. No. 6. November. 560–566.

Trottier, J. -F., Forgeron, D. and Mahoney, M. 2002. Influence of Construction Joints in Wet-Mix Shotcrete Panels. *Shotcrete Magazine. American Shotcrete Association* Fall 2002. 26–30.

Yoggy, G. D. 2001. The History of Shotcrete, Part II. *Shotcrete Magazine. American Shotcrete Association* Spring 2001. 22–23.

Zhang, L., Morgan, D. R. and Mindess, S. 2016. Comparative Evaluation of Transport Properties of Shotcrete Compared to Cast-in-Place Concrete. *ACI Materials Journal.* Vol. 113. No. 3. May. 373–384.

Zynda, C. 2016. Shotcrete Pool Inspection-Checklist. *Shotcrete Magazine. American Shotcrete Association* Summer 2016. 26–29.

Chapter 16

Architectural shotcrete

16.1 INTRODUCTION

Since its earliest days, the versatility of shotcrete has led to its use in a wide range of architectural applications. Shotcrete has been used for architectural purposes in construction of artificial rockscapes, zoo exhibits, water features, domes and shells, buildings and structures, tunnels and caves and sculptures and monuments. Talented architects and craftsmen (designers, nozzlemen, finishers, sculptors and artists) have used carving, texturing, pigmenting and painting (staining) to create some extraordinary architectural features and structures. The sections, which follow, provide examples of the architectural use of shotcrete in the above-mentioned types of applications.

16.2 ARTIFICIAL ROCKSCAPES

Shotcrete has been widely used for ground support in conjunction with soil nailing, or stressed tie-back rock anchors (see Chapter 12) on highway and railway right-of-ways, commercial developments and residential complexes and to stabilize mountain slopes, bluffs and creeks. While natural as-shot shotcrete finishes have been used on most such projects, there are now many projects where the architect or engineer has required the finished shotcrete surface to simulate the appearance of the local surrounding rock. In such applications carved, textured and often integrally pigmented, or post-application coloured shotcrete is used to produce natural-appearing rockscapes (Robbins, 2003; von der Hofen, 2003; Duckworth, 2011a; Strever, 2019). Some examples of such work follow.

Figure 16.1 shows an example of carved and textured shotcrete facing to a highway retaining wall which simulates the local natural rock formations (von der Hofen, 2003). Such work requires a high level of skill from the shotcrete crew. Typically, photographs are taken of local natural rock formations that the owner/authority wants reproduced. Sometimes plaster models

DOI: 10.1201/9780429169946-18

Figure 16.1 Simulated natural rock formation in a highway retaining wall.

(Photo courtesy Marcus H von der Hofen.)

are also made to replicate what is seen in the photographs and the shotcrete contractor then proceeds to produce a scaled-up version of the model. After installation of rock anchors and reinforcing steel, the nozzleman uses shooting wires to establish final line and grade for the structural shotcrete work. The nozzleman then shoots the carving layer, attempting to replicate the undulations and changes in surface profile present in the photographs and (if used) models. The sculptors then proceed to carve the rock to create the required surface profiles. Figure 16.2 shows an example of a sculptor carving initial fracture lines into freshly placed shotcrete (Duckworth, 2011a).

The finishers then follow closely behind, finishing the rockscape to the required surface finish texture. For sedimentary rocks such as sandstones, final finished surface textures can be created by using techniques such as hand rubbing with gloves, followed by brushing with paint brushes or wire brushes. For granitic rock types, the final surface finish appearance has been created by imprinting the prepared shotcrete surface with crinkled heavy-duty aluminum foil to create a dimpled surface texture. The carving layer of shotcrete is often integrally coloured with a pigment to simulate the colour of the local natural rock formations. This is often followed by

Figure 16.2 Sculptor carving initial fracture lines into freshly placed shotcrete. (Photo courtesy Oscar Duckworth.)

hand application of acrylic paints or stains, to provide colour variations representative of the local natural rock.

Another finishing technique used involves applying a sprayed-on retarder to the finished surface, and then when the shotcrete beneath has set, washing off the surface paste to expose the sand grains below (Beaupré and Lacombe, 2000). Yet another technique used is the hand application of mineral sands of different grain sizes and colours into the freshly finished shotcrete surface to achieve a grainy surface texture. In such situations, it is important to use sands representative of the local rock minerology. Figure 16.3 shows an excellent example of a carved, pigmented and textured retaining wall simulating the natural desert rockscape in Al Ain Wildlife Park & Resort in the United Arab Emirates (He et al., 2012).

16.3 ZOO EXHIBITS

The versatility of shotcrete makes it well suited for the construction of a wide variety of different types of zoo exhibits.

Many of the zoos and aquariums in North America have used shotcrete to create natural-looking rockscapes, which serve as enclosures for marine

Figure 16.3 Carved, finished, textured and pigmented shotcrete retaining wall simulating natural desert rockscape, Al Ain Wildlife Park & Resort, United Arab Emirates.

(Photo courtesy Jean-François Dufour.)

and terrestrial animals and birds. Excellent examples of such work can be found at:

- Woodland Park Zoo in Seattle, Washington;
- Point Defiance Zoo & Aquarium in Tacoma, Washington;
- Elephant Lands in Oregon Zoo in Portland, Oregon (Fulford, 2017);
- Bronx Zoo in New York;
- National Aquarium in Baltimore, Maryland (Knipe, 2005);
- Africa Live Exhibit at San Antonia Zoo, Texas (Tucker, 2009);
- Asia Quest at Columbus Zoo and Aquarium, Ohio (Tucker, 2007);
- Mayan Empire Exhibits in Palm Beach and Jacksonville Zoos, Florida (Knipe, 2006); and
- Orca and Beluga Whale pools and rockscapes, Vancouver Aquarium in British Columbia.

Photographic examples and descriptions of some of these projects follow.

16.3.1 Elephant lands, Oregon Zoo

The Oregon Zoo in Portland recently (2016) completed construction of a six-acre park known as Elephant Lands designed to keep the zoo's six

Asian elephants mentally and physically active in an enriched environment (Fulford, 2017). The exhibit includes shotcrete containment walls and water features such as mud wallows and a large 605,000 litres pool, deep enough to allow the elephants to fully submerge. These watertight shotcrete structures were constructed monolithically (no joints) and also used shotcrete to construct pool slab features, with textures that were friendly to elephant feet. The pools are reported to have been effective in inspiring play amongst members of the herd.

The shotcrete walls were designed to be at least 3 m tall, with an overhang to provide containment for the elephants. Considerable effort was expended to make the walls representative of eroding natural embankments in the savannahs and forests of Asia. Relevant images from Asia were obtained, and clay models were developed to replicate specific features. These features were then reproduced in the shotcrete construction of the containment walls and other elements. The walls were constructed using the top-down soil nailing method and were textured with embedded roots and real cobbles to simulate the aesthetic of eroding embankments. The shotcrete was integrally pigmented and then stained to replicate the rich range of colours often present in Asian soils. The shotcrete walls were designed to resist impact from elephants rubbing against them. Figure 16.4 shows part of the herd travelling through their new exhibit.

Figure 16.4 Elephant herd travelling through the elephant lands exhibit at the Oregon Zoo.

(Photo courtesy Turnstone Construction.)

16.3.2 Asia Quest at Columbus Zoo and Aquarium

Asia Quest at the Columbus Zoo and Aquarium is a large animal enclosure exhibit that simulates landscapes ranging from the lush forests of South East Asia to the harsh environment of the Amur River Valley in Eastern Russia (Tucker, 2007). The zoo design architects made extensive use of shotcrete to simulate the naturally occurring rock in the different regions represented in the park. Shotcrete was used to construct artificial rockwork, mud banks, waterfalls, pools and even *faux* trees, creating habitats for a wide range of different animals, including Red Pandas, Sun bears, Asian Elephants and Siberian Tigers.

Some 7670 m² of themed shotcrete rockwork was constructed, using 230 m³ of custom-designed shotcrete. Intricately detailed trees and rocks and other zoo exhibit elements were constructed by hand-shaping reinforcing steel to provide the required forms and shapes. The rebar cages were then covered with metal lath and the shotcrete applied. The freshly applied shotcrete was carved, finished, textured and completed using colours and stains to produce the required visual effects. A particularly impressive exhibit is a 5.8 m high shotcrete waterfall that spills water at 1360 L/min into a moat system that wanders through the park and helps to contain the animals and separate the different exhibit areas. An example of such work is presented in Figure 16.5, which shows a Siberian Tiger reclining on a

Figure 16.5 Siberian Tiger overlooking shotcrete lined pond with *faux* shotcrete tree stump adjacent the pool.

(Photo courtesy The Companies of Nassal.)

Figure 16.6 Russian highland viewing shelter faced with carved and coloured shotcrete resembling stacked stone.

(Photo courtesy The Companies of Nassal.)

shotcrete ledge above a shotcrete-lined pool, with a *faux* shotcrete tree stump in the background.

The shotcrete contractor also simulated ancient Asian architecture such as a Cambodian Temple and Russian highland viewing shelter by first producing the base structure using conventional cast-in-place concrete and block wall construction and then applying, carving and finishing shotcrete to create the required architectural effect. For example, this method was used to construct the Russian Highland Viewing Shelter shown in Figure 16.6. The shotcrete was hand carved and coloured to resemble stacked stone and also included some carved rock detailing.

16.3.3 Mayan Empire Exhibits, Jacksonville and Palm Beach Zoos, Florida

Shotcrete was the dominant construction medium used for creation of ancient Mayan Empire exhibits at the Jacksonville and Palm Beach zoos in Florida (Knipe, 2006). The Jacksonville project, named *The Range of the* Jaguars covers 4.5 acres and took 18 months to build. The exhibit simulated an archaeological dig site and included Mayan artefacts, stone pathways, eroded temple buildings and watertight lagoons, all constructed

Figure 16.7 Jaguar Lair at the Jacksonville Zoo viewed from the zoo restaurant. (Photo courtesy Cemrock.)

with shotcrete, rather than the massive blocks of carved stone used by the ancient Mayans. Even jungle vines and trees were constructed with shotcrete. Figure 16.7 shows a view of the jaguar lair at the Jacksonville zoo, taken from the zoo restaurant.

An even larger and more ambitious project was the *Tropics of the Americas Exhibit* at the Palm Beach Zoo. This exhibit took nearly two years to build. The wet-mix shotcrete process was used in construction of most of the structures and many of the artefacts. At the entrance to the exhibit is a simulated massive stump of a ficus tree constructed with shotcrete (see Figure 16.8). Included in the construction were a shotcrete pyramid, with authentic Mayan historical detail (see Figure 16.9), a full-size Mayan *caracol* observatory building, temples, Mayan *stellae*, and a pre-Columbian village in a pristine state, undamaged by time. Also constructed with shotcrete were a jaguar enclosure, earth retaining walls, simulated ancient ruins and historic carvings and sculptures.

Construction techniques included building structural substrates of steel frames covered by mesh, or walls constructed with cement masonry units or cast-in-place concrete, which were subsequently covered with shotcrete. Shotcrete thicknesses varied from as little as 50 mm to 300 mm or more, depending on the details and amount of relief required in the final feature. Facing mixtures with integral concrete colours were used with final appearance being produced by application of acrylic paints to highlight textures and features. Figure 16.10 shows a jaguar reclining in a nook in a shotcrete-faced ruin which simulates ancient carved rock.

Figure 16.8 Entrance into the Tropics of the Americas Exhibit at the Palm Beach Zoo, through the stump of a massive ficus tree constructed with shotcrete.

(Photo courtesy Cemrock.)

16.4 WATER FEATURES

Shotcrete is well suited to construction of durable, natural-looking water-retaining and conveying architectural structures such as pools, canals, *lazy rivers* (Bezanson, 2008; Brazier, 2017), waterfalls, fountains and above and below water rockscapes (Robbins, 2003; Burns and Ferland, 2005; Duckworth, 2011a). One only has to walk down Las Vegas Boulevard (*The*

Figure 16.9 Shotcrete pyramid with authentic Mayan historical detail at Palm Beach Zoo. (Photo courtesy Cemrock.)

Strip), in Nevada to see a myriad of examples of the use of shotcrete in waterscapes at a number of hotels and casinos. Excellent examples include the *volcanoes* and waterfalls at the Mirage, the Pirate Ships exhibit at Treasure Island and the towering waterfalls at Wynn Hotel and Casino. Shotcrete constructed water features are also very popular in golf course architecture in North America, particularly in California, Arizona, Nevada, Florida and Hawaii (Robbins, 2003; Duckworth, 2011a).

Figure 16.10 South American jaguar in its new shotcrete habitat.
(Photo courtesy Cemrock.)

16.4.1 Mirage Hotel and Casino, Las Vegas

The waterfalls and simulated volcanic eruptions on the Las Vegas Boulevard at the Mirage Hotel and Casino represent one of the most spectacular uses of shotcrete in a waterscape. During the day, massive volumes of water are pumped over the shotcrete waterfalls. Figure 16.11 shows one part of the waterfall exhibit during the day. At night, combinations of water jets and burning natural gas are used to create a volcanic eruption spectacle in the *shotcrete* rockscape.

Figure 16.11 Shotcrete waterfalls at the Mirage Hotel and Casino in Las Vegas. (Photo courtesy Andrea Scott.)

16.5 DOMES AND SHELLS

Curved structures such as domes and shells are difficult and costly to form and construct using the cast-in-place concrete method. This is particularly true for hemispherical structures, such as domes. A wide range of economical and attractive architectural shotcrete structures have, however, been constructed using the shotcrete process. Forms can be either inflated *balloons* or *barrels* shot from either inside or outside, or single-sided rigid forms, constructed from steel, conventional wood and plywood forms, or even permanent precast concrete forms, which become part of the final structure. It is the lack of need for a second confining form, as required for cast-in-place concrete on vertical or steeply sloping surfaces, that makes the shotcrete process so attractive. Creative architects and structural engineers have been able to design and build remarkably strong, thin curvilinear domes and shells with reinforced shotcrete (Flanagan, 2015; South, 2017; Huesler, 2017, 2020). Descriptions and photographs of such applications are provided in the section which follows.

16.5.1 Architectural shells

Award-winning acoustic shells were constructed in a sunken garden beside the beach in Littlehampton, West Sussex, England, using the shotcrete construction process (Flanagan, 2015). The concept for the shells was derived from the traditional British bandstand, popular in the late 1800s and early 1900s. The shells are contiguous, with one shell facing the town and a second smaller structure facing the sea. The larger structure acts as the principal bandstand stage and the smaller shell provides a shelter for listening to the sounds of the sea and for entertainers to perform facing the promenade. The shotcrete shell design was attractive, as it unified the architectural components of the floor, walls and roof into a single entity, which reduced materials, complexity and cost while satisfying acoustic needs of the structure and providing durability in the marine exposure environment. The shells were constructed by first erecting a grid scaffolding of reinforcing bars surveyed to accurately provide the spatial coordinates for the shells. An expanded metal lath was then installed on the rebar where it acted as a stay-in-place formwork which had shotcrete applied from both sides. The thickness of the shells was on average 100 mm but increased to 150 mm at the leading edge to provide structural stability. Once sprayed, the shotcrete was finished to a smooth finish with hand trowels and then painted a white colour and provided with an anti-graffiti seal. Figure 16.12 shows a view of the two completed shells.

Another excellent example of architecturally attractive shotcrete shell construction is the Comfort Stations at the Ayla Golf Resort in Aqaba, Jordan (Huesler, 2017). The vaulted shell buildings were inspired by Bedouin tents and were designed to blend in with the surrounding desert and mountain scenery in the Gulf of Aqaba. The comfort stations provide a snack/refreshment kiosk and restroom facilities. They also served as a precursor for construction of the much larger 3700 m² golf academy and clubhouse,

Figure 16.12 Acoustic shotcrete shells.

(Photo courtesy Flanagan Lawrence Architects.)

Figure 16.13 Shotcrete shell comfort stations at the Ayla Golf Resort in Aqaba, Jordan. (Photo courtesy of Rasem Kamal, Oppenheim Architecture.)

which was later constructed with a complex of six interconnected shotcrete shells (Huesler, 2020). The construction process involved erection of computer-generated flexible thin-gauge steel ribbons, to which reinforcing steel and an outer layer of mesh was added. This was followed by installation of an adjustable *blanket mesh* and a layer of insulation. Shotcrete was then applied from both the interior and exterior to create the final shell finish. Natural local aggregates and pigments were used in the shotcrete to create a natural unadorned appearance that blended in with the landscape. Figure 16.13 shows a view of one of the completed comfort stations.

16.5.2 Architectural domes

In addition to industrial domes (see Section 10.5), a number of architecturally attractive shotcrete domes have been constructed for residential, institutional and commercial buildings. An excellent example of such construction is the new Dome Technology Corporate Headquarters building in Idaho Falls, Idaho (South, 2017). This architectural dome is a stunning example of what is possible using the thin-shell shotcrete construction process. The building has an open free-span shotcrete thin-shell exposed by arching openings with light window glazing around the building perimeter. The building is unique in that the thin shell was constructed using air-formed shotcrete technology without a single conventional concrete form or shore and uses geothermal energy for heating and cooling. The construction process was basically as follows:

After construction of the concrete ring beam, an elliptical polyvinyl chloride (PVC) air form fabric was connected and inflated. Polyurethane

Figure 16.14 View of completed Dome Technology Corporate Headquarters dome in Idaho Falls, Idaho.

(Photo courtesy Dome Technology.)

insulating foam was then applied from the inside of the inflated form to provide a layer 75 mm thick. Multiple layers of reinforcement and shotcrete were then applied from inside the dome in a strategic sequence until the necessary thickness was achieved, and the dome met its strength requirements. Arched openings were achieved by placing a thinner amount of shotcrete and lesser amount of reinforcing steel in the areas to be removed. Later these areas were cut out and removed from the shell, leaving the arched openings. The PVC membrane doubled as the air-supported shotcrete form and a single-ply waterproofing system over the entire shell. Porcelain tile with a 100-year life expectancy provided the final finished exterior surface.

Remarkable features of the building are the heating and cooling systems that are housed within the concrete floor and shotcrete dome. All heating is achieved through in-floor radiant heat with hot water routed through the floor. The innovative cooling system is radiant too. The insulated shell holds heat exceptionally well and excess heat is discharged through some 5 km of PVC tubing that was routed within the shell during the multilayer shotcrete construction process. Groundwater with a temperature of about 13°C is circulated through the PVC tubing during warmer weather to dissipate the heat. The heating and cooling system provides long-term cost savings and a comfortable working environment for employees in the building. Figure 16.14 shows a view of the completed building.

16.6 BUILDINGS AND STRUCTURES

While the vast majority of reinforced concrete buildings and structures, which are comprised predominantly of vertical and horizontal elements, are designed and built using the formed, cast-in-place concrete process, there are, however, certain buildings and structures, with complex shapes and curvatures that are far better suited to construction using the shotcrete process. Excellent examples of this include:

- Refurbishing the auditorium in the Gotheanum in Dornach Switzerland, using structural, pigmented and hand-carved/chiseled dry-mix shotcrete (Hasler et al., 1999);
- Construction of complex curvilinear interior and exterior reinforced shotcrete walls at the Museum of the History of Polish Jews in Warsaw, Poland, using the dry-mix shotcrete process (Czajka, 2013); and
- Construction of the Scottsdale Arch bridge at Indian Bend Wash in Scottsdale, Arizona using barrel arch forms and reinforced shotcrete and use of integral colouring to produce architectural details such as trumpet features on the headwalls (Noland, 2006).

Photographic examples and descriptions of these projects are provided in the section, which follows

16.6.1 Goetheanum

The Goetheanum in Dornach near Basel, Switzerland was constructed between 1925 and 1929 and represents one of the first uses of concrete for monumental sculptured forms (Hasler et al., 1999). It was designed by Rudolf Steiner (founder of the Waldorf Schools) as a world headquarters for the Anthroposophical Society. The building consisted of an outer reinforced concrete structure encasing a very large inner 17,000 m^3 auditorium with seating for more than 1000 people. The inner architecture included free-standing columns topped by sculptured capitals and sweeping architraves, constructed mainly from wood and an expansive suspended ceiling coated with asbestos. In 1993, a decision was made to remove the ceiling (for environmental reasons) and at the same time renew and improve the heating, ventilation and cooling systems and, above all, improve the acoustics, which had always been unsatisfactory. (The ethos of the Anthroposophical Society prohibited the use of any electronic amplification in the auditorium). The architectural brief also prohibited the use of any polymers or chemicals in replacement materials.

Consideration was given to the use of free-standing formed cast-in-place reinforced concrete to recreate the inner auditorium, but this was rejected, as it would have imposed excessively heavy loads on the floor and foundation system and also would have been extremely difficult and costly to reproduce the original carved wood appearance of the auditorium enclosure. This led to the decision to use a system of thin shells constructed with reinforced dry-mix shotcrete to reproduce the complex shapes comprising the auditorium enclosure.

The interior elements of the new auditorium were supported by a structural steel frame of columns and girders that stands on the floor and is anchored to the existing exterior reinforced concrete frame. The complex

Figure 16.15 Reinforcing steel skeleton with metal lath being fixed behind to create *lost formwork*.

(Photo courtesy Hans Hasler.)

shapes for the new auditorium were created with a network of shaped reinforcing steel *baskets*, either prefabricated or constructed in place. The substrate for the shotcrete was an expanded metal lath, fastened behind the steel *baskets* to act as *lost formwork*. Figure 16.15 shows metal lath being fixed behind the reinforcing steel cages. The metal lath was chaired to provide at least 20 mm of clearance behind the reinforcing steel, so that the applied shotcrete, building from behind, could fully encase the reinforcing steel.

The dry-mix shotcrete used was designed to have a reddish/buff colour with a *salt and pepper* colouration when chipped to expose the exterior shotcrete appearance (the first author was involved in the design of this shotcrete mix). This was accomplished by using a dry-mix shotcrete, batched on site, made with nine parts white cement, to one-part hydraulic lime, a 0 to 8 mm maximum size pumice aggregate, a 0 to 3 mm maximum size reddish expanded clay aggregate and a red iron oxide mineral colourant. Figure 16.16 shows the shotcrete being applied at high impacting velocity to thoroughly encase the reinforcing steel skeleton. This shotcrete had a minimum 100 mm thickness. Shrinkage cracking control was provided by installation of a blue glass fibre mesh directly to the shotcreted surface, followed by application of an additional approximately 40 mm thickness of shotcrete. Every square meter of the finished and hardened shotcrete surfaces in the auditorium was then meticulously hand carved with hatchets by a team of some 35 artisans over a period of just over six months to expose the interior character of the applied shotcrete and create the visual appearance required by the architect and surface roughness texture required for acoustical purposes. Figure 16.17 shows sculpting of the shotcrete with a hatchet in progress.

Figure 16.16 Dry-mix shotcrete application to auditorium wall.

(Photo courtesy Hans Hasler.)

Figure 16.17 Hand sculpting column ornamental feature with a hatchet.
(Photo courtesy Hans Hasler.)

Figure 16.18 shows a view of the totally refurbished main auditorium in the Goetheanum. It is an extraordinary unique combination of architecture and sculpture as well as good engineering. Very few restrained shrinkage cracks were found in the entire complex. The final surface texture and appearance was highly uniform and free of defects and satisfied acoustical requirements and the Anthroposophical Society was delighted with their new auditorium.

Figure 16.18 View of the totally refurbished main auditorium in the Goetheanum. (Photo courtesy Hans Hasler.)

16.6.2 The Museum of the History of Polish Jews

Another extraordinary example of architectural shotcrete is a 26 m high curvilinear wall system, with an approximate surface area of 6000 m² which is a major architectural feature of The Museum of the History of Polish Jews in Warsaw, Poland (Czajka, 2013). The curvilinear wall symbolizes the Red Sea parting during the exodus of the Jews from Egypt in biblical times and it forms the main spatial element in the interior of the museum, as well as the main entrance into the museum. Originally, the curvilinear walls were planned to be constructed using resin-cement panels cast ex-situ and then incorporated into a steel curvilinear wall structure with a system of holding elements. Such a system would, however, have been technically and economically difficult to build and an alternative system was proposed by a shotcrete contractor with extensive experience in building curvilinear reinforced shotcrete walls. Structural designs were carried out and static load and fire resistance tests were conducted on a shotcrete model and after satisfactory results were achieved, the shotcrete alternative was accepted.

A substructure comprised of 273 mm diameter vertical pipes and 100 mm diameter horizontal pipes together with reinforced concrete columns was first constructed. Figure 16.19 shows a view of a part of the fire-protected curvilinear wall substructure. The envelope of the curvilinear wall is a 50 mm thick, thin-walled reinforced shotcrete structure with mesh reinforcement. The wall is suspended using a system of rigid anchors embedded in the substructure. Expansion joints were provided which broke the wall

Figure 16.19 Fire-protected curvilinear wall substructure.
(Photo courtesy Wlodzimierz Czajka, SPB Torkret.)

up into plates with areas limited to about 16 to 20 m². The expansion joints formed an important architectural feature in the finished shotcrete wall appearance, as can be seen in Figure 16.20.

The walls were constructed using the dry-mix shotcrete process. The first course of shotcrete was shot using a conventional shotcrete mixture with natural rounded quartz aggregates and Portland Cement. The final finish layer was shot using selected quartz aggregates and a white cement with specially selected pigments to provide a colour similar to that in the Western Wall in Jerusalem. Finishing was performed to provide a light sandstone type appearance, as can be seen in the shotcrete entrance walls to the museum in Figure 16.21. The shotcrete system proved to be a technically and cost-effective means of constructing these high-profile architecturally sensitive elements at the museum.

16.6.3 Scottsdale Arch Bridge at Indian Bend Wash, Arizona

Indian Bend Wash is a major greenbelt floodway that was built by the US Army Corps of Engineers to protect the City of Scottsdale from floodwaters. The Scottsdale Road passes over the wash and a widening of the road envisioned construction of a six-span bridge using AASHTO-type box girders. A design/build contractor specializing in the construction of arched bridges using the shotcrete process submitted a value engineering alternative for construction of the bridge (Noland, 2006). The new design took advantage

Figure 16.20 Finished curvilinear walls in interior of museum.

(Photo courtesy Wlodzimierz Czajka, SPB Torkret.)

Figure 16.21 Curvilinear shotcrete walls entrance into The Museum of the History of Polish Jews in Warsaw.

(Photo courtesy Wlodzimierz Czajka, SPB Torkret.)

Figure 16.22 Wet-mix shotcrete being applied to a steel arch form.

(Photo courtesy Chuck English, president Hunter Contracting Co.)

of the arch shape to reduce shotcrete thickness and quantities of reinforcing steel required. This, together with the utilization of re-useable single-sided steel arch forms for the shotcrete construction resulted in cost reductions, which saved the City of Scottsdale over US$564,000 and allowed architectural enhancements to be added to the project. Architectural enhancements included trumpet features on the headwalls, form liners for aesthetics and integral colouring to the shotcrete. The new design consisted of a six-cell 12.8 m span arch with each cell having a length of 42.4 m and rise of 3.15 m. Figure 16.22 shows wet-mix shotcrete being applied to a steel arch form. Figure 16.23 shows a view of the completed arched bridge structure. It is considerably more attractive than a conventional AASHTO-type box girder bridge structure and represents a technically, economically and architecturally good use of the shotcrete process.

16.7 TUNNELS AND CAVES

As detailed in Chapter 13, shotcrete is widely used for ground support in tunnels and caves and other underground openings. Many view the shotcrete finish in such linings to be architecturally unattractive. This need, however, not be the case. For example, nearly all of the approximately 100 underground metro stations in Stockholm, Sweden are lined with wet-mix shotcrete with a natural as-shot surface finish. The City Council assigned

Figure 16.23 Finished Scottsdale Arch bridge at Indian Bend Wash, Arizona. (Photo courtesy Chuck English, president Hunter Contracting Co.)

Figure 16.24 Artistic painting on shotcrete lined Stockholm Metro stations.

different artists the challenge of a beautification program for these metro stations, and the resultant effects are stunning. With creative use of pigments and paints, the artists transformed over 90 of these rather utilitarian spaces into remarkable works of art. Pictures of a couple of these shotcretes lined and decorated stations are provided in Figure 16.24.

Another popular use of shotcrete, with natural as-shot finishes, is for lining tunnels and wine caves in California and now elsewhere in North America. The tunnels and caves provide almost ideal temperature and humidity conditions for storage of wine barrels and provide substantial

Figure 16.25 California wine cave with natural as-shot shotcrete surface finish. (Photo courtesy Oscar Duckworth.)

savings in energy costs compared to surface structures with ongoing heating, cooling and humidifying costs. The caves provided attractive underground spaces, and many are being used for wine tastings and even weddings and banquets. These tunnels and caves are now predominantly constructed with wet-mix, macrosynthetic fibre-reinforced shotcrete with final finish coats of white or buff-coloured shotcretes. The light-coloured natural finish shotcretes provide architecturally attractive linings, with good acoustical and light reflectance characteristics (Rowland, 2006; Duckworth, 2011b; Zignego, 2016; Townsend, 2018). An example of one such cave is shown in Figure 16.25.

16.8 SCULPTURES AND MONUMENTS

The versatile, free-form character of the shotcrete application process lends itself well to the creation of specialty sculptures and monuments. There are a number of companies that specialize in such work (Burns and Ferland, 2005; Knipe, 2006). Many exotic shotcrete trees have been created with shotcrete in zoos and aquariums, because shotcrete is much more durable than real wood trees in such exposure environments. Good examples include large artificial trees at the Quebec City Zoo in Quebec, as shown in Figure 16.26 and the Tropics of the Americas exhibit at the Palm Beach Zoo in Florida (see Figure 16.8).

Figure 16.26 Artificial shotcrete tree at the Quebec City Zoo.

16.8.1 City of Calgary shotcrete lions

In the City of Calgary, Alberta, four large reclining monumental lions, origi-nally built with concrete in 1916 and placed on pedestals on the Centre Street Bridge, had seriously deteriorated from over 80 years of exposure in the harsh Alberta climate. They were replaced in 2000 with four new lions constructed using a high-performance wet-mix shotcrete (Kroman et al., 2002). The original four lions were patterned after the bronze lions at the base of the Nelson Column in Trafalgar Square, London, England. All four lions were removed from their pedestals and the least deteriorated lion was painstakingly restored to its original detail to serve as a mould for construction of the new hollow shotcrete lions. A rubber latex demould-ing compound was sprayed onto the reconstructed model lion, followed by

Figure 16.27 Rubber latex and glass fiber-reinforced resin moulds stripped from original model lion.

sprayed-on fibre glass-reinforced resin to create a mould. Once cured the moulds were stripped from the model lion. Figure 16.27 shows the stripped mould, which produced a faithful negative image of the model lion.

The moulds were reassembled on hollow precast concrete pedestals that allowed a shotcrete nozzleman access to spray shotcrete from inside the moulds. A special dry-bagged premix shotcrete was used. It had 5 mm maximum size aggregate and incorporated silica fume and micro synthetic fibre. A liquid air-entraining admixture was added to the batch during mixing to provide good durability in this aggressive freezing and thawing and deicing chemical exposure environment. The as-shot air content was typically in the 8–10% range and the parameters of the air void system in a hardened shotcrete sample were 10.9% air content and 0.14 mm spacing factor, which satisfied CSA A23.1–19 requirements for frost-resistant concrete. Values of Boiled Absorption and Volume of Permeable Voids in the hardened shotcrete averaged 4.6% and 9.1%, respectively, which represents very low permeability shotcrete. Compressive strength test results averaged 50.4 MPa at 28 days.

An initial approximately 12 mm thick layer of the wet-mix shotcrete was first applied into the moulds, taking care to thoroughly fill all the fine detail within the mould. After 6 hours of curing a second about 20 mm thick layer of shotcrete was applied and stainless-steel tie wires were inserted into the shotcrete. These ties were used to secure a network of 6 mm diameter stainless steel bars and 40 mm × 40 mm gauge 16 welded wire mesh reinforcement, which was installed throughout the cross-section of the lions. A final layer of shotcrete with a minimum thickness of 50 mm was applied to fully encapsulate all the reinforcing. The shotcrete applied inside the moulds was initially cured with humidifiers to prevent any plastic shrinkage cracking.

Figure 16.28 Completed shotcrete lion.

After stripping from the moulds, the lions were wet-cured for 7 days to protect against drying shrinkage cracking. These curing procedures were effective in that the stripped lions were essentially crack free when mounted on the bridge pedestals. Some fine hairline cracking did subsequently appear on the lions after a few winters of exposure. This was attributed to thermal effects caused by the very severe exposure environment. In winter months, the ambient temperature in Calgary often falls below minus 30°C but can warm up to above freezing in a matter of a few hours when a Chinook wind blows down from the nearby Rocky Mountains. This creates severe differential thermal strains through the thickness of the shotcrete, which can initiate fine hairline cracking. This issue was mitigated by application of a flexible polymer-modified cementitious coating to the lions and they have since shown durable performance. Figure 16.28 shows one of the lions shortly after being stripped from its mould. It is an excellent example of what is architecturally possible with the shotcrete process.

REFERENCES

Beaupré, D. and Lacombe, P. 2000. *Exposed Aggregate Wet-Mix Shotcrete as a Repair Material*. Concrete International. Vol. 22. No. 6. 5p.

Bezanson, W. 2008. The Star Pass Lazy River Project. *Shotcrete Magazine. American Shotcrete Association* Fall 2008. 36–38.

Brazier, Z. 2017. Challenges on the Lagoon at Treasure Island Resort. *Shotcrete Magazine. American Shotcrete Association* Spring 2017. 64–65.

Burns, D. and Ferland, M. 2005. Dream Pools and Spas in Cold Climates: Made a Reality with Shotcrete. *Shotcrete Magazine. American Shotcrete Association* Fall 2005. 4–6.

Czajka, W. 2013. The Museum of the History of Polish Jews. *Shotcrete Magazine. American Shotcrete Association* Winter 2013. 12–17.

Duckworth, O. 2011a. Imitating Nature's Rock Features. *Shotcrete Magazine. American Shotcrete Association* Fall 2011.10–14.

Duckworth, O. 2011b. California Wine Caves Showcase Wet-Mix Shotcrete. *Shotcrete Magazine. American Shotcrete Association* Fall 2011. 26–28.

Flanagan, J. 2015. Acoustic Shells. *Shotcrete Magazine. American Shotcrete Association* Winter 2015. 16–19.

Fulford, J. 2017. Elephant Lands. *Shotcrete Magazine. American Shotcrete Association* Winter 2017. 18–21.

He, H., Miller, J., Beaupré, D. and Dufour, J. -F. 2012. Al Ain Wildlife Park & Resort Retaining Wall and Artificial Rocks. *Shotcrete Magazine. American Shotcrete Association* Spring 2012. 12–15.

Hasler, H., Teichert, P. and Morgan, D. R. 1999. Artistic Shotcrete for a Historic Auditorium. *ACI Concrete International*. Vol. 21. No. 3. March. 29–33.

Huesler, B. 2017. Ayla Golf Resort Comfort Stations. *Shotcrete Magazine. American Shotcrete Association* Winter 2017. 60–62.

Huesler, B. 2020. Ayla Golf Academy and Clubhouse. *Shotcrete Magazine. American Shotcrete Association* Winter 2020. 44–46.

Knipe, D. 2005. Art, Animals and Architecture: Shotcrete Builds the National Aquarium in Baltimore. *Shotcrete Magazine. American Shotcrete Association* Fall 2005. 8–10.

Knipe, D. 2006. The Mayan Empire Rises Again-Shotcrete Buildings Replicate Ancient Monuments. *Shotcrete Magazine. American Shotcrete Association* Winter 2006. 4–7.

Kroman, J., Morgan, D. R. and Simpson, L. 2002. *Shotcrete Lions for Calgary's Centre Street Bridge. Shotcrete Magazine. American Shotcrete Association* Winter 2002. 4–8.

Noland, B. 2006. Scottsdale Arch at Indian Bend Wash. *Shotcrete Magazine. American Shotcrete Association* Spring 2006. 29–31.

Robbins, H. L. 2003. Architectural Shotcrete for Residential and Commercial Development. *Shotcrete Magazine. American Shotcrete Association* Fall 2003. 6–8.

Rowland, L. 2006. Shotcrete for Wine Storage. *Shotcrete Magazine. American Shotcrete Association* Winter 2006. 8–10.

South, J. 2017. Dome Technology Corporate Headquarters. *Shotcrete Magazine. American Shotcrete Association* Winter 2017. 46–48.

Strever, D. 2019. Pampoen Nek Cutting. *Shotcrete Magazine. American Shotcrete Association* Winter 2019. 28–31.

Townsend, F. 2018. Rails Steakhouse Wine Cave. *Shotcrete Magazine. American Shotcrete Association* Spring 2018. 42–43.

Tucker, K. 2007. Asia Quest, Columbus Zoo and Aquarium. *Shotcrete Magazine. American Shotcrete Association* Summer 2007. 32–35.

Tucker, K. 2009. Africa Live! At the San Antonio Zoo. *Shotcrete Magazine. American Shotcrete Association* Fall 2009. 34–35.

von der Hofen, M. H. 2003. Architectural Finishes for Retaining Walls. *Shotcrete Magazine. American Shotcrete Association* Fall 2003. 18–20.

Zignego, J. 2016. Creating a Wine Cave. *Shotcrete Magazine. American Shotcrete Association* Spring 2016. 46–48.

Appendix A

Guide specification for structural shotcrete

Adapted from a publication by D.R. Morgan and L. Totten *Guide Specification for Structural Shotcrete Walls*, Shotcrete Magazine, Winter 2008, pp.18–27

I GENERAL DESCRIPTION AND REQUIREMENTS

1.1 Scope

This specification is for the construction of _____ using the wet-mix shotcrete construction process.

1.2 Qualifications

The shotcrete contractor's crew foreman and nozzlemen shall meet the following requirements.

a) Furnish proof that the shotcrete crew foreman has at least 5 years' experience in reinforced shotcrete construction projects of similar size and character along with three references from persons who were responsible for supervision of these projects. Include name, address and telephone number of references who will testify to a successful completion of these projects by the shotcrete crew foreman.

b) Furnish proof that the nozzlemen are certified by the American Concrete Institute (ACI) for application of shotcrete to vertical surfaces, using the wet-mix shotcrete process, as prescribed in the ACI publication CPP-660.1.

c) Furnish proof that the nozzlemen have successfully completed three projects of similar size and character. The nozzlemen shall also pass a preconstruction mock-up test, described in Section 8.3, demonstrating their ability to satisfactorily construct the reinforced shotcrete structural elements required for this project.

DOI: 10.1201/9780429169946-19

d) If the shotcrete contractor can provide proof to the Engineer that the proposed shotcrete crew, including the foreman and nozzlemen have demonstrated their ability to satisfactorily construct structural shotcrete elements with similar character, size and reinforcing details to that required, using similar means of shotcrete supply and placing equipment, in the past 3 years, then the requirements for construction of the preconstruction mock-up can be waived by the Engineer. An un-reinforced test panel shall, however, still be shot to pre-qualify the shotcrete mix, using the same shotcrete mixture and placing equipment proposed for use on the project.

1.3 Requirements

1.3.1 Furnish all labour, materials and equipment for the following:

a) Demonstrate in preconstruction testing that the submitted shotcrete mixture design(s) satisfies the performance requirements of this specification.

b) Shoot a preconstruction mock-up of the reinforced shotcrete foundation walls to demonstrate that the shotcrete materials, mixture(s), equipment, crew and construction sequence and methods used are capable of producing a product conforming to these specifications and acceptable to the Engineer.

c) Provide quality control services as necessary to ensure compliance of the completed work with the requirements of this specification. Shoot test panels at the frequency specified for independent quality assurance testing by the Engineer.

d) Verify that the reinforcing steel bars in the walls are installed in a manner that is conducive to the shotcrete construction process.

e) Provide all hoarding, covers or other protection devices necessary to protect all fixtures and installations in the shotcrete construction area from contamination, or damage from the shotcrete construction process. In particular, protect such fixtures and installations from impact from the shotcrete nozzle stream, rebound, overspray and shotcrete mist or dust.

f) Provide all scaffolding, platforms, lift equipment or other devices necessary to provide the shotcrete nozzlemen and other crew and inspectors with safe and proper access to the shotcrete work.

g) Provide suitable ventilation, lighting, fans, curtains or other devices necessary to provide the shotcrete nozzlemen and crew with good visibility and control of shotcrete mist, dust, overspray and rebound.

h) Provide all forming, bracing, guidewires and finishing tools necessary to enable construction of the reinforced shotcrete elements to the specified profiles, tolerance and finish.

i) Apply shotcrete to the foundation walls using pre-qualified nozzlemen and crew and approved shotcrete mixture(s).

j) Finish shotcrete to specified finish, dimensions, tolerance and line and grade. Provide moist curing as specified.

k) Provide assistance to Engineer for quality assurance testing including access for any coring required by the Engineer. Remove and replace at no cost to the Owner, any defective shotcrete or work which is non-conforming to the project specifications.

l) Leave completed shotcrete work in a clean condition, free of any deposits of shotcrete, overspray, rebound or other contaminants. Remove all such materials from the work area and dispose of at an approved disposal site.

1.3.2 Implement a health, safety and environmental protection programme which conforms to the requirements of the Engineer and any other authorities having jurisdiction. Such programmes shall include, but not be limited to the following:

a) Ensure that all equipment, scaffolding, shoring, bracing and other devices used on the project meet the requirements of the authorities having jurisdiction.

b) Put in place a mandatory health and safety training programme for all workers, inspectors and other persons entering the workplace.

c) Protect all workers and other personnel from applied shotcrete and rebound during the shotcrete application process. As a minimum, all workers and personnel in active shotcreting areas shall wear appropriate respiratory protection devices as well as appropriate clothing and other protection equipment (hard hats, eye protection, safety boots and reflective vests). Provide eye-wash equipment at shotcrete site (s).

2 SUBMITTALS

2.1 Submit to the Engineer at least 10 working days before commencement of production shotcrete work written documentation which provides the following:

2.1.1 The qualifications of the work crew, including the supervisor, shotcrete nozzleman, pump operator and shotcrete blowpipe operators, and the references for the supervisor required in 1.2 (a).

2.1.2 Test records, showing source and proof of conformance to project specifications for all shotcrete materials, including:

a) Portland cement

b) Supplementary cementing materials (silica fume, fly ash)

c) Aggregates

d) Mix water

e) Chemical admixtures, and

f) Reinforcement

2.1.3 Details of proposed shotcrete mixture(s) shotcrete mixture proportions and means of shotcrete supply.

2.1.4 A list of the proposed shotcreting equipment, including brand name, model and capacity of proposed pump and air compressor.

2.1.5 Results of the preconstruction testing program and a description of the proposed construction quality control testing program including the frequency of specific tests.

2.1.6 Details of proposed scaffolding, man lifts or other temporary support system for workers and inspectors.

2.1.7 Details of proposed forming, bracing, or temporary support systems for construction of reinforced shotcrete elements.

2.1.8 Details of proposed means of preparing surface to receive shotcrete.

2.1.9 A description of proposed curing procedures and protection to be provided to shotcrete.

2.1.10 Details of proposed methods for control and disposal of waste materials, including waste shotcrete, rebound and overspray.

3 REFERENCE DOCUMENTS

3.1 The documents referenced below form a part of this document only to the extent referenced. In the case of conflicts between the referenced portions of these documents and this specification, the requirements of this specification take precedence.

3.2 American Concrete Institute (ACI)

- ACI 506R   Guide to Shotcrete
- ACI CPP660.1 Certification Policies for Shotcrete Nozzleman and Shotcrete Nozzleman-In-Training
- ACI 506.2:   Specifications for Shotcrete
- ACI 506.4:   Guide for the Evaluation of Shotcrete
- ACI 506.6:   Visual Shotcrete Core Quality Evaluation Technote

3.3 American Society for Testing and Materials (ASTM)

ASTM C260:   Standard Specification for Air-Entraining Admixtures for Concrete

ASTM C1140:   Standard Practice for Preparing and Testing Specimens from Shotcrete Test Panels

ASTM C1141:   Standard Specification for Admixtures for Shotcrete

ASTM C1436:   Standard Specification for Materials for Shotcrete

3.4   Canadian Standards Association (CSA)
  CSA A3000:   Cementitious Materials Compendium
  CSA A23.1:   Concrete Materials and Methods of Concrete Construction
  CSA A23.2:   Test Methods and Standard Practice for Concrete
  CSA G30.18:   Carbon Steel Bars for Concrete Reinforcement.

4 DEFINITIONS

4.1   The following definitions refer to words and terms used in this specification. For definitions not covered in this document, refer to ACI
506R and ACI 506.2

ACCEPTABLE, APPROVED OR PERMITTED: Acceptable to approved
or permitted by the Engineer.

BENCH SHOOTING: The practice of shooting thick members of full
section by building from the bottom up.

BLOWPIPE: Air jet operated by nozzleman's helper in shotcrete application to assist in keeping rebound and overspray out of the work.

CONTRACTOR: The person, firm or corporation with whom the
Owner enters into agreement for construction of the work.

ENGINEER: The accepting authority responsible for issuing the project
specifications and administering work under the contract documents on behalf of the Owner.

GUIDE WIRE (ALSO CALLED SCREED WIRE OR SHOOTING WIRE): Small
gauge, high strength wire used to establish line and grade to guide
work.

NOZZLEMAN: Worker on the shotcrete crew who manipulates the
nozzle, controls air addition at the nozzle and controls final deposition of the material.

OVERSPRAY: Shotcrete material deposited away from the intended
receiving surface.

REBOUND: Shotcrete material leaner than the original mixture which
ricochets off the receiving surface and falls to accumulate on the
ground or other surfaces.

ROD: Sharp-edged cutting screed used to trim shotcrete to forms or
ground wires.

SHADOW: Area of porous, improperly consolidated shotcrete behind
reinforcing steel or other embedments.

SHOTCRETE: Concrete pneumatically projected at high velocity onto
a receiving surface.

SLOUGHING (ALSO CALLED SAGGING): Subsidence of shotcrete due
generally to excessive water in the mix or placing too great a
thickness or height in a single pass.

WET-MIX SHOTCRETE: Shotcrete in which all the shotcrete ingredients, including mix water, are mixed prior to introduction into the shotcrete delivery system, and compressed air is introduced to the material flow at the nozzle.

5 MATERIALS

5.1 Cement
  5.1.1 Cement shall conform to the requirements of CSA A3000 Portland Cement Type GU.
5.2 Supplementary Cementing Materials
  5.2.1 Fly ash shall conform to the requirements of CAN/CSA –A3000 Type F or CI.
  5.2.2 Silica fume shall conform to the requirements of CAN/CSA–A3000 Type SF.
5.3 Water
  5.3.1 All water used in shotcrete production shall be of drinking water standard and free of oil and chemical or organic impurities.
  5.3.2 Similarly, all water used for in pressure sprayers for removal of rebound and overspray or green-cutting, and for shotcrete curing, shall be of drinking water standards and free of oil and chemical or organic impurities.
5.4 Aggregates
  5.4.1 Use normal weight aggregates conforming to the requirements of CSA A23.1. Aggregates shall be hard, dense and durable and conform to limits for allowable quantities of deleterious substances as given in CSA-A23.1 Table 12.
  5.4.2 Aggregates used shall not react with alkalis in the cement to an extent that results in excessive expansion of the shotcrete. The requirements of CSA A23.1 and CSA A23.2-27A shall be met.
  5.4.3 Use nominal 10 mm maximum size coarse aggregate combined with a concrete sand to provide a blend which conforms to the following composite gradation envelope:

Metric sieve size	Total passing each sieve % by mass
14 mm	100
10 mm	90–100
5 mm	70–85
2.5 mm	50–70
1.25 mm	35–55
630 μm	20–35
315 μm	8–20
160 μm	2–10

5.4.4 The 10 to 2.5 mm coarse aggregate fraction shall be stockpiled and added separately from the fine aggregate (nominal 5 mm maximum size) during batching operations.

5.5 **Admixtures**

5.5.1 Do not use any admixtures containing chlorides. Do not use any shotcrete accelerators without written authorization by the Engineer.

5.5.2 Air-entraining admixtures shall conform to the requirements of ASTM C260.

5.5.3 Chemical admixtures, such as water reducers, high range water reducers (superplasticizers) and retarders, shall conform to the requirements of ASTM C1141.

5.6 **Reinforcement**

5.6.1 Use reinforcing steel of the type, size and dimensions shown in the drawings.

6 SHOTCRETE PROPORTIONING

6.1 **Mixture Design**

6.1.1 The Contractor shall be responsible for shotcrete mixture proportioning. Submit the proposed shotcrete mixture proportions to the Engineer for review and approval at least 10 working days prior to preconstruction trials; see Section 8.3. As a minimum, for each shotcrete mixture design, submit the following information:

6.1.2 An easily identifiable mix designation, number or code.

6.1.3 Proof that the proposed mixture design is capable of meeting the specified performance requirements.

6.1.4 Performance Requirements

6.1.5 Proportion shotcrete to meet the following performance requirements:

Test description	Test method	Age (days)	Specified requirement
Maximum water/cementitious Materials ratio		—	0.40
Air content – As shot, % *	CSA A23.2-4C	—	4 ± 1
Slump at discharge into pump, mm	CSA A23.2-5C	—	70 ± 20
Minimum compressive Strength, MPa	CSA A23.2-14C	7 28	30 40

* Note: to obtain an *as-shot* air content of 4±1% will require an air content at the point of discharge into the shotcrete pump in the 7% to 10% range.

7 SUPPLY AND EQUIPMENT

7.1   **Batching, Mixing and Supply**
   7.1.1 Batch, mix and supply wet-mix shotcrete by one of the following methods:
   a) Central mixing with transit mix delivery
   b) Transit mixing and delivery
   7.1.2 Central Mixing and Supply

   a) Aggregate, cement and silica fume shall be mass batched in a central mixer in accordance with the requirements of CSA A23.1-14. Water and chemical admixtures shall be batched to the accuracy specified in CSA A23.1-14.
   b) Transit mixers shall be free of excessive accumulations of hardened shotcrete or concrete in the drum or on the blades. Blades shall be free of excessive wear. Transit mix delivery shall conform to the requirements of CSA A23.1-14.
   c) All shotcrete shall be shot within 90 minutes after addition of mix water to the batch. Shotcrete loads shall be of such batch size that this requirement is met. This time limit may be extended, subject to approval by the Engineer, if proper use is made of set retarding or hydration controlling admixtures to maintain workability without re-tempering with water.
   7.1.3 Transit Mixing and Supply

   a) The same requirements in Section 7.1.2 apply for central mixing except that all ingredients shall be added directly to the transit mixer, instead of the central mixer. Transit mixers shall be charged to not more than 70% of their rated capacity, to enable efficient mixing action.

7.2   **Shotcrete Placing Equipment**
   7.2.1 The shotcrete delivery equipment shall be capable of delivering a steady stream of uniformly mixed material to the discharge nozzle at the proper velocity and rate of discharge.
   7.2.2 The use of positive displacement pumps equipped with hydraulic or mechanically powered pistons (e.g. similar to conventional concrete piston pumps), with compressed air added at the discharge nozzle, is the preferred type of wet-mix shotcrete delivery system. Pneumatic feed guns, rotary type feed guns (similar to dry-mix guns) and peristaltic squeeze-type pumps shall only be used if the Contractor can demonstrate that they produce shotcrete meeting all the specified performance requirements.
   7.2.3 The air ring at the nozzle shall be carefully monitored for any signs of blockage of individual air holes. If non-uniform discharge of shotcrete becomes apparent, shooting shall be stopped and the air ring cleaned or other appropriate corrective actions taken.

7.2.4 The delivery of equipment shall be thoroughly cleaned at the end of each shift. Any build-up of coatings in the delivery hose and nozzle shall be removed. The air ring and nozzle shall be regularly inspected and cleaned and replaced if required.

7.3 Auxiliary Shotcrete Equipment

7.3.1 Supply clean, dry compressed air, capable of maintaining sufficient nozzle velocity for all parts of the work and simultaneous operation of a blowpipe.

7.3.2 The air supply system shall contain a moisture and oil trap to prevent contamination of the shotcrete.

7.3.3 Provide auxiliary shotcrete equipment such as materials delivery hoses, blowpipes and couplings as required to complete the work.

7.4 Reinforcing Steel

7.4.1 Reinforcing Steel to be of the type, size and dimensions detailed in the drawings.

7.4.2 Securely tie reinforcing steel bars at locations of intersecting bars with 1.6 mm or heavier gauge tie wire to minimize vibration and prevent movement of steel during shotcrete application. Avoid formation of knots of tie wire which could interfere with proper shotcrete encasement of reinforcing steel.

7.4.3 Tie reinforcing steel to avoid multiple laps or other congestion which could compromise ability of shotcrete nozzleman to properly encase reinforcing steel and embedments.

7.4.4 Submit proposed splice details to the Engineer for review and approval, prior to installation of reinforcing steel.

7.4.5 Clearance between reinforcing bars and formwork to be as detailed in drawings, but not less than 20 mm.

7.5 Alignment Control and Cover

7.5.1 Implement alignment control to establish control over line and grade and ensure that the minimum specified shotcrete thickness and cover to reinforcing steel are maintained. Verify that reinforcing bars are fixed to provide specified cover, prior to application of any shotcrete.

7.5.2 Provide alignment control by means of devices such as shooting wires, guide strips, depth gauges or forms. The proposed means of alignment control shall be submitted to the Engineer for review and approval prior to any shotcrete application.

7.5.3 When shooting wires (also called guide wires) are used, they shall consist of a high-strength steel wire kept taut during shotcreting. Remove shooting wires after completion of shotcreting and screeding operations.

7.5.4 Guide strips and forms shall be of such dimensions and installation configuration that they do not impede the ability of the nozzlemen to produce uniform, dense, properly consolidated shotcrete. In particular, installations which are conducive to the entrapment of rebound or formation of shadows and voids shall not be used.

8 QUALITY ASSURANCE AND QUALITY CONTROL

8.1 Quality Assurance

The Engineer will implement a quality assurance programme which will include:

a) Review of contractor submittals
b) Review and approval of contractor's proposed materials, supply, equipment and crew. In particular, all shotcrete nozzlemen proposed for use on the project shall be evaluated in the preconstruction mock-up testing programme. Only nozzlemen approved by the Engineer shall be used on the project.
c) At start-up of the project examination and approval of areas prepared for shotcreting, including installation of anchors, reinforcement, and devices to control line and grade, prior to application of any shotcrete
d) Provision of intermittent inspections to monitor shotcrete installation at a frequency selected by the Engineer.
e) Regular monitoring of the results of the compressive strength tests conducted by a testing agency appointed by the Owner on cores extracted from standard shotcrete test panels shot by the contractor at a frequency specified by the Engineer.
f) Implementation of a programme for in-place evaluation and acceptance, or rejection, where testing indicates shotcrete is non-conforming to the project specifications
g) Where defective shotcrete is indicated, carrying out appropriate tests which may include compressive strength testing of extracted cores from the in-place shotcrete and visual evaluation of cores extracted from the in-place shotcrete; guidance on the approach can be found in ACI 506.4 *Guide for the Evaluation of Shotcrete (Chapter 10 on the Acceptance Criteria for Shotcrete)*.
h) Monitoring of a programme of remedial works by the contractor, where indicated as being necessary from the results of the quality assurance programme.

8.2 Quality Control

The **Contractor** shall establish and maintain a quality control programme for the shotcrete work to ensure compliance with the contract requirements. Such programme shall include maintenance of test records for all quality control operations. Such records shall be provided to the Engineer for review on request.

8.3 Preconstruction Trials

8.3.1 Implement a preconstruction trial to enable the Engineer to evaluate the ability of the proposed materials, shotcrete mixture, equipment and crew to produce shotcrete conforming to the project specifications. Acceptance of the preconstruction trial results by the Engineer is required prior to application of any shotcrete on the project.

8.3.2 The preconstruction trial shall be used to pre-qualify the nozzlemen proposed for use on the project. Nozzlemen who have not been pre-qualified shall not be permitted to apply shotcrete on the project.

8.3.3 The preconstruction trial shall use the same materials, shotcrete mixture and equipment proposed for use on the project and approximate actual working conditions, configuration, reinforcement and shooting positions as near as possible.

8.3.4 Nozzlemen shall pre-qualify by shooting mock-ups of the reinforced structural wall element. The Engineer shall specify the number, size and locations of cores to be extracted or the locations of saw-cut surfaces.

8.3.5 The acceptance criteria for the mock-ups shall be established by the Engineer. The cores extracted or the saw-cut surfaces must be evaluated by a qualified inspector for acceptance based on the specified acceptance criteria for defects, extent of void sizes, frequency and location, and steel encapsulation. Refer to ACI 506.6 *Visual Shotcrete Core Quality Evaluation Technote* for proper identification of defects.

8.3.6 Pre-qualify the shotcrete mixture by shooting a plain (non-reinforced) test panel with dimensions of 500 × 500 and 150 mm deep. The test panel shall be made from wood and sealed plywood and have 45° sloped edges to permit rebound to escape and facilitate de-moulding.

8.3.7 Cure the test panels in the field, close to the location where shot, for two (2) days before being transported in the form to the testing laboratory. Cure the test panel under wet burlap covered with plastic sheet under field temperatures conditions. Protect the panels from disturbance or damage.

8.3.8 Assist testing laboratory by loading test panels, in their forms, onto their trucks. Test panels and cores extracted from the test panels shall be moist cured in the laboratory at 23±2°C until the time of compressive strength testing.

8.3.9 If the preconstruction test specimens fail to meet the project performance requirements, then make the necessary adjustments in shotcrete materials, mixture design or application, and re-shoot test panels. No work shall commence on the project until the preconstruction performance testing requirements have been meet.

8.4 Construction Testing

8.4.1 Shoot one construction test panel for each 50 m³ of shotcrete production, or for each day of shotcrete production, whichever is more frequent. Shoot the panel in the same orientation as the work being done.

8.4.2 Produce, store, handle and cure construction test panels in the same manner prescribed for preconstruction test panels. Similarly, prepare, handle, cure and test in the same manner prescribed for the preconstruction test panels.

9 SHOTCRETE APPLICATION AND FINISHING

9.1 Provide suitable scaffolding, man lifts, or other devices to provide the nozzlemen, helpers and inspectors with free unhindered access to the work area. Provide safety measures to protect the workers on such devices which comply with the requirements of the authorities having jurisdiction.

    9.1.1 Install sufficient lighting and ventilation to provide the nozzlemen and helpers with a clear, unhindered view of the shooting area. Work shall be terminated and corrective measures adopted if, in the opinion of the Engineer, visibility is unsuitable for the safe application of quality shotcrete.

    9.1.2 Use good shotcrete nozzling technique as detailed in ACI 506R and ACI CPP660.1. In particular:

        a) Use the *bench-gunning* technique. Orient the nozzle at right angles to the receiving surface, except as required to fill corners, cove edges and encase reinforcing steel.

        b) Optimize the combination of air volume at the nozzle and distance of the nozzle from the receiving surface to achieve maximum consolidation of the shotcrete and full encapsulation of the reinforcing steel.

        c) Adjust air volume and distance of the nozzle from the work while encasing reinforcing steel to keep the front face of the reinforcement clean during shooting operations, so that shotcrete builds up from behind to encase the reinforcement without the formation of shadows or voids.

        d) Nozzleman's helper to continuously remove accumulations of rebound and overspray using blowpipe, or other suitable devices in advance of deposition of new shotcrete.

        e) Do not include rebound, hardened overspray or stiffened shotcrete trimmings in the shotcrete work.

9.2 When applying more than one layer of shotcrete trim with a cutting rod, or brush with a stiff bristle broom to remove all loose material, overspray, laitance, or other material detrimental to bonding of the next layer of shotcrete.

9.3 Allow shotcrete layer to stiffen sufficiently before applying next layer of shotcrete. If shotcrete has set and hardened, re-saturate with clean water and bring to SSD condition at time of application of the next layer of shotcrete.

9.4   Use a shooting technique which provides full encapsulation of all reinforcing steel and embedments. Cut out any voids, shadows, sags or other defects from the applied shotcrete while still plastic and re-shoot. Otherwise make good any defects in the hardened shotcrete using light duty chipping hammers (7 kg max) followed by high pressure water blasting (minimum 30 MPa) to remove *bruised* shotcrete surface.

9.5   Trim shotcrete with a cutting rod or other suitable device to the specified line and grade. Finish shotcrete to a sandy texture as approved by the Engineer using suitable finishing tools. Tolerance of finished surface shall be as specified by the Engineer.

9.6   Protect all fixtures and adjacent concrete surfaces from build-up of rebound, overspray and shotcrete trimmings. Remove all such materials from the work area on a daily basis.

9.7   Remove any excess shotcrete applied outside of the specified areas to be shot. Leave the work area in a clean condition on completion of the work, free from contamination by excess shotcrete trimmings, rebound, overspray or slurry from shotcrete operations.

9.8   Construct construction joints to a 45° tapered edge. Cut plastic shotcrete with a trowel or other suitable tool to form a construction joint. Green cut with a 30 MPa water pressure jet the next day, if necessary to remove loose material. Do not featheredge (produce long tapered) construction joints.

10   CURING AND PROTECTION

10.1 Curing

10.1.1   On completion of finishing, prevent shotcrete from drying out by moist curing using fogging or wetting or maintenance of a minimum 95% relative humidity in the area surrounding the shotcrete.

10.1.2   Moist cure shotcrete for a minimum of 7 days. Moist curing shall be accomplished using one or more of the following procedures:

a) Wrap the elements in wet burlap covered with a plastic sheet or a presaturated plastic coated non-woven synthetic or natural fabric.

b) Install sprinklers, soaker hoses or other devices which keep the shotcrete continuously wet. Avoid the use of intermittent wetting procedures which allow shotcrete to undergo cycles of wetting and drying during the curing process

10.2 Hot and Cold Weather Protection

10.2.1 The general requirements for hot and cold weather concreting detailed in CSA A23.1 apply to the shotcrete work.

10.2.2 If the prevailing ambient conditions (relative humidity, wind speed, air temperature) are such that the shotcrete develops plastic shrinkage and/or early drying shrinkage cracking, terminate shotcrete application. Adopt corrective measure such as installation of wind barriers or fogging devices to protect the work, before restarting shotcrete application. Do not proceed with shotcrete application if the rate of evaporation at the shotcrete surface exceeds 1.0 kg/m²/h as detailed in CSA A23.1 Appendix D.

10.2.3 Terminate shotcrete application if the ambient temperature rises above 30°C, unless the Contractor adopts special hot-weather shotcreting procedures which are approved by the Engineer.

10.2.4 During periods of cold weather, shotcreting may only proceed if the concrete substrate to which the shotcrete is applied is above 5°C and the air temperature in contact with the repair surfaces is above 5°C.

10.2.5 Maintain the air temperature at the shotcrete surfaces at 10°C or greater for at least 4 days after application of shotcrete. The means of maintaining the air temperature shall be approved by the engineer. The use of unvented heaters which give rise to carbonation is prohibited.

11 SHOTCRETE ACCEPTANCE AND REPAIR

11.1 Shotcrete Acceptance

11.1.1 The Engineer has the authority to accept or reject the shotcrete work. Shotcrete which does not conform to the project specifications may be rejected either during the shotcrete application process, or on the basis of tests on cores from test panels or the completed work.

11.1.2 Deficiencies observed during the shotcrete application process, such as, but not limited to the following, constitute a cause for shotcrete rejection:

a) Failure to properly control and remove build-up of over-spray and rebound,

b) Incomplete consolidation of shotcrete around reinforcing steel and embedments,

c) Incorporation of shadows, excessive voids, delaminations, sags or sloughing,

    d) Failure to apply shotcrete to the required line and grade and tolerance,

11.1.3 Whenever possible, perform remedial work to correct deficiencies while shotcrete is still plastic.

11.1.4 The hardened shotcrete will be examined by the Engineer for any evidence of excessive plastic or drying shrinkage cracking, tears, featheredging, sloughs or other deficiencies. Sounding shall be used to check for voids and delaminations. If the shotcrete does not meet the specified criteria, the work will be rejected and the Contractor shall implement a remediation programme to correct the deficiency.

11.1.5 If the results of compliance tests from shotcrete test panels, or assessment of the plastic or hardened shotcrete indicate non-conformance of the shotcrete to the project specifications, the Engineer will implement a programme of evaluation of the in-place shotcrete. Such evaluation shall include, but not be limited to:

    a) Extraction of cores from the in-place shotcrete at locations selected by the Engineer and testing of such cores for compliance to the project specifications.

    b) Checking for delaminations using sounding or other appropriate non-destructive testing procedures;

    c) Diamond saw cutting or coring to check the adequacy of encasement of reinforcing steel and embedments.

11.1.6 Shotcrete which is proven to be non-conforming to the project specifications shall be removed and replaced by the Contractor at no cost to the Owner.

11.2 Shotcrete Repair

11.2.1 Shotcrete which is identified as being defective while still plastic shall be removed using trowels, scrapers or other suitable mechanical devices.

11.2.2 Hardened shotcrete which is identified as being deficient shall be removed. Care shall be taken to prevent damage to reinforcing steel bars or embedments and adjacent sound shotcrete. Any embedments and adjacent sound shotcrete damaged during the shotcrete removal process shall be removed and replaced at no cost to the Owner.

11.2.3 All prepared repair areas shall be inspected and approved by the Engineer prior to the placement of any repair shotcrete. Repair shotcrete shall be placed, finished, cured and protected in the same manner specified for shotcrete work.

Index

Printed in the United States
by Baker & Taylor Publisher Services